D0146920

RE-IMAGINING COMPARATIVE EDUCATION

REFERENCE BOOKS IN INTERNATIONAL EDUCATION
Edward Beauchamp, General Editor

RE-IMAGINING COMPARATIVE EDUCATION

Postfoundational Ideas
and Applications for
Critical Times

Edited by Peter Ninnes • Sonia Mehta

RoutledgeFalmer

NEW YORK AND LONDON

Published in 2004 by
RoutledgeFalmer
29 W 35th Street
New York, NY 10001
www.routledge-ny.com

Published in Great Britain by
RoutledgeFalmer
11 New Fetter Lane
London EC4P 4EE
www.routledge.co.uk

RoutledgeFalmer is an imprint of the Taylor & Francis Group.
Printed in the United States of America on acid-free paper.

10 9 8 7 6 5 4 3 2

Library of Congress Cataloging-in-Publication Data

Re-imagining comparative education : postfoundational ideas and
applications for critical times / edited by Peter Ninnes and Sonia Mehta.
    p. cm. -- (Reference books in international education)
    Includes bibliographical references and index.
    ISBN 0-415-94817-7 (hardcover : alk. paper)
    1. comparative education. 2. Postmodernism and education.
I. Ninnes, Peter, 1960- II. Mehta, Sonia, 1966– III. Series.

LB43.R45 2004
370′ .9--dc22   2003019143

Contents

Acknowledgments

Many people have made this project both possible and enjoyable. I would first and foremost like to thank Sonia for her wonderful sense of scholarly adventure and willingness to boldly go where few have gone before (beyond the "Edges, Borders, Boundaries, Brinks and Limits [that] have appeared like a team of trolls... Short creatures with long shadows, patrolling the Blurry End"[1]); for her willingness to carry the load when I could not; for her keen wit and critical eye; and for her endless appetite for Bollywood movies. I am also very grateful to Sonia, Vineet, and Pickin' Dandelions for their superb hospitality during my editorial trips to Ypsilanti and Ann Arbor. Those have been very special, unforgettable times.

Many colleagues have supported this work and encouraged it. In particular I am thankful to all those friends made at conferences in Vancouver, San Antonio, Washington, D.C., Orlando, and New Orleans who have taken an interest in this project.

I also thank all the contributors to this volume, who have worked very hard to meet deadlines and have responded to our editorial prodding with grace and good humor. Thank you for accompanying us on this journey of discovery.

Much of my editorial and research work has been supported by funds provided by the Faculty of Education, Health and Professional Studies at the University of New England. This backing has been invaluable and I am greatly indebted to the Faculty for the opportunities it has provided.

Finally, I wish to thank my partner in life, Fiona, and our children Emily, Michael, Joseph and Thomas, for being kind, generous, and loyal companions on the road.

Peter Ninnes

---

[1] Arundhati Roy, "The God of Small Things" (Hammersmith: Flamingo, 1997), p. 3.

All (this) began with a cantankerous debate about ideological inclusions and exclusions at a CIES conference years ago, and a cup of coffee afterward with someone called Dr. Peter Ninnes. A tentative question from the sidelines, a struggle for articulation, thousands of cups of chai (and a cup of coffee) later, I wish to profoundly thank Peter for throwing open a whole world of scholarship and friendship to me. As a colleague, I raise a cup to a co-editor who is the soul of deep understanding, patience, wit, and really terrible puns, all of which made this book a possibility and a pleasure.

A very special thank you to my husband, Vineet, whose superb technological and organizational skills, and endless patience formed the safety net into which this book frequently fell and came out renewed, as did I. Pickin' Dandelions has my eternal devotion for reminding me that we must play, whenever we can.

I thank Rolland Paulston for his keen insight (and keen sight that found lots of trolls that we missed), his constructive editing, intolerance of nonsense, and constant support throughout this process. I can never forget the friendship and understanding of my dissertation guide and great friend, Lynn Ilon, for her understanding, forbearance, and support when school work and book work overlapped. And over it all, I owe a depth of gratitude to the students and teachers of comparative education who struggle for alternative, inclusive, and meaningful space in their teaching and learning. In the end, your words and your spirit made this volume imaginable.

Sonia Mehta

Kimberly Guinta at Routledge has been marvelous to work with and both of us thank her for her professional help and advice, and for invigorating us at a crucial juncture.

Introduction: Re-Imagining Comparative Education

We conceive this book as being about caring for the field of comparative education and caring for ideas, and in so doing, caring about those who work, study and come in contact with the field. Our care is directed toward exploring the ways in which post-foundational ideas — postmodernisms, poststructuralisms, and postcolonialisms – can open up new possibilities for comparative education. We believe this is an important task for a variety of reasons, not the least of which is we believe that, despite some dissenting voices, the potential of these ideas has rarely been substantively explored in the field. Furthermore, comparative education, with its focus on dynamic relations between education and society, on global and local educational manifestations, and on pluralism and difference, is uniquely located within academia and therefore able to engage with postfoundational issues in unique ways. Thus we hope to show in this volume not only the richness and diversity of postfoundational ideas, but also the powerful contribution they can promise for comparative education. Comparative educators are international in their practice, experience, information sources and skills. It would seem therefore of particular poignancy that the field should hesitate to take up or allow the engagement with postfoundational thinking which directly intersects many areas of interest to comparative educators. Indeed, education at large is arguably international in scope and effect. In our re-imagining of this field, we hope to open many more areas of interest and dialogue across fields.

Through this book we invite all comparative educators — practitioners, teachers, researchers and students — to engage in a new dialogue about the way these perspectives can help to practice our field. These are not necessarily 'new' perspectives, having been in use in the social sciences, cultural studies, architecture, and urban planning studies. A dialogue about them in comparative education, however, is fairly recent, and we felt the need, as the authors in this volume, to continue that dialogue. Compiling such perspectives is the first step. We hope there will be other voices in this debate, and that this dialogue will be continued by those who find themselves in this work, by those who see beyond it and by those who disagree or refute what is said here. Then our purpose will have been served, because we see the educational enterprise as an ongoing process, only as good as the voices informing it. There should be no doubt that such an undertaking is dangerous. It has the potential, of course, to shake what have been the 'foundations' of the field. Thus, it is not to be undertaken lightly. However, 'caring' also implies respecting, all that teachers, students, and researchers have to offer; and so, out of respect for ourselves and for other ideas in and beyond the field, this was a project we had to undertake.

Nel Noddings (1984) argues that to engage in caring for ideas we must be free to pursue these ideas wherever they lead (p. 164). She suggests that when presented with some kind of new conceptualization, if we care about ideas, we can ask not just "what does it mean" but "what shall I do?" (p. 164) One possible response, she suggests, is to shout "run!" and it is certainly the case that in comparative education, this is a very tempting response to post-foundational ideas. Such a response, however, means that we never confront new concepts. Noddings believes that in order to care for ideas, confront and perhaps perform new concepts, we must feel safe to do so, have the will to do so, create time to do so, and not be subject to ridicule as we do so. Furthermore, in order to work through a conceptualization and hence derive understanding and create meaning, we need to operate in two modes. The active mode involves analyzing the concept. In the receptive mode, we allow ideas to come upon us, by watching, and listening, that is, by having an intuitive cast of mind (Noddings, 1984, p. 166). In this book we seek to demonstrate this care for ideas both within and without comparative education in a number of ways. Most important, we provide a safe place for scholars in the field to confront post-foundational ideas. This space allows ideas to be explored in a way that is valued, rather than seen as foolish. It makes possible a space in which to articulate alternative paradigms of thinking without fear of losing legitimacy, credibility, or even alterity. It opens up a space for scholars in the field — both as authors and readers — to let these ideas work upon them, to watch and to listen, in order to develop our understanding of the ideas and create meaning. By creating such a space, we hope to provide comparative and other educators with a wider and more inclusive view of the possibilities for education. We hope, too, that creating this space will allow a greater diversity of scholars to see something of themselves in the work in the field. We hope it will be a space to articulate all that which has not been articulated in comparative education, at least not to any great extent; that is, a space to think what previously had been difficult to think, and an opportunity for "exploring a space of dynamic possibilities" (De Landa, 1993, quoted in Holmes 1998, p. 97).

We do not pretend to be in a position to say that we know all that post-foundational ideas can offer the practice of comparative education. Compiling this collection was a learning process for us, too. But we have observed that in the field, some scholars are starting to engage with post-foundational ideas and employ them in substantive ways to everyday practical educational issues. Thus, we are putting the book together in the hope that what has so far been at the margins will begin to speak within the field. Nor do we see ourselves as proposing an alternative form of comparative education, diametrically opposed to other forms. We are not inverting hierarchies of knowledge in order to set up a different unitary discourse (Foucault, 1980, p. 86). Nor do we wish, in engaging with knowledges that have operated at the margins, to take on the characteristics of oppressors (Freire, 1970) by prescribing the abandonment of large chunks of the panoply of perspectives that comprise the field. However, we are concerned with re-imagining the field of comparative education by constructing knowledge spaces, problematizing the creation, maintenance and reproduction of knowledge in the field, and extending an invitation to everyone in the field to consider anew post-foundational ideas and beyond. Beyond center/margin binaries, we hope to be working in the space between theories and their deployment around issues of the everyday work of comparative educators in research, consultancy, and teaching.

The organization of the book oscillates between general discussions of the place of particular postfoundational ideas in comparative education and specific examples of research projects that employ these theoretical perspectives. In chapter 1, we introduce readers to a range of ideas that commonly are incorporated under the postmodern, poststructural and postcolonial rubrics. Our intention is not to 'pin' each piece of research to its 'post'-something theory, or to converge into definitions of these theories, but to illustrate their use in research already underway in the field. Our aim here is not to be prescriptive, but to open up the discussion of the ways in which these ideas have been performed in situated educational contexts, and to consider their more specific application in the field of comparative education. In chapter 2, Sonia Mehta refines this discussion particularly for the students and teachers of comparative education, by examining the relationship between postfoundational ideas and the experience of pedagogy in comparative education.

The next six chapters primarily engage with poststructural ideas about discourse. In chapter 3, Peter Ninnes explores various ways of conceptualizing discourse and discourse analysis, and reviews strands of educational research that have employed these ideas. Greg Burnett undertakes a critical discourse analysis of education in the Republic of Kiribati (chapter 4), then, in chapter 5, Ayaz Naseem deconstructs discourses of citizenship and gender in Pakistani education. In chapter 6, Nuzhat Amin and Ryuko

Kubota undertake a comparative study of the deployment of native speaker discourses in English education in Japan, Pakistan, Canada, and the USA. In chapter 7 Marianne Larsen presents a comparative analysis of the discursive constitution of the quality teacher in a range of education settings. Chapter 8 rounds off this part of the book. William deJong-Lambert provides an historical analysis of the relationship between power, knowledge, and scientific discourses in the former Soviet Union.

In chapter 9, Gustavo Fischman extends the foregoing examples of the analysis of text by arguing for methods that allow for the analysis of visual culture in comparative education. His piece provides an important expansion of Paulston's (2001, p. 69) call for the field to address the "pictorial" turn. The next four chapters explore issues related to postcolonial theory. Peter Ninnes and Greg Burnett (chapter 10) analyze the extent to which postcolonial theory has been used in research articles published in comparative education journals, and suggest ways in which other postcolonial ideas can be employed. Yoko Mochizuki's postcolonial re-reading of the internationalization movement in Japanese education (chapter 11) provides both a thought-provoking area study as well as a novel analysis of internationalization. Then, in chapter 12, Leona English discusses training educators for cross-cultural work, employing a range of key postcolonial concepts to disrupt the more commonplace conceptualizations of cross-cultural training.

Many comparative educators undertake consultancies in developing countries. Yet much of this work is not informed by contemporary, critical approaches to the concept of 'development.' In chapter 13, Jonathan Makuwira and Peter Ninnes provide a summary discussion of the critiques of development that have become known as 'post-development,' and examine their place in comparative education. Finally, in chapter 14, Jorge Gorostiaga and Rolland Paulston use concepts of both discourse analysis and social cartography to map and compare how issues of decentralization have been understood and represented at the global level, and in particular, in the national context of Argentina. By representing this debate as a space constructed by multiple perspectives, they show how to argue and counter-argue the benefits and pitfalls of different school decentralization policies.

In order to enable the imagination, one needs a point of departure. Our departures come from moving away from Nietzschean 'ressentiment,' or 'resentment,' which Dimitriadis and McCarthy (2001, p. 4) explain as "the practice by which one defines one's identity through the negation of the other." We would like to include, not negate the other, and if that means more rigor in our critique, then so be it. Between action and research, between theory and application, there is the in-between space of imagining. It's not a bad place to be, as we have found, and as the authors in this book have demonstrated.

And behold! Thrones were kingless, and men walked
One with the other even as spirits do,
None fawned, none trampled...
And women, too...
Speaking the wisdom once they could not think.

— From *The Evidence of the Imagination,* edited by Donald Reiman *et al.,*
New York: New York University Press, 1978

References

Freire, Paulo. *Pedagogy of the oppressed.* New York: Seabury Books, 1970.

Dimitriadis, Greg and Cameron McCarthy. *Reading and Teaching the Postcolonial: from Baldwin to Basquiat and Beyond.* New York: Teacher's College Press, 2001.

Holmes, Lucy. "Julia Kristeva: Intertextuality and education." In *Naming the multiple: Poststructuralism and education* (pp. 85-102) edited by M. Peters. Westport, Connecticut: Bergin and Garvey, 1998.

Noddings, Nel. Caring: *A feminist approach to ethics and moral education.* Berkeley: University of California Press, 1984.

Paulston, Rolland. "Imagining comparative education: Past, present, future." Compare 30 (2001): 353–367.

CHAPTER 1

A Meander through the Maze: Comparative Education and Postfoundational Studies

PETER NINNES and SONIA MEHTA

Comparative education has become a field whose work and influence extend well beyond the Euro-American academy and the English-speaking world. In the following reading of the field, we focus on comparative education as it is practiced and discussed in the English-speaking world, primarily the US and Canada, the United Kingdom, and Australia, and Hong Kong. For want of a better term, we refer to this part of the field as Anglo-American Comparative Education, which we shall call CE. We are aware that comparative education as a field has taken somewhat different trajectories in other parts of the world (Cowen, 2000), but because of our own linguistic limitations, we are not in a position to examine these alternative trajectories. We are very much aware that many practitioners and even more students of comparative education studying in English-speaking academies have their origins outside this area. This awareness, however, only strengthens our resolve to address postfoundational issues in comparative education.

Despite pleas for coherence of focus and method (e.g., Cummings, 1999), our view of CE is characterized by eclecticism. It incorporates a range of theories and methods from the social sciences and intersects a range of subfields, including sociology of education, educational planning, anthropology of education, economics of education and education and development (Wilson, 1994; Rust, Soumaré, Pescador and Shibuya, 1999).

The major theoretical positions which have informed CE have been examined by Paulston (1999), who, in his most recent cartographic creation, argues that positions within the field range, among other things, from modernist certainties with essentialist views of reality and identity, to nonessentialist postmodernist destabilizations which view identity as mutable; from approaches which problematize systems to those which problematize actors; and from paradigms which emphasize structural relations, to those which focus on simulations and hyperreality.

Although elements of all of these approaches can be found in articles and books published in CE, at different times in the history of the field, particular theories have tended to dominate. There is general agreement that functionalist and positivist approaches dominated the field during the 1950s, 1960s, and early 1970s (Welch and Burns, 1992; Paulston, 1994; Kelly, Altbach and Arnove, 1982). Other approaches, such as those emphasizing cultural and historical perspectives, were also present in this period, but they were in a relatively subordinate position (Cowen, 1996). One of the main focuses of CE in this period was on the modernization and development of education systems and the societies they served. From the mid-1970s onward, critical approaches began to challenge the dominant positivist and functionalist paradigms (Paulston, 1994; Cowen, 1996). Neo-Marxist approaches were particularly to the fore, and the emphasis expanded from describing the development and social impact of educational systems and structures to analyzing the nature of identity created in part by those systems and structures (Cowen, 1996). The 1980s saw the emergence of what Paulston (1994: 926) calls "a more humanistic Marxism, or radical humanism." This was accompanied by the rise of interpretive, ethnomethodological and interactionist approaches. During the 1990s, debates arose about the place of postfoundational ideas in CE, and it is these debates with which we particularly wish to engage in this chapter.

We take the term post-foundational from St. Pierre and Pillow (2000), and we use it as an umbrella term to incorporate postmodernisms, post-structuralisms, and postcolonialisms. 'Foundational' here refers primarily to the enlightenment idea that human rationality provides the ultimate source or foundation of knowledge. This idea assumes that humans are entirely rational, that language is transparent, that reason can be infallibly employed to overcome conflicts between truth, power and knowledge, and that freedom involves obeying rational laws (St. Pierre and Pillow, 2000, p. 5). Post-foundational, then, refers to the set of ideas which challenge these humanistic enlightenment notions of humanity and the self, and interrogates these in terms of authority, inclusions, and exclusions, and in regard to whose interests these notions serve. Blake, Smeyers, Smith, and Standish (1998) suggest that a rejection of foundations of knowledge is not a result of post-modern attacks, but a result of the problematics of the concept of foundations themselves. Furthermore, adopting a post-foundational stance is not an abrogation of intellectual responsibility, as some critics have claimed. As Blake et al (1998, p. 28) argue, it may be the case that it is "simply the commitment to critique itself, the critical position within the politics of knowledge, that authorizes dissent in the real world of politics." Furthermore, as St. Pierre and Pillow (2000, p. 1) assert, rather than finding "despair, paralysis, nihilism, apoliticism, irresponsibility or immorality" in the ruins of the enlightenment and foundationalism, we can choose to look for "possibilities for different worlds that might, perhaps, not be so cruel to so many people."

We want here to provide a reading of the ways in which CE has engaged with postfoundational studies. How the debates have proceeded and how these theories have been applied are the two main areas in which we are interested. We wish to not only identify what has been discussed and used and how, but also what has not been canvassed. We then want to speculate on the benefits and dangers to CE of a further engagement with these ideas.

Postmodernisms

Within CE it is possible to distinguish more or less three approaches to postmodernism. The first approach tends to oppose postmodernism. This approach, in Paulston's (1999, p. 445) terms, continues to employ "metanarratives of reason, emancipation and progress." A second approach involves a reconceptualization of CE through the selective appropriation or adoption of particular aspects of postmodern thinking while maintaining primarily modernist positions. In Paulston's (1999, p. 445) heterotopic mapping, the position includes the "reflexive modernity adaptations" and the "critical modernist appropriations." A third approach comprises a radical change to CE by giving postmodern thinking a central (although not necessarily exclusive) place within the field.

Peters (1999) argues that modernism is both (1) a development in the arts that involved a breaking away from traditions of naturalism and classical methods and (2) a philosophical movement that believed in scientifically derived progress and the advancement of knowledge. Postmodernity therefore can be thought of as a transformation in the values and practices of modernism, or a period in which this occurs. In this chapter, we focus on postmodernism as a philosophical movement or sensibility involving the transformation of the belief in scientifically derived progress and the advancement of knowledge.

There are two particular aspects of a postmodern sensibility that we wish to emphasize here. One aspect is the so-called incredulity toward metanarratives (Lyotard, 1984; Peters, 1999), that involves a skepticism to all stories which purport to provide a fail-safe, all-encompassing interpretation of the world, humanity, society, culture and so on. Metanarratives include among other things Marxism, Western science, and *inter alia,* Kant's notion of progress based on the natural laws of reason. This skepticism derives from several problematic features of metanarratives. First, as Peters and Lankshear (1996 p. 3) observe, metanarratives mask the will-to-power that underlies their legitimating functions, and almost always involve the exclusion of particular groups' interests. Lyotard (1984) notes that all emancipatory metanarratives have counter signs which are not "progressive," but have been predicated on "the subjugation, domination, exploitation, enslavement, and near-genocide of all those who are not the West" (Bain, 1995, p. 4). The metanarrative of modernity, in particular, is continually being eroded by small narratives. Bain refers to the "disorderly voices that the homogenizing discourses of modernity thought to either domesticate, eliminate or ignore [such as] non-Western peoples, women, African Americans, gays, lesbians, the physically challenged, all those who somehow did not meet the criteria for being the universal subject of history" (Bain, 1995, p. 5).

Second, we wish to examine Lyotard's notion of the differend. Differends are conflicts that cannot be resolved, because of a lack of common perspectives between two parties. The notion of the differend therefore contrasts with Hegel's idea that differences could be resolved through rational discussion. According to Peters (1995, p. xxv), Lyotard considered the aim of philosophy to be to "detect differends (a cognitive task) and to bear witness to them (an ethical task)." However, we do not consider that the notion of difference should be interpreted as if there are only differends and no possibility at all of finding some common ground or consensus. Rather, we argue that complete consensus is an ideal rarely possible, that emphasizing consensus is often done at the expense of a consideration of power relations, and that within all human interactions there is a greater or lesser differend at work.

Within CE the debates about postmodernity have been muddied by the common practice of conflating postmodernism and poststructuralism. In this discussion, we wish to distinguish between the two sets of ideas, but our attempts to do so are hindered by the fact that various contributors to the dialogue do not make this distinction. Two initial and important moments in the debate about postmodernism in CE occurred in the early 1990s. First, Vandra Masemann (1990) called for a consideration of various ways of knowing. Masemann (1990, p. 465) pointed out that comparative education had "willfully" ignored or bypassed whole domains of knowledge, particularly indigenous knowledges, and noted that ideas about what represents valid knowledge are constructed in the academy. Second, Val Rust argued that post-modernism "should be a central concept in our comparative education discourse" (Rust 1991, p. 610) because the 1990s represented a substantively new era "possessing new formal features of culture, a new type of social life, and a new economic order" (Rust 1991, p. 611). Rust argued that comparative education needed to adopt new methods of analysis such as post-modernism to suit this new era since it "may provide a more accurate depiction of reality than existing frameworks" (Rust 1991, p. 625). Rust suggests that the work of French thinkers such as Derrida, Foucault, and Lyotard, which emphasize variability of meaning, and which reject totalizing and universalizing narratives, provide important insights for comparative education, especially in terms of identifying our own metanarratives and their effects on our analyses, examining the roles of minorities in resisting totalizing educational narratives, and analyzing the nature of power and its relationship to disadvantage and inequity.

Since the early 1990s, Paulston has contributed to the debate both theoretically and practically through his mappings of the field of CE (see for example Paulston and Leibman, 1994; Paulston, 1993, 1997, 1999, 2000). His work involves constructing maps representing his reading of the relationships of the various ideological positions found within CE. His work is radical on at least two fronts. First, it represents a construction of the field that is eclectic (i.e., anti-hegemonic), multiple, porous and dynamic. This is in stark contrast to an approach that sees the field of CE as fixed, bounded, unified, coherent, singular, and impermeable. Second, Paulston's work is radical because it does not purport to provide a modernist, objective picture of CE reality. Instead it represents his reading of the field, and as such provides a point of departure for continuing dialogue, rather than a final answer to questions concerning the identity of CE. Third, Paulston's maps are radical in that they open space to multiple ontological, epistemological and axiological choices present in the field's discourse.

A number of authors have sought to appropriate or adopt postmodern ideas within CE (e.g., Cowen, 1996; Young, 1997). Cowen (1996, p. 165), for example, argues that postmodernism "is best read from the contemporary anxieties" of European and European settler societies, and therefore it does have some application within CE to those national contexts, but not others. He also argues that postmodern literature has some use in interpreting and analyzing the "very serious problems" posed by "late modern educational systems" (p. 166) because these systems tend to be overly reliant on economic theory as a foundation for decisionmaking, because they tend to ignore or marginalize difference, and because they form a basis for developing a social contract related to the modernist metanarratives of emancipation and social justice. Furthermore, Cowen (1996, p. 166) argues that the combination of the "late modern educational pattern and the literature on post-modernity highlight for comparative education as crucial areas of attention in a research agenda [the] investigation of transitology, the global, of pedagogic form and of the other." Cowen also suggests that postmodernity highlights the need to search not so much for rules regarding how education systems work, but instead focus on the issue of how various parties within education systems interpret their situations. Although Cowen mentions issues of emancipation and social justice, he eventually argues that comparative education should perhaps be done with emancipating others and instead focus on emancipating itself. Overall, however, the text argues for the appropriation rather than central positioning of particular postmodern ideas for particular purposes.

The texts that resist the engagement of CE with postmodern ideas do so on several major grounds. First, some authors argue that postmodernisms represent an abandonment of all that is good in the modernist project. Comparative education as a field has long engaged with the modernist project by its endorsement of education as a means for spreading democracy, and pursuing 'progress,' including the improvement in people's material, political, social, cultural, and physical well-being. For some authors, an embrace of postmodernism is untenable because it would involve abandoning the desire to improve people's well-being. Hayhoe (2000) for example, argues that we have taken for granted the material and social benefits of modernity. Thus, modernity should not be abandoned but reshaped in the interests of "greater justice, greater harmony, and greater respect for the values of community" (p. 425). According to Hayhoe, this reshaping of modernity's "jagged profile" (p. 424) should be mitigated in part through an engagement with how non-Western societies have dealt with the problems of modernity.

Such arguments arise from a commendable desire to improve the lot of many of the world's people. However, these views present themselves as being caught in a binary comprising 'embrace postmodernity/abandon social justice' or 'embrace modernity/pursue social justice.' We can find an alternative way of conceptualizing the problem if we unpack this binary. First we realize that the modernist project is not homogenous. According to Mouffe (1993) the project of modernity had two major thrusts, namely, a political/democratic project focusing on self-assertion, and an epistemological project focusing on self-foundation. The self-assertion aspect has led to and is the progenitor of explorations of democracy, social justice, emancipation, and so on. The self-foundation aspect of the modernist project focuses on the Kantian construction of the self as rational, transparent, self-knowing, and unified, and on the Hegelian dialectic that posits truth as the product of rational dialogue between self-knowing subjects. As Mouffe (1993) points out, there is no necessity to connect these two parts of the modernist project. It is possible to rethink the self-foundational aspects of the modernist project, while still remaining committed to ideals of democracy and social justice, albeit in a contingent, plural and localized way. As Mouffe (1993, p. 7) argues

> In order to radicalize the idea of pluralism, so as to make it a vehicle for a deepening of the democratic revolution, we have to break with rationalism, individualism, and universalism. Only on that condition will it be possible to apprehend the multiplicity of forms of subordination that exist in social relations and to provide a

framework for the articulation of the different democratic struggles — around gender, race, class, sexuality, environment, and others.

For us, the abandonment of metanarratives does not entail the abandonment of projects of emancipation, but their expansion and diversification. The excitement and challenges of recent and contemporary times are elegantly captured by Laclau and Mouffe (1990), who argued:

> We are living [in] one of the most exhilarating moments of the twentieth century: a moment in which new generations, without the prejudices of the past, without theories presenting themselves as 'absolute truths' of history, are constructing new emancipatory discourses, more human, diversified, and democratic. The eschatological and epistemological ambitions are more modest, but the liberating aspirations are wider and deeper. (p. 98)

Mouffe (1993) also argues for a distinction between political modernity and social modernity. The former refers to political liberalism, especially democracy, whereas the latter refers to economic modernization, particularly in terms of capitalist production. Hayhoe appears not to make this distinction in her assessment of the benefits of modernity, but given the rapacious impact of capitalism on people and the environment, this is an important distinction to make. Furthermore, Hayhoe's argument conceives that postmodernism is against modernism. As various authors have argued, however, postmodernism is better understood as existing alongside and as a response to modernism (see for example Pillow, 2000).

Second, some texts argue that the mistrust of metanarratives leads to "*blasé* ironic detachment" (Welch, 2000, p. 200), relativism, and anti-historicism (Watson, 1998). Yet these views suggest a particular and essentialized reading of a narrow range of postmodern literature. Watson (1998), for example, essentializes the argument and argues that postmodernism "rejects total explanations for causes and events, and as such challenges the concept of historical interpretation" (p. 13). Bain (1995, p. 10), however, observes it is not that a mistrust of metanarratives has resulted in the disappearance of all meaning. Rather, meaning itself, and meaning-making, including the writing of history, become problematized in terms of their construction, effects, legitimation, and their implication in power relations. Rather than being universal, meaning is construed as contingent, locally constituted, and tied up in relations of power. Postmodernism, rather than instigating the abandonment of all meaning-making and a retreat into ironic detachment, brings to the surface contingencies, constitutions, and relations. Furthermore, as St. Pierre argues, the production of an objectivism/relativism binary is based on assumptions that are disputable when truth is thought of as "multiple, historical, contextual, contingent, political, and bound up in power relations" (St. Pierre, 2000, p. 25).

Third, it is argued that postmodernism has descended into a linguistic labyrinth that is of little use to the practical and socially emancipatory concerns of CE (Welch 1999, p. 39–40; 2000, pp. 201ff.). The problems with this argument are first that it sets up a binary between language/text and political engagement (Welch, 2000, p. 203), as if the two were mutually exclusive. Yet language and texts are political, and to be politically engaged means in part dealing with the material effects of language and texts (hook, 2001, MacLure, 2003). Second, the criticism echoes calls for postmodern writing to be somehow more comprehensible. St. Pierre (2000, p. 25) observes that such criticism assumes that the responsibility for intelligibility lies solely with the author, and that "for some reason, these readers expect postmodernism to be readily accessible and coherent within a structure it works against." In addition, it assumes, contrary to poststructuralist ideas, that language simply reflects reality, and that singular, clear readings of texts are possible (MacLure, 2003).

Fourth, it is argued that postmodernism is Eurocentric (Tikly 1999, Cowen, 1996). According to Cowen (1996, p. 165), postmodernism "does not reflect or read the structural socioeconomic conditions, ideological projects, educational systems, or self-society issues of identity in Japan, Taiwan, or South Korea, still less, China. It cannot easily be extended to understand the state projects for the construction of Islamic identity in Algeria, Iran, Malaysia, or Pakistan." The basis for this criticism, presumably, is that Lyotard's "The Postmodern Condition" (1984) focuses on knowledge in advanced industrial societies, and that many post-modern thinkers are Westerners. If so, this argument again sets up binaries between 'the West' and 'the rest,' and between advanced industrial societies and other societies. We should not assume that since a set of ideas develops in one particular geographic area within a particular set of cultural and social contexts, they cannot be applied or adapted in other contexts and places. How curious that we would place this barrier in front of postmodernism but not apply it to the modernist metanarratives of social justice, democracy, and emancipation. Given the extreme historical and contemporary impact of the cultural, political, environmental and economic activities of advanced industrial societies on the rest of the world, and the apparently accelerating exchanges of ideas and people around the globe with advances in communications and transport, from which there appears to be no retreat (Bauman, 2002, p. 19), the suggestion that some how postmodern social analyses are quarantined in and apply only to advanced industrial societies is difficult to support.

What then are the implications of the postmodern condition and a postmodern sensibility for education? Peters (1995, p. xxx) argues that in the postmodern condition, lacking metanarratives to legitimize knowledge and education, the state employs performativity to legitimize science and education. Performativity underpins the monetarism and economic rationalism driving much education reform, and is based on the assumption that "individuals are rational utility maximizers and ... the pursuit of self-interest in the marketplace will yield socially and economically desirable outcomes" (Peters, 1995, p. xxxi). Watson (1999) has rightly called on comparative educators to challenge the dominance of economic thinking driving education reform, and although he warns against the dangers for comparative education of postmodernism, he suggests a solution that is rather Lyotardian. Watson (1999) calls for an insistence on the importance of social, cultural, and historical contexts, rather than quick and easy one-size-fits-all solutions. According to Peters (1995), Lyotard offers a similar approach, namely, legitimation of educational practice by paralogy, that is the study of little narratives and local determinism, or, an emphasis on the way in which people in specific contexts make meaning and make sense of the world around them.

Perhaps, if CE does consider itself serious about issues of social justice as Welch (2000) advocates, it could do well to more seriously engage with postmodern literature, because as Fritzman notes, postmodern sensibilities are centrally concerned with uncovering, resisting, and witnessing oppressions:

The task is not only to resist recognized oppressions but also to invent new self-descriptions, to bear witness to those oppressions that are not now recognized as such, and to testify to the possibility of still unimagined new languages that would call into question currently accepted practices and institutions. (Fritzman, 1995, p. 72)

Poststructuralisms

As noted above, much of the debate in CE about postfoundational studies has tended to conflate postmodernism and poststructuralism. We wish to distinguish between the two sets of ideas because we believe this distinction has important implications for CE. To make this distinction it is important first to distinguish between structuralism and modernism. According to Peters (1999), structuralism has much less to do with aesthetics than modernism. Structuralism developed from literary criticism, discourse analysis and poetics, and challenged the humanist models that interpreted particular texts as the unique expression of an author (Peters, 1999, par. 2.7). Structuralism in its early applications was a structural-functional approach to the scientific study of language, involving a search for relations between elements of language and the inner laws of social and linguistic structures (Peters, 1999). Poststructuralism can perhaps be best thought of as an extension rather than a complete repudiation of structuralism. According to Peters (1999), the two sets of ideas have some common features. Both share a suspicion of philosophical approaches such as phenomenology and existentialism that privilege rationality and human consciousness as a means of deriving universal truths about the world. They share a belief in the subconscious and in hidden structures and forces that constrain and govern behavior. Both view linguistic signs as reflexive rather than referential, and both acknowledge the importance of social, historical, and cultural contexts in constituting people as subjects. On the other hand, whereas structuralism attempted to employ scientific approaches to the analysis of structures in order to unpack history, poststructuralism emphasizes a critical history, especially around questions of ontology (ways of seeing reality or being), and challenges the scientism of the human sciences and foundationalist discourses in epistemology (Peters, 1999).

Peters (1998) argues that 'poststructuralism' is a multifaceted and contested concept. It reacts to and escapes from Hegelian thought. That is, whereas Hegel sought a harmonious whole truth through the transcendence of the dialectic between opposing but related propositions, poststructuralisms affirm difference: "The rule of consensus that governed the Enlightenment narratives and cast truth as a product of agreement between rational minds has finally been rent asunder" (Peters, 1995, p. xxvi).

In analyzing the genealogy of poststructural thought, Peters (1998, 1999) notes poststructuralisms' debt to Nietzsche. Whereas Marx emphasized power and Freud emphasized desire, Nietzsche combines the two. Nietzsche developed ideas around the plurality of interpretation, and power-knowledge relations, including the will to power, the will to truth, and the will to knowledge. Drawing on Nietzsche, Foucault embarked on analyses that resisted the search for essences and origins, Lyotard deconstructed universalizing tendencies, Derrida challenged binary oppositions and binary thinking and their associated hierarchies, while Deleuze focused on pure difference instead of the Hegelian dialectic (Peters, 1999). Peters (1999, par. 4.8) suggests that

> All of these thinkers together emphasize the way meaning is an active construction radically dependent upon the pragmatics of the context and, thereby challenge the universality of truth claims ... [They also challenge the] Cartesian-Kantian humanistic subject as an autonomous, free, and transparently self-conscious subject that is traditionally regarded as the fount of all knowledge, and moral and political agency, [and instead regard the subject as] de-centered within the language system, discursively constituted, and positioned at the intersection of libidinal forces and socio-cultural practices.

A growing body of literature is addressing the issue of the application of poststructuralist thought to educational contexts. Although a number of authors have used poststructural theory to frame their research, there has been little discussion in the comparative education literature of the contributions which poststructuralisms could make to the field, except for our own work over the last few years (Ninnes, 1998; Ninnes and Mehta, 2000; Mehta and Ninnes, 2000; Ninnes and Burnett, 2001; Mehta, 2001; Ninnes and Burnett, 2003).

Peters (1998, pp. 12–13) argues that poststructuralisms' contributions to education include the development of complex ideas about teacher and student subjectivities; new ways of thinking about language, reading, writing, and texts; ideas about the relationships between discourse, power, and knowledge; powerful and novel approaches to analyzing educational policies, institutions, practices, administration, and management; the disruption of binary thinking; the acknowledgement of desire as a component in analyzing education; and new theorizing about difference.

There have been a number of key pieces of research published in the field of CE in recent years that illustrate the application of poststructuralist ideas. As previous research has demonstrated, much of this substantive application has drawn on a number of key concepts developed by a small number of authors, with the works of Foucault dominating the material published in CE journals in the last decade (Ninnes and Burnett, 2001).

To demonstrate the use of poststructuralist ideas in CE in the last decade, we will draw on the work of Ninnes and Burnett (2003) to focus on the substantive use of Foucault's ideas. Foucault's conceptions of power as ubiquitous and inextricably linked to knowledge, and of the state as one nodal point in a complex network of power relations are employed by Davies (1996), Ginsburg, Kamat, Raghu, and Weaver (1992), Magalhães (1995) and Clark (1993). The idea of disciplinary power (Foucault, 1977a, 1977b, 1980), a power which observes, judges, controls, and constitutes individuals as subjects through the creation and maintenance of regimes of truth, is employed by Currie (1998) and Stromquist (1995). Foucault's notion that power is implicated in constituting notions of what is true, that is, in constructing regimes of truth, is shown in Talbani's (1996) analysis of the Islamization of education in Pakistan. The analysis of the relationships between discourses, knowledge, and power is advocated by Rust (1991) and Magalhães (1995) as a means of challenging inequity and disadvantage and of contributing to social change.

Foucault's conception of the subject has been used rather circumspectly in CE. Pineau (1994) examines the relationship between various models of education and the constitution of the subject, while Muller (1998) examines the way in which particular curriculum reforms constitute certain kinds of learners. De Alba (1999) cites a number of authors, including Foucault (1972), to argue that the subject is constituted through discursive practices.

Three broad methodological approaches can be indentified in Foucault's work — archaeology, genealogy and problematization of ethics (Gutting, 1994). Gutting (1994) argues that archaeology is principally about the history of concepts or ideas, e.g. madness, knowledge, and civilization. On the other hand, genealogies are histories of the present, that is, histories of institutions and practices which examine how it is that things came to be the way they are, not in terms of a "grand narrative of inevitable progress [but] by tracing the origins of practices and institutions from a congeries of contingent 'petty causes'" (Gutting, 1994, p. 14). If comparative education should focus on the institutions of education, as Cummings (1999) so passionately argues, then it would appear that genealogical approaches have great potential for expanding the insights available to comparative educators. According to Flynn (1994, p. 37), problematization builds on archaeological and genealogical methods by examining the "truth games" which people play when they construct themselves as subjects, that is, the "way we fashion subjectivity" (Bernauer and Mahon, 1994, p. 143).

There are very few examples of these kinds of methodologies being employed in the CE literature in the last decade, except for Baeck's (1999) archaeology of discourses of development, and Talbani's (1996) and Buenfil Burgos' (1999) genealogical analysis of education in Pakistan and Mexico respectively. The only study approaching a problematization of ethics is Pineau's (1994) examination of the kinds of subjectification involved in various models of education.

In the broader education literature, a number of collections have attempted to apply poststructuralisms to educational issues. Interested readers may wish to examine the collections edited by Ball (1990), Peters (1998), Popkewitz and Brennan (1998), St. Pierre and Pillow (2000), Palermo and McWilliam (2002) and Baker and Heyning (2003). Within these works there are a number of pieces that are of substantial relevance to CE. For example, the collection by Popekwitz and Brennan contains chapters on teacher education in Finland (Simola, Heikkinen and Silvonen, 1998), early childhood education in Sweden (Hultqvist, 1998), the construction of the concept of childhood in US public schools (Baker, 1998), and the social role of the educational intellectual (Blacker, 1998).

Postcolonialisms

As is the case with postmodernism and poststructuralism, there are many ways of conceptualizing postcolonialism. Gandhi (1998) makes a useful distinction between postcoloniality, which is a set of social conditions, and postcolonialism, which is a set of theoretical perspectives for analyzing those social conditions. Postcolonial studies address a range of issues, including the diverse experiences of colonialism and its aftermath. These experiences vary in different societies. For example, postcoloniality in Jamaica is quite different to postcoloniality in Australia (Hall, 1996).

Hall (1996) argues that postcolonial refers to a general process of (de)colonization which has had profound effects both in the colonized and colonizing societies. The binaries of colonized/colonizer, which dominated early works on colonialism and its effects, needs to be re-read because of the multiple, contradictory and complex effects of colonialism.

Postcolonialism requires a global reading of colonialism and its effects as complexly transcultural and transnational. Hall (1996) further suggests that postcolonialism is concerned with the internalization of the effects of colonization within decolonized societies and "the proliferation of histories and temporalities, the intrusion of difference and specificity into the generalizing and Eurocentric post-Enlightenment grand narratives, [and] the multiplicity of lateral and decentred cultural connections, movements and migrations which make up the world today, often bypassing the old metropolitan centres." (Hall, 1996, p. 248).

Whereas colonialism constructs a binary opposition of colonizer and colonized, postcolonialism works to break down that binary, working with the idea that subjects and identities are multiple, diverse, and contested, and that experiences of colonialism are fractured along class, gender, ethnic, and other lines (see, for example, McClintock, 1995). Postcolonial theory, according to Hall, sees colonialism as both a period of rule and a process of European expansion, exploration, conquest, and cultural homogenization. Thus, the task of the postcolonial thinker is to interrupt processes of binary and essentialist identity construction of 'others' and the western grand narratives of modernity and globalization (Hall, 1996).

Gandhi (1998) suggests that to date postcolonialism has made important inroads into breaking down the epistemological exclusiveness of the western academy. However, in doing so it has labeled as marginal those knowledges that are central in the non-west. Gandhi therefore advocates an engagement with "the theoretical self-sufficiency of African, Indian, Korean, [and] Chinese knowledge systems" and the foregrounding of "those cultural and historical conversations that circumvent the Western world" (p. x). Hall (1996) suggests, too, that postcolonialism has not yet taken economic ideas into account. It is as if because the grand narrative of economic foundations has been undermined, economic relations do not exist at all. Yet Loomba (1998, cited in Tikly, 1999) argues that postcolonialism does not ignore economic relations but provides an alternative way of reading or interpreting them.

Comparative education has not shirked from engaging with issues of colonialism and neo-colonialism. The works by Carnoy (1974) and Altbach and Kelly (Altbach, 1971, 1982; Altbach and Kelly, 1978a, 1978b) illustrate the extent to which this engagement has occurred, particularly in terms of dependency theory. As Tikly (1999) has observed, this work "provided a valuable critique of human capital and modernization theory, which had treated the colonial relationship as unproblematic" (p. 609), and linked colonialism, neo-colonialism and education. However, according to Tikly (1999), dependency theory is limited by its fundamentally economic focus and its subsequent lack of engagement with issues of race, culture, identity, and language. It tends not to consider the contradictory effects of relations between the colonized and colonizer nor the development of alternatives and resistance to colonialism, and it employs binary oppositions (colonizer/colonized; center/periphery). Furthermore, it employs the nation state as the unit of analysis, which, as various authors have argued, is becoming highly problematic in this age of 'globalization' (see, for example, Cowen, 2000; Crossley, 1999, 2000; Crossley and Jarvis, 2000; Watson, 1999).

Within CE, there has been a substantive engagement with issues of culture. Yet the concept of culture has been primarily theorized from anthropological perspectives (Masemann, 1982, 1990). Tikly, however, argues that postcolonial approaches offer a more sophisticated alternative to such perspectives, which tend to essentialize culture and view identity as fixed. Postcolonialism problematizes these approaches, and also pays more attention to issues of racism in colonial relations. Within recent CE literature, a number of authors have attempted to substantively apply perspectives from postcolonial theory. These works are reviewed by Peter Ninnes and Greg Burnett (this volume).

References

Abu-Lughod, Lila. "Writing against culture." In *Recapturing Anthropology: Working in the Present.* Edited by R. Fox. New Mexico: School of American Research, 1991.

Altbach, Philip. "Eduction and neocolonialism." *Teachers College Record* 72 (1) (1971): 543–558.
_____. "Servitude of the mind? Education, dependency, and neo-colonialism". In *Comparative Education.* Edited by Philip Altbach, R. Arnove, and G. Kelly. New York: Macmillan, 1982.

Altbach, Philip and Gail Kelly. *Education and Colonialism.* New York: Longman, 1978a.

Altbach, Philip and Gail Kelly. *Education and the Colonial Experience.* New York: Transaction Books, 1978b.

Appadurai, Arjun. *Modernity at large: Cultural dimensions of globalization.* Minneapolis: University of Minnesota Press, 1996.

Baeck, L. "Text and context in the thematization on development." *Prospects* 29 (1999): 459–477.

Bain, William. "The loss of innocence: Lyotard, Foucault and the challenge of postmodern education." In *Education and the postmodern condition.* Edited by M. Peters. Westport, Conn.: Bergin and Garvey, 1995.

Baker, Bernadette. "Childhood" in the emergence and spread of US public schools. In *Foucault's Challenge: Discourse, Knowledge and Power in Education.* Edited by Thomas Popkewitz and Marie Brennan. New York: Teachers College Press, 1998.

Baker, Bernadette and Katharina Heyning. *Dangerous coagulations: The uses of Foucault in the study of education.* New York: Peter Lang, 2003.

Ball, Stephen (Ed.). *Foucault and Education: Disciplines and Knowledge.* London: Routledge, 1990.

Bauman, Zygmunt. *Society under Siege.* Cambridge, UK: Polity Press, 2002.

Bernauer, J. and M. Mahon. 1994. The ethics of Michel Foucault. In G. Gutting (ed) *The Cambridge Companion to Foucault,* Cambridge UP, Cambridge (pp. 141–158).

Bhabha, Homi (Ed.). *Nation and Narration.* London and New York: Routledge, 1990.

Blacker, David. "Intellectuals at work and in power: Toward a Foucaultian research ethic." In *Foucault's Challenge: Discourse, Knowledge and Power in Education.* New York: Teachers College Press, 1998.

Blake, Nigel et al., *Thinking again: Education after postmodernism.* Westport, Conn.: Bergin and Garvey, 1998.

Buenfil, Burgos, R. N. "The spectre of theory in curriculum for educational researchers: A Mexican example." *International Review of Education* 45 (1999): 461–478.

Carnoy, Martin. *Education as Cultural Imperialism.* New York: Longman, 1974.

Chatterjee, P. *Nationalist thought and the colonial world: A derivative discourse.* New Delhi: Oxford University Press, 1986.

Clark, S. "The schooling of cultural and ethnic subordinate groups." *Comparative Education Review* 37(1) (1993): 62–68.

Cowen, Robert. "Last past the post: Comparative education, modernity, and perhaps post-modernity." *Comparative Education* 32(2) (1996): 151–170.

_____. "Comparing futures or comparing pasts?" *Comparative Education* 36(3) (2000): 333–342.

_____. 1999 "Reconceptualising Comparative and International Education." *Compare* 29 (3) (1999): 249–67.

Crossely, Michael. "Bridging cultures and traditions in the reconceptualisation of comparative and international education." *Comparative Education* 36(3) (2000): 319–332.

Crossley, Michael and Peter Jarvis. "Introduction: Continuity, challenge and change in comparative and international education." *Comparative Education* 36(3) (2000): 261–265.

Cummings, William. "The institutions of education: Compare, compare, compare!" *Comparative Education Review* 43(4) (1999): 413–437.

Currie, Jan. "Globalization practices and the professoriate in Anglo-Pacific and North American universities." *Comparative Education Review* 42 (1998): 15–29.

Darville, R. "Knowledges of adult literacy: Surveying for competitiveness." *International Journal of Educational Development* 19 (1999): 273–285.

Davies, J. "The state and the South African university system under apartheid." *Comparative Education* 32(3) (1996): 319–332.

De Alba, Alicia. "Curriculum and society: Rethinking the link." *International Review of Education* 45 (1999): 479–490.

Epstein, Irwin. "Comparative education in North America: The search for other through the escape from self?" *Compare* 25 (1995): 5–16.

Errante, Antoinette. "Education and National Personae in Portugal's Colonial and Postcolonial Transition." *Comparative Education Review* 42 (3) (1998): 267–308.

Fabian, J. *Time and the other: How anthropology makes its object*. New York: Columbia University Press, 1983.

Flynn, T. "Foucault's mapping of history." In *The Cambridge Companion to Foucault*, edited by G. Gutting. Cambridge: Cambridge UP, 1994.

Foucault, Michel. *Archaeology of knowledge*, trans., Sheridan-Smith, A.M., London: Tavistock Publications, 1972.

Foucault, Michael. *Discipline and punish: The birth of the prison*. London: Penguin,1977a.

Foucault, Michael. *Language, counter memory, practice: Selected essays and interviews*, trans., Bouchard, D. F. and S. Simon. Blackwell, Oxford: 1977b.

Foucault, Michael. *Power/knowledge: Selected interviews and other writings 1972–1977*. Ed. C. Gordon. New York: Pantheon, 1980.

Foucault, Michael. "Afterward: The subject and power." In *Michel Foucault: Beyond structuralism and hermeneutics*. Edited by Dreyfus, H. and P. Rabinow. Chicago: The Harvester Press Ltd., 1982.

Fritzman, J. M. "From pragmatism to the differend." In *Education and the postmodern condition* (pp. 59–74). Edited by Michael Peters. Westport, Conn.: Bergin and Garvey, 1995.

Gandhi, Leela. *Postcolonial theory: A critical introduction*. Sydney: Allen and Unwin, 1998.

Ginsburg, Mark et al. "Educators/Politics." *Comparative Education Review* 36 (1992): 417–445.

Gutting, Gary. "Introduction: Michel Foucault – A user's manual." *The Cambridge companion to Foucault*. Edited by G. Gutting. Cambridge: Cambridge UP, 1994.

Hall, Stuart. 1996. "When was the postcolonial? Thinking at the limit." *The Post-colonial question*. (pp. 242–260). Edited by I. Chambers and L. Curti. London: Routledge, 1996.

Hayhoe, Ruth. 2000. "Redeeming modernity." *Comparative Education Review* 44 (2000): 423–439.

Hoffman, Diane. "Culture and Comparative Education: Toward Decentering and Recentring the Discourse." *Comparative Education Review* 43 4 (1999): 464–88.

Hook, Derek. 2001. Discourse, knowledge, materiality, history: Foucault and discourse analysis. *Theory and Psychology* 11, 521–547.

hooks, bell. *Talking Back: Thinking Feminist, Thinking Black*. Toronto: Between the Lines, 1990.

Hultqvist, Kenneth. "A history of the present on children's welfare in Sweden: From Frobel to present-day decentralization projects." In *Foucault's Challenge: Discourse, Knowledge and Power in Education*. Edited by Thomas Popkewitz and Marie Brennan. New York: Teachers College Press, 1998.

Kelly, Gail. P., Philip G. Altbach, and Robert F. Arnove. "Trends in comparative education: A critical analysis." In *Comparative Education*. Edited by P. G. Altbach, R. F. Arnove and G. P. Kelly. New York: Macmillan Publishing, 1982.

Lacalu, E. and C. Mouffe. "Post-Marxism without Apologies." *In New Reflections on the Revolution of Our Time* (pp. 97–132). Edited by E. Laclau. London: Verso, 1990.

Lyotard, J. F. *The postmodern condition: A report on knowledge*, trans., Bennington, G. and B. Massumi. Minneapolis: University of Minnesota Press, 1984.

Magalhães, I. 1995. "Beliefs about literacy in a Brazilian Community." *International Journal of Educational Development* 15(3): 263–276.

Masemann, Vandra. "Critical ethnography in the study of comparative education." *Comparative Education Review* 26 (1982): 1–15.

Masemann, Vandra. "Ways of knowing: Implications for comparative education." *Comparative Education Review* 34 3 (1990): 463–473.

McClintock, A. *Imperial leather: Race, gender, and sexuality in the colonial conquest.* New York: Routledge, 1995.

McConaghy, Cathryn. *Rethinking Indigenous Education: Culturalism, Colonialism, and the Politics of Knowing.* Flaxton, Queensland: Post Press, 2000.

MacLure, Maggie. *Discourse in educational and social research.* Buckingham: Open University Press, 2000.

McHoul, Alex and Wendy Grace. *A Foucault primer: Discourse, power and the subject.* Carlton, Victoria: Melbourne University Press, 1993.

Mehta, Sonia. "Doing comparative education: Positioning possibilities." *Paper presented at the CIES annual conference, Washington DC*, 14–17 March, 2001.

Mehta, Sonia and Peter Ninnes. (forthcoming) "The word became text: Disciplining comparative education." Manuscript submitted to *Comparative Education Review*.

Mehta, Sonia and Peter Ninnes. "Postpositivist debates and comparative education: Resistance, reinvention, revolution." *Paper presented at the CIES annual conference*, San Antonio, Texas, 2000.

Mouffe, Chantal. *The Return of the Political.* London: Verso, 1993.

Muller, J. "The well-tempered learner: Self-regulation, pedagogical models and teacher education policy." *Comparative Education* 34 (1998): 177–193.

Nandy, Ashish. "The psychology of colonialism: Sex, age, and ideology in British India." *Psychiatry* 45 (August) (1982): 192–218.

Ninnes, Peter. "Learning a new dance: The infiltration or otherwise of Foucault's ideas in scholarly articles in comparative and international education." *Paper presented at the Comparative and International Education Society (Western Region) conference*, Vancouver, 11–13 June, 1998.

Ninnes, Peter and Greg Burnett. "Opening comparative education research: Poststructuralist possibilities." *Paper presented at the Comparative and International Education Society annual conference*, Washington DC, 14–17 March, 2001.

Ninnes, Peter and Sonia Mehta. "Postpositivist theorizing and research: Challenges and opportunities for comparative education." *Comparative Education Review* 44 (2000): 205–212.

Palermo, James and Erica McWilliam. *Poststructuralism and the pedagogic moment.* New York: Peter Lang, 2002.

Paulston, Rolland. "Mapping discourse in comparative education texts." *Compare* 23 (1993): 101–114.

_____. "Comparative and international education: Paradigms and theories." In *International Encyclopedia of Education* (2nd ed.), (pp. 923–933). Edited by T. Husén and N. Postlethwaite. Oxford: Pergamon, 1994.

_____. "Mapping Visual Culture in Comparative Education Discourse." *Compare*, 27 2 (1997): 117–52.

_____. "Mapping comparative education after postmodernity." *Comparative Education Review* 43 4 (1999): 438–463.

_____. "Imagining comparative education: Past, present, future." *Compare* 30 (2000): 353–367.

Paulston, Rolland. and Martin Leibman. "An Invitation to postmodern social cartography." *Comparative Education Review* 38 2 (1994): 215–232.

Peters, Michael. "Introduction: Lyotard, education, and the postmodern condition." In *Education and the postmodern condition*. Edited by M. Peters. Westport, Conn.: Bergin and Garvey, 1995.

_____. *Naming the Multiple: Poststructuralism and Education*. Westport Connecticut: Bergin and Garvey, 1998.

_____. "(Posts) structuralism and modernism: Affinities and theoretical innovations." *Sociological Research Online* 4 (1999): 3.

Peters, Michael and Colin Lankshear. "Postmodern counternarratives." In *Counternarratives: Cultural studies and critical pedagogies in postmodern spaces* (pp. 1–39). Edited by H. Giroux, C. Lankshear, P. McLaren, and M. Peters. New York and London: Routledge, 1996.

Pillow, Wanda. "Deciphering attempts to decipher postmodern educational research." *Educational Researcher* 29 5 (2000): 21–24.

Pineau, Gaston. "Histoires de vie et formation de nouveaux savoirs vitaux." *International Review of Education* 40 3–5 (1994): 299–311.

Popkewitz, Thomas. "National imaginaries, the indigenous foreigner, and power: Comparative educational research." In *Discourse Formation in Comparative Education* (pp. 261–294). Edited by J. Schreiwer. Frankfurt: Peter Lang, 2000.

Popkewitz, Thomas and Marie Brennan (Eds). *Foucault's Challenge: Discourse, Knowledge and Power in Education*. New York: Teachers College Press, 1998.

Renan, Ernest. "What is a nation?" In *Nation and narration* (pp. 8–22). Edited by H. Bhabha. London and New York: Routledge, 1990.

Rust, Val. "Postmodernism and its comparative education implications." *Comparative Education Review* 35 4 (1991): 610–626.

Rust, Val., A. Soumar, O. Pescador, and M. Shibuya. "Research strategies in comparative education." *Comparative Education Review* 43 1 (1999): 86–109.

Simola, Hannu, Sakari Heikkinen, and Jussi Silvonen. "A catalog of possibilities: Foucaultian history of truth and education research." In *Foucault's Challenge: Discourse, Knowledge and Power in Education*. Edited by T. Popkewitz and M. Brennan. New York: Teachers College Press (pp. 64–90), 1998.

Spivak, Gayatri. *The post-colonial critic: Interviews, strategies, dialogues*. New York: Routledge, 1990.

St. Pierre, Elizabeth. "The call for intelligibility in postmodern educational research." *Educational Researcher* 295 (2000): 25–28.

St. Pierre, Elizabeth and Wanda Pillow. "Introduction: Inquiry among the Ruins." In *Working the ruins: Feminist poststructural theory and methods in education*. Edited by E. St. Pierre and W. Pillow (pp. 1–24). New York and London: Routledge, 2000.

Stromquist, Nelly. 1995. "Romancing the state: Gender and power in education." *Comparative Education Review* 394 (1995): 423–454.

Talbani, Aziz. "Pedagogy, power and discourse: Transformation of Islamic education." *Comparative Education Review* 40 1(1996): 66–82.

Tikly, Leon. "Postcolonialism and comparative education." *International Review of Education* 45 (1999): 603–621.

Watson, Keith. "Memories, models and mapping: The impact of geopolitical changes on comparative studies in education." *Compare* 28 (1998): 5–33.

_____. "Comparative education research: The need for reconceptualisation and fresh insights." *Compare* 29 3 (1999): 233–248.

Welch, Anthony. "The functionalist tradition in comparative education." *Comparative Education* 21 (1985): 5–19.

_____. "The triumph of technocracy or the collapse of certainty? Modernity, postmodernity and postcolonialism in comparative education." In *Comparative Education: The Dialectic of the Global and the Local* (pp. 25–49). Edited by R. Arnove and C. A. Torres. Baltimore: Rowman and Littlefield, 1999.

_____. "New times, hard times: Re-reading comparative education in an age of discontent." In *Discourse Formation in Comparative Education* (pp. 189–225) edited by J. Schreiwer. Frankfurt: Peter Lang, 2000.

Welch, Anthony and Burns, Robin. 1992. "Introduction: Reflections upon the field." In *Contemporary Perspectives in Comparative Education* (pp. xi–xlv). Edited by R. Burns and A. Welch. New York: Garland Publishing, 1992.

Wilson, David. "Comparative and International Education: Fraternal or Siamese twins? A preliminary genealogy of our twin fields." *Comparative Education Review* 38 4 (1994): 449–486.

Wright, H. K. "Educational Change in Sierra Leone: Making a Case for Critical African Drama." *International Journal of Educational Development* 14 2 (1994): 177–193.

Young, Robert. "Comparative methodology and postmodern relativism." *International Review of Education* 43 5–6 (1997): 497–505.

CHAPTER 2

'Post' Cards from a Pedagogical Edge[1]

SONIA MEHTA

Achilles had overtaken the Tortoise, and had seated himself comfortably on its back.

"So you've got to the end of the race-course?" said the Tortoise. "Even though it does consist of an infinite series of distances? I thought some wiseacre or other had proved that the thing couldn't be done?"

"It can be done," said Achilles. "It has been done! *Solvitur ambulando.* You see the distances were constantly diminishing; and so —"

"But if they had been constantly increasing?" the Tortoise interrupted. "How then?"

"Then I shouldn't be here, " Achilles modestly replied; "and you would have got several times round the world by this time!"

"You flatter me — flatten, I mean," said the Tortoise; "for you are a heavy weight, and no mistake! Well now, would you like to hear of a race-course, that most people fancy they can get to the end of in two or three steps, while it really consists of an infinite number of distances, each one longer than the previous one?"

"Very much indeed!" said the Grecian warrior, as he drew from his helmet (few Grecian warriors possessed pockets in those days) an enormous note-book and pencil. "Proceed! And speak slowly please! Shorthand isn't invented yet!"

---

[1] Apologies to Elizabeth St. Pierre and Wanda Pillow (2000), from whom I borrowed the idea of a 'post' card; apologies as well to the popular movie with a similar name as my title.

> Here the narrator, having pressing business at the Bank, was
> obliged to leave the happy pair, and did not again pass the spot
> until some months afterwards.
>
> — Lewis Carroll, "What the Tortoise said to Achilles," Mind, n.s.,
> 4 (1895), pp. 278–80.

This chapter is about teaching comparative education because it is also
about learning comparative education. My concern in this chapter is to
draw into comparative education discourse, debates about pedagogy in
general, and the pedagogy of comparative education in particular. My
concern is bound up with my argument, which sees pedagogy in this field
on three levels: The contexts of teaching and learning comparative education make pedagogy in this field a performative act, a possible site of articulation for the 'unsaid' and therefore, powerful in all its 'unpredictable
generative potential' (Martusewicz, 2001, p. xiv). As a performative act,
pedagogy takes its life from its context and its moment, where 'context' is
the network of relations around the act of teaching and learning
(Ellsworth, 1997, p. 159). In Todd's conceptualization, pedagogy "argues
for the need to develop an awareness of desire as a mediating factor in the
recognition and enunciation of difference. It regards desire as that which
ceaselessly circulates through the *unsaid* [original emphasis] of classroom
life." (Todd, 1997, p.239). Therefore, pedagogy represents a disruption
whose outcomes cannot be predicted, while yet being rooted in its context
and time, can enable articulation and be generative. Pedagogy, explored
for this, is a broad term covering both the 'vision' and 'instruction' (Gore,
1993) of comparative education, where I take pedagogy to mean all the
'process (es) of knowledge production' (Lusted, 1986, quoted in Gore,
1993, p. 4). That is to say, I focus on pedagogy as producing meaning in
the transference of knowledge that constructs and constitutes us as comparative educators, students and teachers of comparative education. In
appropriating Carroll's appropriation of Zeno's Achilles and the Tortoise, I
present a metaphor for the teaching and learning of comparative education. One might choose to see pedagogy in comparative education as a
race-course, an exercise in competitive (or comparative) mastery with a
finish line that proclaims victory for some and defeat for others. Or one
might choose, as I do in this chapter, to see it simply as a 'course,' a process
that includes and embraces the shifting and multiple layers of identity, of
experience, and the uncertainties and possibilities of education in the global arena of education. This course is dynamic in 'seeking passage,' as
Rebecca Martusewicz (2001) puts it, towards a more inclusive relationship
with the complex world in which we live and work. Thus, I privilege pedagogical processes that do not establish an end-point, but whose 'infinite
number of distances and horizons' increasingly increase, so as to encom-
pass a reflexivity that resonates with the particular opportunities that this
field offers. How can one reconstruct and re-imagine such pedagogies for

the field? I choose to do this from 'deleted' work (Star, 1991), and perceptions of absences, gaps and need from students in comparative education. Therefore, this chapter presents my reading of student subjectivity vis-à-vis their engagements with the field. There are three reasons for crafting pedagogical concepts from a student-learner's point of view: first, to tap into what may be 'silenced' needs and desires in the field. Second, I wish to interrupt the discourse of teaching comparative education by recentering learner experience, difference and desire as 'contexts' informing the pedagogical process. Third, I focus on students in (and not of) the field, because they are actively engaged with the pedagogy of the field, being constructed by it as well as continuously constructing it through a process of interpretation and application. Reading this from postfoundational concepts, which focus on pedagogy as constitutive of desire, difference, identity and Otherness, I then propose a re-imagined pedagogical modality as both 'vision' and 'instruction' (Gore, 1993) for the field. Gore reminds us that every pedagogical approach emphasizes its own social vision for education and schooling. In connecting the micro (instruction) and the macro (vision), she further points out that these two concepts are not mutually exclusive, and that "differences in arguments about pedagogy...do not reflect the empirical realities of pedagogy. For instance, those approaches that emphasize instruction also contain within them a social vision, perhaps not an explicit vision" (p. 4). The chapter is itself organized as a critique of pedagogy, deploying its argument as pedagogy while arguing for particular pedagogical conceptualizations. As I analyze and present analysis, I am aware that I am also in the process of inscribing subjectivities and discourse. Much will be missing from this analysis but it is presented nevertheless as demonstrative of the need for such a debate in the field, and is symbolic of the critical reflexive possibilities such a debate might generate. Picking up from Tikly and Crossley's argument (2001) that comparative education has the strength to stand as a discipline that could inform other disciplines, I suggest that the field, seen through postfoundational lenses, may indeed have a pedagogical 'edge.'

The issue of pedagogy has occupied a particular, if rather marginal place in comparative education. There is a distinction to be made regarding methodologies of *how to compare* and methodologies of *how to teach* comparative education. A substantial amount of written work exists on the former, about the appropriate and experimental methods of comparison (Noah and Eckstein, 1968; Koehl, 1977; Eckstein, 1983; Thomas, 1990). The field is marked by many debates about the kinds of knowledge produced by the field, the process of legitimating and valuing certain kinds of knowledges over others (Masemann, 1986; Rust, 1991), the opening/delimiting of the canon (Epstein, 1983) and the need for the inclusion of interdisciplinary approaches within comparative education studies (Cowen, 1996; Ninnes and Burnett, this volume; Ninnes and Mehta, 2001; Mehta and Ninnes, 2003; Gottlieb, 1989; Rust, 1991;

Paulston, 1994). As such there are useful area studies on pedagogy that address the comparative studies of schools or teachers across a geographic or national border (see for example Tatto, 1996). Of the studies that have addressed the question of *how to teach* comparative education, some signal the need for a more critical questioning (Kazamias, 1972; Springer, 1977; Paulston and Liebman, 1994). Earlier work on teaching comparative education focused on instruction and micro-processes that did not necessarily take into account the more intimate constructions of subjectivities and the role of power in the classroom. Bereday (1958), for example, advocates, as preparation for educators to face the "growing responsibilities of education" (p. 3), to teach through area, or regional approaches, teaching through sequence, for which the goal is unity of and adherence to an adopted linear program of education, through the classification of competencies and historical perspective. King (1959) also centers his discussion of pedagogy on how the professor of comparative education should communicate. This is on three levels, each level following from the previous: 1) communicating the 'essence' (pg. 31) to students, 2) following from that, the use of 'problems' to analyze the real subject matter of comparative education which is people and their institutions. The third level, reached when there is a complete understanding and interpretation of the human condition, is beyond the concern of either the student or the teacher of comparative education, and belongs to the realm of epistemology. Methods and goals in this pedagogical advocacy read the teaching of comparative education as finding the underlying, 'real' 'essence' of complete understanding in research. Where it focuses on process, the debates appear to focus on subject-matter, rather than subject-matter and the reason for this subject-matter. Deficiencies in the debate on pedagogy have been raised. In 1972, Kazamias, in his presidential address, pointed out that the orientation of neutrality in the field had omitted any study of the pedagogical culture present in "teaching, learning, knowledge and classroom interaction" (pp. 406–11). Epstein (1995) mentions the lack of area studies on students and Springer (1977) critiques the lack of studies done on teachers and teaching within the field. While these are valid and useful critiques, they do not address in any substantive manner what might occur in the transfer of knowledge among and between different ontological (perceptions of reality) and epistemological (ways of knowing) in the field. There is also an absence of analysis of the construction of learner subjectivity in the field, and of the discursive potential of power through these dimensions. Perhaps we have assumed that questions of pedagogy as the transfer and configuration of knowledge in the field, is an area safely ignored, or a question that adjusts itself to the demands and functions of the field. However, not only are the functions of the field changing, students are changing as well, as school, work, and society (Dimitriadis and McCarthy, 2001; Broadfoot, 1997). Major centers and universities where comparative education is taught, have a national base, but an international clientele and reference group (Altbach et al., 1982; Cowen, 1990). The field attracts and in fact encourages a multi-disciplinary approach to research (Epstein, 1994; Altbach et al., 1982; Paulston, 1994), and finds in its midst scholars who come from not only differing academic fields, but also from differing cultural and academic traditions, who have differing life experiences and expectations. And yet there remains a lack of inquiry into pedagogy within comparative education classrooms, about the students who make up these classrooms and of learning space constructed by CE classrooms. The next two sections of this chapter are organized around Jennifer Gore's (1993) reflexive method of analyzing pedagogy. According to Gore, pedagogies are themselves critiques of pedagogy. Thus, one can interrogate pedagogy through the inconsistencies between "the pedagogy argued for (claims made about the process of knowledge production in the pedagogy) and the pedagogy of the argument (the process of knowledge production evident in the argument itself" (p. 5). I have chosen to present the pedagogy that informs my argument first, which is my study of student discourse in the field. This is then followed by the pedagogy argued for, in a reversal of Gore's conceptualization.

The Pedagogy of the Argument

There were layers to my purpose in this research. I wanted to understand who the students of comparative education are, as well as to understand their perception of the field and the process of knowledge production in relation to their work in the field. In order to be able to construct such a discourse, I used concepts from qualitative analysis of interview data, stemming from a series of questions. However, unlike most qualitative studies that make use of 'triangulation' to get to the veracity of statements and researcher, I used concepts of discourse to represent as many variations of statements as possible, which means there were as many 'truths' represented as there were interviews. Language became important: Articulation was not meant to rest with a better command of English, but rather with the difference of expression used. This is a critical aspect of 'centering' language in comparative education, a field in which English is not the primary language for many of its students. I focused on presenting each interview as a mosaic of this discourse. I constructed the discourse using the postfoundational idea of centering subjectivity (rather than 'the individual') that signals my own desire to understand the workings of desire within comparative education. The conceptual framework driving my methods here come from a need to be able to access and articulate 'invisibilities' or 'deleted work' (Star, 1991), as much as differences and to be able to reach into a private space of reflection. I was interested in how the students, given their desires, their experiences and diversity, constructed the field, which was in turn constructing them.

Therefore my questions came from the need to be able to tap into the sense of personal space of identification and world-view that each student brought into their course of study; I had to begin with points from which students themselves defined who they were, how they came to be in the field, and why. I asked questions about their upbringing; about their notions of what education should do for the person and for society; how they perceived the engagements of research in the field with global society; and what they wanted out of their experience of comparative/global/international education. Usually, I began asking what Spradley (1979) calls descriptive-structural questions specific to the topics I was seeking a discourse around and, such that would arrange responses around the individuals themselves. For example, my questions included questions about those areas where the students felt they learnt the most, where least, and why they thought this was so, when and how did they sense that something was missing in their education during comparative education courses. The path these interviews would take would bring me into many different and very personal journeys of complexity. I was asked to negotiate and clarify my own meanings as well. Three things worked powerfully to connect me with the students. First, I myself was a student in the act of becoming 'validated' through research and this gained me sympathy camaraderie, and scrutiny. Second, the experience of being 'international' connected us. To the international students I interviewed, it was as if we shared an unspoken space in the field — I was questioned by these students as deeply as I questioned them. For example, they asked me "How did you arrive at these questions?" "Do you miss 'home'?" "Do *you* have problems with the language?" and "What is it you *really* want to know?" A number of students expressed surprise at my study and I heard very often statements such as, "How is it that you began to think about these things?" and "No one has ever asked us questions like this!" These sorts of interview exchanges became very significant in analyzing these stories. I was never a neutral participant in any of these stories and was made very aware of my own inscription of the discourse. I also asked contrast questions. These questions were more focused, more specific. For example, I asked, " If you were to teach comparative education, how would you do it?" "What concepts would you bring to your own students, why?" Twenty-two students responded to my requests for interviews. These were students either in the middle of their programs or at the proposal/dissertation writing stage. In short, my purpose was to elicit ontological positions (perceptions of reality), values toward education (experience and identity), attraction toward the field (desires), and finally explorations of what was missing in their education in the field, a question that was tied in with all the preceding ones (pedagogical advocacy).

It appears that the field attracts particular kinds of students, those who have or who want international and global experience. These were also students who in some sense step out of the boundaries of education as it is defined in parochial, limited terms. Students native to the United States seem to desire another paradigm of education beyond the familiar. Students coming from other countries into the United States are also 'stepping out' of the familiar and the known, either to enrich that familiar space or to venture into other territories of learning and experience. Although I have broadly conceptualized them, each student embraced at least two levels of global experience, and in themselves had a variety of complicated, intricate, and merged experiences of the world. The themes of desire, difference, experience, and power are merged intricately in these stories.

> "I used to dream about this adventure around the world. Of doing things for people, of different languages... I speak several Kenyan languages and want to learn about other languages. But things are different. I come from a different culture, societal background; values are also different. But it is different. There is a lot going on in comparative education, the old fathers and some new fathers as well. What were really enriching were the different perspectives of the students because they come from everywhere. But I had to choose where to belong."

The students I interviewed came from many countries but to varying degrees they all expressed a certain lack or suffered some struggle that had brought them into the field. For some it was the lack of 'another place' to be, a lack of opportunity, or lack of affirmation, of broader perceptions, of not having, of not being able to act in certain ways, to think in certain ways, or of not being able to 'see' beyond one's own experience ("I want to know more," "I saw that as a women I would need to prove myself," and "There is no program like comparative education where I was"). The desire for knowledge, as Todd (1997) points out, has been imbedded in the notion of education since the classical notion of education was propounded. It appears that this desire, for many students in the field, is the desire to know the Other. Varied experiences of 'othernesses,' apart from the experiences of being the 'others' in a different country and 'other' in the heterogeneous comparative education groups of peers, were stories that rarely found their way into the comparative education classroom. Denying these subjectivities meant that students perceived a certain loss of self, perhaps even of skill, in their comparative education experiences. 'Otherness' of knowing, alterity and difference were discussed as if they were 'issues' in education and 'out-there,' disconnected, in many cases, from their identities and experiences of those who learn. In conversation with a Korean student, I learnt that she had come to the comparative education program in the United States to learn more about what to do with educational problems in her country. She went on to relate what she had learnt and would take back to Korea. When I asked her if she felt she could use her knowledge to address problems in Korea, she told me that in order to address problems you have to know the context intimately. As she was speaking she paused and said:

> I don't think this program can tell me anything about Korea! I have learnt to measure things, but there are only a few articles on Korea and I can say more about Korea than them. I could teach so very much about Korea- comparative education cannot really teach me anything. We studied Korea as part of Asia week, but so what?

This student realized, perhaps in that moment, that the difference that made up part of her identity was vaster than the appearance or treatment it received in the classroom. Some spoke to me about their observations of the effects of difference. 'Difference' is a word used to mark a separation or alternative to a 'mainstream,' a norm or a center. Difference, then, became not just a differentiation, simply an expression of neutral differentiation; it was used as a term to denote the degree of desirability (of the difference) of that position. Difference was often perceived as a disadvantage when it was affirmed by being separated from the approval or sanction of an authority figure (such as the instructor). On the other hand, difference became a strength when it was seen as contributing to learning, or by a professor who legitimated that difference:

> Now finally, the field is giving me what I want, because I learn how to communicate with others. My professor showed me how to communicate. I watched him, I took every class with him. In the beginning, to bring me into the discussion, he tried to rephrase everything I said. I usually accepted. He respected me, but soon I realized that the way it was being rephrased was a little different than what I wanted to say. So I said "no," and then he recognized that this student was understanding much more.

The power of the professor is evident in this narration. Building one's identity, or indeed one's difference around the legitimacy of an authority figure is part of what Foucault (1983) calls power/knowledge, where power is located within the regimes of discourse and practice (Marshall, 1998). Within this 'regime' through which 'truth' is constituted, technologies of domination work through professionals and experts who have the authority to constitute the self into particular desired subjectivities (Marshall, 1998, p. 73). In relation to Foucault's concept of power/knowledge, it is also useful to think of Ellsworth's (1997) exploration of the promise and possibilities of a student-teacher relationship as a mode of address. "Modes of address," according to Ellsworth (p. 6), "is one of those intimate relations of social and cultural power that shapes ...who teachers think student are, and who students come to think themselves to be." There is a range of literature that speaks of the mobilizing forces of difference (Belenky, 1986; Friedman 1998; Gore, 1993; hooks, 1994; Kelly, 1997; Martusewicz, 2001). However, if difference (or diversity) in the construction of subjectivity is obfuscated as a pedagogical possibility, there are pedagogical effects: the inability to position oneself in relation to other experiences of difference. Sharon Todd's (1997) text makes an important distinction between 'difference,' meaning 'non-same,' and 'disparity,' meaning 'unequal in difference' (p. 240), resisting the temptation to essentialize difference. Thus, it is not enough to simply acknowledge diversity, which is itself a complex and problematic term it is also necessary to mobilize and make generative, identifications of diversity and difference. The following quote addresses this point in comparative education:

> I am faced with so many theories, but I ask myself, where am I in all this? If I 'place' myself somewhere, there is another question: what about what I know or have known, what about experiences and looking at the world through your eyes-- and why can't I see what others know as well? I see only what is in front of me; I cannot see the experiences of other students.

This student desired to be able to participate in the diversity, of theory and experience, not only as validation of those differences in himself, but as learning about those experiences that did not belong to him. Having to position himself securely within theory denied him the ability to "see the experiences of other(s)."

Experience, as desire, was cited as being a profound motivator and value creator. The word 'experience' was used to signal diversity, and learning sites and marked significant events in the students' past and present condition of being a student, of understanding and conceptualizing knowledge in their relationships with themselves and with the field.

> I believe in my own experiences as a wealth of knowledge. Because that is who I am that is my identity, and my experiences teach me how to look at the world. If I say that something is based on my own experiences, then I believe that that is a source of knowledge. Few (teachers) did encourage me in this perspective. But there were more that were not willing to encourage me. We better redefine 'scientific': the thinking process is scientific as well and you can't leave out something.

The issues of identity building and understanding are seen to be part of the construction of a world view, the building blocks of values, beliefs, and desires, all of which bring to bear not only on the construction of 'place' in the world, but are a source of knowledge and meaning. Most of the students I spoke with brought life experience into stories of how and why they were learning.

Desire was a powerful motivator in determining the value of one's education: that education is enriching, which resonates with one's desire:

> What is the point of all this knowledge if you cannot use it to help something, someone. If I have a great education that cannot prepare me to work in the way I want to, it is an empty education.

This student describes the link between her values (to help someone, something), and the need for engagement with the world. In her view, education should enable her to act upon the world. Connected with the need to be able to act on the world, these students expressed a need for adventure and pleasure. They reveled to me the need for a space from which the world may be understood through many lenses. As one student put it, "local stuff (in the US) is too closed off, too boring, just not enough." The notion of being able to access the Other, to be able to know that Other was perceived as being able to step out, or to be able to 'adventure' into territory largely unknown. This meant to experiment, and to create 'new' solutions, methods or understandings. Many students were in fact attracted to risk and imagination ("You have to really challenge what's going on and what's being done, not necessarily because you are a revolutionary, but because you may think there's something wrong here..."). They expressed the desire to transgress boundaries, or to reconceptualize boundary making. Primary among these beliefs was that comparative education as a knowledge space was perceived to be characterized by a vast degree of heterogeneity in terms of the diversity of its student body and membership, the plurality of their experiences and varied cultural and professional lives, and the diversity of disciplines that influenced the field. All these were seen as highly attractive to the students. Even the much-debated issue of the canon was addressed: intangibility was seen by some as an opportunity to interpret. For others, such fluidity was unacceptable because it left them without a compass in a sea of theories. This group felt lost and disenfranchised and without the discipline with the 'high seriousness' of an established discipline, unlike other groups who felt lost because of the inability to 'see' the experiences of others. The idea of intangible-interpretive perceptions of the field signals the need for an opening of spaces, the play of difference and personal interpretations of the field. This is one of the 'ruptures' that could be introduced into the established discourse of the field by bringing in pedagogies from cultural studies, postcolonialism, postmodernism, postfeminisms and others.

> Because the field is so marginal the people who have a voice are the experts in the field who are established in the field. The danger is that that makes up a microcosm and gives the impression that we are sufficient — that we do not need any other inputs.

Interestingly, the data show that students made a distinction between the conceptualizations of 'expert' and 'teacher.' A 'teacher' was seen as someone who mediated between the expert body of knowledge and the non-expert receiving that knowledge, that is, the students. This is not to say that the teacher was never conceived of as an expert; however, there was a degree of differentiation. The teacher-educator was seen as, variously, 'the guide,' 'advisor,' 'mediator,' 'interpreter' — in effect, the active, dynamic agent. The idea of a steep hierarchy culminating in the 'best' was problematized:

> The problem with being the expert is you see that as the end of knowledge. This is never the case — you are always learning. The impression I get sometimes of being at the receiving end of 'expertise' is that I am not well, I have to be cured. So you in turn tend to doctor things and you end up with something not your own. You have your own experience and you have a language for that. I feel I have to learn another language for something else and I am then a lost person without the true confidence...

The end of knowledge is perceived as the end of learning, a goal when reached impinged on what she calls her 'process.' The danger of such a 'cure' can be read such that this method of producing knowledge, produces translated intellectuals, or worse, recreated intellectuals, who are both obedient and disenfranchised. Here is a student struggling to find a passage through the silence created by an expert discourse:

> People who are seen as the experts who own the field are essentially living in their own ivory tower and the discourse they have created is incomprehensible to even their students. I am not questioning the arguments that are made, I'm just questioning the way they are made: the language used. We are looking up to these people and since we have no other choice, we have to grapple with this. Certainly there are other discourses and they must be heard, but no one knows where they are. So, in addition to excluding people who are already excluded, I mean, here they are simply off the map. We might be doing some real damage by proceeding on a path that assumes this exclusion is OK.

Constructing and producing knowledge is seen as producing expertise of some kind. However, this student points to a very crucial problematic — the idea that kinds of language forms are used in the transmission of knowledge: Truth and knowledge claims, in effect, construct the field for this student. She also mentions 'other' discourses and the fact that they seem to be invisible in the expert knowledge space. This is seen as a lack, or a gap. This student perceives an established process of knowledge production, in which this knowledge continues to be 'produced' or legitimated, notwithstanding the agency, or perhaps, interruption of the learner. Sometimes 'passage' (Martusewicz, 2001) is found, and it usually comes from the desire to resist inscription. This is desire 'against the grain' as it were (Todd, 1997, p. 4), "maintaining a balance between how subjects are inscribed, and yet they refuse such inscriptions as potential agents of change."

As if speaking to this resistance, here is one such agent of change:

> Start with the texts — but that's not a good start, the texts are not good — they come from wherever the specific authors come from. It is incredible how sparse the material about smaller, indigenous, third world cultures is. Or even how the people who write these articles are from a university or organization that is in the industrialized regions. You don't have a chance of reading European authors in America. But then, I guess you don't read American authors in Europe, ha ha. But seriously, it is incredible to me the who that is writing and the who that is being addressed. The who that is being addressed is the elite student — [these texts] highlight the Other and all that, but to this elite majority, not the Other who comes in, bringing with them their cultures.

It became apparent that difference itself was an important component of being able to construct pedagogies for and about difference, in a multicultural, global classroom. Students reported that this idea was not really addressed within their classrooms. Students focused on the idea that the *unknown* may in fact be the *unique*, but that this feature difference is fragile within the classroom situation:

> In CIE there is a great variation, diversity in learning styles and perceptions. The underlying expectation is that we (those who know) will be able to enlighten someone. There was this student once in class who came in conflict with the professors because they were waiting for him to have an epiphany or something, so that he would begin to do things like everyone else. It's difficult sometimes for professors to accept different approaches to understanding — this student was so unique. In classes it's all a debate about knowledge, of knowledge, for knowledge; but I think we need to understand also what's really going on, where people are coming from. It's good to get all the ideas out there, but when it comes to a point where we begin to meddle with the unique, I think there's something wrong there.

This text indicates that there is no real language or space in which to include this knowledge, that is, the expression of knowledge which is linked with identity (and perhaps different histories). Students defined a particular dynamic inscribed within the workings of an academic field constituted of diverse and plural theoretical and methodological constructs. Multiple theoretical considerations were seen as a force overshadowing the actual constructions of knowledge. It would seem that student identity was based primarily on the academic construct of knowledge and adherence to the theory available to them, and this arrangement was not necessarily a relevant or desired link. The process of becoming educated (or becoming an expert) was seen as a process separate from the experiential knowledge of these students' lives, as the construction of knowledge and understanding in the classroom was seen as separate from the available theoretical constructs. There was a perception of a distinct lack of a pedagogical method to understand difference:

> I don't think pedagogy addresses ideas of 'difference' as such.
> There's no real conversation. I mean, what's 'difference'? I mean we
> are given books to read, and articles and so on, but at the level of
> actually bringing in those voices… It remains an interesting idea to
> me. The field is very much driven by a few notable scholars and
> that has a dominating effect. I would not even know if someone
> was being 'silenced.'

According to this student, notions of 'difference' were attached to groups, peoples, and cultures outside herself. That is to say, the constructions of 'difference' that she had engaged with, were still exotic notions belonging to Other imagined communities. Perhaps, however, the realization of a twice-removed layer of 'invisibility' ("I would not even know if someone was being silenced") is a disturbing one: It seems to introduce a degree of malignancy to continued ignorance of or inadmissibility of the Other. This text points to a rather large gap in the constructions of inclusive (or relevant) knowledges and pedagogies in which voices that were never 'known' are concealed. Consider the invisibility present in another statement:

> First I could not understand anything. Then I tried to translate and
> then no one could understand me when I tried to say that I had a
> different… opinion. You have to say it or you are left behind. So I
> tried to learn — translations of the articles, everything that was
> being discussed. But I was always somewhere behind, thinking
> something else. Really, no one can understand you, not even your
> family sometimes. It's very difficult. So, you have to be able to say
> something so that you can be there, wherever you want to be. Or
> you can't … exist. If you have no voice, you don't exist.

This points to a blanketing effect of perceived pedagogy over the diversity of voices. Even more remarkable is the observation by this student that 'existence' in the classroom depends on being able to be heard. A chilling corollary is the idea that those who have no voice, or who cannot be heard, have no existence. Even more disturbing, given that the construction of knowledge is such a personal, sophisticated and fragmented process, the only aspects of knowledge that come into existence are those that are legitimated and find expression and audience. The inadmissibility of experience, struggle, and desire, linked with the need and ability to act, be and become creates problems within the personal spaces of engagement with comparative education such as when writing a dissertation and framing research problems. This has the effect of marginalizing and shrinking these personal spaces, for one thing, and for another, has a debilitating effect on the creativity of the student and on the joy and pleasure of the process of becoming educated in the field. These unattended spaces also, therefore, have the effect of placing limits on the learner's ability to be self-critical and self-reflexive.

Gaps or invisibilities were described by student data in three broad areas: knowledge production, the construction of the expert, and pedagogy. Perceptions about the nature of the gaps in comparative education discourse are really a description of the nature of disjuncture and conflict experienced within the field. The sense I received after talking with the students in various programs was that there was a kind of journey that takes place in the student's passage toward being validated. This journey involved deficiencies and falsities that they came across as students that became, in effect, the spaces of fugue and disconnection that were experienced along this passage. I call this 'the gap,' and I see it as constituted of disconnections and absences. The gap also encompasses the spaces in-between experienced dichotomies. Therefore, the gap also comprises liminal spaces the most learning seems to take place where linkages are made between widely differing concepts; where bridges are built, attempts are made to connect, and opportunities are perceived to merge knowledges and entities. In a sense, the 'gap' is also a fluid, plastic conception, representing disconnection with purpose, values, and wholeness. It signifies rupture and yet in another sense represents the physical dislocation from the established discourse of the field. This is actualized in the writing of a thesis and dissertation proposals, for example, which made students seek different kinds of knowledge to inform their construction of a research 'problem.'

To be more precise, the engagement with this 'gap' occurs in 1) the realization of the disconnect and an attempt to bridge it with work, either as research or academic projects, or in some cases by the professor, and 2) the places of community action among students when they come together to work on 'interpretations.' The positioning of the gap is important in a time-space measure: most students experienced this, when they were at the end of their program, especially when they are called upon to frame their own research questions, and during the taking of courses at the beginning of a CE program.

In trying to arrive at what symbolizes the many values and processes and ideas of 'what is missing,' there was an astonishing re-occurrence of two major concepts: diversity of experience and need for connection in order to make meaning out of experience and newer, more experimental themes.

The Pedagogy Argued for

In Lacan's conceptualization (Peters, 1998), desire issues in relationship with the Other of one's self, with the imagined promise of fulfilling some lack in the subject. According to Foucault, (1985), who broke with the traditional (and taken as 'constant') notions of sexuality, desire or the 'desiring subject' is constituted through "the establishment of a set of rules and norms — in part traditional, in part new — which found support in religious, judicial, pedagogical, and medical institutions: and changes the way individuals are led to assign meanings and value to their conduct, their duties, their pleasure, their feelings and sensations, their dreams" (p. 4). Desire, therefore is seen as discursive. Kelly's work (1997), takes this concept further to show the pedagogical or 'material' or 'schooled' (p. 21) dimensions of desire, which are "the language practices through which desire is named, constituted, spoken." In this respect, it is useful to understand the workings of power, an alternative view offered by Foucault. According to Foucault (1980), every relation is a power relationship. Power is practiced, rather than 'present' or dormant, and so it circulates and passes through the forces in this relationship. Power is therefore not necessarily repressive and could be generative; positive, depending on the force it passes through. According to this, students have power as well as teachers or experts. Sharon Todd (1997) focuses this idea on the concept of desire as being a relationship of lack. She argues,

> for the need to develop an awareness of desire as a mediating factor in the recognition and enunciation of difference. (The argument) regards desire as that which ceaselessly circulates through the *unsaid* of classroom life…even as it intersects with the symbolic and spoken discourses uttered by student and teacher alike. Desire is, therefore, not only produced…nor is it only an "impulse" projected upon the pedagogical scene." It is occasioned by (and made apparent through) another kind of textuality as well: a body discourse where gesture informs any teaching and learning experience (p. 239).

Todd, in linking desire to difference in this way, sees beyond the concept of desire as Lacanian ontological lack, rather sees it as a dialectic, with transformative potential, as desires are formed and reformed in social organization. Following Ellsworth (1997, p. 110) then, one could ask both of teachers and students in comparative education, "How are the workings of desire operative within any given pedagogical practice? How, and for what, is the educational gaze desiring? On every educational site, in what ways do knowledge, power, desire and pedagogy intersect and impact at the level of the subject? In what ways are these effects limiting and/or enabling of this critical issue?" As shown in Kelly's work (1997, pp. 105–110), the discursive dimension of desire also works to construct difference (or the Other) as identities. Comparative and international education deals with a great deal of difference. One might say that the field has a 'project of difference' but it does not have a *pedagogy* of difference. Says Kelly (1997), "the pedagogical project of difference is a resignifying project; the project's genesis is culture, representation, the day-to-day mediations of the everyday returned to us through strictures of signification." (p. 105)

And yet, as we look to alternative, postfoundational pedagogies such as radical, transformative, critical and feminist pedagogies to inform our own, Jennifer Gore (1993) reminds us of the postmodern resistance against closure as well as the danger of another pedagogical modality becoming yet another grand narrative. Gore analyzed radical feminist and critical pedagogies around notions of empowerment and authority, using Foucault's 'regimes of truth,' to show how even these most marginalized of pedagogies can have dominating effects, because they may read the world in delimiting ways. The idea then, is simply not to be content with arriving and taking a position; or even advocating one pedagogy over another. The idea is to find the language and the concepts by which to analyze and interrogate any pedagogical construct. This is where postmodern and poststructuralist literature becomes powerful tools through which one can think not only critically, but also reflexively. And so my point is not to name the postmodern pedagogy to be used. The point is to rather name and situate a space and a process in comparative education where students and teachers can engage with these concepts in practice. Thus, there might finally be an opening from which could emerge languages of knowing that do not wait to be inscribed by either the stasis of an outcome based pedagogy, or an abstraction of distant theoretical genealogy.

And so to a Re-Imagination

The 'invisible space' that Star (1991) advocates includes ways of knowing the expression of which has been closed off or blocked by discursive controls, what cannot be said, in other words, because of the power of particular discourses. These 'invisibilities' come from the marginalized and the disinherited or devalued ways of knowing, such as alternate views of education-society relationships, and experiences of disorders, victimization, exclusion, artistic vision, musicality, difference, disenfranchisement, and so on. While I will avoid for now the socio-moral judgments attached to the discourses of these ways of knowing (if they are even seen as such), I wish to point out that they have effects, in some shape or form, on identity construction, and therefore need to be considered as pedagogical possibilities. In this sense, the understanding of 'invisibilities' as defined by Star, is a significant pedagogical activity. Invisible knowledges are also those ways of knowing that represent the Other of scientific discourse and therefore cannot be expressed within discourses of scientific expression. Feminist and postcolonial texts are examples of such knowledges forging their own expression in academia/academe to the great advantage of pedagogy, as illustrated by Dimitriadis and McCarthy (2001), Todd (1997), Gore (1993) and Martusewicz (2001). For our time, signifying a break with comparative education's metaphoric classical past, I suggest a tailored version of Stronach and MacClure's (1997, pp. 50–52) description for a postmodern research agenda as pedagogical 'vision' :

"We need to abandon the old ways of futuring." The discourse of CE (or canon) usually contains a history of the field. A re-reading of these histories (such as has been done by Ninnes (2002) need to be undertaken as part of the taught syllabi.

"Our concern should be with how educational questions 'issue,' rather than some shopping list of alleged 'issues.'" Comparative education has long been engaged in methods of 'problem-solving,' whether as 'development' issues or others. It would be far more useful to understand and teach the genealogies and 'histories' of how questions are formulated, why they are maintained and which ones are more valued than others.

"All inheritances reformed or not are conservative in tendency. We need not to favor some new orthodoxy, but remain in favor of experimentation, creativity and risk." From this point of view, which is incidentally one that appears to address at least one of the desires expressed by some of the students that I interviewed, the pedagogical process locates power, as a dialectic and dynamic construct, with teachers, students, and the troublesome 'expert,' who ceases henceforth to be a troublesome adversary to the student (or perhaps even the teacher).

This vision certainly deserves a separate and more detailed debate that is beyond the focus of this chapter. However, more can be said about some methods of application, or 'instruction,' following the above 'vision.' Two poststructuralist methods have already been described in this volume, which I will appropriate for their pedagogical, instructional value. These methods are critical discourse analysis (Ninnes, this volume), and postmodern social cartography (Gorostiaga and Paulston, this volume).

As I was doing my own analysis of texts, I realized that to be able to recognize the presence of discursive power technologies in the language and structure of the texts is only one aspect of 'action' upon the text. The second aspect is to be able to articulate a place from outside the discourse presented in terms that could indeed interrogate the text, either through other literatures and constructions, or from other and different configurations of knowledge. Furthermore, critical discourse analysis is always incomplete and this is its great value as a pedagogical tool. It is incomplete in the sense of being *one* individual's action upon *one* reading of the text. This has been a drawback of my own analysis, but as a pedagogical tool used by students of different languages, for example, it makes the analysis richer and a more dynamic play of different knowledge perceptions upon a given text, releasing more relevance with the inclusion of more and more 'interpreters.' The analysis might then become fluid and destabilized itself. In this sense, also, the action of critical discourse analysis by a group of learners upon a text assumes the motion of a kind of map, radiating from a text to many texts (of the analyzers) into a space of intertextuality.

Gorostiaga and Paulston (this volume) demonstrate how maps can be used to present findings, as well as how the mapping process leads into an opening of critical reflexive and inter-textual possibilities for analysis. Using those same concepts, I suggest that maps have great value in the process of investigating subjectivities and in finding positions relative to the field (or the pedagogy used). Mapping, re-mapping and counter-mapping inter-textual fields may expand student's choices for 'positions'. Paulston describes how "…a spatial turn in comparative studies would focus less on formal theory and competing truth claims and more on how contingent knowledge may be seen as embodied, locally constructed, and re-presented as oppositional yet complementary positionings in shifting fields" (p. xviii). Thus, the use of mapping as a pedagogical tool to teach the field mobilizes the diversity of the field while allowing students to mobilize and analyze their own desires and identities relative to education work. Following from this, here are my proposals for re-imagined pedagogy in comparative education.

Proposal 1: The use of critical discourse analysis upon the reading material used in comparative education classrooms. The sharing and remapping of concepts, ways of knowing can be done, following from this, creating spaces of interaction in which both students and teachers participate. Students can, thus, teach and reconstruct as well as deconstruct 'difference,' a particularly powerful tool in the diverse, international comparative education classroom.

Proposal 2: The mapping process, as pedagogy, allows for possibilities of the emergence of invisible knowledges (Star, 1991), of the 'minute particulars' of Paulston, (1996), and of 'invisible scholars' (Altbach, 1999). Maps, to extend their pedagogical value, include the metaphoric abilities of the web to be able to see many things at once, including both modern and postmodern sensibilities, action and research, theory and practice, all of which have the possibility to inform each other in the inter-textual space created by a map.

Cleavages occur when ontological stances are set up against each other. Therefore, Proposal 3: The issue of concern is, while these stances interact and exist in a common space of possibilities, the learner need not have to choose a position either with or against the professor or in deference to any other perceived authority, but rather can choose in conjunction with their own ontological journeys, perhaps those of their colleagues in similar knowledge communities. This allows the learner to actually engage and craft multiple, plural or liminal ontologies, perhaps to even reach into new and different ways of perceiving reality.

Proposal 4: Theoretical stances can be interrogated on the bases of values, beliefs, experiences, struggles, marginalities — themes that were seen to be invisible in the pedagogy of the field by the students in this study. Based on this approach, maps may be constructed in public (classrooms) and private spaces (as a students' private self-critique) with the intention of remapping.

There are sites of learning other than the 'classroom' that are possible for comparative education, the particular power of cyberspace being just one. And this, as is abundantly clear, can be a dangerous place. Perhaps it would be more dangerous if the tools of analysis were obsolete or irrelevant. Pedagogical processes in one context may not make sense in another, however attention to processes that facilitates and opens up learning can certainly continue as a focus. The process of learning then becomes, as Shakespeare would say, the 'thing.'

I will have more to say. I'm sure others will, too. Against closing this debate, which this chapter has hopefully re-opened, perhaps the only 'safe' place to end is with Achilles and the Tortoise, who may not provide us with an easy course either.

> The Tortoise was saying, "Have you got that last step written down? Unless I've lost count, that makes a thousand and one. There are several million more to come. And would you mind, as a personal favour, considering what a lot of instruction this colloquy of ours will provide the Logicians of the (Twentieth) Century — would you mind adopting a pun that my cousin the Mock-Turtle will then make, and allow yourself to be renamed TAUGHT-US?"
>
> "As you please," replied the weary warrior, in the hollow tones of despair, as he buried his face in his hands. "Provided that you, for your part, will adopt a pun the Mock-Turtle never made, and allow yourself to be re-named A KILL-EASE!"

References

Abercrombie, Nicholas, S. Hill, and B. Turner. *Dictionary of Sociology*. London: Penguin, 1994.

Altbach, P. G. "Trends in Comparative Education." *Comparative Education Review* 35, no. 3 (1991): 491-507.

Altbach, P. G., R. F. Arnove, and G. Kelly. "Introduction: Approaches and Perspectives." In *Comparative Education*. Edited by P. G. Altbach, R. F. Arnove, and G. Kelly, 3–14. New York: Macmillan Publishing Co., Inc., 1982.

Altbach, Philip G., Robert F. Arnove, and Gail Paradise Kelly. *Comparative Education*. New York: Macmillan, 1982.

———. *Emergent Issues in Education: Comparative Perspectives, Suny Series, Frontiers in Education*. Albany, N.Y.: State University of New York Press, 1992.

Altbach, Philip G., State University of New York at Buffalo. Comparative Education Center, and State University of New York at Buffalo. Dept. of Higher Education. *The Academic Profession: Perspectives on an International Crisis (with Bibliography), Occasional Papers Series / Comparative Education Center, State University of New York at Buffalo; No. 5.* Buffalo, N.Y.: Dept. of Higher Education Faculty of Educational Studies State University of New York at Buffalo, 1979.

Altbach, Philip G., Eng Thye Jason Tan, et al. *Programs and Centers in Comparative and International Education: A Global Inventory.* Rev. ed, *Special Studies in Comparative Education; No. 34.* Buffalo, NY, USA: Graduate School of Education Publications Comparative Education Center State University of New York at Buffalo, 1995.

Apple, Michael W. "Ideology, Reproduction, and Educational Reform." In *New Approaches to Comparative Education*, edited by P. G. Altbach and G. Kelly, 51–72. Chicago: University of Chicago Press, 1986.

Apple, Michael. *Cultural Politics and Education.* New York: Teachers College Press, 1996.

———. *Education and Power.* Boston: Routledge & Kegan Paul, 1982.

Arnove, Robert F., Philip G. Altbach, and Gail Paradise Kelly. *Emergent Issues in Education: Comparative Perspectives, Suny Series, Frontiers in Education.* Albany, N.Y.: State University of New York Press, 1992.

Bain, William. "The Loss of Innocence: Lyotard, Foucault and the Challenge of Postmodern Education." In *Education and the Postmodern Condition*, edited by M. Peters, 1–20. Westport: Bergin and Garvey, 1995.

Bakhtin, Mikhail, ed. *The Bakhtin Reader.* Edited by Pam Morris. London: Arnold, 1994.

Ball, Stephan J. *Education Reforms: A Critical and Post-Structural Approach.* Buckingham: Open University Press, 1994.

Barnett, Ronald. *Improving Higher Education: Total Quality Care.* Philadelphia: Society for Research into Higher Education: Open University Press, 1992.

Belenky, Mary F. *Woman's Ways of Knowing: The Development of Self, Voice, and Mind.* New York: Basic Books, 1986.

Bloom, Allen. *The Closing of the American Mind.* New York: Simon and Schuster, 1987.

Bohm, Gernot. "The Structures and Prospects of Knowledge Societies." *Social Science Information/Information Sur Les Science Sociales* 36, no. 3 (1997): 447–69.

Broadfoot, Patricia. "Comparative Education for the 21st Century. Retrospect and Prospect." *Comparative Education* 36, no. 3 (2000): 357–71.

Castells, Manuel. *The Information Age: Economy, Society and Culture.* Oxford: Blackwell Publishers, 1998.

Clark, Burton. "Values. Higher Education Research Group Working Paper #1," (1987).

Cowen, R. "Last Past the Post: Comparative Education, Modernity and Perhaps Post-Modernity." *Comparative Education* 32, no. 2 (1996): 151–70.

———. "The National and International Impact of Comparative Education Infrastructures." In *Comparative Education: Contemporary Issues and Trends.* Edited by W. D. Halls, 370. London: Jessica Kingsley Publishers, 1990.

———. "Comparing Futures or Comparing Pasts?" *Comparative Education* 36, no. 3 (2000): 333–42.

Dei, George J. Sefa. "Knowledge and Politics of Social Change: The Implication of Anti-Racism." *British Journal of Sociology of Education* 20, no. 3 (1999): 395–409.

Dimitriadis, G. and Cameron McCarthy. *Reading and Teaching the Postcolonial: From Baldwin to Basquiat and Beyond.* New York: Teachers College Press, 2001.

Elton, Lewis. "Can Universities Change?" *Studies in Higher Education* 6, no. 1 (1981): 23–33.

Epstein, E. "Currents Left and Right: Ideology in Comparative Education." *Comparative Education Review* 27, no. 1 (1983): 3–29.

Epstein, I. "Comparative Education in North America: The Search for the Other through the Escape of the Self ?" *Compare* 25, no. 1 (1995): 5–16.

Fairclough, Norman. *Critical Discourse Analysis: The Critical Study of Language.* London: Longman, 1996.

Fairclough, Norman, and Ruth Wodak. "Critical Discourse Analysis." In *Discourse as Social Interaction.* Edited by van Dijk, T. A., 258–84. London: Sage, 1997.

Foucault, M. *The Archeology of Knowledge.* New York: Pantheon Books, 1972.

——. *Power/Knowledge: Selected Interviews and Other Writings 1972–1977*. Edited by C. Gordon. New York: Pantheon, 1980.

Freebody, Peter, Sandy Muspratt, and Bronwyn Dwyer, ed. *Difference, Silence and Textual Practice: Studies in Critical Literacy.* Cresskill: Hampton Press, 2001.

Friedman, Susan, S. *Mappings: Feminism and the Cultural Geographies of Encounter.* Princeton. Princeton University Press, 1998.

Friere, Paulo. *Pedagogy of the Oppressed.* New York: Herder and Herder, 1972.

Game, Ann, and Andrew Metcalfe. *Passionate Sociology.* London: Sage, 1996.

Goodenow, Ronald. "The Cyberspace Challenge: Modernity, Post-Modernity and Reflections on International Networking Policy." *Comparative Education Review* 32, no. 2 (1996): 197–216.

Gore, Jennifer. *The Struggle for Pedagogies: Critical and Feminist Discourses as Regimes of Truth.* New York: Routledge, Chapman and Hall, Inc., 1993.

Gottlieb, Esther E. "The Discursive Construction of Knowledge: The Case of Radical Education Discourse." *Qualitative Studies in Education* 2, no. 2 (1989): 131–44.

Haekesworth, Mary E. "Feministepistemology: A Survey of the Field." *Women and Politics* 7, no. 3 (1987): 115–27.

Heise, Hildegard. "The Ambivalent Starting Point for Feminist Science." *Soziologische Revue* 21, no. 4 (1998): 455–61.

Hendry, Graham D. "Constructivism and Educational Practice." *Australian Journal of Education* 40, no. 1 (1996): 19–45.

Hofer, Barbara K., and Paul R. Pintrich. "The Development of Epistemological Theories: Beliefs About Knowledge and Knowing and Their Relation to Learning." *Review of Educational Research* 6, no. 1 (1997): 88–140.

Hoffman, D. "Culture and Comparative Education: Toward Decentering and Recentering the Discourse." *Comparative Education Review* 43, no. 4 (1999): 464–88.

Kazamias, Andreas M. "Introduction: The State of the Art: Twenty Years of Comparative Education." *Comparative Education Review* 21, no. 2 & 3 (1977): 151–52.

Kelly, G. P., P. G. Albach, and R. F. Arnove. "Trends in Comparative Education: A Critical Analysis." In *Comparative Education.* Edited by P. G. Albach, R. F. Arnove, and G. P. Kelly. New York: Macmillan, 1982.

Kelly, Gail Paradise. "Debates and Trends in Comparative Education." In *Emergent Issues in Education: Comparative Perspectives*, edited by R. F. Arnove, P. G. Altbach, and Gail Paradise Kelly, 13–24. Albany: State University of New York Press, 1992.

Kelly, Ursula Ann Margaret. *Schooling Desire: Literacy, Cultural Politics, and Pedagogy.* New York: Routledge, 1997.

Koehl, Robert. "The Comparative Study of Education: Prescription and Practice." *Comparative Education Review* 21, no. 2 & 3 (1977): 177–94.

Laska, John A. "The Future of Comparative Education: Three Basic Questions." *Comparative Education Review* 17, no. 3 (1973): 295–98.

Lecompte, Margaret D., Judith Preissle, and Renata Tesch. *Ethnography and Qualitative Design in Educational Research.* Second Edition. London: Academic Press, Inc., 1993.

Luke, A. "Open and Closed Texts: The Ideological/Semantic Analysis of Textbook Narratives." *Journal of Pragmatics* 13 (1989): 53–80.

Luke, A. and C. Walton. "Cross-Cultural Study of Education." In *International Encyclopedia of Education*, edited by Torsten Husen, Postlethwaite, Neville T., 1208–198. Oxford: Elsevier Science Ltd., 1994.

Luke, Allen. "Critical Discourse Analysis." In *Issues in Educational Research.* Edited by J. P and Lakomski Keeves, G. New York: Pergamon, 1999.

Marshall, J. and M. Peters. "Postmodernism and Education." In *International Encyclopedia of Sociology of Education.* Edited by L Saha, 88–92. Oxford: Pergamon, 1997.

Martin, Warren. *Alternatives to Irrelevance: A Strategy for Reform in Higher Education.* Nashville: Abingdon Press, 1968.

Martusewicz, Rebecca. *Seeking Passage: Poststructuralism, Pedagogy, Ethics.* New York: Teachers College Press, 2001.

Masemann, V. "Critical Ethnography in the Study of Comparative Education." In *New Approaches to Comparative Education.* Edited by P. G. Altbach and G. P. Kelly, 11–26. Chicago: University of Chicago Press, 1986.

———. "Ways of Knowing: Implications for Comparative Education." *Comparative Education Review* 34, no. 4 (1990): 465–73.

McFee, Graham. "Reflections on the Nature of Action-Research." *Cambridge Journal of Education* 23, no. 2 (1993): 173–83.

McHoul, A., W. Alex, and Allen Luke. "Discourse as Language and Politics." *Journal of Pragmatics* 13 (1989): 323–32.

McHoul, A., and W. Grace. *A Foucault Primer: Discourse, Power and the Subject.* Carlton, Victoria: Melbourne University Press, 1993.

Meynert, M. "Postmodernism and the Modernization of Tradition: Pedagogical Implications." *Education and Society* 16, no. 2 (1998): 32–46.

Murphy, Peter F. "Cultural Studies as Praxis: A Working Paper." *College Literature* 19, no. 2 (1992): 31–43.

Ninnes, Peter. "Origin Stories and the Discursive Constitution of Comparative Education." Stanford: Stanford University, 2002.

Noah, H., and M. Eckstein. *Doing Comparative Education: Three Decades of Collaboration.* Hong Kong: The University of Hong Kong Press, 1998.

Noah, Harold J., and Max A. Eckstein. *Toward a Science of Comparative Education.* New York: Macmillan, 1968.

O'Dowd, Mina. "Re-Tracing the Path to Third Order Knowledge: How Did We Get There and Can We Move On?" *Compare* 31, no. 3 (2001): 279–93.

Paulston, R. "Comparative and International Education: Paradigms and Theories." In *International Encyclopedia of Education.* Edited by T. Husen and Neville T. Postlethwaite, 923–33. Oxford: Pergamon, 1994.

———. "Mapping Comparative Education after Postmodernity." *Comparative Education Review* 43, no. 4 (1999): 438–63.

———. *Social Cartography: Mapping Ways of Seeing Social and Educational Change.* Edited by R. Paulston. New York: Garland Publishing, 2000.

Paulston, R., and M. Liebman. "An Invitation to Postmodern Social Cartography." *Comparative Education Review* 38, no. 2 (1994): 215–32.

Paulston, Rolland G., *Mapping Ways of Seeing Social and Educational Change.* Edited by Edward Beauchamp. New York: Garland Publishing, 1996.

Peters, M. *Naming the Multiple: Poststructuralism and Education.* Edited by M. Peters. Westport, Conn.: Bergin and Garvey, 1998.

Peters, R. S. *The Concept of Education.* London: Routledge & Kegan Paul, 1967.

Phenix, Philip. *Philosophies of Education.* Edited by P. Phenix. New York: Wiley, 1961.

Popkewitz, T. and M. Brennan. "Restructuring of Social and Political Theory in Education: Foucault and a Social Epistemology of School Practices." In *Foucault's Challenge: Discourse, Knowledge and Power in Education,* edited by T. Popkewitz and M. Brennan, 3–35. New York: Teacher's College Press, 1998.

Postlethwaite, T. Neville. *The Encyclopedia of Comparative Education and National Systems of Education.* 1st ed., *Advances in Education.* Oxford [Oxfordshire]; New York: Pergamon Press, 1988.

Raivola, Reijo. "What Is Comparison? Methodological and Philosophical Considerations." *Comparative Education Review* 29, no. 3 1985: 362–374.

Roche, George Charles. *The Fall of the Ivory Tower: Government Funding, Corruption and the Bankrupting of American Higher Education.* Washington, D.C.: Renery Publishing, 1994.

Rokeach, Milton. *Beliefs, Attitudes, and Values: A Theory of Organization and Change.* San Francisco: Jossey-Bass, 1968.

———. *Understanding Human Values: Individual and Societal.* Edited by Milton Rokeach. New York: Free Press, 1979.

Rust, Val. "Postmodernism and its Comparative Implications." *Comparative Education Review* 35, no. 4 (1991): 610–26.

Schriewer, Jürgen. *Discourse Formation in Comparative Education, Komparatistische Bibliothek; Bd. 10 = Comparative Studies Series; Vol. 10.* New York: P. Lang, 2000.

Shapiro, Svi. "Pedagogy in a Time of Uncertainty: Post-Modernism and the Struggle for Community." *Curriculum & Teaching* 6, no. 2 (1991): 23–38.

Spradley, James. *The Ethnographic Interview.* New York: Harcourt Brace Jovanovich College Publishers, 1979.

Springer, Ursula. "Education, Curriculum and Pedagogy." *Comparative Education Review* 21, no. 2 & 3 (1977): 358–69.

Star, Susan L., Ed. *The Sociology of the Invisible: The Primacy of Work in the Writings of Anselm Strauss*. Edited by D. R. Maines, *Social Organization and Social Process: Essays in Honor of Anselm Strauss*. New York: Aldine de Gruyter, 1991.

Stehr, Nico. *Knowledge Societies*. London: Thousand Oaks, 1994.

Strauss, Anselm. *Qualitative Analysis for Social Scientists*. Cambridge: Cambridge University Press, 1996.

Stromquist, Nelly P. "Romancing the State: Gender and Power in Education." *Comparative Education Review* 39, no. 4 (1995): 423–54.

Stronach, Ian and Maggie MacClure. *Education Research Undone: The Postmodern Embrace*. Buckingham: Open University Press, 1997.

Tatto, Maria Teresa. "Examining Values and Beliefs About Teaching Diverse Students: Understanding the Challenges to Teacher Education." *Education Evaluation and Policy Analysis* 18, no. 2 (1996): 155–80.

Terren, Eduardo. "Postmodernity and Education: Legitimacy Problems of Discourse." *Politica y Sociodad* 24 (1997): 121–39.

Thomas, R. Murray. *International Comparative Education: Practices, Issues & Prospects*. 1st ed. Oxford [England]; New York: Pergamon, 1990.

———. "The Nature of Comparative Education." In *International Comparative Education: Practices, Issues and Prospects*. Edited by R. Murray Thomas, 337. New York: Pergamon Press, 1990.

Torres, C. A., and T. R. Mitchell. "Introduction." In *Sociology of Education: Emerging Perspectives*. Edited by C.A. Torres and T. R. Mitchell, 1–18. Albany: State University of New York Press, 1998.

Torres, Carlos Alberto, and Robert F. Arnove. *Comparative Education: The Dialectic of the Global and the Local*. Lanham, MD: Rowman & Littlefield, 1999.

Usher, R., and R. Edwards. *Postmodernism and Education*. London: Routledge, 1994.

Watson, Keith, Ed. *Doing Comparative Education: Issues and Problems*. Oxford: Symposium Books, 2001.

Welch, A., and V. Masemann. "Editorial Introduction. (Special Issue on Tradition, Modernity and Postmodernism in Comparative Education)." *International Review of Education*. 43, no. 5–6 (1997): 393–99.

Wilson, David N. "Comparative and International Education: Fraternal or Siamese Twins? A Preliminary Geneology of the Field." *Comparative Education Review* 38, no. 4 (1994): 449–86.

Woolman, D. "Understanding the Modern World with Implications for Education." *Education and Society* 17, no. 1 (1999): 25–36.

Wright, Handel Kashope. "(Re)Conceptualizing Pedagogy as Cultural Praxis." *Education and Society* 13, no. 1 (1995): 67–81.

CHAPTER **3**

Critical Discourse Analysis and Comparative Education

PETER NINNES

In his article on imagining comparative education, Rolland Paulston (2000, p. 63) argues for comparative educators to engage with new developments in theory and methodology in the social sciences by going to work on "the linguistic, the spatial, and the pictorial turns." In this chapter I want to contribute to this work by opening up a discussion of the contributions which critical discourse analysis can make to the kinds of issues and problems that many comparative educators consider to be central to the field. I hope to show that critical discourse analysis provides a powerful set of conceptual and methodological tools with which to gain new insights into areas such as the contexts of education, educational policy, issues of difference (Crossley, 1999, 2000; Crossley and Jarvis, 2000; Grant, 2000); the movement of educational ideas across and within national boundaries (Little, 2000; Popkewitz, 2000); and some of the political concerns of comparative educators such as social justice and emancipation (Welch, 1999, 2000; Blake et al, 1998). I have used certain forms of critical discourse analysis in my research for a number of years, but it is a broad set of approaches over which I am unwilling to claim mastery.[1] My desire here is to facilitate the commencement within comparative education of a substantive engagement with and broad discussion of the benefits for comparative education of the various forms of critical discourse analysis. To do so, I wish to first examine the scope and theoretical tapestry of critical discourse analysis. I then review a number of studies which have employed critical discourse analysis to examine a range of relevant educational topics, namely, policy analysis; the global circulation and local manifestation of educational ideas; classroom studies; analyses of school subjects and curriculum materials; student and teacher subjectivities; and the rise and fall of educational discourses.

Discourse and Critical Discourse Analysis

Critical discourse analysis has been greatly influenced by the work of the French thinker Michel Foucault. In his earlier work, Foucault (1972) conceptualized discourse as the entire set of statements about a topic. These statements could comprise oral or written words, graphics or symbols, that is, texts. For example, we can think about the discourse of 'development' or 'education.' But nested within such broad discourses there are more specific discourses, such as, 'poverty alleviation,' 'women and development,' 'life long learning,' or 'rates of return.' It is useful, too, to distinguish between a discourse and a theory. The set of statements, that is, discourse, about a particular topic can include diverse or competing theories. For example, the discourse on development can include statements derived from both human capital theory and dependency theory. At the same time, within particular theoretical positions, there can be various discourses. For example, within human capital theory we can find a set of discourse around such topics as methodology, schooling, vocationalism, and so on.

As well as comprising sets of statements, discourses contribute to the construction of academic disciplines. Thus, we can talk about the discipline of sociology whose boundaries, parameters, and limits are constructed by what sociologists and others say sociology is. Sociology does not exist as an objective fact. Rather, it is constituted through the discursive practices of people, including sociologists (see Game and Metcalfe, 1995). The same can be said of comparative education. In response to the question, "What is comparative education?" I would simply reply that it is whatever comparative educators and other people who engage with the field say it is. Of course, this is a highly contested issue, as a detailed reading of the comparative education literature shows (see for example Paulston, 1997, 1999, 2000; Broadfoot, 2000; Crossley, 1999, 2000; Welch, 1999, 2000; Watson, 1998; Saha, 2001; Mehta and Ninnes, 2000; Marginson and Mollis, 2001). But like other disciplines, comparative education is constructed through the process of people talking and writing about its "nature."

In his early work, Foucault focused on examining the ways in which discourses and disciplines changed over time, how it was that particular statements and discourses and not others arose in particular contexts, the specific conditions of this arousal, and the relations between particular discourses such as "their coexistence, their succession, their mutual functioning, their reciprocal determination and their independent or correlative transformation" (Foucault, 1972, p. 29). These kinds of descriptions of the rise of and relations between discourses are often referred to as 'archaeologies' (Foucault, 1980; Bain, 1995; Marshall, 1990). In later work, Foucault added an approach that he called 'genealogy,' that is, the analysis of the relations of power that imbue and inscribe discourses and discursive formations (Marshall, 1990). Bain suggests that genealogy unpacks the taken for granted, examines the way human life and history are essentialized through discourses, and reveals history as a process involving "struggles, conflicts, contingencies, and reversals" (Bain, 1995, p. 13). This view of history is quite different from more traditional views, in which history was interpreted in terms of continual linear progress, or major overarching themes and processes. The political agenda of genealogical approaches is amply demonstrated by Foucault's own work examining the techniques of oppression and control employed with and against marginalized social groups, such as prisoners, the insane, the sexually 'deviant,' and so on. For Foucault, genealogy involved uncovering knowledges which had been hidden or suppressed by dominant discourses; the application of intellectual analysis to the knowledges and perspectives of the oppressed produced a "union of erudite knowledges and local memories which allows us to establish a historical knowledge of struggles and to make use of this knowledge tactically today" (Foucault, 1980, p. 83).

Critical discourse analysis is a major tool of genealogy, and is part of a wider set of techniques of linguistic analysis, namely, discourse analysis, within which McHoul and Luke (1989) identify two major schools. Some authors such as MacLure (2003, p. 190) suggest that these two schools are "irreconcilable," although some research does tend to draw on ideas and techniques from both schools (e.g., Luke, 1989). The Anglo-American school closely aligns discourse analysis with empirical linguistics, focusing on precise analysis of actual discourses. The so-called Continental Tradition (i.e., developed by thinkers based in continental Europe) takes a more critical approach, and tends to focus on the social, historical, and political contexts and effects of discourse. It examines issues such as the discourses that occur in institutions like schools; the way discourse affects how humans see themselves and others (i.e., human subjectivity); and the relationships between discourses and, for example, power and knowledge. It is to this school that we can most readily attach most of Foucault's work. Luke (1999) develops some of these 'continental' ideas more fully. He argues that critical discourse analysis focuses on the role of written and spoken texts in the constitution of knowledge, power, social relations, and identity. These ideas are further developed by Fairclough and Wodak, (1997), who suggest that critical discourse analysis practices and theory have eight broad features and assumptions: discourse constitutes society and culture; discourse does ideological work; discourse is historical; power relations are discursive; the link between text and society is mediated; discourse analysis is interpretive and explanatory; discourse is a form of social action; and critical discourse analysis addresses social problems.

Critical discourse analysis is derived in part from poststructuralism, which, as can be seen from the previous discussion (and in contrast to critical theory), recognizes the centrality within social analysis and social practices of discourse and language (Luke, 1999; van Dijk, 2001). Fairclough (1996) points out that within institutions there tend to be dominant ideological discursive formations, which become naturalized and thus seen as 'common sense.' Many foundational educational theories, including those in comparative education, are examples of such dominant ideological discursive formations, whose truth claims are open to questioning (Luke, 1999). One important task of critical discourse analysis therefore is to 'denaturalize' such formations by showing the web of relations between discourses and social structures (Fairclough, 1996). In applying critical discourse analysis to comparative education, we can interrogate dominant ideologies and discourses by addressing questions such as how various spoken, written and symbolic texts constitute and define knowledge, student, teacher and institutional identities, social relations and relations of power, and the social and historical conditions by and in which these discourses have arisen. Because of the dialectical relationship between discourses and social and historical conditions, we can also examine the effect of particular discourses on society.

Critical discourse analysis can take a number of forms, but each of these is distinguishable from other forms of discourse analysis. Fairclough and Wodak (1997) provide a wide-ranging review of the scope and theoretical underpinnings of critical discourse analysis and suggest that there are two key differences. First, critical discourse analysis views language as a form of social practice. That is, discourses and social situations are dialectically and mutually constituted. Social situations here include knowledges, identities, subjectivities, relationships, ideologies, and so on. Thus, discourses have material effects, especially in terms of power, which means that discourses can shape, constitute, maintain, reproduce and disrupt relations of inequality. One of the aims of critical discourse analysis is to identify and critique these aspects of discourse, which are sometimes considered 'common sense' or 'natural.' Fairclough and Wodak (1997) further argue that critical discourse analysis is actively involved in intervening in social practices. That is, it is politically engaged on the side of the oppressed and openly declares itself to be so.

Critical Discourse Analysis and (Comparative) Education Research

In order to illustrate the concepts of discourse and critical discourse analysis, I now wish to turn to a review of research that has employed various forms of critical discourse analysis to the examination of issues and problems commonly addressed in the field of comparative education. In particular I focus on policy analysis, the global circulation and local manifestation of educational ideas, the analysis of classroom and interview texts, the analysis of particular school subjects, and the politics of education, especially discursive construction and governmental effects of educational fields, disciplines, and concepts.

Policy Analysis

Some forms of discourse analysis focus only on actual texts. The application of such an approach to the analysis of educational policy therefore involves only the analysis of policy documents. Critical discourse analyses, however, are concerned with not only the contents of the documents, but also the processes of policy development and evaluation, and the outcomes or impacts of policy implementation (Ball, 1994). Thus, a critical discourse analysis of educational policies examines among other things who produced the documents, by what means, under what circumstances, for what purposes, and with what consequences. We can then work out what and how particular kinds of knowledges informed the policy, how particular perspectives were included and excluded, and who benefited and who was disadvantaged by these inclusions and exclusions. Ball (1994) explores the notion of policy as both *text* and *discourse*. If we adopt such a view, then educational polices are not objective, fixed, and static documents with only one possible reading. Furthermore, as Luke, et al (1993) observe:

> What policy texts represent, simulate, and do is never self-evident, literal or fully transparent. Particularly in dealing with policy ostensibly sympathetic to the plights of marginal groups, we cannot construe it as a simple set of truths or distortions and misrepresentations that reveal or hide unambiguous structural realities about social relations, relations to the means of production, and cultural domination (p. 140).

As noted earlier, critical discourse analysis views discourse as constitutive; it creates social relations, relations of power, ideas about what is true, and so on. Thus, we can think of policies and their discourses not as reflecting some objective truth about education, but instead as part of the process of the production of what people believe to be the truth about education. Polices produce truth by prescribing and proscribing "what can be said and thought ...[and] who can speak, when, where and with what authority" (Ball, 1994, p. 21). In Ball's terms, statements in educational policies such as what knowledge is useful, how students learn, and what are effective teaching methods *produce* the truth (and, by implication, the "false") about teachers, students, learning and schooling. The idea that discourses produce the objects of which they speak is derived from Foucault (1972). However, as Luke, et al (1993) remark, this concept should not lead to the spurious conclusion that if everything is circumscribed by discourse, that all there is is discourse. For indeed subject construction ultimately leads back to consequential effects: how the subjects, clients and problems of policy are constituted and positioned in the discourse of policy, becomes an actual act of power and regulation over those very subjects in the world (Luke, et al, 1993, p. 141)

If we extend Ball's and Luke, et al's analyses to issues that often concern comparative educators, we can suggest that education policies also contribute to the production of the truth about what education systems should be achieving, how to effectively manage education systems, the relationship between culture and education, what constitutes (and how education systems should respond to) educational inequality, and so on.

While Ball (1994) argues that it is useful to consider policies as both texts and discourses, he does not address in detail how policy analysis based on these notions might proceed. Codd (1988) provides a means for analyzing policy documents that takes account of the idea that policies are both text and discourses. According to Codd (1988), orthodox approaches to policy analysis imply an idealist view of language in which it is considered possible to communicate clearly and explicitly by using correct language to express particular thoughts. Once this correct language is found and used, exact and shared meanings can be created between the text and the receiver of the text (reader or listener). However, such a view of language is quite inadequate because it does not take into account the social practices of language, the social effects of language, or how language produces and transforms notions of what is true. Drawing on Saussure, Codd argues that language is a system of signs, concepts, and sound images that is both arbitrary and socially constructed. Once we start to think of language in this way, we can better appreciate the notion of discourse and its real effects (or *materiality*). Codd provides an example of a deconstructive approach to educational policy analysis which involves the interpretation of documents "in terms of their implicit patterns of signification, underlying symbolic structures, and contextual determinants of meaning" (p. 243) and an explicit recognition of the historical and political context in which the documents arose. Thus, in his analysis of key documents in the review of core curriculum in New Zealand, Codd describes the political context of the documents and charts the procedures which took place in their development, including processes of consultation and statements made by key figures. He then examines particular pieces of text from the documents, looking for how various discourses about curriculum are taken up, how contradictions within and between discourses are handled, and the statements which are made about notions such as the learner, the role of schools, centralization and decentralization, and basic educational principles.

More recently, Taylor (1997) has made further contributions to ways of thinking about the critical discourse analysis of educational policies. Taylor (1997) argues for an approach to discourse which looks at all levels of policy, emphasizes the political nature of policy development, and takes into account culture and practice. She advocates for the usefulness of Fairclough's focus on the links between discursive practices, events and texts, and social structures and relationships. Discourse analyses can enhance critical policy analyses, Taylor suggests, in several ways. Since the focus is on policies as texts, this leads to a focus on the processes of text production within broader social frameworks. Furthermore, if policymaking is viewed as a struggle of meaning-making involving the strategic and tactical deployment of particular discourses, then policy texts can be viewed as the outcome of these struggles and deployments. In addition, if we view language from poststructuralist perspectives, then texts such as policies are considered to be open to multiple readings, thus producing multiple effects and ongoing interpretations and reconstitutions of the policy. Finally, Taylor argues that an important focus for research needs to be the conditions under which particular discourses rise to prominence within particular fields of power/knowledge. I will examine some concrete examples of this approach later in the chapter. In a somewhat more specific light, however, Taylor argues for the use of discourse analysis to explore the historical context of policies, the discursive construction of educational 'problems,' the ways in which particular issues become important, how social contexts influence how policies are framed, and what happens in the policy implementation process, that is, "how policies are read and used in context" (Taylor, 1997, p. 29) or the politics of policy implementation. Interestingly, for comparative educators, Taylor suggests there is a need for more comparative studies, for example, in terms of policy development, who is involved, whose discourses are admitted and whose are marginalized. Such comparisons could wed a fine-grained poststructuralist approach to an analysis of broader contexts, thus dovetailing with political and social justice emphases (Taylor, 1997).

Luke, et al (1993) examined the way in which discourses in the National Aboriginal and Torres Strait Islander Education Policy (DEET, 1989) position and construct groups and communities, and the effects of these policies. They begin by examining the context of the policy. This context they characterize as one in which there was growing skepticism over the efficacy of the welfare state, and complex and contested views on the identity and rights of Indigenous peoples. In their thematic analysis they look for "the discourse strategies and moves used to suture over, hide, and appropriate difference, and those strategies which are deliberately polysemous, which can be read differently as referring to and operating in the interests of competing audiences" (p. 141). In particular they look for discourses that construct notions of Indigenous peoples and their others, universal rights, preferred educational practices and goals, and what counts as successful policy implementation.

In terms of the discursive construction of Indigenous peoples and their others, Luke, et al (1993) found that the policy constructed Indigenous peoples as homogenous by employing the blanket term 'Aboriginal' to include both Aboriginal and Torres Strait Islander peoples, by paying only lip service to diversity within Aboriginal and Torres Strait Islander groups, and by ignoring differences of gender and class. The policy employed a discourse that focused on the supposed lack experienced by ATSI peoples within education systems when compared to an imaginary norm. In terms of rights, the policy discussed international human rights treaties, but omitted to mention the human rights context of Australia, in which governments have been unable to legislate to provide teeth to their international obligations. The discourses around preferred educational goals and practices present Indigenous cultures as having been eroded. The use of this metaphor both elides the agents of this erosion and depicts the process as somehow natural. Luke, et al (1993) argue that the document fails to name education systems and the state as part of the cause of 'erosion.' Although schooling is implicated, it is only in terms of cultural misunderstanding, rather than in terms of the effects of state power on Indigenous social disintegration. Finally Luke, et al's (1993) analysis identifies within a discourse of corporate managerialism and human capital whose "very operation militate against diversity, local flexibility, and communication" (p. 147). They argue that the problem with using performance indicators to assess the policy is that they elide the play of difference. Furthermore, an emphasis on outputs as measured by performance indicators deflects questions of teaching, learning, pedagogy, curriculum, and policy.

The global circulation and local manifestation of educational ideas

The rubric of globalization and the global/local binary are beginning to have a prominent place in comparative education (see, for example, the collection edited by Arnove and Torres, 1999). Yet Saha (2001) argues that the discussion of globalization within comparative education has been undertaken primarily on the basis of neo-liberal assumptions. However, many of these assumptions are challenged by poststructuralist approaches to identity, subjectivity, and language. A different way of examining the global circulation and local manifestation of educational ideas is suggested by Popkewitz (2000). His notion of comparative studies is "to explore how knowledge systems of 'reason' circulate historically across and within institutions and national boundaries to order the principles of action and participation" (p. 262). This exploration involves unpacking how images and narratives that are perceived as universal cross national boundaries and become embedded and naturalized in local contexts. Thus, comparative education could map the circulation and local manifestation of ideas about curriculum, schooling, the ideal student, the professional teacher, the good citizen, and so on. According to Popkewitz, such an approach would also reveal how these discourses of education contributed to the construction of the ways in which citizens of a nation view themselves vis-à-vis the nation, i.e., to the construction of national imaginaries, national identity, collective memory, and subjectivity. Furthermore, the effects of these national imaginaries are not confined to the boundaries of the nation, but reveal cultural anxieties and mutually constituted relations of the global and the local. This is because national imaginaries are hybrids of multiple overlapping discourses that are both local and global. An example of the kind of globally circulating discourses to which Popkewitz alludes involves the invocation of the "indigenous foreigner" (p. 277), a concept which suggests "a particular type of hero and heroic discourse" (p. 277), which is deployed in educational reform movements as a means of legitimizing the reform. Popkewitz suggests that such "heroes" include Dewey, Vygotsky, Freire, Foucault, Habermas, and Arendt. His point is that the works of these authors are often used without any sense of their historicity or contingency. From this I conclude that an interesting and important task for comparative education involves an analysis of the ways in which the works and names of particular reformers are invoked in particular educational contexts; what aspects of their work are deployed; what omissions occur; what are the social, cultural and educational effects of these discursive moves; and how would it have been possible to think otherwise. Of course, such an analysis could be extended beyond simply examining the circulation and local manifestation of the educational ideas of "heroes." In addition it could be applied to educational concepts in general, as the following work by Christie shows.

Pam Christie (1997) provides an analysis of the competency debates that have occurred in South Africa in the last decade. She argues that in South Africa these debates have local manifestations and contexts that differ from other countries. The paper explores the specificities of these debates and their intermingling with international debates, trends. and experiences. The aspects of the locally complex context of South Africa include, first, a high level of educational policy development by a range of actors in the post-apartheid era, such as the ANC; and second, the construction of what constitutes educational problems has been the result of employing both new and old concepts. New concepts, Christie argues, have been introduced into South Africa via, for example, academic literature, visits by South African educationists to other countries, and by foreign consultants. The construction of competence-based education as a new problem in South Africa was directly influenced by Australian debates, and it is this connection that she teases out in more detail. As well as demonstrating the mechanisms and complexities of the movement of educational ideas and discourses across national borders, Christie's paper also shows how particular discourses can be deployed for different political purposes. While competence-based ideas may be linked to neo-liberal agendas of accountability in education, in South Africa they were linked to ideas of social justice. Because the population in the immediate post-apartheid era was very diverse in terms of its educational needs, it was argued that a competence-based approach was appropriate in order to develop an articulated education system in which a wide range of educational backgrounds and pathways could be accommodated. Finally, this study highlights the inadequacy of an approach which identifies only global trends, similarities, and so on, or which focuses only on globalization as an homogenizing process. It demonstrates the value of examining the local educational specificities of globalized discourses such as competence.

Critical discourse analysis of classroom texts

Broadfoot (2000) points out that while Western models of education have been very successful for some parts of the population, the problem of delivering education for all still remains, as does the role of schooling in creating and perpetuating social inequality, and the problems of the quality of education, of boredom among students, or an overemphasis on performativity. She argues that comparative education should have a much more explicit social science perspective with a greater emphasis on the processes of learning, rather than the provision and organization of education. Critical discourse analysis can contribute to understanding teaching and learning processes because it can be used to examine discursive formations both in schools in general and in classrooms in particular. Three studies are discussed below that illustrate some of the ways in which this can be done.

Lee (1994) applied critical discourse analysis to the enactment of the curriculum in classrooms. She examined gendered discourses in the geography classroom and their relationship to the ongoing production of student identity, or what Lee calls "identity-work." She attempts to combine linguistic micro-analysis with a wider and broader examination of the workings of the discourses of geography. Although Lee is interested in deconstructing the discourses that occur in the geography classroom, her aim is not simply to criticize and problematize. She is also interested in "possibilities for transformation" (p. 27). Lee examines the way in which different students' ideas are affirmed or thwarted by the teacher. Second, she examines the ways in which the various speakers position themselves and are positioned. Third, Lee reflects on the text in light of the wider context of the geography curriculum and geographical discourses, especially what she refers to as "economics" and "bio-philosophy" (p. 37). Fourth, and concurrently with the other techniques, Lee examines the genderedness of the classroom discourse. Lee's reading of her data present a complex picture of how masculine privilege is achieved, but it is a picture which instead of relying on "simple theories of gendered conspiracy" reveal ruptures and contradictions in these social processes. By specifying the genderedness of particular speech strategies, and their links with the discourses circulating in the subject of geography, Lee is able to identify and open up spaces for contestation of these strategies and discourses.

The idea of curricular discourses interacting with "identity-work" also occurs in Davies' (1993) research regarding the ways in which young children read and explain gendered discourses that they encounter in texts. Whereas Lee reported on her reading of events in and around geography classrooms, Davies reports on strategies that teachers can use to work with students to identify and disrupt oppressive discourses in texts. This work provides an example of practical classroom work in which teachers and students can engage, and demonstrates the possibilities for collaborative comparative studies of the implementation of curricula in ways that challenge contemporary oppressions. It does this by providing strategies that can be used to enact particular policies (e.g., concerning gender and education), and engage both deconstructively and reconstructively with curriculum materials through the provision of opportunities for classroom discussions about oppressive and resistant discourses.

Comber's (1997) study is important because it demonstrates how macro-scale discourses, in her case, literacy and managerialism, impact on the everyday work of students and teachers. Comber is interested in how the new discourses of literacy impact teacher and student practices in the classroom and how these discourses discipline the work of student and teachers, particularly in terms of the uses that are made of the discourses and if and how they are resisted. She argues that critical discourse analysis is an important technique in this case because it is "active analysis of how and where…discursive practices insinuate themselves in the minute details of everyday life and so to suggest how and where resistance happens" (p. 390). Her work was undertaken in a socioeconomically disadvantaged community in South Australia. She focuses particularly on the deployment of managerialist discourses in the construction of the 'disadvantaged child.' She concludes that managerialist discourses actually were a disservice to disadvantaged students because they focused on work habits and attitudes. But even students with good work habits and positive attitudes were not always successful at attaining high levels of literacy. This literacy failure was hidden, particularly in students' reports, by the positives evaluations ('hard-working,' 'good attitude') arising from the deployment of the dominant managerialist discourse and by the absence of discursive resources that could name and suggest remedies for the failure.

Critical discourse analysis of school subjects and curriculum materials

A wide range of opportunities present themselves for the critical comparative analysis of school subjects and curriculum. In the section below I discuss a discursive analytic study of the implementation of curricular reforms and teachers' resistance to them. In this section I want to focus on the work I and my colleagues have done analyzing curriculum materials, especially in terms of the representations of indigenous knowledges and identities in high school science textbooks in Australia, Canada, and New Zealand, and the conditions of the production of these representations.

Using concepts such as essentialism and othering drawn from postcolonial theory (see, for example, Gandhi, 1998), we examined the ways in which science textbooks attempted to respond to the culturally diverse societies in which they were located. We examined a range of contemporary junior high school science textbooks used in the three countries, particularly in terms of how they represented indigenous legends and myths, technology, knowledge of the natural world, and social life (Ninnes, 2000, 2001; Ninnes and Burnett, 2001). Although we found that in some instances the textbooks were highly inclusive of this kind of material, we also identified several problems associated with the various approaches taken. In some cases the textbooks essentialized indigenous people. That is, they created the impression that indigenous groups were homogenous, thus masking the diversity within and between indigenous groups. In other cases the textbooks overcame or avoided this problem by referring to the knowledges and practices of specific indigenous groups. The second problem arose from the deployment in some textbooks of discourses of traditionality. In other words, some textbooks placed an emphasis on traditional indigenous lifestyles and practices and elided contemporary ones. Such an emphasis, in our reading, ascribes authenticity to particular forms of indigeneity, and, following McConaghy (1998), we suggest that this kind of discursive deployment is a means of controlling and constraining indigenous people's identities and possibilities. We identified a third problem through the application of systemic linguistics approaches advocated by Luke (1989). Our analysis of grammatical devices employed by the authors revealed that in some cases past tense was used to discuss extant indigenous knowledges and practices. The problem here is that this gives the impression that indigenous knowledges and practices have been superseded by "scientific" knowledges and practices, or as McClintock (1995:40) phrases it, "superannuated by history."

A fourth problem which our initial research on the representations of indigenous knowledges and practices in science textbooks revealed involved the issue of the politics of the production of the textbooks. The textbooks, for example, gave very little information about the processes of textbook production. We were not satisfied with simply examining the discourses contained in the textbooks because we saw that the appropriateness or otherwise of particular representations of indigenous knowledges and practices could not be objectively assessed. Rather, these representations are contingent and contextualized. For example, following Spivak (1990, 1993), we viewed the question of essentialism as highly complex. It may be that particular kinds of representations are neither right nor wrong; what is crucial is who is deploying them, for what purpose, and with what effects. It may be that an essentialist representation of indigeneity is part of an important political process engaged in by or with the consent of indigenous people that brings to the fore indigenous knowledges that had previously been marginalized or made invisible. To this end, we surveyed a small sample of authors of textbooks that had relatively extensive frequency of representations of indigenous knowledges and practices (Ninnes, 2001). Our aim was to find out the reasons for the inclusion of these discourses of indigeneity in the textbooks, who was involved in the process, and in what way. The results revealed a wide diversity of views among authors regarding the merits of including the perspectives of indigenous and minority groups in science textbooks. Some authors argued that the barriers to the inclusion of more material of this kind included their own lack of knowledge about indigenous issues and inadequate time to increase their knowledge, and conservatism on the part of publishers, who were willing to follow government and curriculum directives, but not take an ideological lead in incorporating diverse perspectives. One of the major incentives for the inclusion of material of this kind was provincial or state curriculum prescriptions. However, almost all of the authors who did incorporate multicultural perspectives relied on secondary source material. As a result, Indigenous people and members of other minority groups were almost never directly involved in the process of textbook production, which suggests that the incorporation of their perspectives on knowledge, culture, and science often amounts to appropriation with little change in the power relations between the holders of dominant and subjugated knowledges.

Variations in the kinds of representations of indigenous and non-indigenous minority groups found in the textbooks and differences in the processes of textbook production in Australia, New Zealand, and Canada can be explained by reference to the differing political and policy contexts of the three nations. In New Zealand, the textbooks made substantial reference to Maori knowledges, but much less attention was paid to the knowledges of non-Indigenous minorities. A similar approach was taken in one of the series of textbooks used in New South Wales, Australia. In the New Zealand case, the privileging of Maori knowledges and language is a reflection of the precedence given to Maori identity and culture in Aotearoa New Zealand and the fact that since 1987 Maori and English have both been recognized as official languages in Aotearoa, New Zealand; this was one response to the Waitangi Tribunal's finding that although the Treaty of Waitangi guarantees preservation of Maori *taonga* (treasures), the Maori language was in substantial decline (McKinley, et al. 1992). In the Australian case, the authors at the time were working within a context in which the NSW Aboriginal Education policy recommended Aboriginal perspectives be incorporated across the curriculum, but did not mandate this. The authors chose to do so out of a sense that it was the right thing to do. In the Canadian case, provincial education policy required that a multicultural perspective be presented, but there was no specific requirement to present Indigenous perspectives.

Subjectivity and Governmentality

The work by Comber described above shows the way in which particular categories of students are constituted through discourses and the interaction of those and other discourses to prescribe and constrain students' educational futures. That is, it shows how people are constituted as particular kinds of subjects through discourse, and how populations are categorized and controlled or governed. There are a number of other works that examine the role of education in this intersection of subjectivity and governmentality that provide useful models for the application of critical discourse analysis in comparative education. Interested readers may wish to read the works by Tait (1993) on the construction of the categories of 'child' and 'adolescent,' Jones (1990) on the 'good teacher,' McCallum (1993) on the 'problem child,' Troyna and Vincent (1995) on 'social justice,' Tyler (1993) and Baker (1998) on 'childhood,' Fendler (1998) on the 'educated subject,' and Wagener (1998) on 'the body.' In order to illustrate this kind of work, I review Tait's (1995) work on the processes and effects of the construction of the category of 'at-risk youth.'

Tait (1995) examines the discursive construction of both the category of 'at-risk youth' and the supposed solutions to this problem. Tait argues that the problem and the solution are constituted through the collection of statistical data identifying risk within populations, and along with subsequently developed programs, the discursive construction of the category and its attendant data collection constitute a technology or apparatus [dispositif] for governing youth. Thus, Tait argues, " 'youth' is not a stage of life but is instead an artifact of various forms of government" (p. 132).

The concept of 'risk' replaces the concept of 'dangerous' in the governance of populations. According to Tate's sources, nineteenth-century forms of government were concerned with identifying 'dangerous' individuals in the population and preventing them from wreaking havoc. The problems with this approach were its inability to either predict or prevent outbreaks of dangerous behavior. The category of 'risk,' on the other hand, is much more useful in these regards. This is because the measurement of the frequency of dangerous behaviors within various strata of society can be used to identify which sections of the population are most at risk of exhibiting these behaviors. These sections of the population can then be subject to specific programs of prevention. Tait (1995) identifies three crucial implications of this discursive shift. First, factors, rather than the characteristics of individuals, are used to predict levels of risk. The 'delinquency' of individuals is therefore constituted not through individual characteristics, but their location within a constellation of factors. Second, the task of identifying 'risk' falls as much into the hands of government administrators who calculate risk factors as the hands of specialist practitioners. Third, Tait believes that the concept of risk represents a more powerful and indeed efficient technology of governance than the kinds of surveillance represented by the panopticon[2] and other carcereal institutions. Risk is more calculable, specific and versatile. Risk is everywhere and everyone is at risk of something. Therefore everyone is legitimately within the bounds of government intervention.

Tait examines the deployment of this category of 'at risk-youth' in a key report published in Australia in the early 1990s. The so-called Finn Report (Finn, 1991) was commissioned by the Australian Education Council Review Committee and examined the participation of 'youth' in post-compulsory education and training. Tait (1995) found that the risk to which youth were subject, according to this report, was of not making the transition from compulsory to post compulsory education, which was seen as an essential component of making the transition from 'youth' to adulthood. Although the report indicated that all youth were potentially at risk, it identified certain groups who were especially so. Tait notes that the Finn report reveals how statistical calculations are used to identify the proportion of youth who are 'at risk,' and observes that "this exhaustive and meticulous collection of data ... is the very mechanism by which knowledge is acquired concerning the social body" (p. 128). In turn these statistical calculations are used to justify the deployment of particular levels of governmental funding to prevention programs. Tait also observes the distinction between the discourses of 'risk' and 'disadvantage.' The latter has much greater possibilities for justifying government intervention because whereas 'disadvantage' is constituted as a category measured against a norm, and therefore only occupied by a certain segment of the population, 'at risk' is a category in which anyone can be placed.

The rise and fall of educational discourses

Critical discourse analysis can be used to identify the ways in which particular educational discourses come to prominence, their effects, and how to disrupt them. For example, Simola, Heikkinen and Silvonen (1998) in their study of Finnish education, used curriculum documents, particularly committee reports, from 1925, 1952, 1970, 1985, and 1994, to show how ideas about the good teacher changed over time. However, in this section I wish to focus on a research study that demonstrates the use of critical discourse analysis in exploring the ways in which teachers resist particular discourses at the classroom and school levels. Gvirtz and Narodowski (1998) examined the implementation of curricular reforms and policies during Peron's first two terms of government in Argentina (1946-1955). In these reforms, an authoritarian approach was adopted to education in which Peronist ideology was explicitly inserted into a range of curriculum areas and in which Peronistas were rewarded and promoted and anti-Peronistas were demoted or moved out of their preferred positions. Gvirtz and Narodowski looked particularly at how textbooks were used, how the partisan contents were presented, and responses to centrally-derived directives.

Despite Peronist attempts to impose homogeneity and the exertion of authoritarian pressure by the state at the macro-political level, there was substantial resistance at the micro-political level. Even the use of police power and propaganda could not ensure that the impacts of these policies were either entirely direct or uniform. Using class notebooks as the major data source, Gvirtz and Narodowski identified three types of resistance tactics with two common features. First, these tactics occur in teacher work in a range of different places, that is, they appear to have arisen independently, and second the tactics are manifest in pedagogical methods rather than in open proclamations of opposition.

The three tactics employed by teachers involved, first the "depoliticization of content" (pp. 236–7). This tactic involved removing the overt political content from lessons to give an appearance of political or ideological neutrality. For example, in composition and other language exercises which Gvirtz and Narodowski analyzed in the students' notebooks, teachers employing this tactic focused on features such as formal correctness of grammar and ignored aspects of the political 'correctness' of the text. The second tactic involved what Gvirtz and Narodowski term "disrupting the logical stabilization of statements" (pp. 237–8). They argue that students' class notebooks were meant to be logical, unambiguous and internally consistent. However, in the Peronist era, the notebooks start to first, include "imprecise, ambiguous or simply self-contradictory statements" (p. 237), which confuse the educational policy which the teachers were meant to implement; and second, the teachers tended to use one passage to contradict another. The final tactic was indifference. Gvirtz and Narodowski (1998, pp. 238–239) identify instances involving the explicit exclusion of Peronist material, partial inclusion or superficial coverage. For example, some teachers excluded material related to the rise of power of Peron (in the 1943 coup) in a section on Argentine history that was intended to cover the period 1853–1949. There were also instances of indifferent grading. That is, teachers sometimes did not give any grades for explicitly Peronist material; or they just corrected the spelling errors in that kind of material and did not give a grade.

The discursive analysis conducted by Gvirtz and Narodowski reveals aspects of resistance to particular ideologies that would not have been revealed through other means, such as the study of the contents of policy documents or the proclamations of government and opposition political parties. This is because the resistance which they uncovered was not based on enunciating an opposing ideology, but on getting rid altogether of the overtly ideological elements in the curriculum. The resistance arose from a professional attitude to what was appropriate curriculum content, rather than through the workings of structured political institutions such as political parties or trade unions.

Final Remarks

My aim in this chapter has been to explore the meanings of discourse and critical discourse analysis, and to provide some examples of the use of critical discourse analysis in exploring issues that are commonly of concern to many comparative educators. In particular, I have reviewed works that use critical discourse analysis to explore issues related to policy analysis; the global circulation and local manifestation of educational ideas; classroom studies; analyses of school subjects and curriculum materials; student and teacher subjectivities; and the rise and fall of educational discourses. These forms of analysis are powerful because discourses have material effects. Discourses impact the ways students are treated in schools; the ways education policies impact on teaching, learning, and administrative practices, the ways in which teachers see themselves and their students; and the kinds of learning experiences that students have. As such, critical discourse analysis brings a fertile and challenging range of methods to the field of comparative education, which have the potential to provide new and powerful insights into issues of concern to the field.

Endnotes

1. For a discussion of the problematics of claiming mastery, see Cixous and Clément (1975/ 1986, pp. 136 ff.).
2. A panopticon was a design for a prison in which prisoners could be watched by guards in such a way that the prisoners were unaware of whether they were being watched or not. The prisoners thus became self-disciplining. The panopticon is used as a metaphor for any system of surveillance in which subjects come to assume or know they are being watched and hence discipline themselves. See Foucault (1977).

References

Arnove, Robert and Carlos Alberto Torres. *Comparative Education: The Dialectic of the Global and the Local.* Lanham, MD: Rowman and Littlefield, 1999.

Bain, William. "The Loss of Innocence: Lyotard, Foucault and the Challenge of Postmodern Education." In *Education and the Postmodern Condition.* Edited by Michael Peters. Westport, Conn.: Bergin and Garvey, 1995.

Baker, Bernadette. "'Childhood' in the Emergence and Spread of US Public Schools." In *Foucault's Challenge: Discourse, Knowledge and Power in Education.* Edited by Thomas S. Popkewitz and Marie Brennan. New York: Teachers College Press, 1998.

Ball, Stephen, J. *Education Reform: A Critical and Post-Structural Approach.* Buckingham: Open University Press, 1994.

Blake, Nigel, et al. *Thinking Again: Education after Postmodernism.* Westport, Conn.: Bergin and Garvey, 1998.

Broadfoot, Patricia. "Comparative Education for the 21st Century. Retrospect and Prospect." *Comparative Education* 36(2000): 357–371.

Christie, Pam. "Global Trends in Local Contexts: A South African Perspective on Competence Debates." *Discourse: Studies in the Cultural Politics of Education* 18(1997): 55–69.

Cixous, Hélène and Catherine Clément. *The Newly Born Woman.* Translated by Betsy Wing. Minneapolis: University of Minnesota Press, 1986.

Codd, John. A. "The Construction and Deconstructions of Educational Policy Documents." *Journal of Educational Policy* 3 (1988): 235–247.

Comber, Barbara. "Managerial Discourses: Tracking the Local Effects on Teachers' and Students' Work in Literacy Lessons." *Discourse: Studies in the Cultural Politics of Education* 18(1997): 389–407.

Crossely, Michael. "Bridging Cultures and Traditions in the Reconceptualisation of Comparative and International Education." *Comparative Education* 36(2000): 319–332.

_____. "Reconceptualising Comparative and International Education." *Compare*, 29 (1999): 249–67.

Crossley, Michael and Peter Jarvis. "Introduction: Continuity, Challenge and Change in Comparative and International Education." *Comparative Education* 36(2000): 261.

Davies, Bronwyn. *Shards of Glass: Children Reading and Writing beyond Gendered Identities.* Sydney: Allen and Unwin, 1993.

Fairclough, Norman. *Critical Discourse Analysis: The Critical Study of Language.* London: Longman, 1996.

Fairclough, Norman and Ruth Wodak. "Critical Discourse Analysis." In *Discourse as Social Interaction.* Edited by Teun A. van Dijk. London: Sage, 1997.

Fendler, Lynn. "What is it Impossible to Think? A Genealogy of the Educated Subject." In *Foucault's Challenge: Discourse, Knowledge and Power in Education.* Edited by Thomas S. Popkewitz and Marie Brennan. New York: Teachers College Press, 1998.

Finn, B. *Young People's Participation in Post-Compulsory Education and Training: Report of the Australian Educational Council Review Committee.* Canberra: Australian Government Publishing Service, 1991.

Foucault, Michel. *The Archaeology of Knowledge*, translated by A. M. Sheridan Smith. London: Tavistock, 1972.

Foucault, Michel. *Discipline and Punish: The Birth of the Prison*, translated by A. Sheridan. London: Penguin, 1977.

Foucault, Michel. *Power/Knowledge: Selected Interviews and Other Writings 1972–1977*, translated and edited by Colin Gordon. New York: Pantheon, 1980.

Gale, Trevor. "Policy Trajectories: Treading the Discursive Path of Policy Analysis." *Discourse: Studies in the Cultural Politics of Education* 20(1999): 393–407.

Game, Ann and Andrew Metcalfe. *Passionate Sociology.* London: Sage, 1996.

Gandhi, Leela. *Postcolonial Theory: A Critical Introduction.* St. Leonards, NSW: Allen and Unwin, 1998.

Grant, Nigel. "Tasks for Comparative Education in the New Millennium." *Comparative Education* 36(2000): 309–317.

Gvirtz, Silvina and Mariano Narodowski. "The Micro-Politics of School Resistance: The Case of Argentine Teachers Versus the Educational Policies of Peron and Evita." *Discourse: Studies in the Cultural Politics of Education* 19(1998): 233–241.

Jones, D. "The Genealogy of the Urban School Teacher." In *Foucault and Education: Disciplines and Knowledge.* Edited by Stephen Ball. London and New York: Routledge, 1990.

Lee, Alison. "Gender and Text in Educational Research." *Australian Educational Researcher* 21(3, 1994): 25–46.

Little, Angela. "Development Studies and Comparative Education: Context, Content, Comparison and Contributors." *Comparative Education* 36(2000): 279–296.

Luke, Allan. "Open and Closed Texts. The Ideological/Semantic Analysis of Textbook Narratives." *Journal of Pragmatics* 13 (1989): 53–80.

Luke, Allan. "Critical Discourse Analysis." In *Issues in Educational Research.* Edited by John P. Keeves and Gabriel Lakomski. Amsterdam: Pergamon, 1999.

Luke, Allan, et al. "Policy and the Politics of Representation: Torres Strait Islanders and Aborigines at the Margins." In *Schooling Reform in Hard Times.* Edited by Bob Lingard, John Knight and Paige Porter. London: Falmer Press, 1993.

MacLure, Maggie. *Discourses in Educational and Social Research.* Buckingham, UK: Open University Press, 2003.

Marginson, Simon and Marcella Mollis. " 'The Door Opens and the Tiger Leaps': Theories and Reflexivities of Comparative Education for a Global Millennium." *Comparative Education Review* 45 (2001): 581–615.

Marshall, James D. "Foucault and Educational Research." In *Foucault and Education: Disciplines and Knowledge.* Edited by Stephen Ball. London and New York: Routledge, 1990.

McConaghy, Cathryn. "Constructing Aboriginality, Determining Significant Difference. In *The Context of Teaching* (2nd ed.). Edited by Thomas W. Maxwell and Peter Ninnes. Armidale, NSW: Kardoorair Press, 2000.

McCallum, David. "Problem Children and Familial Relations." In *Child and Citizen: Genealogies of Schooling and Subjectivity.* Edited by Denise Meredyth and Debra Tyler. Brisbane: Griffith University Institute for Cultural Policy Studies, 1993.

McHoul, Alex W. and Allan Luke. "Discourse as Language and Politics." *Journal of Pragmatics* 13 (1989): 323–332.

McKinley, Elizabeth, Pauline M. Waiti and Beverley Bell. "Language, Culture and Science Education." *International Journal of Science Education,* 14 (1992): 579–595.

Mehta, Sonia and Peter Ninnes. "Postpositivist Debates and Comparative Education: Resistance, Reinvention, Revolution." Paper presented at the Comparative and International Education Society annual conference, San Antonio, Texas, March 2000.

Ninnes, Peter. "Representations of Indigenous Knowledges in Secondary School Science Textbooks in Australia and Canada." *International Journal of Science Education.* 22 (2000): 603–617.

_____. "Writing Multicultural Science Textbooks: Perspectives, Problems, Possibilities and Power." *Australian Science Teachers' Journal.* 47(4, 2001): 18–27.

_____. "Representations of Ways of Knowing in Junior High School Science Texts Used in Australia." *Discourse: Studies in the Cultural Politics of Education* 22(2001): 81–94.

Ninnes, Peter and Greg Burnett. "Postcolonial Theory and Science Education: Textbooks, Curriculum and Cultural Diversity in Aotearoa New Zealand." *New Zealand Journal of Educational Studies* 36(1, 2001): 25–39.

_____. "Mapping Visual Culture in Comparative Education Discourse." *Compare* 27 (1997): 117–52.

_____. "Mapping Comparative Education after Postmodernity." *Comparative Education Review* 43(1999): 438–463.

Paulston, Rolland. "Imagining Comparative Education: Past, Present, Future." *Compare* 30 (2000): 353–367.

Popkewitz, Thomas S. and Miguel A. Pereyra. "An Eight Country Study of Reform Perspectives in Teacher Education: An Outline of the Problematic." In *Changing Patterns of Power: Social Regulation and Teacher Education Reform.* Edited by Thomas S. Popkewitz. Albany: SUNY Press, 1993.

Popkewitz, Thomas S. "National Imaginaries, the Indigenous Foreigner, and Power: Comparative Educational Research." In *Discourse Formation in Comparative Education,* edited by Jurgen Schreiwer. Frankfurt am Main: Peter Lang, 2000.

Saha, Lawrence. "The Sociology of Comparative Education." In *Sociology of Education Today.* Edited by Jack Demaine. Basingstoke: Palgrave, 2001.

Simola, Hannu, Sakari Heikkinen, and Jussi Silvonen. "A Catalog of Possibilities: Foucaultian History of Truth and Education Research." In *Foucault's Challenge: Discourse, Knowledge and Power in Education.* Edited by Thomas S. Popkewitz and Marie Brennan. New York: Teachers College Press, 1998.

Soucek, Victor. "Educating in Global Times: Choice, Charter and the Market." *Discourse Studies in the Cultural Politics of Education* 20(1999): 219–234.

Spivak, Gayatri. *The Post-Colonial Critic: Interviews, Strategies, Dialogues.* New York and London: Routledge, 1990.

_____. *Outside in the Teaching Machine.* New York and London: Routledge, 1993.

Tait, Gordon. "Sex Education: Some Political Ambiguities." In *Child and Citizen: Genealogies of Schooling and Subjectivity,* edited by Denise Meredyth and Debra Tyler. Brisbane: Griffith University Institute for Cultural Policy Studies, 1993.

Tait, Gordon. "Shaping the 'At-Risk Youth': Risk, Governmentality and the Finn Report." *Discourse: Studies in the Cultural Politics of Education* 16(1995): 123–134.

Talbani, Aziz. "Pedagogy, Power and Discourse: Transformation of Islamic Education." *Comparative Education Review* 40 (1996): 66–82.

Taylor, Sandra. "Critical Policy Analysis: Exploring Contexts, Texts and Consequences." *Discourse: Studies in the Cultural Politics of Education* 18(1997): 23–35.

Troyna, Barry and Carol Vincent. "The Discourses of Social Justice." *Discourse: Studies in the Cultural Politics of Education* 16(1995): 149–166.

Tyler, Deborah. "Making Better Children." In *Child and Citizen: Genealogies of Schooling and Subjectivity*. Edited by Denise Meredyth and Deborah Tyler. Brisbane: Griffith University Institute for Cultural Policy Studies, 1993.

van Dijk, Teun A. "Critical discourse analysis." In *The Handbook of Discourse Analysis*. Edited by Deborah Shiffrin, Deborah Tannen, and Heidi Hamilton. Oxford: Blackwell, 2001.

Wagener, Judity Rabak. "The Construction of the Body through Sex Education Discourse Practices." In *Foucault's Challenge: Discourse, Knowledge and Power in Education*. Edited by Thomas S. Popkewitz and Marie Brennan. New York: Teachers College Press, 1998.

Watson, Keith. "Memories, Models and Mapping: The Impact of Geopolitical Changes on Comparative Studies in Education." *Compare*, 28 (1998): 5–33.

Welch, Anthony. "The Triumph of Technocracy or the Collapse of Certainty? Modernity, Postmodernity, and Postcolonialism." In *Comparative Education: The Dialectic of the Global and the Local*. Edited by Robert Arnove and Carlos A. Torres. Lanham, MD: Rowman and Littlefield, 1999.

Welch, Anthony. "New Times, Hard Times: Re-Reading Comparative Education in an Age of Discontent." In *Discourse Formation in Comparative Education*. Edited by Jurgen Schreiwer. Frankfurt: Peter Lang, 2000.

CHAPTER 4

Deconstructing Educational Discourse in Kiribati: Postcolonial Encounters

GREG BURNETT

Colonial Discourse and Education For All

The recent scheme in the Republic of Kiribati to universalize Junior Secondary education is possibly the largest intervention since the introduction of missionary schooling in the 1800s. The desires that motivated this move, however, appeared much earlier in the 1950s when I-Kiribati began to participate in colonial governance. Parliamentary records reveal numerous petitions by I-Kiribati representatives lobbying for expansion of educational services and subsequent rejections by British officials whose approach to colonial administration was at best miserly (Tabai, 1987). However, the political expediency of opening up secondary schooling has been recognized by a series of post-independence Kiribati governments. After the departure of the British in 1979 the number of secondary schools increased, albeit barely within what economic conditions would allow, until, by the mid 1990s, fifty percent of primary students were placed in secondary schooling. The government's quantum leap in 1997 to universalize secondary schooling was made justifiable, despite continuing economic constraints, by wider global pressures to provide basic 'education for all' (EFA).

Education authorities have received EFA uncritically, not only in the industrialized West which dominated its envisioning, but in parts of the world where basic education enrollment has never been complete. EFA has also gained the consent of a range of NGOs, for example, Oxfam (see

Watkins, 1999) and *New Internationalist* (see May, 1999, Special Education issue). Within the field of Comparative and International Education, criticisms of EFA have been few. Where they have occurred, EFA rationale has been perceived as laudable but unrealistic for economic reasons (Vlaardingerbroek, 1998; Burchert, 1995). or in terms of inadequate teacher preparation (Ndawi, 1997). Critiques directed at the politics of knowledge and the Eurocentricity of the intervention (see, for example, Brock-Utne, 1999) tend to slide toward 'cultural relativism' (Hoffman, 1999; McConaghy, 2000). In these instances critics advocate interventions that attempt to re-indigenize curricula and the languages of schooling according to perceived cultural and identity differences.

Re-indigenization in response to universalization discourse runs the risk of further marginalizing the formerly colonized (Nakata, 1999). Desires for indigenization can be tied to anthropological discourses that either seek to maintain colonial power structures (McConaghy, 2000) or in many cases are the result of 'primitivist' desires (Torgovnick, 1996) by dis-located Europeans and non-European elites. In either case, desires are based on essentialized assumptions about non-Western cultures and identity (Appadurai, 1988). Furthermore, desires for re-indigenization are often at odds with the desires of many people in former colonies who seek Western forms of schooling and competence in English language for their children. Thus, re-indigenization is largely a project of the socially dominant elite. Following Spivak (1988), and despite the 'indigenous' veneer of the debates, the subaltern cannot speak but must continue to be spoken for.

I argue that EFA is an inadequate response to educational needs, not just in Kiribati, but also globally. It becomes most problematic when it is paraded by governments, NGOs, and local educational authorities as not just a panacea for a nation's educational ills, but as a means toward national development and personal prosperity. I argue that EFA is a simplistic intervention that refuses to dismantle older, long standing structural inequalities that continue to exist. In Kiribati, older discourses of education, initiated in colonial times will, despite EFA, have free reign to shape education *because* of greater access. The persistence of colonial discourse in education, I argue, results in a continued uneven distribution of privilege in Kiribati society. Colonial discourses such as those identified in this chapter are causal factors in a system that favors students along multiple axes of gender, class, location, and language competence.

The claim that privilege is unevenly produced along these axes is not necessarily grounded in the observations of either the author, who occupies the historically problematic subject position in the Pacific of academic European male, nor those in the most recent comprehensive education sector report (Team Report, 1992). Rather, the reality of differential privilege emerges when more than a decade of educational trends (see Tekawa, 1999) are compared with the many statements concerning 'inclusivity' and 'democracy' found in documents authored by or consented to by I-Kiribati, such as education mission statements (see Ministry of Education Training and Technology, 1998) and the nation's constitution (ROK, 1979). There is disjuncture between the openly stated aims of governance and its institutions, for example, education and actual student outcomes. Though all I-Kiribati students might be present in classrooms because of secondary EFA, educational statistics (Tekawa, 1999) indicate male students from families where parents are English competent and working in the cash sector in the urban center of Tarawa will continue to accrue benefits. Other groups, such as females, I-Kiribati language speakers, and rural students, at the same time continue to, on average, accrue deficits.

Education planning needs to move beyond just placing all students in classrooms or alternatively 'reindigenizing' educational practice. Rather, equitable educational futures are more likely when students are allowed access to the ways particular discourses have attempted to shape educational and social life and identities over time (Willinsky, 1998). Knowledge production and ways of knowing are not neutral, but can and have been marshaled by socially dominant groups, both I-Kiribati and non-I-Kiribati, to maintain positions of power and status. Discourses here mean the ways I-Kiribati and in particular students have been made subjects in the educational deliberations of socially dominant missionaries, administrative officials, and I-Kiribati authorities. At the same time socially dominant groups have also created subject positions for themselves, often in terms of simple binary opposites, for example, rational/irrational, superior/inferior or moral/immoral (see Blaut, 1993, p. 17 for a greater list of colonial subject positions). These ideas derive from the work of Michel Foucault (see, for example, Foucault, 1983) and have been applied specifically to interrogating colonial relations, for example, by Edward Said (1978, p. 5) who argues:

> The Orient [read Kiribati] is an idea that has a history and a tradition of thought, imagery and vocabulary that have *given it a reality* and presence in and *for the West* (Said, 1978, p. 5, italics mine).

These subject positions are merely imaginings, passed off as 'givens' and used accordingly to naturalize colonial social formations and particular ways of schooling. The following critical postcolonial discourse analysis of Kiribati education seeks to cast 'doubt' (Patterson, 1997) on the way I-Kiribati identity and educational practice have been legitimized. This process is a pre-requisite to imagining democratic educational futures that move beyond the 'more of the same' reforms of EFA.

I identify here three major discourses in contemporary educational practice in Kiribati: the embodied I-Kiribati, cultural authenticity, and development. Their genesis or 'genes' (Jóhannesson, 1998, p. 301) can be traced to colonial times when formal schooling was instituted. I use a "problematizing" (Dean, 1994) approach to historiography where the educational and social past is examined for the ways in which "human beings are made subjects" (Foucault 1983, p. 208), which are then stratified by what Foucault (1983, p. 208) calls dividing practices. Foucault emphasizes, 'the subject is either divided inside [within the individual] or divided from others' (1983, p. 208). I argue it is imperative that students critically understand how these dividing practices have impacted not only contemporary educational practices, social relations and identities in Kiribati, but how the process of naturalization works.

Abject Bodies, Abject Minds: Education and the Civilizing Mission

Universalization and its emphasis on numbers at the expense of the more substantive aspects of schooling, for example, whose knowledge, and for whose purposes, reflects an obsession with bodies and a subsequent erasure of what Franz Fanon (1967) calls an 'otherness of being,' that is, the moral, spiritual and emotional. Universalization is fundamentally about positioning bodies in schools, and thus presenting equality in terms of opportunity only. It fails to recognize the effects differences across multiple axes have on the teaching and learning process *after* all bodies are present in the classroom. Tied to universalization is an insistence on tailoring education in Kiribati to suit national human resource requirements. This educational rhetoric is very persuasive when linked, as it often has been, to nationalism and the desire to replace with I-Kiribati the number of non-I-Kiribati that are still relied upon for expertise. A jobs-driven system of schooling where positions need to be filled denies the possibility of a broader education that attempts to meet students' 'otherness.'

On a micro-scale discourses of the body can be identified in school management practices. Until universalization all students participated in boarding school rituals, which to a large degree were common to all schools. In many cases even those who lived adjacent to the school compound or were children of staff were required to enter into a lifestyle of dormitories, mess rooms, preps and fatigues. Universalization has meant that all students up to Form Three level have become day students and are thus free of many of these routines. However, the boarding ritual will continue for those students in senior secondary levels (Tataua, T. 2000, pers. comm., 4 Jan). According to my experience as a teacher in two boarding schools, it is a ritual that students wear uniforms and prominently display their school's motif. Departure from standard dress is noted at formal evaluations by student leaders and teaching staff. Students often march around the compound to the orders of head boys and head girls who have been carefully selected on the basis of the extent to which they reflect the values and desires of staff, administration, or church. Rolls are called each teaching period, meal, prep, and in the dormitory. Temporal and spatial boundaries are adhered to with the threat of physical punishment.

Students in the wrong place at the wrong time run the risk of punishment in the form of labor or the stick. Bells divide the day into eating, worshipping, learning, working, studying, and sleeping periods. Boundaries are clearly demarcated by sea and lagoon or by a distinct line of tamed bush where the compound has been distinguished from forbidden village spaces by the meticulous weeding of students at work or in punishment.

From the earliest times of the missionary and administrative presence, discourses of the embodied I-Kiribati, such as these, can be identified and linked to the establishment and maintenance of colonial power structures. George Pierson, an American missionary, was sent to assess Kiribati for a permanent mission station. With many references to countenances, smiles, nudity, tattooing, high foreheads, eyes and appearance in general, his journal demonstrates the emphases on the body. Pierson's descriptions of I-Kiribati stopped at the body, since that was considered enough to assess what lay beyond. This type of observation held indigenous morphology to be a kind of 'text,' which once read, provided details about intellect, character, and morality (Wade, 2000). Missionaries and many colonial administrators may not have used empirical body readings, (for example, craniometry and skull measurement; see Tylor, 1881, p. 60) used by anthropologists of the time; however, the same basic principles still applied.

Franz Fanon's (1967, p. 110ff) reflections on being 'read' by Europeans in this superficial way are instructive here. His "meeting [of] the white man's eyes" is considered a negating experience where "the countless facets of [his] being" desire to burst forth. Every time Pierson peered at the I-Kiribati countenance, observed the smile and the high forehead, he denied the breadth of being behind such superficialities. The gaze here is not only reductive, but results in the perception that all difference encountered in the colonial interaction is part of the natural order of things or 'fixed' (Fanon, 1967, p. 116). The following statement from Pierson is evidence of his perceived link between the inner state of I-Kiribati he met and their appearance:

> But the natural appearance of any people be it ever so revolting to our feelings is not to be compared with the moral corruption and wickedness there is in the heart (Pierson, 1855b).

Colonial logic dictated that since all looked the same, all were the same in every other way. Very early in his journal Pierson remarked that observations of the appearance, character, and customs of the people on the first island visited 'apply to the whole group and hence have not [sic] repeated hereafter' (Pierson, 1855a, p. 26). The tendency to essentialize indigeneity was a recurring practice throughout Empire, facilitating the imposition of European values, ways of knowing and governance. To borrow from Edward Said (1978, p. 102), it was as if a bin called 'Kiribati' existed into which all the authoritative, Western attitudes to Kiribati were unthinkingly dumped.

This deliberate confusion of human traits with appearance and the substitution of the whole for a physical make-up is a form of fetishization. As Stuart Hall (1997, p. 266) suggests, fetishization is significant for masking with qualities less malevolent something 'dangerous and powerful' in the recipient of the gaze. I argue the many references made to the outward appearance of I-Kiribati can be read as a disavowal of a rational, moral, and spiritual I-Kiribati presence that opposes and challenges the missionary's presence. The fetishization process also reveals a barely hidden colonial fear and anxiety, which I discuss in the next section.

The British administration's involvement in schooling was also marked by emphasis on the body, in particular hygiene, disease management, and physical education. Of all the posts that needed filling by I-Kiribati in early civil service expansion, the priority was for native medical dressers (see McClure, 1923, pp. 3–4). Only after an adequate supply were produced were other positions such as scribes, magistrates, and even law enforcement officers filled. The training of local medical personnel reflected colonial beliefs concerning the abjectivity (McConaghy, 2000) of the colonized, desires to maintain racial purity and health, and fears of contamination and the backward flow of degeneracy to the colonial center (McClintock, 1995). After training, key I-Kiribati were expected to stand in the breach between the abject colonized masses and a small colonial administration that realized its own vulnerability.

In the 1930s and 1940s, as the colony grew, I-Kiribati men were needed for non-medical civil service positions which in turn mounted a further challenge to colonial authority. As a result, a special role for I-Kiribati women began to emerge as protectors of the hearth and conveyors of what Anne McClintock (1995, pp. 34–35) calls the 'cult of domesticity' (see also Davin, 1997). The colonial authorities believed that educating I-Kiribati females in conservative domestic values countered the risks of having a socially mobile male population. To achieve this, European females in the colony, often as spouse and mother, were expected to model European notions of the family and domesticity. John Smith, the Governor of the Colony, told wives of expatriates in 1974 that through "ample opportunities in the home," such as, "running playgroups" and "dress making" they could play a vital role in the advancement of the Colony ('Expats Told to Impart Skills,' Atoll Pioneer, 25th April 1974, p. 2). Formal schooling was also used to achieve I-Kiribati female domesticity. Missionaries openly admitted educating girls to provide "suitable marriage partners" for the male graduates of their schools (Pateman, 1937, Eastman, 1941, p. 29). The government was no less subtle when in 1959 it deliberately built their girls' school next to the already established boys' school. In the words of one administrator this was partly "to provide girls suitable [as] wives for graduates of the boys' school and others who proceed for higher training abroad [and] to ensure principles taught shall be handed down to the next generation" (Maude, 1945, p. 18). To achieve these aims, curricula for girls at both mission and government schools emphasized housekeeping, child rearing and disease management, thus attempting to achieve the same ends as the earlier training of native dressers.

Authentic Identities: Education and Cultural Preservation

Discourses of authenticity and preservation of culture and identity are not easy to identify in educational practices, given the universalization of a particularly European model of schooling. These discourses, however, are locatable in Kiribati social life and around the edges of educational debates. The Kiribati president's valorization of the "village way" at the *2000 Pacific Islands Conference of Leaders* (see Tito, 2000) is one example. His appeal for Pacific people to embrace their villages because of the supposed values of 'community' they embody, to which other Pacific leaders consented, could be read as a prescription of authentic I-Kiribati identity. The unstemmed flow of people from rural outer islands to Tarawa and universalized secondary education suggests, in Kiribati at least, that many people reject this subject position. Appeals to 'traditional' culture and identity such as this can be read as an attempt to place people in the past (Fabian, 1983; McClintock, 1995). Europeans gazing into the Pacific are not the only ones guilty of attempting to museumize its inhabitants in this way. In terms of education, discourses of authenticity are also identifiable in the rhetoric of regional educators (see Nabobo, 1994, 1998; and Thaman, 1991, 1992, 1998) who argue for the reindigenization of school curriculum and the recovery of Pacific languages, values, and cultures. In Kiribati I was the instigator of a local skills program at one secondary school in the mid-1990s. Elderly people from nearby villages were invited to teach weaving, fishing, agriculture and a variety of other 'traditional' skills. Upon reflection, my motivation stemmed from my European positionality and what I perceived as 'relevant' schooling for islander students. When the scheme was working I experienced a level of satisfaction in seeing islanders doing islander 'things.' There is often, however, more at stake than merely satisfying personal yearnings. Discourses of authenticity, when articulated by socially dominant authorities, potentially bring into play a politics whereby some individuals and groups are marginalized by such 'authenticity,' while others maintain status and power.

Significantly, many I-Kiribati reject the 'authentic/traditional' frames that socially dominant groups construct for them, desiring instead more of the same from their children's schooling. Similarly, students in 'my' local skills program showed initial enthusiasm, but over the weeks the interest of many waned to such an extent that the scheme was scrapped. Similarly, many parents consider enough is already being done in secondary schools in terms of cultural education and they become critical of schooling that attempts to transmit cultural knowledge (see also Burnett, 1998).

However, not all people reject the 'cultural' all of the time. Apart from those for whom these practices are an everyday lived reality, others adopt 'authentic' culture or identity positions at one stage or another to achieve some purpose. In Kiribati many people are realizing the value thatch has in small-scale tourist operations. Europeans visiting Kiribati prefer to stay in open *kiakia* rather than concrete block and iron roofed houses desired by many I-Kiribati for their own dwellings. In another example, people may request support from financially buoyant overseas relatives to pay for a child's school fees, a fare to Tarawa, or a new outboard motor. That request, or *bubuti*, often cannot be refused when it is presented in culturalist terms. Then there are those individuals whose mobility takes them into alien surroundings, often because of secondary or tertiary education. Feelings of uncertainty and insecurity felt by those who have ventured away are dealt with by learning a dance, singing a song, buying fish, and getting together with I-Kiribati within a wide radius.

Certainly in some of the examples just cited, 'culturalism' helps bind people together, for example, when confronted with the unfamiliar (see, for example, hooks [1990, p. 28ff], and what McConaghy [2002 pers. comm, Feb. 20th] calls 'anti-anti-essentialism') or for strategic purposes in seeking political advancement or compensation for past wrongs (see, for example, Spivak [1984/85, p. 184ff]). However, there are other uses of 'culturalism' that mask asymmetrical power relations and are used to license injustice. As Patricia Nelson-Limerick (1997, p.1) states, "the assertion that 'my culture made me do it' proves to have remarkable power as a defense strategy and a mechanism for dissolving responsibility." As well as maintaining asymmetrical power relations, discourses of cultural authenticity in education, as with culturalist discourses generally, could also be the product of the 'primitivist' desires of the socially mobile. Torgovnick (1996, p. 5) describes primitivism as "the utopian desire to go back and recover irreducible features of the psyche, body, land, and community — to reinhabit core experiences." These features, she argues, are perceived by many Westerners as existing in non-Western societies largely due to the partial narratives of returned travelers and colonials. Torgovnick (1996, pp. 10–12) further suggests that destabilizing events in the West, such as the World Wars, have assisted the intensification of the West's desire for primitivism. The alienating features of globalization as it impacts many individuals in the West also fuel wistfulness for things 'primitive.'

From the 1920s a dualistic education system was established in Kiribati, in order to produce a small number of local elites to work in the civil service while keeping the majority within their village and atoll environments. Contrary to popular beliefs that colonial schooling helped eliminate indigenous languages and cultural practices (see Mühlhäusler, 1996; Pennycook, 1998), schooling for the majority of I-Kiribati was conducted in the vernacular and consisted of knowledge deemed relevant to atoll life. Many officials believed Kiribati would never, due to its perceived isolation and lack of resources, play anything but a minor role on the world stage. The words of one colony official, who later became Chair of Pacific History at Australia's national university, summed up this attitude:

> Since, then, there is no possibility of a native having to pit his brains in competition with members of a higher culture there is no need to train him to be able to do so (Maude, 1936, p. 8).

These ideas can alternatively be read in terms of colonial governance and as a fear of the 'unruly' I-Kiribati. At more reflective moments colonial administrators admitted to the possibility of political unrest eventuating from an approach to education in which English language and the knowledges of the colonizer were widely transmitted. The following thinly veiled statements from prominent long serving members of the colonial administration attest to this fear:

> But when the pupil leaves school he becomes exposed to influences over which little or no control can be exercised, and it is his reaction to such fortuitous influences that will determine his ultimate value as a citizen. Herein seems to lie the chief danger of bringing the native into intimate contact with a literature which is not his own, and with visitors whose political views can find no healthy application in his islands (Grimble, 1930, p. 2).
>
> My experience is that a native with a knowledge of English seldom develops a taste for reading good literature and those few who do are not assisted to become contented members of the native society to which they belong (Maude, 1936, p. 9).

By the 1970s, with decolonization occurring on an Empire-wide scale, desires for cultural authenticity began to be expressed in terms of 'relevance.' The persuasive discourse of 'relevance' and the desires by the socially dominant groups to see I-Kiribati doing I-Kiribati 'things' can be identified in the Community High School (CHS) scheme. Again a separate stream of schooling was created for students who, it was perceived, would never participate in the higher echelons of Kiribati social and economic life. The CHS attempted to equip students with the 'cultural' and 'vocational' resources required in an atoll environment. Significantly, parents recognized that these schools would never allow their children entry into cash employment and social privilege on South Tarawa and they successfully forced their closure (Tata, 1980;Hindson, 1985).

Human Resources: Education and Development

Kiribati national development plans have often perceived education as a tool in the economic growth of the country (see IMF, 2001). This is a particularly de-humanizing perspective on education that fails to recognize ways of knowing related to an individual's 'otherness of being.' In these plans, schooling and students are invariably constructed as "human resources" (GEIC, 1973b, p. 20), "skilled manpower" (GEIC, 1973b, p. 85), "manpower needs" (GEIC, 1971b, p. 47), "specialized manpower requirements," "output" (GEIC, 1973b, p. 90) or alternatively "waste" (GEIC, 1970c, p. 61, ROK, 1983, p. 17). The plans also demonstrate the unwillingness of successive governments to think beyond participation, albeit small, in global and regional trade markets. It is difficult to think otherwise when so many of those responsible for education policy have successfully negotiated the academic secondary schooling/cash employment pathway themselves. As a result, I-Kiribati students are given little lateral space to create their own life-ways outside those prescribed by national development plans.

It is a logic of human resource development that economic concerns both drive educational practice and result from them. The key issues in present debates about educational reform are funding levels and sources and the material resources, for example, classrooms, textbooks, and teacher training that will produce desired outcomes. In turn, outcomes are often measured in similar material terms, that is, the degree of localization and increased trade figures. Evidence for this can be seen in the recent education action plan produced by the Pacific Islands Forum Secretariat, to which Kiribati was a signatory. While the plan does to a degree attempt to address problems concerning "the most vulnerable and disadvantaged children" (Pacific Islands Forum Secretariat, 2001, p. 2), it nevertheless does so within old frameworks of jobs-driven schooling, "development," "qualifications," "exams," "benchmarks," "social cohesion" and most notably, "human resource development" (Pacific Islands Forum Secretariat, 2001, pp. 1-4).

In this administrative and educational style, a modernizing teleology lingers that appears to meet with little resistance. Internal migration to Tarawa continues unabated to the point where the population density long ago passed that of Hong Kong (Teasdale, 1985). The fragile Tarawa atoll land base cannot support older subsistence lifestyles. Therefore, fuel for cooking, building materials, and basic food items, including fish must be purchased from elsewhere. While this lifestyle is not always called 'progressive' or 'modern,' the alternative outer-island lifestyle is often termed 'backward' by I-Kiribati youth. Apart from the Banabans, included in the Kiribati group in 1916, few people see the flaws in decades of modernization. Although for a time the Banabans experienced relative wealth and prosperity from phosphate royalties, they now experience rusty machinery, crumbling concrete, and displacement (Teaiwa, 1999). Like many mining ventures, development's upward trajectory abruptly stopped when the minerals ran out, the mining company rationalized their operations, and the colonial administration withdrew. Parts of Tarawa, in particular

Betio, are fast catching up in terms of 'modernization.' It, too, has its share of rusty car bodies, broken machinery, overcrowding, dust, and noise. The results of 'development' discourses and practices here are particularly visible and crude whereas other discourses identified in this chapter are veiled and subtle. This high visibility itself could perhaps be the rallying point used by I-Kiribati to critique policies and practices flagged by the word 'development', not merely in education but in wider governance.

Though present to varying degrees since the Second World War, development discourse began to forcefully shape educational practice and sociality in the 1960s. Development discourse, it needs to be stated, was not confined to the administration of Kiribati at this time but part of a global discourse in the post-Second World War period. Its Euro/North American teleological and industrial rationale became the basis for the new post-war world order, driven by European and North American Cold War fears. It is a particularly resilient global discourse that is rarely challenged in both rich and poor parts of the world, despite the glaringly uneven distribution of wealth and resources resulting from so-called development (Escobar, 1995).

In the 1960s there was a common belief in the West generally, adopted by the colonial administration in Kiribati, concerning the strong role education should play in the development process. This link was particularly emphasized in the work of Clarence Beeby, a New Zealand educational administrator, who traveled widely in the Pacific region as an educational consultant. Beeby's seminal 1966 work, *The Quality of Education in Developing Countries* (Beeby, 1966), mapped the stages of growth that systems of schooling passed through in developing countries as their economic circumstances changed. Beeby's stages-of-growth theory was a direct take on Rostow's (1960) key stages of economic growth analysis. Though Kiribati did not receive a visit from Beeby himself during the 1960s and 1970s, his published work influenced educational planning in the colony, including recent work on teacher training in Kiribati (see Taribo, 1998, pp. 10–11). Beeby's staged teleological growth of education systems and the link to economic growth is representative of modernization discourse and the drive to adopt educational practices that 'work' for developed countries in the hope they will also 'work' for everyone. 'Development' here resembles Eurocentric teleologies in earlier times, especially social Darwinism that underwrote much eighteenth-century colonial expansion (McClintock, 1995). Beeby's ideas on schooling in the Pacific were based on prescriptive beliefs that current schooling was at a stage already superceded by school systems in the West. Such beliefs further legitimized Western tinkering in Pacific educational affairs and in many cases continues to do so.

Similar beliefs about education and development were embraced by a number of I-Kiribati whose rise in status confirmed the appropriateness of a similar education for others. However, not all I-Kiribati were as enthusiastic about education's potential for accelerating economic growth. The scarcity of resources, small land mass, isolation, and the limited injection of funds from Britain were sometimes stated as reasons for a more 'relevant' education system. In the 1960s and 1970s secondary education's sole purpose was to produce an elite cadre of I-Kiribati who could eventually replace the Europeans. However, this was only possible if the majority of I-Kiribati remained in a lifestyle appropriate to an atoll environment. Primary schooling therefore focused on socializing people to accept their particular lot in life with separate streams of education culminating later in the period with the establishment of the CHS scheme mentioned earlier. If any benefits were to accrue from development then they would, as a matter of design, be unevenly distributed across the Kiribati community. Initiatives in adult education also began at this time, but behind the facade of greater educational opportunity, these initiatives had the sinister role of 'educating' an older generation into accepting the dualistic education system and the aims of national development. In the words of the 1970 Director of Education:

> The Adult and Social Education Section was a sort of information and propaganda service to the adult community, putting over to them the meaning of the Development Plan, the need to change attitudes in these changing times and to help them understand what is happening round about (GEIC, 1970b, p. 102).

An uncritical belief within the European administration in the link between education and national development meant that expansion of educational services largely took place at the secondary and tertiary levels. This emphasis was justified to I-Kiribati by using the enticement of localization mentioned earlier. If I-Kiribati were to ever replace European officers in the civil service and other senior positions in the Colony, then an education system was needed to produce suitable local replacements. Some I-Kiribati questioned the emphasis on secondary education for the few, and this led to interventions in the primary sector, but only in terms of 'relevance' and socializing students into village roles.

The resilience of such a tenuous link between education and development is on the surface baffling. However, as Douglas Noble (1997) suggests, there are strategic reasons why governments and business believe economic reform and development hinge on education systems and jobs-related training. First, Noble suggests educational reform linked to greater employment provides politicians with a "risk-free agenda" (Noble, 1997, p. 207). Certainly in Kiribati there has been widespread and longstanding community desires for more schooling and cash employment. Second, Noble suggests that in making educational reform the engine that drives the economy, the responsibility for economic progress is put squarely on the workforce and the educational achievements of its workers (Noble, 1997, p. 206). This shifts responsibility away from governments and business management that in many cases might be to blame for a country's slow rate of 'progress.' In the Kiribati past, colonial administrators were extremely reluctant to inject funds and resources into developing a local economy, something that has hindered post-independence 'development' efforts (Tabai, 1987). Third and perhaps more significant here is Noble's suggestion that the focus on human resources is profoundly limited by the type of economic future leaders of government and business envisage (Noble, 1997, p. 207). Debates about economic futures in Kiribati have been and are chiefly concerned with fitting Kiribati into a European dominated capitalist system. Accordingly, students in Kiribati have only been given educational opportunities deemed relevant by colonial administrations and post-independence authorities. There is little scope for students to step out of allotted career paths and make their own futures and in turn collectively shape an altogether different form of development.

A careers booklet distributed to students in secondary school further illustrates the constitutive work of development discourse in relation to education. In 1970 the administration produced a booklet entitled *Careers in the Gilbert and Ellice Islands* (GEIC, 1970a), which illustrates the type of development the colonial administration envisaged for the Colony. Reflecting the functionalist views of the administration the booklet encouraged students to choose from a narrow range of civil service careers rather than in an entrepreneurial way pursue other life-ways. The booklet also demonstrated the earnestness the administration had for persuading I-Kiribati to accept that particular type of development. With its emphasis on white-collar civil service careers the booklet enforced a distinction between what constituted valid work in the Colony. The subsequent down-playing of blue-collar work reflected the class orientation of the European administration in the Colony.

The booklet helped forge a lingering link between a particular form of education and privilege in Kiribati society. In the booklet's words, the type of education the students received had value, whereas most of their peers and many of their elders had received something far less worthwhile in whatever experience of schooling or informal education they may have had:

> Those of you who will read this booklet belong to a privileged minority. You have had the advantage of an education which will equip you to do an interesting and worthwhile job. Most of the people of your age and almost all your elders are less lucky. Most of them have not had the advantage of learning English to the stage where they can enter anything other than laboring employment (GEIC, 1970a, p. 1).

The careers booklet also reflected desires for a growth in nationalism along Eurocentric lines. Young graduates were encouraged to see a link between themselves, their experience of schooling, the career they were to pursue, and the colony's progress. They were obliged to accept the Eurocentric vision of the future because effort and resources had been expended on them:

> Those of you who have been fortunate enough to have secondary education will owe a debt to the community because although you may have paid your school fees, these represent only a small proportion of the total cost of your education. It therefore behooves you to think in terms of how you can contribute to the development of the country and how you can help to ensure that all the people benefit from your education (GEIC, 1970a, p. 1).

Teachers also needed to adopt this vision, since they were best placed for transmitting it to the students in their care and the communities in which they worked. In 1971 a newspaper advertisement encouraged graduates to take up teaching since it afforded them the opportunity to "serve their country and mould its future" ("Applications Wanted," CIN, 26th August 1971, p. 7).

The careers booklet ironically suggested that their privileged position was the result of luck and good fortune and thus it denied the selective characteristics of secondary education. This was also a view held naively by some of the I-Kiribati elites in parliament. Tito Teburoro in a June 1973 meeting of the House of Assembly spoke of the granting of educational opportunity as a "better gift from God" (GEIC, 1973a, p. 204). A few critical observers, however, saw the uneven distribution of educational privilege in more realistic terms of control and gate keeping. Ioane Kaua told the Legislative Council in 1971:

> The best pupils are catered for in Government schools, the second best in missions while the rest continue in primary until they are 16. As far as the pupils are concerned, they have writ their academic epitaph on the dull Doomsday Book. Whatever career they choose is determined by the type of education they have been forced into. We as educators, politicians, teachers and parents are largely responsible for their destiny (GEIC, 1971a, p. 72).

The careers booklet also encouraged students to work hard and to perceive their job as "the main source of satisfaction throughout most [of their] lifetime" (GEIC, 1970a, p. 2). Perhaps with similar reasoning those students who eventually went overseas for training were bonded to serve a specified number of years in the Colony civil service upon their return. Bonds still apply to students who have received training outside of Kiribati, ensuring a degree of loyalty to aims outlined in national development plans.

Critical Futures: Education and Coming to Voice

This chapter has identified and problematized the dominant educational and social discourses pertaining to the embodied I-Kiribati, cultural authenticity, and development. The troubling of these discourses opens up a space whereby other forms of social relations and education that move beyond simplistic provisions of greater access can be imagined. The dominant discourses and associated technologies and logics of colonialism, although I have situated them in a particular time frame, continue to work in contemporary times largely unfettered by the current scheme to universalize secondary schooling. Each discourse has either provided a foundation for a particular set of social relations and educational practices that came later or that remain influential in present social relations and educational practices.

The above process of deconstructing educational discourses in Kiribati does not merely clear a space whereby other ways of talking about and doing education can be imagined. There is potency in the deconstruction process itself that is transformative. Nevertheless there is one substantive implication for educational futures. I draw in part upon recent work by John Willinsky (1998), whose basic premise is not merely historical but one that loosely draws on perspectives of critical pedagogy. Looking forward, according to Willinsky, has as its most vital pre-requisite looking back. Educational futures are infinitely more imaginable when the role education has played in the past becomes clear to those participating in the debates. Here Willinsky does not mean reading the educational and colonial past as "non-fiction" (p. 245), that is, a neat chronologically ordered set of facts. Instead, the past is considered problematically in terms of how educational practice has been complicit in dividing and subjectifying people. The educational past is examined for the processes of bestowing an identity upon people and then hierarchically arranging them into categories that legitimize the colonial presence generally and colonial forms of education in particular. It is a past that has denied many I-Kiribati the right to participate in formulating their own subject positions in relation to that of the various dominant groups. Educational practice as well as various forms of administration governing I-Kiribati lives were put in place based on the "textual inventions" (Nakata 1998:287) of the colonizer in the many differentiated forms that group has taken over time. As Homi Bhabha (1994, p. 63) might suggest, I-Kiribati students need to "re-member" not just the educational past, but the past generally, that is, put it together and see their place in it differently to the version largely authored along Eurocentric patriarchal lines.

A re-membering of the past allows the previously constructed subjects of educational and colonial practice in Kiribati a greater chance to break free from those discourses that have sought to limit and bind. This can occur if those people most closely involved in secondary education in Kiribati develop a critical agency, one defined by McLaren and Giroux (1997, p. 20) as:

> The ability of individuals to analyze subjectivity, reflect upon subject positions they have assumed and choose those which are the least oppressive to themselves, to others and to society as a whole.

The imperative to create a critical facility in students who are canny, alert, and politically conscious is great in these present times where old colonial tropes in Kiribati are still present in subtle ways and where discourses of globalization, in many ways similar to those of colonization (see Firth, 2000), are increasingly having an influence on the young in overt and blatant ways. Whether or not I-Kiribati secondary school students who wear baggy clothes, baseball caps, and dance to techno music at school socials have made a conscious decision to adopt those particular cultural practices or not is perhaps beside the point. The fact that they are visible in Kiribati social life, as examples of wider globalizing influences in the arts, economy, language use, and education, suggest the need by those engaged in the affirmation of such practices to recognize what is being silenced or negated and the ideological positioning behind them.

Certainly much work is needed to translate these ideas into classroom practices. The language choices of much critical pedagogy have been criticized for its disjuncture between theory and practice. As Matthews (1996, p. 44), for example, has argued, its very vocabulary has been "hyper-abstracted" and beyond implementing by educational practitioners on the ground in real teaching/learning contexts. However, in practical terms, John Willinsky (1994) suggests a "postcolonial supplement" to existing curricula that exposes students to a sensitive and critical reading of the colonial and educational past. Willinsky (1998, p. 256ff) has recently suggested a more detailed schema of the postcolonial supplement in terms of "domains of inquiry," "disciplines," "identity concepts," and a "project grid." The idea of a supplement is significant as it means retaining present curriculum practices, an important concession to parental desires for current forms of schooling. In addition, retaining present practices circumvents to some extent the interest and partiality that would otherwise be implicated in the complete replacement of the old with the entirely new.

There is also a danger of creating a role for those who direct the critical gaze "in the rear view mirror" (Willinsky, 1998, p. 251) that has the potential to reproduce colonial oppressions and a hierarchal binary of enlightened/unenlightened self/other. It is a role adopted by "an intellectual class or class of interlocutors who are simultaneously able to speak on behalf of the oppressed and conscientise them" (McConaghy, 2000, pp. 238–239). Associated with this role there can be, as Jennifer Gore (1992, pp. 61–62) argues, a high level of "arrogance" based on a rationale of "what we can do for you!" This role is based on a belief that subalterns cannot speak for themselves or have a true awareness of their subjugated position. These beliefs also come very close to suggesting that the majority of I-Kiribati have been duped by the discursive activity of socially dominant groups over time and need the veil of false consciousness lifted from their eyes, or in the words of emancipatory discourse, must undergo a decolonization of the mind. These criticisms are certainly important and need to be allowed to temper the debates concerning educational futures. However, I argue that educational futures in Kiribati can still be imagined loosely around the notion of critical pedagogy. Educational leaders lead the gaze back only, leaving futures in the hands of individuals and groups historically on the subjugating end of colonial discourse. Educational consultants or elites, familiar with the constitutive work of discourse, acting with the highest levels of reflexivity, merely facilitate debates by directing students' gaze to the past. Actual reforms, changes, or interventions become more the task of the individual subaltern. The nature of debates about futures becomes what Ellsworth (1997, p. 127) calls "response-able." A degree of care needs to be taken for the Other and the talk needs to be far more dialogic, that is, evoking a response.

There have been other criticisms of critical pedagogy in the past decade, particularly from a feminist perspective. These include critical pedagogy's inherent patriarchal nature (Luke, 1992) and its basis in Eurocentric enlightenment rationality (Ellsworth, 1989, 1997) that has the potential to lock critical pedagogy into a binary with an irrational non-European other. However, the 'critical' is not necessarily a Western trait monopolized by the rational European subject. Contemporary I-Kiribati elites, for example, have been described by one recent educational adviser (Luke, A. 2001 pers. comm., 18 Aug), as being very critically astute, particularly in the way these individuals play what he called the "foreign aid game." To claim the critical as solely a European trait and its opposite characteristics, such as passivity, fatalism, or at worst naivety, as traits possessed by non-European others is to fall into the trap of binary thinking identified earlier. To withhold the critical as a possible alternative to education in non-European contexts because of a belief that the critical is an artifact of Western enlightenment and therefore not applicable or relevant to non-European people is to reproduce colonial discourse in education. To do so would be to limit and bind educational and social futures for non-European peoples in much the same way as the discourses of colonialism identified in this chapter. I advocate here a widening of critical discourse among all I-Kiribati. Those individuals most central to Kiribati education are then equipped to participate in debates about educational futures and are granted a greater freedom to construct their own subject positions. As a result those traditionally dominant groups and individuals, such as the administrators, labor market experts, aid donors, and educational consultants, including the European male researcher, in turn become 'bit' players in debates about futures.

There is much validity in terms of transformation, empowerment, and justice by encouraging a critical awareness in I-Kiribati students. It is achievable directly in proportion to the level those involved recognize what Ellsworth describes as not just their own interestedness but also partiality. As Ellsworth (1989) has previously argued, "critical awareness" needs to be something that is constantly strived for despite the difficulties. As she states:

> If you can talk to me in ways that show you understand that your knowledge of me, the world, and 'the right thing to do' will always be partial, interested, and potentially oppressive to others, and if I can do the same, then we can work together on shaping and reshaping alliances for constructing circumstances in which students of difference can thrive (1989, p. 322).

As this chapter demonstrates, the texted educational and colonial past in Kiribati is the result of a chiefly Eurocentric male discursivity and accordingly can only be described at best as 'a' history or perhaps at worst something bordering on the fantastic. Perhaps part of the value in this chapter's identification of discursivity in Kiribati education will be realized if those most closely involved in educational practice in Kiribati echo Martin Nakata's (1993, p. 59) reaction to the ways in which he and members of the Torres Strait Islander community have been represented in various European authored accounts of their educational and colonial past, that is, "a sick feeling inside when you're thinking — 'but this isn't me' — 'this isn't how I perceive my position' — 'this wasn't my predicament.' " The discourses, technologies, and logics of educational discourse in Kiribati identified here have been presented in a way ultimately flawed and partial by the positionality of the author. However, they are nevertheless offered for consideration and for equipping students, parents, and teachers with an astuteness necessary in an ever globalizing world that tends to silence, negate, and flatten knowledges and ways of knowing that are not generated from a Euro/North American center.

References

Appadurai, Arjun. "Putting Hierarchy in Its Place." *Cultural Anthropology* 3, no.1 (1988): 36–49.
Applications Wanted. *Colony Information Notes*, August 26th (1971): 7.
Beeby, Clarence. *The Quality of Education in Developing Countries*. Cambridge: Harvard University Press, 1966.
Bhabha, Homi. *The Location of Culture*. New York: Routledge, 1994.
Blaut, James. *Colonizer's Model of the World: Geographical Diffusionism and Eurocentric History*. New York: Guildford Press, 1993.

Brock-Utne, Birgit. *Whose Education for All? The Recolonization of the African Mind*. New York: Falmer Press, 2000.

Burchert, Lene. "The Concept of Education for All: What Has Happened After Jomtien?" *International Review of Education* 41, no. 6 (1995): 537–49.

Burnett, Greg. "Knowledge, Schooling, and Post-School Opportunities: An Exploration of I-Kiribati Parents' Perceptions of Secondary Education," a thesis submitted in partial fulfilment of the requirements of the degree of Bachelor of Education Honours, of the University of New England, Armidale, 1998.

Davin, Anna. "Imperialism and Motherhood." In *Tensions of Empire: Colonial Cultures in a Bourgeois World*. Edited by F. Cooper and A. L. Stoler. Berkeley: University of California Press, 1997.

Dean, Mitchell. *Critical and Effective Histories: Foucault's Methods and Historical Sociology*. London: Routledge, 1994.

Eastman, George. *In Times of Trial: Being the Decennial Review of the Work of the Gilbert Islands and Nauru Mission*. Rongorongo: LMS Press, 1941.

Ellsworth, Elizabeth. "Why Doesn't This Feel Empowering? Working Through the Repressive Myths of Critical Pedagogy." *Harvard Educational Review* 59, no. 3 (1989): 297–324.

Ellsworth, Elizabeth. *Teaching Positions: Difference, Pedagogy and the Power of Address*. New York: Teachers College Press, 1997.

Escobar, Arturo. *Encountering Development: The Making and Unmaking of the Third World*. Princeton: Princeton University Press, 1995.

"Expats Told to Impart Skills." *Atoll Pioneer*, April 25th (1974): 2.

Fabian, Johannes. *Time and the Other: How Anthropology Makes its Object*. New York: Columbia University Press, 1983.

Fanon, Franz. *Black Skin, White Masks*. New York: Grove Press, 1967.

Firth, Stewart. "The Pacific Islands and the Globalisation Agenda." *The Contemporary Pacific* 12, no.1 (2000): 178–89.

Foucault, Michel. "Afterward: The Subject and Power." In *Michel Foucault: Beyond Structuralism and Hermeneutics 2nd ed.* edited by H. L. Dreyfus and P. Rabinow. Sussex: Harvester Press, 1983.

GEIC. "Careers in the Gilbert and Ellice Islands." 1970a.

GEIC. "Proceedings of the Gilbert and Ellice Islands Colony House of Representatives, First Meeting of the Third Session." February 26th–March 6th. 1970b.

GEIC. "Development Plan 1970–1972." 1970c.

GEIC. "Proceedings of the Gilbert and Ellice Islands Colony Legislative Council, First Meeting of the First Session." 14th–15th April. 1971a.

GEIC. "Proceedings of the Gilbert and Ellice Islands Colony Legislative Council, Second Meeting of the First Session," 22nd-30th July 1971b.

GEIC. "Proceedings of the Gilbert and Ellice Islands Colony Legislative Council, First Meeting of the Third Session," 28th May-7th June. 1973a.

GEIC. "Development Plan 1973–1979." 1973b.

Gore, Jennifer. "What We Can Do For You! What Can We Do For You?: Struggling Over Empowerment in Critical and Feminist Pedagogy." In *Feminisms and Critical Pedagogy*. Edited by C. Luke and J. Gore. New York: Routledge, 1992.

Grimble, Arthur. "Letter to His Excellency the High Commissioner for the Western Pacific, Suva, Fiji." October 15th, 1930.

Hall, Stuart. "The Spectacle of the 'Other.' " In *Representation: Cultural Representations and Signifying Practices*. Edited by S. Hall. London: Sage Publications, 1997.

Hindson, Colin. "Post Primary School Non-academic Alternatives: A South Pacific Study." *Comparative Education* 21, no. 2. (1985): 135–55.

Hoffman, Dianne. "Culture and Comparative Education: Toward Decentering and Recentering the Discourse." *Comparative Education Review* 43, no.4. (1999): 464–88.

hooks, bell. "The Chitlin Circuit: On Black Community." In *Yearning: Race, Gender, and Cultural Politics*, edited by b. hooks. Boston: South End Press, 1990.

International Monetary Fund. "Staff Report for the 2001 Article IV Consultation." Prepared by the Staff Representatives for the 2001 Consultation with Kiribati. June 8th, 2001.

Johannesson, Ingólful. "Genealogy and Progressive Politics: Reflections on the Notion of Useful-ness." In *Foucault's Challenge: Discourse, Knowledge, and Power in Education*, edited by T. S. Popkewitz and M. Brennan. New York: Teachers College Press, 1998.

Luke, Carmen. "Feminist Pedagogy in Radical Pedagogy." In *Feminisms and Critical Pedagogy*. Edited by C. Luke and J. Gore. New York: Routledge, 1992.

Matthews, Julie. "Radical Pedagogy Discourse: A Skeptical Story." *Curriculum Perspectives* 16, no. 1 (1996): 39–45.

Maude, Harry. "Culture Change and Education in the Gilbert and Ellice Islands." *A paper delivered to the Seminar-Conference on Education in Pacific Countries*, Honolulu. 1936.

Maude, Harry. "Memorandum on Post-War Reorganisation and Administrative Policy." 1945.

McClintock, Anne. *Imperial Leather*. New York: Routledge, 1995.

McClure, Henry. "Memorandum: Education in the Gilbert and Ellice Islands Colony." 1923.

McConaghy, Cathryn. *Rethinking Indigenous Education: Culturalism, Colonialism and the Politics of Knowing*. Flaxton: Post Pressed, 2000.

McLaren, Peter, and Henry Giroux. "Writings from the Margins: Geographies of Identity, Peda-gogy, and Power." In *Revolutionary Multiculturalism: Pedagogies of Dissent for the New Mil-lennium*. Edited by P. McLaren and H. Giroux. Boulder: Westview Press, 1997.

Ministry of Education Training and Technology. "Junior Secondary Education: Strategic Plan for 1999, 2000, 2001." 1998.

Mühlhäusler, Peter. "Linguistic Ecology: Language Change and Linguistic Imperialism in the Pacific Region." London: Routledge, 1996.

Nabobo, Unaisi. "Exploring Yalomatua: Fijian Education and the Missing Link." *Directions* 16, no.1 (1994): 41–54.

Nabobo, Unaisi. "Cultural Values and Some Implications for Classroom Learning in the Pacific." *Pacific Curriculum Network* 7, no.1 (1998): 18–22.

Nakata, Martin. "An Islander's Story of a Struggle for 'Better' Education." *Ngoonjook: A Journal of Australian Indigenous Issues* 9 (1993): 52–66.

_____. "The Cultural Interface: An Exploration of the Intersection of Western Knowledge Systems and Torres Strait Islander Positions and Experiences." PhD thesis, James Cook Uni-versity, Townsville 1998.

_____. "Issues of Literacy in Indigenous Communities." Keynote address at Postcolonial Ped-agogies for Community-Based Indigenous Teacher Education Workshop, 12–13 August, University of New England, Armidale, NSW, 1999.

Ndawi, Op. "Education For All by the Year 2000 (EFA 2000) in Some Countries in Africa: Can Teacher Education Ensure the Quantity, Quality, and Relevance of that Education?" *Inter-national Journal of Educational Development* 17, no. 2 (1997): 121–28.

Nelson-Limerick, Patricia. "The Startling Ability of Culture to Bring Critical Inquiry to a Halt." *The Chronicle of Higher Education* 24 (1997): A76.

Noble, Douglas. "Let Them Eat Skills." In *Education and Cultural Studies: Towards a Performative Practice*. Edited by H. Giroux and P. Shannon. New York: Routledge, 1997.

Pacific Islands Forum Secretariat. "Pacific Islands Forum Basic Education Action Plan 2001." 2001.

Pateman, May. "Rongorongo Girls' School." In *In Times of Trial: Being the Decennial Review of the Work of the Gilbert Islands and Nauru Mission*. Edited by G. Eastman. Rongorongo: Beru, 1941.

Patterson, Annette. "Critical Discourse Analysis: A Condition of Doubt." *Discourse: Studies in the Cultural Politics of Education* 18, no. 3 (1997): 425–35.

Pennycook, Alastair. *English and the Discourses of Colonialism*. London: Routledge, 1998.

Pierson, George. "Journal of a Voyage from the Sandwich Islands through the Kingsmill and Mus-grave Islands to Strongs Island in the Caroline Group." 1855a.

Pierson, George. "Personal Correspondence to Faree, Rev. G. M. of the American Board of Com-missioners for Foreign Missions." 1855b.

ROK. "The Constitution of Kiribati." 1979.

ROK. "National Development Plan 1983–1986." 1983.

Rostow, Walt. "*The Process of Economic Growth*." Oxford: Clarendon, 1960.

Said, Edward. "Orientalism: Western Conceptions of the Orient." New York: Pantheon, 1978.

Spivak, Gayatri. "Criticism, Feminism and the Institution: An Interview with Gayatri Chakravorty Spivak." *Thesis Eleven: A Socialist Journal* 10/11 (1984/85): 175–88.

_____. "Can the Subaltern Speak?" In *Marxism and the Interpretation of Culture*, edited by C. Nelson and L. Grossberg. Board of Trustees of the University of Illinois, 1988.

Tabai, Ieremiah. "The Ethics of Development: A Kiribati View." In *The Ethics of Development: The Pacific in the 21st Century Vol. 1*. Edited by S. Stratigos and P. Hughes. Papua New Guinea: University of Papua New Guinea Press, 1987.

Taribo, Abitorama. "Program Evaluation : A Case Study of the Kiribati Teachers' College." A thesis submitted for the degree of Master of Education: Administration at the University of Queensland. 1998.

Tata, Ieremiah. "New Policies For Classes 7, 8 and 9 in Kiribati Primary Schools." *Directions* 5 (1980): 26–35.

Teaiwa, Katarina. "Out of Phosphate: The Diaspora of Ocean Islanders." *Address presented on behalf of the History/Politics Department and the Pacific Concerns Resource Centre*, Suva, 24th Nov. 1999, University of the South Pacific, Suva. 1999.

Team Report. "Kiribati Education Sector Review." Governments of Kiribati, New Zealand, and United Kingdom. 1992.

Teasdale, G. R. "Education For Poverty: The Case of the South Pacific." *A paper presented at the Annual Conference of the Flinders University Centre for Development Studies*, 1985.

Tekawa, Kirata. "Digest of Education Statistics 1999." Tarawa: Ministry of Education, Training and Technology, 1999.

Thaman, Konai. "Towards a Culture Sensitive Model of Curriculum Development for Pacific Island Countries." *Directions* 13, no.1 (1991): 1–12.

_____. "Cultural Learning and Development Through Cultural Literacy." In *Voices In a Seashell: Education, Culture and Identity*, edited by G. Teasdale and J. Teasdale. Suva: Institute of Pacific Studies, 1992.

_____. "Learning to Be: A Perspective from the Pacific Islands." Keynote address at Education for the 21st Century in the Asia-Pacific Region. Melbourne UNESCO Conference. 1998.

Tito, Teburoro. "The Pacific Village Way." Statement by His Excellency the President of Kiribati at Special Meeting of the Standing Committee of the Pacific Islands Conference of Leaders Honolulu, 16-17th March. 2000.

Torgovnick, Marianna. *Primitive Passions: Men, Women, and the Quest for Ecstasy*. New York: Alfred Knopf, 1996.

Tylor, Edward. *Anthropology: An Introduction to the Study of Man and Civilisation*. London: Macmillan, 1881.

Vlaardingerbroek, Barend. "The 'Myth of Greater Access' in Agrarian LDC Education and Science Education: An Alternative Conceptual Framework." *International Journal of Educational Development* 18, no.1. (1998): 63–71.

Wade, Maurice. "From Eighteenth to Nineteenth-Century Racial Science: Continuity and Change." *Race and Racism in Theory and Practice*. Edited by B. Lang. Landham, MD: Rowman and Littlefield Publishers, 2000.

Watkins, Kevin. "Education Now: Break the Cycle of Poverty." Oxfam International, [cited November 1999] Available from World Wide Web: (http://www.caa.org.au/oxfam/advocacy/education/report/execsum.html)

Willinsky, John. "After 1492–1992: A Postcolonial Supplement for the Canadian Curriculum." *Journal of Curriculum Studies* 26, no. 6. (1994): 613–29.

_____. *Learning to Divide the World: Education at Empire's End*. Minneapolis: University of Minneapolis, 1998.

CHAPTER 5

State, Education and Citizenship Discourses, and the Construction of Gendered Identities in Pakistan[1]

MUHAMMAD AYAZ NASEEM

Introduction

A major theme that runs through the Pakistan social studies and history curricula, from grades 1 through 10, relates to the place of women in the social system of the country. Women are portrayed as mothers, sisters, and wives whose primary duties include childbearing, childrearing, and other household responsibilities. Their virtues include sacrifice, devotion, religiosity, and dedication to family. They exist and operate exclusively in the private domain and totally outside the 'practical' domains of politics and economics. Even their roles as educators are confined to the four walls of 'home.' In recent years, emphasis on religion and nationalism has also been added to the school texts.

In this chapter, I examine subject construction and subject constitution in the educational discourse in Pakistan, specifically how these processes are articulated with respect to women. Of particular concern are the processes of governmentality in relation to the educational discourse through which gendered identities are constructed. Finally, I am interested in looking at how these discursive identities in turn reproduce the educational discourse, among other discourses.

In this respect I posit that the educational discourse is neither unitary in terms of its object and structure, nor in terms of its conceptual architecture and fundamental philosophical choices. I also posit that in order to understand the educational discourse and the construction of gendered identities in and through it, we have to understand its formation criteria for multiple objects, operations, concepts, and theoretical and philosophical options and choices. It is also important to place this discourse in its proper history and in relation to the histories of other discourses.

In order to accomplish this I draw conceptual insights from post-structuralist theory, particularly feminist post-structuralist theories of the state. I do so with the contention that these theories provide the best conceptual juncture from which to look at and examine oppression in any society. In taking gender as the central concept, albeit as a mobile, fragmented, non-universal one, they also provide a useful space where different forms of oppression (class, race, gender, and so on) can be seen in their cumulative form.

The chapter is divided into three sections. I begin by laying down the conceptual map of the arguments to follow. In this respect I provide a brief discussion of state and governmentality. Based on Foucauldian conceptualization of governmentality I explore whether this conceptualization can be extended to a post-colonial state. I also briefly examine feminist post-structuralist theories of the state in order to see how the state could be conceptualized both as an actor as well as the arena where identities are and can be negotiated.

In the second section I chart the historical location of the educational discourse among other discourses in Pakistan. In this respect I focus on discourses of citizenship and nationalism. My focus on discourses of citizenship and education does not mean that other discourses, such as those of defense, nationalism, health care, development, and so on are not important, nor that they are less instrumental in the construction of gendered identities and perpetuating unequal gender relations. My contention is that these discourses complement, supplement, and feed into each other. Constraints of space, however, do not permit a fuller treatment of these. I refer to them when and where necessary.

Similarly, although it is imperative to locate the discourses in their proper historical perspective, the constraints mentioned above restrict a detailed analysis in this respect, too. I thus only briefly lay down the historical context. Finally, while one cannot ignore the fact that these discourses not only produce women's identities and that the male identities produced by them interact in meaningful ways with the female identities to produce and reproduce gendered power relations in the society, I concentrate more on the production of women's identities, leaving the other part for a future venture.

In the third section I examine how gendered objects are constituted in and through the educational discourse in Pakistan and how in turn they constitute the educational discourse (among other discourses).

State and Governmentality

For Foucault, power is a relation between and within discourses. The state, to him, can be conceptualized as an "apparatus of social control which achieves its regulatory effects over everyday life through dispersed, multiple and often contradictory and competing discourses."[2] For him discourses form the objects of which they speak. They neither identify objects nor are they about objects. Discourses constitute objects. It is thus through discourses that the social production of meaning takes place, subjectivity is produced and power relations are maintained.[3] For Foucault, the state initially was conceptualized as singular and external to the population. Thus, it was also conceptualized as fragile and perpetually under threat, since the external enemy wants to dismantle it and the internal population has no *a priori* reason to accept its rule. As a corollary, the state remained in a constant effort to exercise power in order to reinforce, strengthen and protect itself.[4] To this was added the emphasis on territory and sovereignty (internal and external) in the seventeenth century. The conception of the state thus came to be dominated by the structures of sovereignty or the 'reason of state.' These structures however were circular in that the end of sovereignty was sovereignty itself. It did not, per se, include the task of government. Following the juridico-legal and rights based conceptualizations in seventeenth and eighteenth centuries a transition in the discourse of the state took place. It replaced a regime dominated by structures of sovereignty by one ruled by techniques of government. In this transition, however, sovereignty did not disappear. It continued to exist along with the exegesis of government. As Foucault puts it:[5]

> ...we need to see things not in terms of the replacement of a society of sovereignty by a disciplinary society and the subsequent replacement of a disciplinary society by a society of government; in reality one has a triangle, sovereignty-discipline-government, which has as its primary target the population and its essential mechanism the apparatuses of security.

Foucault terms this as governmentality, which is both external as well as internal to the state. It refers to the governmentalization of the administrative state of the fifteenth and sixteenth centuries. It is through governmentality that the continual definition and redefinition of what the state can or cannot do is achieved. The state thus can only be understood in its survival and its limits on the basis of the general tactics of governmentality.[6] Government in this sense has to do less with governance of territory and population. It rather becomes a complex amalgam of men (sic) and things. The complexity of this amalgam lies in the way men (sic) are related to things and vice versa. As Foucault explains:[7]

> The things with which in this sense government is to be concerned are in fact men [sic], but men [sic] in their relations, their links, their imbrication with those other things which are wealth, resources, means of subsistence, the territory with its specific qualities, climate irrigation, fertility, etc.; men [sic] in their relations to that other kind of things, customs, habits, ways of acting and thinking etc.; lastly men [sic] in their relations to that other kinds of things, accidents and misfortune such as famines, epidemics, death, etc.

There are however two things that need to be noted in the above conceptualization. First, Foucault does not mention men [sic] in relation with gender, race, and class relations. Governance or governmentality not only regulate these relations in order to manage 'men in relation to things' but in more ways that are conceived of, it is in turn constituted and regulated by these complex relations. This is where the feminists 'discipline' Foucault[8] while appropriating him.

Second, the criteria of formation, transformation, threshold, and correlation of the discourses of the state and governmentality in the Third World are starkly different from that in the West. Whereas it was the Christian pastoral model and the Westphalian military-diplomatic technique that ushered in the state and the discourse of governmentality in the West, in the world of ex-colonies the local discourses of state and government were disrupted by the imperial and colonial discourses of state and the government.

Third, in a Foucauldian conceptualization of the state and governmentality, men and things in relation to each other matter only in the internal context of the state. In the case of the Third World states, the criteria of formation were also influenced by how its men and things related to men and things outside the state. Thus one has to see the criteria of formation of the Third World States' discourse in relation to the meta discourses of the Cold War, Containment, the UN, international finance, international development, and so on.

Thus, even if we do subscribe to Foucault's notion of governmentalization of the state, we might have to re-investigate and redefine the notion in accordance with the criteria of formation, transformation, and correlation. Furthermore, this investigation also must be located in relation to the larger discourses with which the discourse of the state came in contact, once the process of decolonization started. This is important because more often than not the investigation regarding the state and other discourses in the Third World have been affected by the super-imposition of the larger discourses on the local ones.

State and the Liberal Feminist Theory

Liberal feminists view[9] the state as a natural and unproblematic entity. For them the state is a natural actor and an arbiter between different individuals and groups who are in a state of contestation over reallocation of resources and allocation of values. It is thus natural for them that women should use the state in order to claim and gain rights that are due to them as equal citizens. They basically seek initiatives (by the state itself), legislation, and policies that have the potential for addressing gender inequalities. It is thus essentially a reformist view of the state.

Radical Feminism and the State

Radical feminists have disputed the liberal feminist assumptions about the state and its role as a neutral arbiter. They do so on the grounds that not only is the state a male construct, but that oppression and patriarchy are both reflected in and maintained by the state. For radical feminists, the state especially in its liberal persona is essentially hostile to the articulation as well as the realization of women's goals.[10]

Marxist/Socialist Feminism and the State

Marxist/socialist feminist views of the state and that of the relationship between women and the state is interesting as well as paradoxical. In as much as it is the liberal state, it is indeed an agent of exploitation and that of oppression. It exploits through capitalism and oppresses through patriarchy. Notwithstanding the above mentioned debate within feminism in general and Marxist/socialist feminism in particular regarding the nature of the relationship between capitalism and patriarchy, Marxist feminists believe that the provision of welfare is the cheapest possible means to reproduce labor. The capitalist/patriarchal state not only appropriates female labor at the work place it also perpetuates their economic dependence on males by reinforcing their domestic responsibilities.[11]

Postmodern Feminism and the State

Postmodern feminists are divided about the potential role that the state can play to help women ward off oppression. Those who work within a Foucaldian framework argue that power rests in and is exercised at various points in society. It is thus natural that resistance to power (though in a strict Foucauldian sense the relation between the two is neither natural nor automatic) shall also be located all across society and not at any one given point.[12] For them, and following Foucault, placing the state either above or outside the society is not only to gloss over its significance, but also to assume that there is homogeneity in the operation of power.

Foucault "warns that we should not assume that 'the sovereignty of state, the forms of the law or the overall unity of domination are given at the outset; rather these are only the terminal forms power takes. Power does not reside in institutions or structures and rather than there being a 'unity of state power,' there is a complex strategical situation in a particular society."[13] Watson and Pringle also note that unlike many of the poststructuralists who concentrate exclusively on language, Foucault, as a historian of power, was much more interested in discourses and practices concerning the state.[14]

One reading of Foucault suggests that since there is no centralized authority, the notion of using (liberal feminist) or rejecting (radical feminist) the state does not make sense. As Allen argues,[15]

> the state is a category of abstraction that is too aggregative, too unitary and too unspecific to be of much use in addressing the disaggregated, diverse and specific (or local) sites that must be of more passing concern to feminists... the state has not been an indigenous category of feminist theory. Rather, it is an import, and for some commentators and in some instances, an uneasy amalgam: partly the liberal state, partly 'the state' as formulated by contemporary Marxism; but either way a theory of the state with definitions, parameters and analytic tasks forged for political positions other than feminism.

An advantage of looking at the state in this manner is that it facilitates a search for particular levels or institutions of the state that are oppressive or those that can be beneficial for women. As Sonia Alvarez has argued in the case of Brazil, often enough the local state is more beneficial for women than the national state.[16]

An alternative reading of Foucault suggests that instead of looking at the state as a monolith that wields power and oppresses, it can and should be understood at various levels that are local.[17] It is at these levels that subversive activity can be directed.[18] In this sense the state does not merely reflect and bolster gender inequalities, it constitutes them through its practices at the same time. As Pringle and Watson put it, "gender practices become institutionalized in historically specific state forms."[19]

In my opinion, it is more beneficial to look at the state in terms of an arena for engagement. There are then further sub-arenas where the state can be engaged—for instance local government, state education, broadcasting, and so on. The state in this sense becomes a site where meanings and identities are or can be contested, and where engagement with institutions could take place. Thus, the state is important, albeit in a redefined manner, and it is more useful to engage it rather than doing away with it. As Bryson argues, "From a post-modern perspective state agencies and institutions are also particularly important because of the ways in which they help construct and enforce the meaning of what it is to be a man or a woman in …society."[20] Watson argues that the state, by responding to some demands and not to others actually constructs these demands.[21]

Recognition of the state in this sense is also important because only then can women hope and aim to 'get in' and work from within the state, at whatever level, to make a difference. As the experiences of femocrats in Australia show, this can mean success for the feminist cause, no matter how restricted or limited.[22] It should, however, be noted that for femocrats or those working with the state, the basic objection was on the adjective male and not on the noun state.[23] Consider for instance Hester Eisenstein's position, according to which "it is inaccurate to say that the state is male but it is accurate to say that up to now the state has been male if by that we mean that until recently public power has been wielded largely by men and in the interest of men…."[24]

The postmodern feminists also argue that instead of looking at the state as a coherent entity that either influences a coherent set of interests that are formed outside it or represents or embodies them, it is more useful to view it as a domain where such interests are articulated and defined.[25] These interests are evoked and constructed through discourses. Furthermore, these interests are not unitary and do not represent unitary entities, e.g., men, women etc. "Interests are not merely reflected in political sphere, they have to be continuously constructed and reproduced. It is through discursive srategies, that is, through creating a framework of meaning, that interests come to be constructed and represented in certain ways."[26]

Discourses in turn are themselves constructed in this discursive space and construct the state at the same time. The discourses that construct the state assume a masculine subject rather than self-consciously defending or creating men's interests. A lengthy quote from Pringle and Watson clarifies this point[27]:

> If the state is to be perceived as an object of feminist strategy, it requires an analysis which breaks with the various kinds of functionalism of the past. This will be one which examines the ebb and flow of power, its twists and turns, nodes, and concentrations. It will not foreground the state but will instead situate it amongst the variety of strategies employed by men in constructing their interests. The state apparatuses here intersect with other levels and practices which have to be treated in their specificity rather than a reproduction of given structures.

Third World Feminists and the State

One group of feminists that has predominantly, but not exclusively, worked with the poststructuralist feminist paradigm is that of third world feminists. These can broadly be divided into those who are located in various diaspora and work mainly on issues related to women in diaspora and multiculturalism, and those who are located in the developing societies and work primarily on issues related to women within developing countries. I will concentrate on the latter group as it is their context that is closer to my area of study.

Some Third World feminists have argued that Western feminist theory by and large ignores the experience of Third World women, especially those under the postcolonial state.[28] Following postmodernist feminists, the Third World feminists view the state not as a unitary monolith, but as a loose network of power relations that are both in cooperation and contestation with each other. These relations are situated in a grid of economic, political, legal and cultural forms.[29] The state thus can be seen and understood in the context of social relations which are affected by systems of power and that affect the system of power through their agency. This conceptualization of the state has an added advantage for the Third World feminists because it allows "a space within which to give importance to the 'form' that states take in different historical contexts."[30] However, as Third World feminists note, the feminist debate regarding the relationship between women and the state has largely ignored conceptualizing the relationship between Third World women and the postcolonial state.

Third World feminists argue that the relationship between women and the state is defined by the history of the relationship between women (as colonial subjects) and the colonial state and by the history of relationship between women and the postcolonial nationalist state. In the relationship between women and the nationalist state, the latter took over the modernizing framework of the colonial state and thus normalized "the colonial modernist and Orientalist discourse."[31] The postcolonial/nationalist state took over women's bodies as reference points to legitimize and validate the 'nationalist' movement and then the postcolonial state after decolonization. For most postcolonial women, the state figures marginally in their lives.[32] "It looms large only when women transgress the boundaries set by the state in various areas of public and private life that it has jurisprudence over. Therefore, for the majority of women the question is not whether or not to approach the state. *It is they who are approached by the state in many instances in a brutal way and violent way.*"[33]

While there is a lot of merit in Rai's argument,[34] the point remains that to conceive of the relationship between women and the postcolonial state in this framework amounts to robbing women of their agency and falling once again into the structural functionalist trap. Second, to assume unintentionality on the part of the state is not correct either. The intentionality is there and it comes from the "success with which various groupings are able to impose them and is always partial and temporal."[35] As Waylen explains[36]:

If the state is not a homogeneous entity but a collection of institutions and contested power relations, it is far better to see it as a site of struggle, not lying outside of society and social processes, but having, on the one hand, a degree of autonomy from these which vary under particular circumstances, and on the other becoming permeated by them. Gender (and racial and class) inequalities are therefore buried within the state, but through part of the same dynamic process, gender relations are partly constituted through the state. The state therefore partly reflects and partly helps to create particular forms of gender relations and gender inequality. State practices construct and legitimize gender divisions and gendered identities are in part constructed by the law and the private discourses which emanate from the state.

Once it is recognized that states and the relationship between state and gender relations is not fixed and immutable, battles can be fought in the arena of the state. As Alvarez has shown, one can still look for and find space within which the state can act (or be made to act) for a positive change in gender relations.[37]

Setting the Context: State, Citizenship, and Identity

In Pakistan it is the state that constructs or determines the 'reality' and the official truth. It monopolizes the production of truth and rationality by defining what is rational, reasonable, and credible. This is accomplished mainly by discourses that arrange the society into various levels and forms of inequalities and differences. These differences are then compartmentalized into mutually exclusive areas. Religious and educational discourses hierarchize the society in terms of class, gender, and other inequalities. While initially these discourses were largely exclusive of each other, from the mid-1970s onward they started to amalgamate under the state sponsorship in such a way that the influence of the religious discourse on the education has become predominant. This development started with the advent of General Zia-ul-Haq's martial law in 1977 and has continued until the present. These identities reproduce the masculine state, the tribute-gathering economic structure and the patriarchal value system and are reproduced by them. It is thus important to have a brief look at the evolution, the nature and the character of the post-colonial state in Pakistan in order to understand how and why gendered identities are constructed by it.

The state of Pakistan emerged onto the world scene with what Noman calls a schizophrenic personality.[38] On the one hand it was a theological demand that served so well as the basis for the new state and on the other hand was the league leadership, especially Jinnah, who was categorically opposed to the idea of a theocratic state.

The new state had a highly centralized political structure, with Jinnah[39] retaining for himself the position of the Governor General. It went about consolidating its power in consonance with a predominantly colonial liberal-secular ideology totally at odds with the religious symbolism it had adopted during the independence movement. Jinnah time and again reiterated in categorical terms that his vision of the political system of the new state had little to do with Islam as a political system. The religious leaders who had initially opposed the idea of a separate state for the Muslims of India now lobbied for a theocratic state.[42] While the nationalist leadership was not willing to concede its newly won political power to the religious lobby, the latter fought hard to regain its position as the interpreter of Islam for the society. It was essentially a contest over setting the rules and limits of the relationship between the religious discourse and that of the state. The contestation between the nationalist and the religious discourses over construction of meaning laid down the formative criteria for citizenship and other discourses in Pakistan. During the phase of state consolidation in Pakistan (1947–1958), successive governments redefined Islam as a state ideology in inclusionary terms. This was in direct contrast to the exclusionary concept of religion (Muslims versus Hindus) that was used by the Muslim League leadership during the independence movement. This shift signifies the desire of the state to assert its role as the arbiter of values and the interpreter of religion. While the 'Hindu' other was maintained, its nature shifted from the communal other to the 'state' or the national 'other.' This is not to argue that the inclusionary criteria were gender, class, or minority sensitive. The religious lobby on the other hand had to create an 'other' in order to regain the status they enjoyed in the undivided India (where they were accepted by the colonial state as the sole arbiters of religious values). Women and minorities (especially the upwardly mobile dissident sect of *Ahmadis)* were constructed as the other.

In the post-Bangladesh period (post–1971), Bhutto's nationalist and internationalist aspirations led him to construct an identity that was exclusionary both internally and externally. Internally, this was achieved by the declaration of the Ahmadiya community as non-Muslims, and externally it was through an ideological identification with the Muslim world and thus the creation of an 'other' that now included the west along with India. This identification with the Muslim world implicitly strengthened the exclusion of women from the norm of citizenship. An interesting facet of Bhutto's identity construction that has often either escaped attention of researchers or has been ignored is that it was he who overtly masculinized political discourse in Pakistan.

The military government of General Zia-ul-Haq, which assumed power on the pretext of averting a civil war, expanded the exclusionary construction of identities. Zia's construction of a national identity is significant at three levels. One, by co-option of Jamaat-e-Islami (the leading religio-political party) and the *de facto* labeling of the secular as anti-nation, anti-state, and anti-Islam, the secular elements, along with those who did not agree with the regime, were excluded. The second exclusion was much more subtle and implicit. By repeatedly berating political activity as vanity and thus against Islam, by berating the politicians and the political parties as anti-state and un-Islamic, the regime excluded the political self of the Pakistani people from the national identity. On a third level, the regime excluded women from citizenship by confining them to the private world of *Chador* and *Chardewari* (the veil and the four walls of home). Citizenship and 'national' identity was now defined essentially in religious, masculine, militaristic, and apolitical terms.

It is interesting to note the internalization of this discourse by different strata of society. On the one hand the religious overtones further deepened the dichotomous cleavage between the secular and the religious and on the other aggravated the already unequal gender relations. A manifestation of the former was the overshadowing of the class conflict by the religious/communal conflict. This brought into the political arena new religio-political parties that were willing to tow the regime's line against the mainstream political forces and in return get a piece of political power and patronage. The confinement of women to *Chador* and *Chardewari* gave the disenfranchised male (mainly belonging to the middle and the lower middle classes) a farcical sense of power and a target for the exercise of this power. It kept the attention of the masses diverted from issues of political disenfranchisement and economic hardship. This is not to imply that all Pakistani males were disenfranchised. The military regime, soon after taking the helm, co-opted the feudal, religious, and industrial elite. The middle class that was at the forefront of the movement against the Bhutto regime soon found itself ignored and disenfranchised by the military junta. Cognizant of the fact that this was the segment of the society that could once again rise up in protest, the military government delegated authority to the males of these classes over women and thus mitigated the feeling of disenfranchisement by giving them a sense of empowerment. This was done quite methodically. Under the banner of Islamization of the society new legislation was enacted. This legislation was based on a strict interpretation of religious edicts on personal behavior. The centerpiece of this legislation was the subjugation and subjectivity of women. These laws not only restricted the agency, mobility, and behavior of women under the farce of *Chador* and *Chardewari*, whereby the conduct of women outside these confines was to be under public (that is, male) scrutiny, but they also placed the onus of proof of innocence on women.

With respect to the last point, in a number of cases where women reported rape cases, not only the onus to prove rape was put on them but it was also they who were punished with public lashings and imprisonment when they could not prove the rape.[43] A common assumption in the media and the society was that such cases would not take place if women were to remain within the confines of *Chador* and *Chardewari*. The moral and social duty of keeping women within these confines was passed on by the state to the men in general. Once men could not perform this duty, the state came in with legal weapons such as the infamous 'Hudood' Ordinance.[44] The regime, furthermore, laid the basis for the militarization of the society by its portrayal of the Afghan civil war as a *Jihad* (holy war) and by its meddling in that war on the pretext of religious obligation in return for US aid.

Zia's strategy to gain legitimacy through the so-called Islamization was targeted primarily at middle- and lower-middle-class males. It was designed to generate a symbolic hope as well as a symbolic/psychological sense of power for this disenfranchised class. By giving the members of this class power over women (through construction of an identity for women that was subservient to the male identity), the state warded off pressure from and reaction by a disenfranchised class.[45] The 'Islamization' of the legal system, with its essential and anti-women bias, was designed to generate a false sense of power in the Pakistani male. Though it is argued by a number of scholars[46] that the 'Islamization' process failed to generate the desired legitimacy and/or popular support for the Zia regime, I contend that this is at best only partly true. While it can be said with confidence that his politics of Islam did not win him a mass base that could make him feel confident to let the political process go on,[47] his Islamic rhetoric, its impact on gender relations, and the consequent strengthening of the patriarchy did win him a large following.[48] Zia's patriarchal legacy lives on. This has been proven by the fact that four elected governments could do little or nothing to repudiate this legacy.

This legacy has had far reaching effects on the state-society relations in Pakistan.[49] First, it eroded the conception that the state did not enforce conformity with religion and with it Jinnah's secular ideal for Pakistan. Second, fusion of religious and political authority created the basis of the state's encroachment on and redefinition of the public/private sphere. Third, the state has become the dominant ideological force in the society.[50]

Thus the state wrested the mantle of the arbiter of religious values from the *Ulema* and became the sole interpreter of religion. It also assumed the role of the patriarch. As Khattak puts it, to govern effectively, it generated discourses such as those of defense, health, development, religion, and education, the cumulative effect of which was marginalizing of women through physical and psychological seclusion and legislative discrimination.[51] These discourses, according to Khattak, discriminated against the women on two levels: "the symbolic and the physical. The former ha(s) to do with the concept of women as a collective social being and the concept of femininity, the latter with the concrete being of women." [52] In the following section I discuss how through one of these discourses, namely education, the state constructed gendered identities that marginalize women and strengthen patriarchy in Pakistan.

Educational Discourse and the Construction Of Gender Identities

A common assumption in development circles and the development literature in Pakistan (as elsewhere) is that education empowers women.[53] I argue that in Pakistan this is more of a myth than reality. While I do not argue that it actually disempowers them, for that requires an assumption that they did have power at some point, I argue that the educational discourse in Pakistan negatively affects the position of women in terms of power relations. While the sexist hindrances with respect to access to education have eased a little, the sexual discrimination in the school, the curricula, and the textbooks continue. The quantitative façade is used to mask the qualitative discrimination.[54] It is thus imperative that the research focus should also shift from 'how much education women get' to 'what, how and for what purposes women are taught'.[55] According to Luykx[56]:

> Academic sexism's greatest significance may no longer be in the effects that can be measured numerically, but rather in the construction of gender identities and hierarchies, the internalization of social norms, and the expectations placed upon male and female students. Such effects are subtle but powerful, and may be all the more insidious when they occur under the cloak of superficial equality.

Thus, while female 'literacy' rates almost doubled in twenty years, from 1972 to 1992, and increased another 50% in the decade since then,[57] females' quality of life does not reflect any considerable change. If any, the change has been for the worse. Physically and psychologically, they have been, by and large, excluded from the national citizenship. Under the *Hudood* Ordinance, even their physical security is at the discretion of the male members of the society. In any case the rise in the female literacy is relative.

Sexual discrimination is inherent in the educational discourse in Pakistan. Curricula are designed to reproduce the dynamics, institutions, and structures of power and inequality. They represent the ideology and interests of specific cultural, social, and class interests. The knowledge these produce is neither neutral nor objective as is argued to be the aim. Through this knowledge, the state intervenes in the consciousness of citizens and creates identities that serve to enforce and reinforce internal control. In the following space, I briefly discuss the construction of gendered identities by the educational discourse[58].

While the pre-Zia era policies looked at women as fixed categories both in terms of personhood and obligations, and justified motherhood as a national duty, the post-'Islamization' policies started to justify the fixed category of motherhood in religious terms as well. While the patriarchal value system and division of labor is a constant theme in Pakistan's education policy and discourse throughout its existence, the Zia and post-Zia

period saw the intensification of gender inequality and the marginalization of women in and through the educational discourse.[59] An analysis of
the Urdu curriculum of the Punjab Textbook Board, for instance, shows
that 23% of all topics from class I to VIII deal directly with religion, and
another 18% with national, patriotic, and militaristic ideas.[60] This has a
special significance for the construction of gender identities as I show later.

The religious content increases by one third and the militaristic-nation-
alist content doubles as the child progresses from sixth to eighth grades.
Up to this stage the total percentage of topics that deal with science is a
mere 3.3%, compared to the religious, moral, and nationalist content of
75%. The reality constructed by text in the curricula is very much in line
with the citizenship discourse of the state. The citizenship discourse inter-
acts with the educational discourse on the site of textbooks to produce
mechanisms of internal control for the authoritarian state. These textbooks signify, through content and form, particular constructions of reality, and particular ways of selecting and organizing that vast universe of
possible knowledge. They embody someone's selection, someone's vision
of legitimate knowledge and culture that in the process of enfranchising
one group's cultural and political capital disenfranchises another's.[61]

The social studies curriculum in Pakistan primarily constructs gendered identities through a gendered construction of time and space.
Binary categories of before/after, pre/post construct the time dimension of
the nationalist identity. It is then linked to the religion in that the before is
always before the 'advent' of Islam, either in Arabia or in India. The before
is also symbolized by darkness, while the after/post are always characterized by light. Since it is a gendered construction, the dark before is sinful
and polluted and thus feminine, while the after represents the light of virtue and cleanliness and thus represents masculine qualities. The social
studies textbook of the Punjab Textbook Board for class VII, for instance
states that[62]:

> Prior to the advent of Islam, peoples of the world were in a bad
> state. The rulers were permanently engaged in pleasurable pursuits.
> Superstition and ignorance were everywhere. Goddesses and gods
> were worshipped. The *Barahmins* dominated the subcontinent.
> The caste system was prevalent and the *Shudras* were in a bad state.
> Humans were sacrificed for goddesses and gods. People engaged in
> bad customs. The Kaa'ba was full of clay idols. The Arabs had no
> ideals and constantly indulged in bad social customs. They fought
> over small things; they were racist. Slavery was common and slaves
> were treated badly. Women were not respected and female infanti-
> cide was common.

This is depicted as the life before the dawn of Islam. Once Islam spread
things changed for the better. In this discourse pleasure (feminism) was

defeated by virtue (masculine). The dominant Muslim male changed the condition of both the Indian *Shudras* as well as the Arabian slaves. Gallantry thus is a male virtue that can destroy the vices (through his masculinity) and that can also help free the weak (feminist) from tyranny. The condition is just one: submission to the masculine. The Muslim and by default Pakistani male appears in the role of conqueror, the liberator and eventually the benevolent subjugator.[63] The Pakistani male is thus like the historical Muslim hero Muhammad Bin Qasim who came to India in the eighteenth century to save the honor of Muslim women from the Hindu Rajas, or like Zia-ul-Haq (the military dictator) who saved the honor of the Pakistani nation from the debauch political leaders. And this is the message and the aim of the educational discourse in Pakistan.

This submission serves to reproduce patriarchy and also produce internal control for the authoritarian state. It also creates specific identities and their position in the power equation between the genders. Submission is to be accorded. This works well on two levels. On the level of the state versus the society it means submission to the state and on the level of the patriarchal society it means submission to men by women. This process starts right at the beginning of the educational process and continues throughout the educational career of the students. The illustrations in the kindergarten primer for instance show men in all the professions (shopkeeper, barber, doctor, postman, and dry cleaner) that are included in the primer. Though the professions are included to teach the children the basic alphabet, the hidden text has other motivations. The only female illustration in the primer is totally out of place.

Another theme that runs through the texts books, especially the ones taught at the primary level, is the hierarchical nature of the family. The family is, in most if not all cases, a joint patri-local family. It is always the paternal grandparents that live with the family and never the maternal ones, something typical of a patriarchal social structure in Pakistan. The emphasis is on the maintenance of this hierarchy. The term 'good' children, for instance places a premium on discipline. Once again 'good' children are the ones who are extremely disciplined to the point of being regimentized.[61] Boys are shown playing outdoor games, going out with their fathers, and even being naughty. The girls on the other hand are shown to be domesticated. Their usual activities are either playing second fiddle to their brothers or remaining indoors and helping out their mothers.

A very subtle way of reinforcing stereotypes and producing identities is through the imagery in the textbooks, especially at the primary level. A class three textbook of 138 pages has an illustration on almost all pages, but has only six illustrations of women. All six are shown with their heads covered. Only one picture shows a woman in a professional role as a nurse. Here, too, she is shown standing meekly behind a male doctor. One woman is shown working in the fields with a heavy load on the head (a sight that is not uncommon in rural areas). And one illustration shows a girl putting henna on her hand. The Punjab Textbook Board's textbook for class two is similar. The hidden message in these textbooks is more than evident. A good family is hierarchical and patri-local. Good children live with their paternal grandparents. They are disciplined and regementized. Boys play outdoor sports, are adventurous, and naughty. Girls are supposed to be, by contrast, 'good' and meek. All professionals are men and the place of women is in the home or in professions that are 'suitable' for them (such as a nurse).

In other words these texts are designed to construct a discourse that reproduces the patriarchal culture of the Pakistani society. Extensive depictions in the textbooks of a particular version of religious and nationalist content, right from the very beginning, serve to reproduce citizens in accordance with the criteria laid down by the discourse of the state. This assumes added importance if we keep in mind the target population of these texts, namely, the children of the working and lower middle classes. They constitute the future working and subordinate classes. As discussed earlier, their reproduction as passive citizens is imperative for the interests of the dominant classes and the state. It is also necessary to pacify them because they are also the potential protesters of the future. The men are given a false sense of power by giving them a sense of superiority over women. The dominant ideology and culture is thus continuously reproduced and perpetuated.

Concluding Thoughts

At the time of Pakistan's independence from the British rule the dominant discourse at the global level was that of the Cold War between the USA and the Soviet Union. This discourse was partially imposed on India and Pakistan, and partially it was adopted by the intelligentsia and academia in the two countries. At the same time, the nation-state discourse, along with the structures of the colonial state in India were carried over as colonial legacies. The governmentalization of the state in Pakistan was different from that in the West in that the government was characterized by extra political and extra constitutional forces, mainly the military bureaucracy oligarchy. These forces understood and managed 'men' in relations with things differently from the socio-political forces that achieved independence from colonial rule.

The criteria for the formation of the educational discourse were also significantly influenced by the legacy of colonial education. The discourses of the colonial state and government thus reflect heavily in the archaeology of educational discourse in Pakistan. The early contestation over the definition and shaping of the discourse of the state brought out gender and gender relations as the main symbol and arena of this contestation. Both the nationalist and religious forces in Pakistan strived to define gender in and through nationalist and religious discourses respectively. This has permeated into and is reflected in the educational discourse. The identities thus created in and by the educational discourse are gendered with negative connotations for women. The educational discourse in Pakistan as it exists today actually disempowers women. Despite an increase in the female literacy rates, women are still on the lighter side of the power balance.

The arguments and analysis I have presented here show that analyzing educational discourse from a post-structuralist standpoint has important implications for educational research, especially in the developing world. Such analyses have the potential to shift the focus of educational research from ahistoric quantitative analysis to an understanding that is grounded in the history, culture, and socio-politics of particular societies. It also has the potential to avoid construction and/or employment of meta-narratives of why a particular educational system has remained underdeveloped. Furthermore, post-colonial/post-structuralist discourse analysis brings out the dynamics of relationships between different discourses and how they individually and collectively constitute subjects that are central to educational research.

Endnotes

1. Parts of this paper were presented at a panel on: Re-imagining Discourse: Post-foundational Ideas for Comparative Education (II) at the 46th Annual Meeting of the Comparative and International Education Society, Orlando, Florida, USA. March 6–9, 2002. Travel to Orlando was made possible by the Alma Mater Travel Grant from the McGill University, Montreal.
2. Kenway, J. Feminist theories of the state: to be or not to be? In M. Blair and J. Holland with Sue Sheldon (Eds.). *Identity and diversity: gender and the experience of education.*
3. Ibid.
4. Foucault, M. 'On Governmentality.' in G. Burchell, et al. The Foucault Effect: studies in governmentality: with two lectures and an interview with Michel Foucault.
5. Ibid.
6. Ibid.
7. Ibid.
8. Bartky, S. L. 'Foucault, femininity and the postmodernization of patriarchal power.' In I. Diamond and L. Quinby (Eds.) *feminism and Foucault: reflections on resistance.*
9. Main proponents of liberal feminism include but are not restricted to: Friedan (1986), Eisenstein (1981), Okin (1990), Wolf (1993). Early feminists that can be broadly classified in this category are Mary Astall (1666–1731), Mary Wollstonecraft (1759–97), Elizabeth Cady Stanton (1815–1902), Susan Anthony (1820–1906) and Harriet Taylor (1807–58). Note that Eisenstein is also considered by some as a radical feminist. Her framework however is more close to liberal feminist tradition.
10. Chalton, et al (1989) have categorized state policies vis-à-vis gender relations in three broad categories. One, policies that are aimed particularly at women, subordination for instance; laws regarding childbirth, maternity, etc. In other words construction and regulation of bodies by the state — or in a Foucauldian way bodies are defined and controlled through discourses such as educational discourse, media, law, etc. Two, policies that deal with the relationship between men and women, particularly property rights, sexuality, family relations. In this sense gender relations are often institutionalized. Three, policies that are supposedly gender-neutral, such as diplomacy, foreign and defense policies, trade,

communication, etc. Women are excluded from all of them. They are excluded from some on the premise of high politics and from others because of lack of masculine traits.

11. Eisenstein, Z. *The radical future of liberal feminism*.
12. See Foucault, M. *Power/Knowledge: selected interviews and other writings 1972–1977*; edited and translated by Colin Gordon.
13. Foucault in Burchell, et al. Op. cit.
14. Pringle, R. and S. Watson. 'Women's interests and the poststructuralist state.' In M. Barrett and A. Phillips (Eds.) *Destabilizing theory: contemporary feminist debates*.
15. Allen, J. 'Does feminism need a theory of the state?' In S. Watson (Ed.) S. Watson (Ed.) (1990). *Playing the state: Australian feminist intervention*.
16. Alvarez, S. Endangering democracy in Brazil: women's movements in transition politics.
17. Bryson, V. *Feminist debates: issues of theory and political practice*. Also see Watson, S. 'The State of Play: An Introduction' in S. Watson (Ed.) (1990). *Playing the state: Australian feminist intervention*.
18. Bryson Op cit.
19. Pringle & Watson Op cit.
20. Bryson (1999) Op cit.
21. Watson 1990 Op cit.
22. Not all femocrats can be termed liberal. See for instance Franzway, S. 'With problems of their own: femocrats and the welfare state' In *Australian Feminist Studies*. 3, Summer, 1986, Connell, R. W. *Gender and power*. Watson, S. (Ed.) *Playing the state: Australian feminist intervention*.
23. Allen, J. 'Does feminism need a theory of the state?' In S. Watson (Ed.) S. Watson (Ed.) (1990). *playing the state: Australian feminist intervention*.
24. P. 115 cited by Allen Ibid
25. Pringle & Watson Op. Cit.
26. See Watson and Pringle Op cit., Also see Fraser, N. Nicholson, L., Social criticism without philosophy: an encounter between feminism and postmodernism.' In L. Nicholson (Ed.) *Feminism/Postmodernism*. New York, London: Routledge, 1990, Nicholson, L. (Ed.). *Feminism/Postmodernism*; Kenway, J. 'Feminist theories of the state: to be or not to be?' In M. Blair and J. Holland with Sue Sheldon (Eds.). *Identity and diversity: gender and the experience of education*.
27. Watson and Pringle Op cit. p. 230.
28. Rai, S. 'Women and the state in the third world: some issues for debate.' In S. Rai and G. Lievesley (Eds.) *Women and the state: international perspectives*.
29. Ibid.
30. Ibid.
31. Ibid, p. 10.
32. Ibid.
33. Ibid, p. 32.
34. Ibid.
35. Pringle and Watson Op cit., p. 229.
36. Waylen, G. 'Democratization, Feminism and the state: the establishment of SERNAM in Chile.' In S. Rai and G. Lievesley (Eds.) *Women and the state: international perspectives*, p. 7.
37. Alvarez, S. Endangering democracy in brazil: women's movements in transition politics.
38. Noman, O. Pakistan: political and economic history since 1947. p.3.
39. Jinnah, a secular Muslim barrister was the main leader of All India Muslim League the vanguard party that led the Muslims of India to a Muslim in demanding and achieving an independent state carved out of the Muslim majority areas of India in August 1947, once British imperialism retreated.
40. While he is widely credited to have led the demand for a separate Muslim homeland in the Indian sub-continent, some (Jalal, 1986) contend that Jinnah was mainly interested in getting a special and permanent political role for Muslims in a combined India once the British left India after World War II.
41. *Hudood* Ordinances were a series of laws introduced by the regime of General Mohammad Zia ul Haq through martial law decree. These laws promulgated through presidential/Chief Martial Law Administrator ordinances, which basically consist of five criminal laws; the Offences against Property Ordinance deals with crimes of theft and armed robbery; the

offence of Zina Ordinance deals with rape, abduction, adultery, and fornication; Qazf that deals with false accusation of Zina; the Prohibition Order that deals with cases of alcohol and narcotic consumption; and finally the Execution of Punishment of Whipping Ordinance that prescribes the mode of whipping for those convicted under the *Hudood* Ordinances. These controversial laws were especially detrimental to women both in their spirit and in application. For an excellent account, see Jahangir, Asma and Hina Jilani. *The Hudood Ordinances: A Divine Sanction?*

42. Some scholars have argued that the religious leaders distrusted the secular League leadership and thus were opposed to the idea of a separate state (Noman, 1990: 6). Others have argued that this leadership had, during the colonial time, created a niche for itself by refusing to let the colonial state interfere in the Muslim personal law and thus had assumed the role of the interpreter of personal religion and thus were not comfortable with the idea of foregoing this status to a new state (Brass, 1991).

43. Rape could only be proved if evidence of four 'pious' men who had not committed the same crime could be provided. The public lashings were usually witnessed by an almost exclusively male crowd.

44. The emergence of the Movement for Restoration of Democracy (MRD) as a major political movement against the Zia regime toward mid-1980s is forwarded as an argument against this line of argument. I contend that the appeal of the MRD was limited as far as the middle and lower middle classes were concerned. These classes that had been the mainstay of an earlier movement against Z. A. Bhutto, by and large supported the Zia regime. This is however, not to argue that the symbolic power over women acted as an opiate for these classes. Just that it did ward off and perhaps delayed the reaction of the disenfranchised classes.

45. Noman, Op cit., Jalal, A. The Convenience of subservience: women and the state of Pakistan. In D. Kandiyoti (Ed.) *Women, Islam and the state*. Also see Jalal, A. *Democracy and authoritarianism in South Asia: A comparative and historical perspective*.

46. He disrupted the process again in the late 1980s by dismissing his hand-picked Prime Minister and the assemblies elected on the basis of his preferred non-party elections formula.

47. This was evident at the time of his death and subsequent death anniversaries, and more significantly in the fact that Muslim League (one of the two major political parties in Pakistan) has borne Zia's political legacy and has won power on its basis twice.

48. Noman, Op cit., p. 213.

49. Ibid, p. 214.

50. Khattak, S. G. 'A reinterpretation of the state and statist discourse in Pakistan: 1977–88. In N. S. Khan, R. Saigol, and A. S. Bano (Eds.). *Locating the self: perspectives on women and multiple identities*, p. 33.

51. Ibid.

52. Evidence from other parts of South Asia suggests that education (in the form that it exists) may not be a source of empowerment or even upward mobility. Jeffery and Jeffery (1997) have demonstrated in the case of North India that education per se might not lead to empowerment of women. For a dissenting view, see Caldwell, Reddy, and Caldwell (1988). Caldwell, et al study, however, focuses on South India.

53. See for instance Adeel, U. K. & Naqvi, M. H. Pakistani women in development: a statistical mirror.

54. As cited in Luykx, A. *The Citizen factory: schooling and cultural production in Bolivia*. p. 159.

55. Ibid.

56. Adeel & Naqvi, Op cit., p. 113.

57. In the non-discursive domain, discrimination with respect to gender exists at the infrastructural level. Pakistan has a tiered education structure both along class and gender dimensions. Along the class dimension the so-called 'English medium' schools owned and operated by the private sector cater only to those who can afford to pay high tuition fees. The majority of the Pakistani children (those who go to school) attend state run schools where the medium of instruction is Urdu (the national language of Pakistan). The net effect is strengthening of the class system. Male children are preferred to be educated over female children by the parents. The discrimination is also evident at the systemic level where not only a segregated school system exists, but where the number of schools for female children is much less than the corresponding number for the male children. A third type of discrimination is evident in the availability of fields of study open to males and females. The

'career' oriented, technical, and professional subjects are open more to the male students than their female counterparts. In professional institutions such as medical colleges a quota of twenty percent is reserved for the women. The justification for this policy is that it will allow more women to enter the medical profession. Ironically, women applying to medical colleges can only apply against the seats reserved for them, thus effectively creating an 80 percent quota for the male students. The educational discourse determines the fields that are considered more 'appropriate' for women. These include fields such as home economics, humanities, fine arts, etc. Technical and vocational fields that are considered 'appropriate' for the female students include nursing, seamstress, typing, and secretarial work, etc.

58. Saigol, R. *Knowledge and Identity: articulation of gender in educational discourses in Pakistan*. Aziz, K. K., *The murder of history: a critique of history textbook used in Pakistan*. Rouse, Shahnaz (1994), "Gender(ed) Struggles: The State, Religion and Society." In Kamla Bhasin, Ritu Menon, and Nighat S. Khan (Eds.) *Against All Odds: Essays on Women, Religion and Development from India and Pakistan*. Also see Rouse, Shahnaz (1998), "The Outsider(s) Within: Sovereignty and Citizenship in Pakistan." In Patricia Jeffery and Amrita Basu, *Appropriating Gender: Women's Activism and Politicized Religion in South Asia.*

59. Saigol, Op cit.

60. Apple, M. W. and L. K. Christian-Smith. The politics of the textbook. In M. W. Apple and Linda K. Christian-Smith (Eds.). The politics of the textbook. (1991). Also see Sleeter, C. E. and C. A. Grant. Race, class, gender and disability in current textbook. In M. W. Apple and Linda K. Christian-Smith (Eds.) *The politics of the textbook.*

61. Punjab Textbook Board. *Muasharati Uloom* (Social Studies) for Class VIII. pp. 7–8. (I have used Saigol's translation which is fairly accurate.)

62. It is interesting to note that when Muslims were successful it was due to their bravery, valor, faith etc. When they failed, however, it was due to the intrigues against them. Intrigue and deceit being feminine qualities. (For a detailed description and explanation, see Saigol 1994, also 1995.)

63. See for instance the Primer for Class 2, Punjab Textbook, Board.

References

Adeel, U. K. and M. H. Naqvi. Pakistani women in development: a statistical mirror. Academy Town Peshawar: Pakistan Academy for Rural Development, 1997.

Allen, J. 'Does feminism need a theory of the state?' In S. Watson (Ed.) (1990). *playing the state: Australian feminist intervention*. London: Verso, 1990.

Alvarez, S. *Endangering democracy in Brazil: women's movements in transition politics*. Princeton: Princeton University Press, 1990.

Anwar, M. *Images of male and female roles in school and college textbooks*. Islamabad: Women's division. Government of Pakistan, 1982.

Apple, M. W. and L. K. Christian-Smith. The politics of the textbook. In M. W. Apple and Linda K. Christian-Smith (Eds.). *The politics of the textbook*. New York, London: Routledge. (1991).

Apple, M. W. *Teachers and texts: A political economy of class and gender relations in education*. New York, London: Routledge, 1988.

Aziz, K. K. *The murder of history: a critique of the history textbook used in Pakistan*. Lahore: Vanguard, 1993.

Bartky, S. L. 'Foucault, femininity and the postmodernization of patriarchal power.' In I. Diamond and L. Quinby (Eds.) *feminism and Foucault: reflections on resistance*. Boston: Northeastern University Press, 1988.

Basu, A. Appropriating gender. In P. Jeffery and A. Basu. (Eds.) *Appropriating gender: women's activism and politicized religion in South Asia*. New York, London: Routledge, 1998.

Bryson, V. *Feminist debates: issues of theory and political practice*. New York: New York University Press, 1999.

Burchell, G., et al. The Foucault Effect: studies in governmentality: with two lectures and an interview with Michel Foucault. Chicago: University of Chicago Press, 1991.

Connell, R. W. *Gender and power*. Sydney: Allen and Unwin, 1988.

Eisenstein, Z. *The radical future of liberal feminism*. London: Longman, 1981.

Foucault, M. *Power/Knowledge: selected interviews and other writings 1972–1977.* Edited and translated by Colin Gordon. New York: Pantheon Books, 1980.

Franzway, S. 'With problems of their own: femocrats and the welfare state.' *Australian Feminist Studies.* 3, Summer, 1986.

Fraser, N. and L. Nicholson. Social criticism without philosophy: an encounter between feminism and postmodernism.' In L. Nicholson (Ed.) *Feminism/Postmodernism.* New York, London: Routledge, 1990.

Government of Pakistan. *Report of the Commission on the status of women.* Islamabad, 1985.

Gumbert, E. B. (Ed.). *Expressions of power in education: studies of class, gender and race.* Atlanta: Georgia State University, 1984.

Hoodbhoy, P. A. and A. H. Nayyar. 'Rewriting the history of Pakistan.' In M. A. Khan (Ed.). *Islam, politics and the state: the Pakistan experience.* London: Zed Books Ltd., 1985.

Hussain, N. 'Women as objects and women as subjects within fundamentalist discourse.' In N. S. Khan, R. Saigol, and A. S. Bano (Eds.). *Locating the self: Perspectives on women and multiple identities.* Lahore: ASR, 1994.

Hussain, N. and N. Shah. Women, media and the production of meaning. In Fareeha Zafar (Ed.). *Finding our way; readings on women in Pakistan.* Lahore: ASR, 1991.

Jahangir, Asma and Hina Jilani. *The Hudood Ordinances: A Divine Sanction?* Lahore: Sang-e-Meel Publications, 2003.

Jalal, A. 'The Convenience of subservience: women and the state of Pakistan.' In Kandiyoti. D. (Ed.) *Women, Islam and the state.* UK: Macmillan, 1991.

Jalal, A. *Democracy and authoritarianism in South Asia: A comparative and historical perspective.* Cambridge: Cambridge University. Press, 1995.

Jeffery, P. 'Agency, activism and agenda.' In P. Jeffery and A. Basu (Eds.) *Appropriating gender: women's activism and politicized religion in South Asia.* New York, London: Routledge, 1998.

Jules, D. Building democracy: content and ideology in Grenadian educational texts: 1979–1983. In M. W. Apple and Linda K. Christian-Smith (Eds.). *The politics of the textbook.* New York, London: Routledge, 1991.

Kenway, J. 'Feminist theories of the state: to be or not to be?' In M. Blair and J. Holland with Sue Sheldon (Eds.). *Identity and diversity: gender and the experience of education.* Cleredon, Philadelphia, and Adelaide: Multilingual Matters Ltd. in association with The Open University, 1995.

Khan, N. S. 'Reflections on the question of Islam and modernity. 'In N. S. Khan, R. Saigol. and A. S. Bano (Eds.). *Locating the self: Perspectives on women and multiple identities.* Lahore: ASR, 1994.

Khattak, S. G. A reinterpretation of the state and statist discourse in Pakistan: 1977–88. In N. S. Khan, R. Saigol, and A. S. Bano (Eds.). *Locating the self: perspectives on women and multiple identities.* Lahore: ASR, 1994.

Luykx, A. *The Citizen factory: schooling and cultural production in Bolivia.* Albany: State University of New York Press, 1999.

Metcalf, B. D. 'Mandering *Madrassahs*: knowledge and short-term itinerancy in the *Tablighi Jama't.*' In N. Crook (Ed.). *The transmission of knowledge in South Asia: essays on education, religion, history and politics.* Bombay, Calcutta, Madras: Oxford University Press, 1996.

Nicholson, L. (Ed.). *Feminism/Postmodernism.* London: Routledge, 1990.

Noman, O. *Pakistan: political and economic history since 1947.* London: Kegan Paul, 1990.

Powell, A. 'Perceptions of the South Asian past; ideology, nationalism and school history textbooks.' In N. Crook (Ed.). *The transmission of knowledge in South Asia: essays on education, religion, history and politics.* Bombay, Calcutta, Madras: Oxford University Press, 1996.

Pringle, R. and S. Watson. 'Fathers, brothers, mates: the fraternal state in Australia.' In S. Watson (Ed.) *Playing the state: Australian feminist interventions.* London, New York: Verso, 1990.

Pringle, R. and S. Watson. 'Women's interests and the poststructuralist state,' in M. Barrett and A. Phillips (Eds.) *Destabilizing theory: contemporary feminist debates.* Cambridge: Polity Press, 1992.

Punjab Textbook Board. *Civics* for Class IX. Lahore, n.d.

Punjab Textbook Board. *Civics* for Class IX-X. Lahore, n.d.

Punjab Textbook Board. *Muasharati Uloom* (Social Studies) for Class VIII. Lahore, n.d.

Punjab Textbook Board. *Mutaliya Pakistan* (Pakistan Studies) for Class IX-X. Lahore, n.d.

Punjab Textbook Board. Primer for Class I. Lahore, n.d.

Punjab Textbook Board. Primer for Class III. Lahore, n.d.

Punjab Textbook Board. Primer for Kindergarten. Lahore, n.d.

Quddus, S. A. *Education and national reconstruction of Pakistan*. Lahore: S. I. Gillani, 1979.

Qureshi, I. H. *Education in Pakistan: an inquiry into objectives and achievements*. Karachi: Ma'aref Ltd., 1975.

Rai, S. 'Women and the state in the third world: some issues for debate.' in S. Rai and G. Lievesley (Eds.) *Women and the state: international perspectives*. London: Taylor and Francis, 1996.

Rouse, Shahnaz (1994), "Gender(ed.) Struggles: The State, Religion and Society." In Kamla Bhasin, Ritu Menon, and Nighat S. Khan (Eds.) *Against All Odds: Essays on Women, Religion and Development from India and Pakistan*. New Delhi: Kali for Women.

Rouse, Shahnaz (1998), "The Outsider(s) Within: Sovereignty and Citizenship in Pakistan." In Patricia Jeffery and Amrita Basu, *Appropriating Gender: Women's Activism and Politicized Religion in South Asia*. New York, London: Routledge.

Saigol, R. Knowledge and Identity: articulation of gender in educational discourses in Pakistan. Lahore: ASR, 1995.

Showstock, S. A. (Ed.). *Women and the state: the shifting boundaries of public and private*. London: Hutchinson, 1987.

Sleeter, C. E. and C. A. Grant. 'Race, class, gender and disability in current textbook.' In M. W. Apple and Linda K. Christian-Smith (Eds.) *The politics of the textbook*. New York, London: Routledge, 1991.

Smith, R. L. 'Implementing qualitative research in Pakistan: international teamwork.' In Crossley, M. and G. ulliamy (Eds.). *Qualitative educational research in developing countries*. New York and London: Garland Publishing Inc., 1997.

Walderkine, V. Sex, power and pedagogy. *Screen Education*. 38, pp. 14–24, 1981.

Warwick, D. P. and R. Fernando. *Learning in Pakistan's primary schools*. London: Westport, 1995.

Watson, S. (ed.) *Playing the state: Australian feminist intervention*. London: Verso, 1990.

Watson, S. 'The State of Play: An Introduction.' In S. Watson (Ed.). *Playing the state: Australian feminist intervention*. London: Verso, 1990.

Waylen, G. 'Democratization, Feminism and the state: the establishment of SERNAM in Chile.' In S. Rai and G. Lievesley (Eds.) *Women and the state: international perspectives*. London: Taylor and Francis, 1996.

Zafar, F. 'Women's education: problems and prospects.' In Fareeha Zafar (Ed.). *Finding our way; readings on women in Pakistan*. Lahore: ASR, 1991.

Zaman, U. S. . Karachi, 1981.

CHAPTER 6

Native Speaker Discourses: Power and Resistance in Postcolonial Teaching Of English To Speakers Of Other Languages

NUZHAT AMIN and RYUKO KUBOTA

Introduction

The field of English Language Teaching (ELT) worldwide has been dominated by colonialist ideologies of who is a legitimate speaker of English, who can be a valid English language teacher, and who is the final authority on ELT pedagogies. Eurocentric theories embedded in the imperialist worldview that "native speakers" from the predominantly English-speaking countries of the West have more ownership of English than "nonnative speakers" from the non-West[1] inform the theories and pedagogies in this field. The native/nonnative division is also situated in global power relations and ideologies. For example, in critiquing the linguistic imperialism of English, Phillipson (1992) argues that the division between "core English-speaking countries" of the West (the U.S., the U.K., Canada, Australia, and New Zealand) and "periphery-English countries," where English is used as an international link language (e.g., Japan and Sweden) or where English was imposed in colonial times and now exists as indigenized varieties (e.g., Pakistan and Nigeria), parallels the relationship between the dominant rich countries and the dominated poor countries. Moreover, because core English-speaking countries of the First World are predominantly Anglo societies, the "native speaker of English" is often a code word for White speakers of English (cf. Paikeday, 1985). Native speaker ideologies and discourses in applied linguistics tend to position native speakers of English as White people speaking standard, good, correct, real English with a standard accent, whereas nonnative speakers are constructed as people of color speaking nonstandard, deficient, inferior English with a nonstandard, inferior accent.

The superiority of the native speaker in ELT, however, has been critically scrutinized. Critics argue that it has an unsound linguistic basis (e.g., Canagarajah, 1999; Christophersen, 1988), is embedded in linguistic imperialism (Phillipson, 1992), and is constructed by discourses of colonialism and racism (e.g., Kachru, 1997; Pennycook, 1998). One notion that challenges the native speaker myth is World Englishes, or different varieties of English used globally (e.g., Kachru, 1990, 1992). The notion of World Englishes signifies the diasporic and hybridized nature of English and attempts to validate marginalized varieties of English. Furthermore, critics have applied poststructuralist notions such as multiplicity of meanings and subjectivities to ELT and proposed postcolonial resistance through appropriating English for counter-hegemonic purposes (Canagarajah, 1999; Pennycook, 1998, 2001). Despite these critiques and proposals, the concepts and ideologies of the division between native vs. nonnnative speakers continue to circulate in ELT, as seen in teaching materials and teacher hiring practices. ELT thus is a site where discourses of colonialism, racism, and imperialism intersect to produce and mark women and men from the non-West as permanent Others when they speak English, which was once the language of the colonizers but is now very much an institution of the countries with or without a history of British and American colonialism.

In this chapter, we as two non-White women teachers from periphery-English countries offer comparative mini-narratives to explore the effect of native-speaker-of-English-discourses on teaching and learning English in postcolonial Pakistan and post-World War II Japan. We also describe the personal challenges presented by these discourses in our teaching in Canada and the U.S. and explore ways to resist native speaker ideologies. Our narratives and analyses are grounded in our local knowledge (Canagarajah, 1993), the knowledge that non-Western writers bring from their local contexts, attempting to bring the margin to the center (hooks, 1990; Spivak, 1990). Because our personal experiences are different in terms of time, space, and nature, it is not possible to draw a perfect parallel between teaching English in Pakistan and Japan or teaching in Canada and the U.S. Amin, who immigrated to Canada from Pakistan in the late 1970s and has taught English to immigrants in Canada, will focus mostly on native speaker discourses in Canada, whereas Kubota, who moved to the U.S. from Japan in the late 1980s and has interests in educational policies in Japan, will mostly focus on native speaker discourses in teaching English in Japan. Although our foci are slightly different, it becomes clear that with the power of English arising from colonial legacies and postcolonial globalization, native speaker discourses are influencing teachers, learners, and academics from both a former English-speaking colony and a non-colony.

Our critical analyses of native speaker discourses are informed by postcolonial and poststructuralist perspectives. As briefly discussed above, the field of ELT has begun to incorporate postfoundational perspectives just as the field of comparative education has (e.g., Ninnes and Mehta, 2000; Paulston, 1999, 2000; Popkewitz, 2000). Our critical analysis of the native speaker construct parallels comparative education's recognition that postcolonial and poststructuralist perspectives are useful in exposing issues of power, knowledge, and discourse in relation to social practices in education. Thus our inquiry critically scrutinizes discursive construction of the fixed norm and colonial construction of the images of Self and Other or the native speaker and the nonnative speaker. It also explores postcolonial resistance in order to bring marginality to center stage and to appropriate or subvert the norm from within. Our inquiry into the native speaker construct also addresses issues of race, identity, culture, and language, the topics often neglected by comparative education's inquiry into colonialism which has been influenced by neo-Marxist dependency theory and globalization theory (Tikly, 1999; Ninnes and Burnett, this volume).

We first historicize the native speaker construct and argue that this construct was mobilized at decolonization as an exclusionary measure against people of color from various ex-colonial countries who were gathering in core countries and making demands for inclusion in the nation state. We then describe how native speaker discourses affect the construction of subjectivities in Pakistan (based on Amin's own experiences) and the practices of teaching English in contemporary Japan (based on Kubota's critical analysis). Next we analyze the challenges we face as non-White women teachers (Amin in Canada and Kubota in the U.S.) in a profession that privileges native speakers. Finally, we examine some of the resistance strategies to the hegemony of the native speaker.

Historicizing the Native Speaker

In the context of core countries, the native speaker construct is embedded in the larger discourses of nativism that position visible minority immigrants from periphery countries as nonnative to the nation, and hence nonnative to English. Similar ideologies are maintained in periphery countries through what we term "native speaker discourses" that maintain the hegemony of White native speakers of English by positioning them as intrinsically knowing better English than nonnative speakers ever can and also knowing how to teach English better than nonnative speakers (see Widdowson, 1994).

Nativist discourses entered the fields of linguistics and applied linguistics, inventing the native speaker through Eurocentric scientific inquiry of language and colonial cultural politics. Pennycook (1992) argues that a) the concepts used in modern linguistics have their origins in language as understood in Europe; b) the notion of language as it grew up in Europe was intimately tied to the growth of the nation state; and c) the notion of a language as a homogeneous unity shared by the inhabitants of a nation state was finally to be taken up and given a "'scientific' blessing as the twentieth century witnessed the emergence of linguistics in its modern form" (p. 97). According to Pennycook (1992), linguistics and applied linguistics developed as fields because they were interested in controlling and disciplining the English language; he suggests that originally the focus was to produce and maintain clear distinctions between the lower and upper classes in England and that standardization became important in order to discipline a language that had been introduced to the elites in Britain's colonies.

It is significant that the first recorded use of the term "native language" surfaced when the new world order was being established between the two world wars, when decolonization was imminent, and when the concept and notion of who is native to a nation state became important. According to Davies (1991), the first recorded use of native speaker is the following definition by the American linguist Leonard Bloomfield: "The first language a human being learns to speak is his native language, he is a native speaker of this language" (see Bloomfield, 1933, p. 43). Cook (1999) indicates that such a definition is similar to that of modern sources such as *The Oxford Companion to the English Language* and *Collins COBUILD English Dictionary*. What is noticeable about such definitions is that they emphasize conditions and qualities such as birth, parentage, childhood, and intuition, and these meanings appear to be embedded in the original meaning of native as "natural." Davies (1991) draws attention to the fact that the cognate of native is "naïf" (through Old French) meaning natural, with "the sense of not being able to help it" (p. ix). The emphasis in these widely accepted definitions is on the intuition of native speakers, who cannot help knowing what they do about English. This intuition is seen as being tied to the fact that their "mother tongue" or "first language" is English.

In sum, linguistics as a scientific and colonial quest for regulating a language system reflected and reinforced the discourses of nativism. The native speaker concept is embedded in nativist discourses that position only speakers of English native to core countries as having legitimate claims to belonging to the nation state and of having English as their native language. The contemporary native speaker discourses can be placed on a continuum of the colonial discourses of nativism.

The Native Speaker of English in Core Countries
(Amin, in Pakistan and in Canada)

I am an ethnic Pakistani woman and grew up in Karachi, Pakistan.[2] The experience of growing up in a postcolonial British society informs how I negotiate native speaker discourses in Canada where I live and where I have taught English as a Second Language (ESL). Hence, in this section I first reflect on my English-language schooling in postcolonial Pakistan, in which I received colonial messages of native speaker superiority. Then I describe my language-related experiences in Canada as well as the parallel experiences of minority women who are constructed as Other to the nation and Other to ESL in Canada. Finally, I discuss ways to resist native speaker discourses.

A Postcolonial Education

I grew up in postcolonial Pakistan, where, as a member of the middle/ upper middle class, I internalized messages of the "indubitable superiority and the impregnable infallibility of the 'native speaker'" (see Nayar, 1994, p. 4). I attended convent schools for 14 years; in these schools English was the medium of instruction. The English taught at these convent schools was not just *any* English. It was modeled on British native speaker English; the ideal was clearly Received Pronunciation (RP), emblematic of which was the BBC. The ghost of Macaulay haunted the corridors and the classrooms: We were supposed to speak only English and local languages were looked down on or laughed at. Those girls who shone in the English class had a reputation of being intelligent and cultured; those who did well in Urdu were either ignored or identified as being from a lower class. However, within the walls of these convent schools, it was made very clear that native speakers were the real and true speakers of English, and Pakistanis could never make such a claim. We understood also that only White people were native speakers. These messages of the superiority of the White native speaker were not restricted to the convent schools. I went on to do two master's degrees in English — in literature and then language. During the latter program, the native speaker was no longer a phantom presence but a flesh-and-blood person, embodied by the visiting White scholars who flew into Karachi to give a few talks. The language laboratory that we frequented for our phonetics course was headed by a White man. A great deal of effort went into ridding students of the pollutant half-*v*/half-*w* sound of Urdu and trying to replace it with two distinct sounds — *v* and *w* — in order to make us sound like native speakers.

I am not aware even now if there was resistance to the native speaker norm through using an indigenized variety of English. Resistance, if at all, was practiced by those among us who went to study in England and the U.S., and came back thinking that English was the master's tool and hence not to be used. Similarly, I do not recall any struggle to have the local variety of English recognized as a valid indigenized variety of English (IVE). Baumgardner (1993) appears to be mocking the examples of Pakistani English that he found in English language newspapers during his stay in Pakistan. When living in Pakistan, I would probably have considered these nativisms to be "incorrect English" or "Urdu-English." No one then said that nonnative speakers can, and do, speak equally good English as native speakers. I conflated native speaker with good English, and nonnative speaker not as different, but deficient. Kachru (1992) is insightful on such experiences and attitudes. He identifies the following four stages in the development of nonnative Englishes: 1) non-recognition of the local variety; 2) the local model is somewhat recognized but is still low on the attitudinal scale; 3) slow recognition of the local variety as the norm; 4) recognition of the local variety. According to Kachru, South Asian societies began to approach the fourth stage only 20 years or so ago — after I left Pakistan. The observations that I have made about my experiences and attitudes to English in Pakistan would probably fall in the first and second stages of South Asian Englishes.

Language-Related Experiences in Canada

I would describe my initial language-related experiences in Canada, in the late-1970s, as difficult, as I was constructed as Other to the norm of native speaker of English and native speaker accent. These encounters with linguistic nativism had an extremely negative effect on my identity formation as I felt that my years of experience as an announcer and news reader in English on Radio Pakistan and my two master's degrees in English seemed to be wiped away overnight by being identified as a speaker of nonnative/nonstandard English. I have taught ESL to adults in Toronto in both credit and noncredit courses in programs run by community colleges and by school boards. There were many differences in these programs in terms of goals, duration, and curriculum. The students in these programs varied in terms of age, gender, ethnicity, linguistic background, level of education, ability in English, and length of stay in Canada. A common thread in these very different teaching situations was that many of the students murmured the term "native speaker" with awe. I received the message that however hard I might work at preparing competent lessons, my teaching could not be as good as that of a native speaker. I experienced the discomfort of having to use tapes with "native speaker" accents, for students to model themselves on, the ignominy of students storming out of the class and demanding a "real" English teacher, and the embarrassment of having to rely on supervisors to pacify angry students with an unconvincing "all our teachers are very qualified... "

Race, Accents, and New Racisms: Construction of the Nonnative Speaker

As indicated above, in the context of core countries, the discourse on the "nonnative speaker" is embedded in the larger discourses of nativism; these position visible minority immigrant women from periphery countries as nonnative to the nation, and hence nonnative to English. To borrow Brah's (1996) words in the context of England, racial minority immigrants are seen as living "in" Canada, but are not seen as being "of" Canada. According to Ng (1990), although the term "immigrant women" refers to women with a particular legal status, those who are seen to be immigrant women by members of society are "'visible minority' women, women who do not speak English or who speak English with an accent (other than British or American), and women who work in low-paid menial jobs" (p. 21). Ng concludes that the "common usage of the word embodies class, ethnic, and racial biases" (p. 21). Ng thus indicates how racism and sexism as systems of oppression and domination in Canada construct minority women as Other.

A marker of being an immigrant woman and of being nonnative to core societies is an immigrant woman's race. I argue that this experience of Otherness is reproduced in ESL through the imagining of the native speaker as White. This discourse pervades all aspects of ESL programs in Canada, as seen in the teaching, classroom materials, and relations between the teacher and learners. In this site, as Rockhill and Tomic (1995) state, the referent is "White, Anglo, male" (p. 210). The race of the idealized native speaker is spelled out by Leung, Harris, and Rampton (1997), who, building on Rampton's earlier (1990) research, argue that there is an "abstracted notion of an idealized native speaker of English from which ethnic and linguistic minorities are automatically excluded. (p. 546)

Another marker of being nonnative is having an accent that is different from the norm of the Canadian ESL classroom. As Brutt-Griffler and Samimy (1999) argue, "national origin and accent" (p. 416) are crucial characteristics that are socially held to represent those of the native speaker. I argue that accents, like race, are socially constructed, are a linguistic manifestation of nativism, and constitute a new and effective form of racism. I need to first lay out what accents symbolize in core societies. Matsuda (1991) states: "Everyone has an accent, but when an employer refuses to hire a person 'with an accent,' they are referring to a hidden norm of non-accent" (p. 1361). Matsuda then explicates this norm of non-accent: "People in power are perceived as speaking normal, unaccented English. Any speech that is different from that constructed norm is called an accent" (p. 1361). As a law professor in the U.S., Matsuda listened to a number of stories about people who had been born outside the U.S. and had been denied a particular job in their country of adoption because of having a "heavy accent"; she came to the conclusion that "accent discrimination is commonplace, natural, and socially acceptable" (p. 1348). Lippi-Green (1997) takes this line of argument further and states that "accent serves as the first point of gatekeeping" into American society because it is no longer legal to discriminate on the basis of ethnicity, race, and homeland, and hence "accent becomes a litmus test for exclusion" (p. 64). She thus establishes that accents are a legal and acceptable form of exclusion of certain groups of people. The next question is which group of people this is. Citing the case of a Columbian man who was attending accent-reduction classes, Lippi-Green (1997) states: "It is not *all* foreign accents, but only accents linked to skin that isn't white, or which signals a third-world homeland, that evokes such negative reactions" (pp. 238–39). These observations establish that the nonnative speaker is constructed as a person of color with periphery-country status, and that contemporary racism has taken on a new discourse that replaces race with linguistic background as a legitimate reason for discrimination.

Colonial Discourses on Race and Language of East Indians and Postcolonial Resistance

Fiction writer Bharati Mukherjee, who is originally from India and now lives in the U.S., grounds much of her fiction in her encounters from 1966 to 1980 with the legacy of colonial discourse in Canada. She distils her experience of being a linguistic and racial Other in her short story "Hindus" (Mukherjee, 1985). In this story, we meet a well-assimilated, upper-class East Indian woman named Leela who lives in the U.S. Leela tells the reader that her job at a publishing house is "menial," but she has the "soothing title" of Administrative Assistant. One day, a White colleague of similar low standing in the publishing house says to her:

> "I had no idea you spoke Hindu. It's eerie to think you can speak such a hard language… I keep forgetting that you haven't lived here always." (p. 140)

Our protagonist doesn't respond, but thinks:

> I keep forgetting it too. I was about to correct her silly mistake… but then I thought, why bother? Maybe she's right. That slight undetectable error, call it accent, *isn't part of language at all.* I speak Hindu. No matter what language I speak it will come out slightly foreign, no matter how perfectly I mouth it. There's a whole world of us now, speaking Hindu. (p. 140, my emphasis)

The protagonist expresses well what I am saying: that mouthing English perfectly does not automatically put the speaker in the native speaker category. An East Indian immigrant woman's English is heard as the English of a foreigner, a Hindu. In these few sentences Mukherjee is able to capture the essence of nativism; for, as Leela says, the undetectable error that constructs her as immigrant, foreigner "isn't part of language at all."

Leela's experience of being constructed as speaking "Hindu" reflects that of East Indians living in Britain. In the context of British schools, Rampton (1988) maintains that Indian and Pakistani students who are proficient in English continue to be put in ESL classes because of their "deceptive fluency" (pp. 503–529). In arguing for ESL training for such students, educators, according to Rampton, unwittingly subscribe to the imperial stereotype of *babu* for Indians and Pakistanis, which was developed during colonial rule of India. Rampton (1988) gives the *Oxford English Dictionary*'s definition of *babu*:

> A native Hindoo gentleman; also (in Anglo-Indian use), a native clerk or official who writes English; sometimes applied disparagingly to a Hindoo or more particularly, a Bengali with a superficial English education (p. 513; see also Kachru, 1990, on colonizers' condescending attitudes to the nativized Englishes of South Asians).

Rampton lists a number of reasons why ethnically Asian children are never considered to speak "normal" English, which are all related to the fact that ESL in Britain cuts its teeth on children of Asian parentage, who remain prototypical ESL learners in the public and professional mind. Rampton points to further evidence of biases against the Indian/Pakistani population: "Only a brief glance at press or TV reveals the wide prevalence and strength of pejorative sociolinguistic images of South Asians" (p. 508).

There are indications that similar pejorative sociolinguistic images of East Indians exist in Canada. Here I need to refer to a recent study that I conducted with ESL teachers in Toronto. From 1998 to 1999 I conducted interviews with eight minority immigrant women who had taught or were teaching ESL to adult immigrants in government-financed language programs known commonly as "Settlement ESL." The purpose of my research was to investigate how nativism, in particular the concept of the native speaker, is manifested in the context of ESL and how minority immigrant women teachers of ESL negotiate this linguistic manifestation of nativism (see Amin, 2000, for details of the study). My participants grew up in the Third World and immigrated to Canada as adults. These women had backgrounds similar to mine in that English was a major language in their lives in their countries of origin and continued to be a major language in their lives in Canada. The participants were randomly selected, and data collection consisted of open-ended semi-structured interviews. The participants were from China, Egypt, India, Jamaica, Kenya, Pakistan and Surinam. My research questions were as follows: 1) How is nativism, in particular the concept of the native speaker, manifested in the context of ESL? and 2) How do visible minority immigrant women teachers of ESL negotiate nativism and the native speaker construct?

The narratives of the teachers point to the following findings: a) Colonial messages of the supremacy of the White native speaker pervade the ESL classroom for adult immigrants in Canada and negatively impact on the minority teacher's identity formation; b) the teacher participants felt that they were effective teachers despite initial nonacceptance by their students on the basis of their race and nonnative speaker status, and despite being constantly judged against the native speaker norm. A tentative finding of my study was that the East Indian participants in my study perceived a stronger, more overt form of nativism than did the participants from other ethnic and racial groups, indicating that East Indian women in Canada continue to feel positioned as *babus* (see Amin, 2000, for further discussion).

The forms of nativism that the East Indian women in my study experienced might well be linked to the continuing British hegemony in Canada, especially in Toronto where this study was conducted. Hurst (1999), writing in the *Toronto Star*, suggests that despite the recent decline in number, people of British descent still hold considerable economic and political power in Canada and especially in Toronto. In other words, although Toronto may be less overtly a British city than it used to be, the British legacy still remains. Thus, the East Indian participants' encounters of linguistic nativism are an indication that nativist discourses of the *babu*, which has a colonial origin in England, may still have an influence in Canada. This indicates that the pejorative comments about my "East Indian" accent and comments on the intelligibility and comprehensiveness of my speech that I experienced when I first immigrated to Canada (see Amin, 1999), may have been embedded in colonial and imperial discourse on South Asians; my interlocutors constructed me as speaking *babu* English.

I am aware that in my country of adoption — Canada — I have to negotiate the nativist discourses that position me as Outsider. I am aware that these nativist discourses of the larger society are reflected in ESL through the positioning of immigrant women, and especially of East Indian women, as nonnative speakers of English with all the implications of subordination. In addition, I have to interrogate colonial discourses of the superiority of the White native speaker that I received in the convent schools that I attended for 14 years in Pakistan. These are indeed strong discourses of disempowerment and marginalization, and could well oppress minority women ESL teachers like myself in Canada.

But I model my resistance strategies to these oppressions on the successful pedagogies described by the teachers in the study that I have referred to above (see Amin, 2000). These teachers challenged the notion that the native speaker is the only valid teacher of English by building effective pedagogies on their ascribed nonnative speaker status. They felt that they were, in fact, more effective in the classroom when they built their pedagogies on their nonnative identities, rather than when they tried to follow the native speaker norm. A particularly successful classroom strategy employed by the teachers was to tell their students that they had learned English in school, thus disrupting native speaker myths that one has to be born in an English-speaking family and that English has to be the first language of a parent in order to know English well. Another way they demythologized the native speaker was by disrupting stereotypes of what accent a teacher should have. In place of commercial audiotapes that use "White" accents, the teacher participants in the study self-consciously used tapes with a variety of accents, thus encouraging their students to rethink their understanding of a Canadian accent. All the teachers worked very hard to prepare effective lessons, thus demonstrating to their students that teaching is a craft that has to be learned and is not a genetic endowment of native speakers. These teachers' narratives indicate their resistance to native speaker discourses by setting up a counter-discursive and counter-hegemonic paradigm in their ESL classroom.

The Native Speaker of English in a Periphery Country (Kubota, in Japan and in the U.S.)

Japan has never been a colony of Britain or the U.S., except that the U.S. occupied Japan between 1945 and 1952 after Japan's defeat in World War II.[3] Nevertheless, perceived superiority of the native speaker of English, similar to the case of Pakistan, does exist, although the linguistic and cultural model, particularly since the end of the war, has been an American rather than a British variety. This is largely due to the strong political, economic, and security ties between the U.S. and Japan in post-war politics. As a native-born ethnic Japanese woman, I received primary through undergraduate education in Japan during the 1960s and 1970s. After teaching English as a foreign language in public schools, I moved to North America in the late 1980s as a Japanese language instructor and a graduate student and later became a university professor in the U.S. As such, I am largely a product of Japanese schooling, including English as a foreign language instruction from grade 7 through undergraduate education. The English language instruction I received in Japan was quite different from the current situation, because at that time, opportunities to interact with native speakers or non-Japanese nonnative speakers of English were quite limited (see Kubota, 2001, for my learning experiences). Nonetheless, all the audiotapes accompanying English textbooks and radio English conversation programs that I was exposed to had voices and accents of only native speakers, mostly Americans. In these audio media, the actual speakers were invisible but their voices gave me the message that they were the ideal, and thus the model that I should follow. It was not until many years later that I read criticisms of the dominance of English in Japan and the superiority of the native speaker of English.

In this section, I will first review recent criticisms of the discourse of native speaker superiority and explore how this discourse is manifested in ELT in Japan. Second, I will discuss how the native speaker construct is being challenged and resisted in two discourses: the affirmation of World Englishes, particularly Asian or Japanese varieties, and the opposition to English linguistic imperialism or the imperialist domination of

English worldwide. Finally, shifting the focus from Japan to the U.S., where I currently teach, I will describe my own experience of being positioned as an illegitimate nonnative speaker of English in one context and as a legitimate native speaker of Japanese in another. Based on these experiences, I will discuss how counter-hegemonic pedagogy can be envisioned. But first, I will provide a brief background to current ELT in Japan.

English Teaching in Japan: A Background

In the post-war Japanese education system, English has been taught as a major foreign language in junior and senior high schools and colleges. In addition, there are numerous private companies that offer instruction of *eikaiwa* or English conversation for various groups of the population: business people, women clerical office workers, housewives, and those preparing for specific careers or study abroad. With globalization of the economy, an emphasis on ELT has intensified, particularly in the past two decades. This emphasis is observed most recently in the introduction of teaching "English conversation" in the elementary school curriculum in 2002 as an optional instruction for promoting "international understanding." (see Kubota, 2002a, for more detail). Another example of an emphasis on English can be seen in a proposal made in January 2000 by a private advisory council to the Prime Minister. The report proposed the future possibility of making English the second official language of Japan and setting goals for enabling every Japanese to communicate in English.[4] Although the former proposal has not been discussed or implemented further, it indicates Japanese leaders' frustration toward English language education that has not successfully fostered communication skills necessary in the global market.

I mentioned earlier that the current situation is quite different from that when I was growing up. One notable change is the introduction of the Japan Exchange and Teaching (JET) Program for public schools. Initiated by the Japanese government in 1987, young people have been recruited from abroad to assist Japanese teachers of foreign languages (mostly English) in schools throughout the country. Until recently, the government recruited teachers only from six countries: the U.S., Canada, the U.K., Australia, New Zealand, and Ireland, although the door is now open to some other countries. Of 5,676 English Assistant Language Teachers (ALTs) in 2002–2003, about 61.7 percent are from North America (the U.S. and Canada), 21.8 percent from the U.K., 14.6 percent from Australia, New Zealand, and Ireland, and the remaining 1.8 percent are from South Africa, Jamaica, Singapore, Israel, Italy, India, and Finland (Ministry of Education, Culture, Sports, Science and Technology, 2002).

Critiques of Native Speaker Discourses in Japan

The native speaker concept, along with English linguistic imperialism, has been widely problematized in predominantly English-speaking countries since the 1990s (e.g., Phillipson, 1992; Rampton, 1990). Such criticism has appeared in Japan as well. For instance, Oda (1995) has pointed out that people's belief in the superiority of native speakers had been strengthened since the 1980s, when the number of people traveling abroad increased and the development of oral English skills began to be emphasized as seen in the creation of "Oral Communication" as one of the courses in high school English curriculum. For commercial *eikaiwa* schools, learning English from native speakers has become a powerful selling point. Oda (1995) cites the following phrase found in an *eikaiwa* school advertisement: "We want you to master real English; all our foreign instructors are native speakers" (p. 24; translated from Japanese). The hidden message in the words "real English" and "native speakers" is that English spoken by nonnative speakers is "fake" and thus "inadequate" and "inferior."

Criticisms of native speaker discourses, however, had appeared much earlier. Perhaps one of the earliest criticisms was expressed in an essay titled "*Ideorogî to shite no eikaiwa* [English conversation as an ideology] by Douglas Lummis (1976). As an American, Lummis reflected on his own observations and experiences as an "English conversation" teacher in Japan in the 1960s. He critiqued the prevalence of the trivialized and idealized treatment of American culture that appeared in dialogues (e.g., drugstore, supermarket, and hamburger stand) with no attention paid to social issues that may reveal dark aspects of American society. Lummis also stated that White Americans were likely to get jobs more easily than non-White Americans and that White American teachers with no experience received more salaries than Japanese teachers with extensive experience. Lummis states: "The world of *eikaiwa* is racist …. It is racist in terms of its method of employment, pay, and advertisement as well as its ideology prevalent in textbooks and classrooms" (p. 22; translated from Japanese). He goes on to say that the concept of "native speaker" is deceptive because it only refers to "Whites" despite the fact that non-White Americans as well as people from the Philippines, Singapore, or India can be native speakers.

Since this publication, diversity among English teachers has certainly increased. However, the concept that only White people are native speakers persists. In an ethnographic study of the JET Program, McConnell (2000) observed a "White bias" in the program particularly during the initial years. For instance, an African American ALT was frequently asked by Japanese teachers, "Can you speak standard English?" (McConnell, 2000, p. 80). A newsletter circulated among JET participants criticized the Japanese government's hypocrisy that was evident in its efforts to promote "internationalization" while limiting racial diversity of the participants (see also Mochizuki, this volume). The White bias, or the notion that only White Americans or Britishers are native speakers, is also criticized by Japanese critics of English linguistic imperialism (Ishii, 1998; Oishi, 1990; 1993; Tsuda, 1990). It is important to note that the concepts of native speaker and Whiteness share an underlying ideology; that is, each represents an unmarked yet privileged and powerful norm considered superior to other speakers or other races, despite the fact that the native speaker *does* speak with a certain "accent" and Whiteness *is* a "color."

Yet there is another dimension to the equation between native speaker and Whiteness. Not all White native speakers have a privileged status; only so-called North American or British Standard English speakers are regarded as a legitimate model. In other words, American or British Standard English represents the *idealized* native speaker. Thus, teachers from Australia, New Zealand, and Ireland often face biases with regard to their accent. Some Australian participants of the JET Program, for instance, were told by Japanese teachers to reduce their accent by listening to tapes (Juppé, 1995) or to use only American English while teaching (McConnell, 2000). The preference of North American or British native speakers, as noted earlier, is demonstrated in the distribution of the countries of origin among the English ALTs—that is, 83.5 percent of all English ALTs are from the U.S., Canada, and the U.K. This suggests that the native speaker superiority is not simply tied to the White race, but is produced by and reflected in neocolonial American and British cultural politics.

Resistance to the Native Speaker

The native speaker construct and the dominance of English, particularly that of the American and British varieties, has met with resistance in Japan. The resistance can be categorized into two strategies: (1) promotion of World Englishes, particularly Asian or Japanese varieties, and (2) refusal to use English with foreign visitors and residents in Japan. First, drawing on the notion of World Englishes (Kachru, 1985), Asian varieties of English have been identified as a target of research and learning (Honna, 1990). The Japanese Association for Asian Englishes has been established for exploring and discussing such issues as the spread of English, language policy, and linguistic features of Asian varieties of English. This focus acknowledges linguistic hybridity and opens up possibilities of appropriating English for indigenous expressions. Taking this approach further, Takao Suzuki proposes using a Japanese variety of English called "Englic" or English-like language (e.g., Suzuki, 2001). This variety, for example, omits "s" for the third-person singular form of a verb (e.g., "She run" instead of "She runs") and permits "ed" for irregular verbs (e.g., "goed" instead of "went"). Suzuki argues that Englic, which has no native speaker, would be much simpler for Japanese people to learn and would allow them to talk about Japan and themselves more easily than English does.

Second, among critics of English linguistic imperialism, Tsuda (1993) mentions three possible forms of resistance to the dominance of English: (1) internationalizing the Japanese language, (2) promoting World Englishes; and (3) promoting linguistic equality. The first approach is seen in the argument for establishing Japanese as an official language of the United Nations (Suzuki, 2001). The second approach is appropriation of English as seen in Englic, which, according to Tsuda, may fail to completely reject native speaker discourses in the learning process. Similarly, in mentioning Honna's (1990) affirmation of Asian varieties of English, Oishi (1993) points out that this approach fails to resist the dominance of English because it ultimately legitimates the spread of English.

The third approach includes validation of the mother tongue. Tsuda supports the use of the mother tongue of the country one is in, suggesting that the Japanese should speak only in Japanese with foreigners in Japan. This approach, however, disregards many non-English speaking foreigners in Japan (e.g., Korean, Chinese, Brazilian, Peruvian, etc.) who are marginalized in the economic, cultural, and linguistic hierarchy of power. Tsuda's proposal demonstrates a strong resistance to the domination of English, but it neglects one's relative position within relations of power and could lead to conservative nationalism or reverse imperialism.

One point of resistance that is common between the promotion of World (Asian or Japanese) Englishes and the critique of English linguistic imperialism is the argument that the Japanese should disseminate information about Japan and Japanese culture to the rest of the world. This is a reaction against the past tendency of foreign language teaching to focus solely on receiving information from the West rather than sending out messages. Again, these proposals to disseminate Japanese culture to the world and to use only Japanese in Japan ignore multiple Japanese identities and multilingualism in Japan and feed into a conservative agenda of identity politics (cf. Kubota, 2002a). As Miura (2000) puts it, these views support monoculturalism and monolingualism that reflect a "zero-sum," rather than "plus-sum" game.

The above review shows that the points of resistance to the native speaker are multiple yet they are within the existing power relations rather than an outside position in relation to that power (Foucault, 1978) and that they reflect varied strategies seen in postcolonial literature—i.e., appropriation and abrogation (cf. Ashcroft, Griffiths, and Tiffin, 1989). One form of resistance affirms multiple "native speakers" of English and a "Japanese" variety of English, appropriating the power of English as the international language. A radical form of resistance is an abrogation discourse that rejects English altogether. This form of resistance, however, problematically promotes Japanese monolingualism. Both forms of resistance tend to share the desire to preserve the "Japanese culture" and disseminate it to the world, ending up using the same discursive strategy as the native-speaker-of-English discourses they are challenging: i.e., essentialism. In native speaker discourses, the native speaker of English is essentialized as the White speaker of Standard American or British English. However, the argument for preserving "the Japanese language and ways of thinking" presupposes the existence of a monolithic Japanese language and identity. In the complex colonial and postcolonial relations of power in which Japanese, English, and other languages are differently positioned in relation to one another, such resistance is quite problematic from a perspective of additive multilingualism and multiculturalism.

While many academics resist native-speaker-of-English discourse in Japan, Japanese individuals confront the same discourse in core English-speaking countries just like Amin did in Canada. The following section describes my own experience as an instructor in a university in the U.S.

Nonnative Speaker, Marginality, and Appropriation of Marginality for Resistance

As a Japanese professor in a predominantly White campus in the U.S. engaging in second language teacher education, I have faced a great deal of student resistance (see Kubota, 2002b, for more details). In my class on foreign language teaching methodology, which enrolled mostly undergraduate female American students wanting to become K–12 teachers of Spanish or French, some complained that I spoke neither Spanish nor French.[5] The team-teaching arrangement with a White woman colleague, a Spanish teacher educator who had more experience of teaching the same course than I did, perhaps exacerbated the difficulty. I was viewed as a less competent teacher. Moreover, these students perceived me as an illegitimate nonnative speaker of English. In the course evaluations, students commented that my English proficiency was a "barrier" and a "limiting factor" in understanding and answering students' questions. The perceived limitation of my English language skills was also equated with "little or no interpersonal skills."

These experiences are sharply contrasted with my experience of teaching Japanese as a foreign language. I usually receive respect from my American students learning Japanese and even compliments about my English (although I conduct my class mostly in Japanese). Speaking in English in one instructional setting positions me as an illegitimate and inferior nonnative speaker, whereas speaking in Japanese in another setting gives me a privileged status as a native speaker. This indicates the pervasiveness of native speaker discourses in language teaching in general. It also indicates that my cultural and linguistic capital is valued in one context but not in the other. In other words, cultural capital as well as power exercised through language is always relational. The value of cultural capital is perceived differently depending on one's positioning in particular relations of power. Power indeed manifests itself as "the multiplicity of force relations immanent in the sphere in which they operate" and the states of power engendered by the moving substrate of force relations are "always local and unstable" (Foucault, 1978, p. 93).

If power "is not a certain strength we are endowed with" and can be confronted (Foucault, 1978, p. 93), how can a marginalized nonnative teacher resist the power manifested in native speaker discourses in English-medium classrooms? Paralleling the teachers in Amin's study, I have appropriated my marginality to advocate additive multilingualism and multiculturalism. I currently prepare K–12 teachers of English as a second language. In my teaching, I devote a significant amount of time of the first day of class to explaining my cultural and linguistic background. I emphasize to the students that their interacting with me enables them to affirm difference and develop intercultural communicative skills. I reiterate these points over the duration of the course and often share my own experiences and perspectives as a nonnative speaker teacher of English. By doing so, I am encouraging the students to assume their share of communicative responsibility as native speakers (cf. Lippi-Green, 1997). This is a strategy to bring my marginality to a central location and turn it into a tool for advocating diversity. This constitutes a counter-hegemonic cultural practice in which marginality is chosen "as a site of resistance, as a location of radical openness and possibility" (hooks, 1990, p. 22). In this counter-hegemonic pedagogy, turning marginality into a center location does not parallel the reactionary approach to identity politics seen in the resistance to the native speaker and the dominance of English. It envisions an additive multilingual and multicultural society in which multiple positionalities are recognized as relative to each other in power relationships and multiple differences are affirmed as important.

Conclusion

In this chapter, based on our own experiences and situated analysis, we have shown that native speaker discourses are pervasive in core English countries as well as in a former English-speaking colony and a non-colony, despite increased scholarly interrogations of these discourses found in applied linguistics and ELT. We have argued that native speaker discourses do not only refer to linguistic phenomena; they are tied closely and in complex ways with issues of race, identity, and national origin in colonial and neocolonial cultural politics. These discourses construct immigrant visible minority women as nonnative speakers regardless of their English language proficiency, while constructing White English speakers as those from U.K. in the case of Pakistan and those from the U.S. and the U.K. in the context of Japan as native speakers who possess more ownership of English than others.

However, there are various forms of resistance being offered to the superiority of the native speaker both on the larger societal level and by individuals as classroom teachers. In Japan, resistance to the native speaker construct and the dominance of English can be seen in the arguments for appropriation and abrogation of English: that is, promotion of Asian and Japanese varieties of English and refusal to use English with foreign visitors and residents in Japan, although such resistance tends to support reactionary identity politics. On the individual level, we have indicated that a powerful form of resistance employed by us as well as racial minority women teachers in Canada is to foreground our nonnative identities to our students and to build effective pedagogies on our ascribed nonnative status, thus subverting existing power relations and creating new meanings regarding who are valid English speakers and which forms of English are legitimate.

Our chapter can offer some creative forms of inquiry to the field of comparative education. First, we engaged in comparative mini-narratives grounded in our local knowledge that we acquired from our non-Western background and lived experiences as women teachers of color. Through our analysis, we were able to find common threads and reveal discourses that produce certain positionalities and images of languages and people. Second, a postfoundational approach through comparative narratives allowed us to focus on critical issues of race, identity, and language. As mentioned in the beginning, these foci can become an important addition to scholarly inquiries in comparative education. Third, nonnative women's lived experiences in teaching against the grain which we described in this chapter provide a basis for further exploration on how postcolonial counter-hegemonic pedagogies are conceived and practiced by various teachers in multiple contexts. As Ninnes and Mehta (2000) argue, such a process of teaching can be an important area of inquiry in comparative education.

Both the writers of this chapter are constantly negotiating our nonnative speaker-of-English status with all its implications of subordination, in classrooms in the U.S. and Canada, where we have chosen to bring our marginality to a central location and turn it into a tool for advocating diversity. Thus our pedagogies are a counter-hegemonic cultural practice in which we have chosen marginality as a site of resistance and possibility with the aim of empowering not only ourselves but also our students.

Endnotes

1. Our use of the terms "West" and "non-West" is an attempt to make transparent the continuing power inequalities between the region with a predominantly Anglo population and the region with a non-Anglo population that produce and maintain dichotomies such as native-nonnative speaker. In this chapter, the terms West and non-West are not interchangeable with the terms "First World" and "Third World." To us, the latter binary division refers to economic inequalities, while the former suggests linguistic and cultural hegemony, although many of the countries of the West are First World and many countries of the non-West are part of the Third World. For example, Pakistan is subjugated economically, culturally, and linguistically to the West and the Anglo world largely as a consequence of being a former British colony. Conversely, Japan is part of the First World in terms of economy, but

is non-West because it suffers from cultural and linguistic subjugation to the West. We realize that these binary terms are problematic, potentially perpetuating and recreating the division of "center" and "margin" (Spivak, 1993), but we decided to use these and other binaries, such as non-White women-White women; core-periphery, strategically (Spivak, 1993) in order to highlight the continuing power inequalities between the two spheres.

2. Pakistan was formed from the predominantly Muslim areas of India in 1947. At the same time, India gained independence from British rule.

3. It is important to note that Japan colonized a number of Asian countries from the beginning of the twentieth century through the end of World War II. The Japanese language was imposed on these colonies just as English was in the British colonies. As in the case of English, issues of standardization arose from the need to establish a model for language dissemination. A number of Japanese publications have begun to uncover Japanese colonial language policies (e.g., Kawamura, 1994; Tai, 1999; Yasuda, 1997).

4. Making English the second official language of Japan is a rather odd proposal given that there is no first official language specified by law.

5. The class recently opened its door to students who want to become licensed to teach Japanese. I no longer teach this course, but I have heard no complaint from these students that the current instructor speaks no Japanese.

References

Amin, Nuzhat. "Minority women teachers of ESL: Negotiating white English." In *Non-native educators in English language teaching*. Edited by George Braine. Mahwah, NJ: Lawrence Erlbaum Associates, 1999.

Amin, Nuzhat. *Negotiating nativism: Minority women ESL teachers and the native speaker construct.* Unpublished doctoral dissertation. Toronto: Ontario Institute for Studies in Education of the University of Toronto, 2000.

Ashcroft, Bill, Gareth Griffiths, and Helen Tiffin. *The empire writes back: Theory and practice in postcolonial literatures.* London: Routledge, 1989.

Baumgardner, Robert J. "The indigenization of English in Pakistan." In *The English language in Pakistan.* Edited by Robert J. Baumgardner, 41–54. Karachi: Oxford University Press, 1993.

Bloomfield, Leonard. *Language.* New York: Holt, Rinehart and Winston, 1933.

Brah, Avtar. *Cartographies of diaspora: Contesting identities.* London and New York: Routledge, 1996.

Brutt-Griffler, Janina, and Keiko Samimy. "Revisiting the colonial in the postcolonial. Critical praxis for nonnative-English-speaking teachers in a TESOL program." *TESOL Quarterly* 33 (1999): 413–431.

Canagarajah, A. Suresh. "Up the garden path: Second language writing approaches, local knowledge, and pluralism." *TESOL Quarterly* 27 (1993): 301–306.

—————————. "Interrogating the 'native-speaker fallacy': Non-linguistic roots, non-pedagogical results." In *Non-native educators in English language teaching.* Edited by George Braine, 77–92. Mahwah, NJ: Erlbaum, 1999.

Christophersen, Paul. "'Native speakers' and world English." *English Today* 15 (1988): 15–18.

Cook, Vivian James. "Going beyond the native speaker in language teaching." *TESOL Quarterly* 33 (1999): 185–209.

Davies, Alan. *The native speaker in applied linguistics.* Edinburgh: Edinburgh University Press, 1991.

Foucault, Michel. *The history of sexuality. Volume 1: An introduction.* New York: Vintage, 1978.

Honna, Nobuyuki, ed. *Ajia no eigo* [English in Asia]. Tokyo: Kuroshio Shuppan, 1990.

hooks, bell. *Yearning: Race, gender, and cultural politics.* Boston, MA: South End Press, 1990.

Hurst, Lynda. "All the king's horses." *Toronto Star,* August 21, 1999: J1–3.

Ishii, Satoshi. "Nihonjin to eigo no kankei: kako to genzai to mirai" [The relationship between the Japanese and English: Past, present, and future]. In *Nihonjin to eigo: Eigo-ka suru nihon no gakusai-teki kenkyû* [The Japanese people and English: Japanese academic studies being Anglicized]. Edited by Yukio Tsuda, 37-44. Kyoto: International Research Center for Japanese Studies, 1998.

Juppé Jr., Robert. "An incomplete 'Perestroika:' Communicative language teaching in Japan." *Gendai Eigo Kyôiku* [Modern English Language Education] June (1995): 18–19.

Kachru, Braj B. "Codification and sociolinguistic realism: The English language in the Outer Circle." In *English in the world: Teaching and learning the language and literatures*. Edited by Randolph Quirk and Henry G. Widdowson, 11-30. Cambridge: Cambridge University Press, 1985.

_____. *The alchemy of English: The spread, functions and models of non-native Englishes*, 2nd ed. Oxford: Pergamon, 1990.

_____. *The other tongue: English across cultures*, 2nd ed. Urbana: University of Illinois Press, 1992.

_____. "English as an Asian language." In *English is an Asian language: The Philippine context*. Edited by M. L. S. Bautista, 1-23. Manila, Philippines: Macquarie Library, 1997.

Kawamura, Minato. *Umi o watatta nihongo: Shokuminchi no "kokugo" no jikan* [Japanese language that went across the ocean: The "national language" period in colonies]. Tokyo: Seidosha, 1994.

Kubota, Ryuko. "My experience of learning to read and write in Japanese as L1 and English as L2." In *Reflections on multiliterate lives*. Edited by Ulla Connor and Diane Belcher, 96–109. Clevedon [England]; Buffalo, N.Y.: Multilingual Matters, 2001.

_____. "Impact of globalization on language teaching in Japan." In *Globalization and language teaching*. Edited by David Block and Deborah Cameron, 13–28. London: Routledge, 2002.

_____. "Marginality as an asset: Toward a counter-hegemonic pedagogy for diversity." In *Women faculty of color in the white college classroom*. Edited by Lucila Vargas, 293–307. New York: Peter Lang, 2002.

Leung, Constant, Roxy Harris, and Ben Rampton. "The idealised native speaker, reified ethnicities and classroom realities." *TESOL Quarterly* 31(1997): 543–560.

Lippi-Green, Rosina. *English with an accent: Language, ideology, and discrimination in the United States*. London: Routledge, 1997.

Lummis, Douglas. *Ideorogi to shite no eikaiwa* [English conversation as an ideology]. Tokyo: Shôbunsha, 1976.

Matsuda, Mari. "Voices of America: Accent, antidiscrimination, law, and a jurisprudence for the last reconstruction." *The Yale Law Journal* 100(1991): 1329–1407.

McConnell, David L. *Importing diversity: Inside Japan's JET Program*. Berkeley, CA: University of California Press, 2000.

Ministry of Education, Culture, Sports, Science and Technology *Heisei 14 nendo JET Program shinki shôchisha no kettei ni tsuite* [On the decisions regarding the invitees for the JET Program 2002-2003]. 2002. <http://www.mext.go.jp/b_menu/shingi/chousa/shotou/020/sesaku/020701d.htm> (14 July, 2002).

Miura, Nobutaka. "Prorôgu: Shokuminchi jidai to posuto shokuminchi jidai no gengo shihai" [Prologue: Language domination in colonialism and postcolonialism]. In *What is linguistic imperialism?* Edited by Nobutaka Miura and Keisuke Kasuya, 7–24. Tokyo: Fujiwara Shoten, 2000.

Mukherjee, Bharati. "Hindus." In *Darkness*, edited by Bharati Mukherjee. Markham: Penguin, 1985.

Nayar, P. Bhaskaran. "Whose English is it?" *TESL-EJ*, 1(1), F-1. [Online serial]. <http://berkeley.edu/-cwp>. (1994).

Ng, Roxana. "Racism, sexism, and visible minority immigrant women in Canada." In *Zeitschrift der Gesellschaft fuer Kanadastudien*, 10 Jahrgang, Nr. 2, 21–34. Neumuenster, Germany: Karl Wachholtz Verlag, 1990.

Ninnes, Peter and Sonia Mehta. "Postpositivism theorizing and research: Challenges and opportunities for comparative education." *Comparative Education Review*, 44 (2000): 205–212.

Oda, Masaki. "Native speaker to nihon no eigo kyôiku" [Native speaker and English education in Japan]. *Gendai Eigo Kyôiku* [Modern English Language Education], June 24–26: 1995.

Oishi, Shunichi. *"Eigo" ideorogî o tou: Seiô seishin to no kakutô* [Questioning the ideology of "English": Struggle with the Western mind]. Tokyo: Kaibunsha Shuppan, 1990.

Oishi, Shunichi. " 'Eigo shihai' shûen ni mukete no kojin teki sônen" [Personal thoughts on the termination of "English domination"]. In *Eigo shihai e no iron* [Oppositions to English domination]. Edited by Yukio Tsuda, 69-118. Tokyo: Daisan Shokan, 1993.

Paikeday, Thomas M. *The native speaker is dead*. Toronto: Paikeday Publishing, Inc., 1985.

Paulston, Rolland G. "Mapping comparative education after postmodernity." *Comparative Education Review*, 43(1999): 438-463.

_____. "Imagining comparative education: Past, present, future." *Compare*, 30, 3(2000): 53–367.

Pennycook, Alastair. *The cultural politics of teaching English in the world*. Unpublished doctoral dissertation. Toronto: Ontario Institute for Studies in Education of the University of Toronto, 1992.

Pennycook, Alastair. *English and the discourses of colonialism*. London: Routledge, 1998.

Phillipson, Robert. *Linguistic imperialism*. Oxford: Oxford University Press, 1992.

Popkewitz, Thomas S. "National imaginaries, the indigenous foreigner, and power: Comparative education research." In *Discourse formation in comparative education*. Edited by Jürgen Schreiwer, 261–294. Frankfurt am Main: Peter Lang, 2000.

Rampton, Ben. "A non-educational view of ESL in Britain." *Journal of Multilingual and Multicultural Development*, 9 (1988): 503–529.

_____. "Displacing the 'native speaker': Expertise, affiliation, and inheritance." *ELT Journal*, 44 (1990): 97–101.

Rockhill, Kathleen and Patricia Tomic. "Situating ESL between speech and silence." In *Gender in/forms curriculum: From enrichment to transformation*. Edited by Jane Gaskell and John Willinsky, 209–229. New York: Teachers College Press, 1995.

Spivak, Gayatri Chakravorty. *The postcolonial critic: Interviews, strategies, dialogues*. New York: Routledge, 1990.

Spivak, Gayatri Chakravorty. *Outside in the teaching machine*. New York: Routledge, 1993.

Suzuki, Takao. *Eigo wa iranai!?* [We don't need English!?]. Tokyo: PHP *Kenkyûjo*, 2001.

Tai, Eika. "Kokugo and colonial education in Taiwan." *Positions: East Asia Cultures Critique*, 7 (1999): 503–530.

Tikly, Leon. "Postcolonialism and comparative education." *International Review of Education*, 45 (1999): 603–621.

Tsuda, Yukio. *Eigo shihai no kôzô* [Structures of English domination]. Tokyo: Daisan Shokan, 1990.

Tsuda, Yukio. "Eigo shihai e no chôsen joron" [Introduction to challenges against the domination of English]. In *Eigo shihai e no iron* [Oppositions to English domination]. Edited by Yukio Tsuda, 13–68. Tokyo: Daisan Shokan, 1993.

Yasuda, Toshiaki. *Teikoku nihon no gengo hensei* [Linguistic organization of the Imperial Japan]. Yokohama: Seori Shobô, 1997.

Widdowson, Henry. "The ownership of English." *TESOL Quarterly*, 28 (1994): 377–388.

The class recently opened its door to students who want to become licensed to teach Japanese. I no longer teach this course but I have heard no complaint from these students that the current instructor speaks no Japanese.

CHAPTER 7

Making the Twenty-First Century Quality Teacher: A Postfoundational Comparative Approach

MARIANNE LARSEN

The Bush administration agenda for a quality teacher in every classroom begins by claiming that "every child in America deserves a quality teacher. In an era of increasing standards and accountability in education, teacher quality and teacher training will be more important than ever" (U.S. Federal Government 2002, p. 5). Elsewhere in the English-speaking world, education policymakers have paid similar close attention to the idea of forming a high quality teaching profession as the basis for reforming education systems (Alberta 1999; Commonwealth Department, 2000; DfEE, 1998, 2001; New Zealand, 1999b; Ramsey, 2000). These contemporary commitments to revitalize and modernize the teaching profession — to create the quality teacher — mark a shift in the ways that we write, speak, and think about teachers and teaching.

This chapter provides a comparative study of the discursive construction of the teacher in a variety of English-speaking countries including Australia, Canada, England, Scotland, New Zealand, and the United States, at the start of the twenty-first century.[1] A set of reforms is examined: the establishment of professional and ethical standards, teacher testing, performance appraisal, and mandatory professional development schemes, and the collection of data about teachers by registration boards. While there are some differences in form between these policies and in local 'take-up' across the countries studied here, the main argument is that they all function as regulatory technologies to create and govern the teacher as a transparent, calculable, performing, and self-governing subject.

Post-Foundational Aims

"Each time I have attempted to do theoretical work it has been on the basis of elements from my experience, always in relation to processes that I saw taking place around me. It is because I thought I could recognize in the things I was, in the institutions with which I dealt, in my relations with others, cracks, silent shocks, malfunctionings . . . that I undertook a particular piece of work, a few fragments of autobiography." (Foucault 1988, p. 156)

Box 1:
March 2002

Dear Linda,

I have thought long and hard about the choice that the Toronto District School Board has put before me: to return to secondary school teaching in September or tender my resignation. It is with regret that I feel there is little option but for me to resign my teaching position. I cannot foresee completing my dissertation before September, which is my present goal. If there is anything else that I need to do, please let me know. Thank you again for taking the time to send me the e-mail, as I know this is an extremely busy time of the year for you. Please give my best regards to my colleagues in the history department and let them know of my decision.

Sincerely,
Marianne Larsen

There are three broad post-foundational aims to this multidimensional study. The first aim is to challenge assumptions concerning what counts as data, objectivity, reliability, and validity in comparative research. The chapter stems from three sets of experiences: as a secondary school teacher, a doctoral student in comparative education, and a university tutor. The auto-biographical, the anecdotal, and the academic, merge in this narrative as they have within me. Thus, in writing this chapter, I am responding to Lather's call for "an interrogative text which reflects back at its readers the problems of inquiry at the same time as an inquiry is conducted, striking the epistemological paradox of knowing through not knowing, knowing both too little and too much" (Lather 1997 in Morgan 2002, p. 209). When referring to my experiences as a secondary school teacher alongside other texts and secondary data, I aim to explore my responses to the different ways in which the teacher has been discursively constructed and controled (see Box 1, for example), while remaining reflective about the social implications of foundational approaches to comparative research.

The second aim is to demystify how it is that we have come to view teachers and teaching in the ways that we do at this particular historical moment. The chapter questions what it means to be a teacher by shaking up our assumptions about the nature of concepts such as quality, accountability, and performance. There is nothing natural or necessarily neutral about the standards approach to improving education systems. Within the countries under study, accountability and performance-driven education policies and processes have come to be seen as not only *the most efficient* means to raise student outcomes, but the *only* mechanisms to reform education systems. In turn, the quality of teachers and student achievement scores have become inextricably linked to one another. By calling into question the sole association of teaching with quality, accountability and performance, I aim to contest those limits of how we think, speak, and act toward teachers and open new discursive spaces to this end.

The final aim of this chapter is to suggest alternative ways of thinking about the relationship between power, knowledge, and the subject. The productive and integrated nature of power and knowledge, and how identities and entire selves or subjects are socially and historically constructed informs the conceptual framework of this post-foundational research. This is not a comparative analysis of the similarities and differences of education policy reforms, nor a study of socialization processes, but rather an analysis of *how* teachers have come to be constituted as objects of knowledge and targets of power through a set of regulatory technologies.

These two ideas mirror the two aspects of the subject discussed here. The first draws our attention toward the ways that have made it possible for the teacher as subject to become an object of knowledge to herself and to others. The focus is therefore on the systems of reasoning, rules, and standards by which the meaning of the concepts 'teacher' and 'teaching' have been constructed. The second aspect of the term subject relates to the notion of being subjected to someone or something through a set of discursively constituted regulatory power/knowledge technologies.

Technologies are all of the processes, procedures, actions, and apparatuses that are utilized to make and govern individuals. This chapter focuses on the link between external technologies and technologies of the self, within which power and knowledge operate to produce the teaching subject. The former are the methods and techniques used by others to shape and make the subject; the latter permits individuals to operate on their own bodies, souls, thoughts, conduct, and ways of being in order to govern and transform themselves (Foucault 1994, pp. 224–225). Through these dual subjectification processes, the teacher is transformed into a divided, accountable, performing, and self-governing subject.

The Quality Teacher as a Professional and Ethical Subject

Assessment and accountability measures have been fundamental to reform efforts to create a high-quality teaching profession. Teacher assessment, according to the World Bank, is now "central to modern education systems" (World Bank 2001, p. 5). Hence, governments have become preoccupied with determining not only what quality means, but with how teaching quality can be quantified.

Box 2:
To Do List - April 2002 - Pay $105
Ontario College Teachers' Fee

Procrastinating about paying my registration fee to the OCT. Ostensibly a self-regulating, professional body, I still view it as yet another means by which the government controls and regulates my profession. Yet how to sift out the difference between autonomous professional accountability and external control? Does it really matter who or what controls my profession, setting the standards for appropriate behavior both within and outside of the classroom? I recall receiving the Standards of Practice booklet from the College two years back. It didn't seem to have any direct impact on my daily teaching routine. Yet, I can see now that this document is central to the entire process of ensuring that teachers in Ontario remain accountable to their students and to the public at large. Still, I wonder if quality can be best ensured through the process of strictly defining what it means to be a teacher.

Quantifying quality means translating the notion of quality into a set of measurable professional and ethical standards. Professional teaching standards and codes of ethics documents address the issue of teacher quality, nationally in Australia, England, New Zealand, and the United States; and within the Canadian provinces of Alberta, British Columbia, and Ontario, and the Australian states of Victoria and Queensland (Australian College, 2001; Australian College, 2002; Alberta, 1997; Australian College, 2001, 2002; National Board, 2003; New Zealand, 1999b; Ontario, 2000a; Teacher Training, 2002b; Victorian, 2002).[2]

The development of teaching standards has been a part of the larger shift toward accountability within educational systems. In most cases, teaching councils, such as the Ontario College of Teachers that I refer to in Box 2, have been mandated by government legislation to develop standards documents for newly qualified and experienced teachers. The assumption behind the statutory formation of teaching councils is that teachers on their own have been unable to modernize their profession, and therefore require the state's assistance to develop and set out the terms for self-regulation. Mandated standards and codes of ethics documents therefore act as technologies for the self-governing of the profession, by claiming to allow teachers to demonstrate their own professional status to others and raise the status of their profession through conformity to 'self-imposed' standards (Smyth and Dow, 1998; Ramsey, 2000).

Box 3:
Strikes and Standards
30 March 2002

During the Fall of 1997, teachers across the province of Ontario stopped working. We were protesting the government's new 'Education Quality Improvement Act,' which we felt did little to ensure quality, and did a lot to regulate and control what happens in the classroom. Not surprisingly, the press was largely unsympathetic to our demands. I realized that the quality teacher who cares for and is committed to her pupils is not supposed to go on strike. Reminded of those days picketing outside my school by a report I heard on the BBC today. Estelle Morris, England's Minister for School Standards, told delegates at the National Union of Teachers' conference that calling for strikes would damage teachers' relations with pupils and parents. After being warned that strike action would lower the public standing of the profession, one teacher responded, 'It is no good Estelle Morris telling us off like naughty schoolchildren.'

Professional standards are generally defined around sets of taken-for-granted propositions or dimensions of teaching: commitment to student learning and motivation, and professional development; classroom management; knowledge of subject matter, teaching practice/methods, and assessment mechanisms; demonstration of leadership, cooperation with colleagues and contributions to the wider community. Codes of ethics documents specify the correct relationships and commitments that teachers are to maintain with students, parents, guardians, principals/head teachers, other colleagues, and the community at large (General Teaching Council, 2002a, 2002b; Ontario College, 2000a; Wellington, 1999). Hence the act of teaching is constituted by a set of techno-rational standards, and the teacher through a set of carefully prescribed ethical assumptions.

Agreement over standards that appear to be self-evident is translated into professional norms that guide behaviors and practices. For instance, the standard that quality teachers have high expectations of their pupils, and are committed to their students and their learning, generates particular principles of action and inaction. Such judgments act as effective mechanisms ensuring teachers' willingness to work additional hours after school and on weekends, to conform to standardized curricular requirements, and to support the testing of pupils as the most effective means to raise educational standards. Moreover, such standards, as Box 3 illustrates, also constrain actions such as strikes and other forms of work to rule.

These standards enclose the quality teacher within a particular discursive space that both enables and constrains professional and ethical actions. While the standard that teachers cooperate with their colleagues may enable fruitful dialogue and relations between colleagues, the standard that teachers must demonstrate leadership skills could possibly act to constrain professional relations. The point is that standards as technologies are productive. They produce a particular type of teacher, but not through external threats and disciplinary action. Rather, the internalization of norms defining the professional and ethical teacher is usually sufficient to ensure acceptance and compliance.

Assessing the Quality Teacher

Decisions that are made regarding teaching standards form the basis by which teachers can be assessed and made accountable throughout their career. Teachers are now required to demonstrate that they have reached or surpassed the appropriate standards in order to be trained, certified, licensed, appraised, and promoted throughout their careers. While in most cases (for example, Australia, Canada, New Zealand, and the United Kingdom), teachers are assessed and made accountable from the time they begin their training, in a few telling examples from the United States, teacher assessment begins *before* training commences. In these cases, accreditation and/or state funding of teacher training institutions is dependent upon the assessment of candidate's skills prior to admission. These mechanisms are put in place to control entry of candidates, and to ensure that only those capable of passing exit certification examinations will be admitted into training, guaranteeing successful completion before training commences (American Federation 2000; National Council 2002).

While the testing of candidates prior to training remains the exception rather than the rule, mandatory testing of newly trained teachers for licensing and certification purposes has become common practice, and in many countries is big business. Forty-two U.S. states, a few Canadian provinces, and England all report the use of a written assessment at some point in the certification and licensing of new teachers (Daley 1999, p.1–4; National Research Council 2001, p. 50; Ontario Provincial 2002a).[3]

There are three general categories of tests: ready-made, standardized tests administered by a private agency; standardized tests that have been customized for use by a particular educational jurisdiction; and those that combine the first two approaches. Licensing tests are generally administered immediately after the first induction or qualifying year of teaching. These multiple choice/short answer, paper and pencil assessments are designed to provide information about the extent to which prospective teachers possess the skills and knowledge considered appropriate for the beginning teacher. In some cases, beginning teachers are tested to ensure competence in basic literacy and numeracy skills (for example, in England

and California) for full entry into the profession. Other jurisdictions, such as Ontario, Texas, and Massachusetts test new teachers' knowledge of curriculum subjects and teaching strategies, including communication and classroom management skills (Hextall and Mahony, 2001, p. 222; National Research Council, 2001, pp. 45; Ontario Provincial, 2002a; Teacher Training Agency, 2002a).

Box 4:
Teachers and Testing in Texas

In 1994–95, I spent a challenging and very rewarding exchange-year, teaching high school in El Paso. Most of the time was spent preparing students for tests, one after another throughout the year. At the end of the year, the principal, facing a teacher shortage, urged me to stay. Texas has been testing teachers since the 1980s. If I had decided to stay, I would have had to write a qualifying test to assess my knowledge and basic skills. As well, since the 1980s, classroom teachers have had to write basic-skills tests in Texas. Other jurisdictions have more recently followed Texas' lead and implemented standards-based teacher tests, for both new and in some cases qualified teachers. I decided to return to Ontario to teach, where up until recently, teacher testing has only been a south of the border phenomenon.

Once licensed and certified, teachers continue to be governed throughout their careers, through standards-based, high stakes testing. Texas, as Box 4 shows, has led the way in testing teachers and claims to be the heartland of high stakes testing. Experienced teachers are tested in some U.S. states to maintain certification, earn additional pay, and other professional rewards such as promotions. Targeted testing of teachers in low performing schools as a strategy to raise student test scores has also occurred across some states (Daley, 1999, p. 1; Hickok and Poliakoff, 1999).

Examinations act as technologies of power to construct and govern the accountable teacher. They and other forms of assessment (discussed below) yield 'truths' about teachers, which place them in hierarchies, organized around the idea of quality teaching. Through these tests, teachers can be compared, judged, measured, and ranked against one another. Information about them is recorded and published in the popular press, government policy reports, academic publications, and the Internet. Tests provide not just information about what the teacher knows, but also information about teachers and teaching. Through these testing technologies, the teacher as object is constructed as a knowable and hence governable subject.

The Quality Teacher as Performer

While testing experienced teachers remains the exception rather than the rule, other accountability mechanisms exist to assess the classroom teacher. While the culture of performance is perhaps most highly visible in England and the United States, other English-speaking countries have also embraced, to varying degrees, the business world paradigm of performance. The overlapping combination of standards-based assessment mechanisms, including tests, self, peer and other external forms of appraisal, performance-related pay schemes, mandatory professional development schemes, and inspections (in the case of England), create an all-encompassing and perpetual performance ethos within school systems. Within this twenty-first century classroom the teacher is reconstructed as a performer.

Performance appraisals, based on professional standards discussed above, have become a persistent part of teachers' lives within the countries examined for this study. A look at three pay-for-performance schemes reveals that despite differences in orientation, they all function as regulatory technologies to shape and define teachers as always ready-to-be accountable performers. The recently established teacher performance appraisal system in Ontario includes pre- and post-observation meetings between the teacher and principal, classroom observation, a review of parental and student input, and the completion of a summative report. While each teacher must have an evaluation every three years, principals may choose to conduct appraisals in addition to those required under the legislation at any time throughout the teacher's career (Ontario Provincial, 2002b).

Performance appraisals are high-stakes. Following an unsatisfactory appraisal rating in Ontario, the principal must explain to the teacher what is lacking in and expected of his or her performance, and prepare a written improvement plan. After two unsatisfactory appraisals, the teacher is put on review status during which a third appraisal is conducted. If that last appraisal is also unsatisfactory, then the principal must recommend termination of the teacher's employment to the board of education (Ontario 2002b).

In other jurisdictions, unsatisfactory teacher performance appraisals can lead not only to termination of contracts, but also provide a barrier to increases in salary. New Zealand and England differ in approach toward performance-based pay; the former is a locally-based model, while the latter is more centralized. The annual assessment procedure in England is based on centrally determined threshold standards that are used to demonstrate high-quality teaching and commitment to professional development. The teacher that performs correctly will reach the performance threshold, and enter the new upper pay range (DfEE 1998, pp. 31–37). In New Zealand, accountability is located at the local level, with staff and senior management generating their own context-specific performance indicators and methods for collecting information. Like Ontario, all school-staff undergo annual performance appraisals, which include observation of teaching, self-appraisal, and an appraisal interview. A variety of other mechanisms can also be used, including peer appraisal, parent and student feedback, students' performance results, and documentary evidence (New Zealand Government, 1999a). While performance-related pay schemes differ in approach in these two educational settings, in both cases normalization technologies determine and standardize the type of teacher who will successfully reach the performance threshold or upper pay scale.

Box 5:
Stress and Teaching in the Inner City London
February 2002

Supply teaching in London has given me some new insight into the stresses that teachers face. In my ten years of teaching, I have never come across more stressed out, demoralized and discouraged teachers. Performance appraisals are viewed with cynicism, resulting in another mandatory, massive load of additional paperwork to reach the performance threshold. Being forced to comply with preparing lesson plans two weeks in advance for the inspectorate, and spending time that doesn't exist complying with other administrative expectations, exhausts and frustrates teachers that are already overworked. I don't need to read the research that's out there revealing how teachers perceive a lack of control and ownership over their work, frustration with low levels of trust, autonomy and meaningful consultation, and increased levels of stress and tension. I can see it for myself, especially in the schools that rank low in the league tables. Given the constant stream of new accountability demands that teachers have faced over the past 15 years, it doesn't surprise me at all that England, like many other countries, faces an enormous teacher shortage.

Performance appraisals place many new demands on teachers' daily working lives. There is much evidence to suggest, both anecdotal (see Box 5) and that which is more 'academic' (Fitzgerald 2001; Jeffrey & Woods, 1998; Travers and Cooper, 1996; Troman, 2000, Smyth and Dow, 2000; Storey 2000) that these reforms have left teachers feeling more demoralized, stressed, and under pressure.

A look at expectations concerning lesson planning reveals how productivity and perform-ativity is now quantified and measured. Teachers in England are provided with clear guidelines outlining how lesson plans are to be organized and presented, and even encouraged to download ready-made weekly plans from authorized Internet sites to this end. One teacher, interviewed for a nationwide workload study, admitted to developing two separate lesson plans: an 'official' plan downloaded from the Internet for the school planning files, and her other personal daily lesson plans which she used for her own teaching (Larsen, 2002). While teachers interviewed for the workload study generally regarded planning as being essential to good teaching, many viewed the additional detailed paperwork "in large part documentation required by others rather than something that supported their own teaching" (PricewaterhouseCoopers 2001, p. 23). Such dual practices create a teacher who must always be one step ahead of the appraisal process, neglecting their own teaching in order to provide documentation of the performance standards required for potential external evaluation.

In this way, plans are not necessarily for the teacher's own classroom use, nor are they strategies conducive to 'good' teaching practice. The crucial point is that the quality teacher is not someone who plans, but someone who can *demonstrate*, in an appropriate way, that they plan and perform correctly. Those who are unable to demonstrate that they fit into the appropriate, measurable model are denied entry, sanctioned, or prevented from passing through the various "gateways" of their profession (Hextall and Mahony, 1999, p. 2).[4]

In the quest to measure quality teaching, performativity provides information about teachers. In this new regime of truth, form and style of lesson plans take precedence over content, as teachers begin to internalize the expectation that planning is as, if not more, important as teaching. As Popkewitz found in his study of the 'Teach for America' program, "The technologies of the lesson plan 'make' sense because of the grid around which the 'reason' of the teaching practice is normalized…The lesson plan ordered and divided the capabilities of the teacher who [is] administered" (Popkewitz, 1998, p. 83). Hence, teaching is constructed as a process of efficiently planning and managing time, rather than engaging in meaningful knowledge production.

The Quality Teacher as Lifelong Learner

Traditionally, the production of knowledge has been one of the teacher's main roles. Today, teachers' employment and promotion are still to a large degree based on the knowledge that they possess and are able to impart to their students. According to the English document 'Professionalism and Trust — the future of teachers and teaching,' the modern professional possesses a body of knowledge about what works best and why, and engages in regular training and development opportunities to keep up to date (DfEE, 2001).

Outside of England, the quality teacher has also been refigured as a lifelong learner, and is similarly exhorted to engage in perpetual professional training to maintain certification (Commonwealth Department, 2000; National Board, 2003; Ontario College, 2000a, 2002b). While the idea of the teacher as a learner is far from new, the difference at the beginning of this century is that the type of knowledge considered most appropriate and how it is to be obtained is much more strictly standardized and defined.

Mandatory and measurable ongoing professional training has become an important part of education reforms within the countries under study here, as well as in Germany, Ireland, Sweden, Switzerland, and Japan. For example, forty-seven U.S. states have mandatory professional development requirements for teacher re-certification; the norm is six semester credits every five years (Ontario College, 2000b, p. 2). Lifelong learning is now an obligation. Hence, teachers' contracts of employment in England include a duty to keep their skills up to date (DfEE, 1998, p. 44).

Some educational jurisdictions allow the teacher flexibility to choose courses best suited to their individual strengths and priorities. In Alberta and Nova Scotia (Canada), teachers are obliged to develop personal plans stating which courses they intend to take to improve their skills, and they need to successfully complete these courses to maintain certification (Fenwick, 2000, p. 1). In England, each new teacher must develop a Career Entry Profile and Individual Learning Account (DfEE, 1998). New York and Ontario law requires teachers to successfully complete a set of professional development courses over a five-year period, in order to maintain certification (Ontario College, 2002b; New York, 1998). These types of activities enable teachers to reflect upon their own learning strengths and priorities and design learning plans that are best suited to individual needs.

Box 6:
12 July 2002

Received a letter from the Ontario College of Teachers today reminding me that the new Professional Learning Programme (PLP) begins in September. To maintain my teaching certificate I have five years to complete the 14-course programme. I'm told that this is not a competency test, but a programme of ongoing professional training. Implicit in that assertion is the assumption that teachers do not engage in professional learning on their own initiative. Yet, I (and nearly all of my colleagues) have consistently throughout our careers, enrolled in additional qualifications courses at night and summer school. I can only select from the list of officially approved courses, most of which are based on curriculum knowledge and practical skills. (These include special education, technology in the classroom, curriculum, student assessment, teaching strategies, communicating with parents and students, and classroom management and leadership.) Moreover, PLP courses must be consistent with Ontario professional standards, contribute to student achievement, and include an assessment component. An M.A. and Ph.D. in Comparative Education do not directly relate to the officially approved course categories, or to raising student achievement scores. In this way, the last few years of my study will not necessarily make me the high-quality teacher that the College expects.

However, while these personal growth plans may appear to be the product of autonomous individuals acting in their own best interest, there is also strong encouragement to engage in learning that can be "demonstrably applied in the classroom" (Ontario College, 2000b, p. 3). In that respect, more clearly defined professional development programs and those that allow teachers to develop their own learning plans, may not be as different as they first appear. In most settings, the scope and type of professional learning considered appropriate for the teacher is mandated directly by the government or through teaching councils. (See Box 6 for a description of Ontario's mandated Professional Learning Programme.)

Professional development programs include outcomes that are linked to improving student achievement, and in the case of England, to salary increases. To reach the performance threshold, teachers in England are expected to meet a set of standards in five areas: knowledge and understanding, teaching and assessment, wider professional effectiveness, professional characteristics, and pupil progress. The latter is defined as a standard whereby teachers show that as a result of their teaching, "their pupils achieve well in relation to their prior attainment, making progress as good or better than similar pupils nationally" (DfES, 2000, p.1).

The fact that professional development courses must include formal assessment means that only explicit and measurable knowledge matters. This techno-scientific paradigm defining what knowledge is valued acts as a regulatory technology. Mandatory professional development schemes construct the teacher as a rational and instrumental technician, able to demonstrate competencies related to the curriculum, teaching strategies, and classroom management techniques. The knowledge that is expected of teachers must be measurable and useful knowledge: knowledge that can raise student achievement scores, and be quantified according to performance standards. The key here as with all of the performance-driven reforms, is that quality has come to be associated most closely with efficiency. Constructing the twenty-first century teacher has more to do with maximizing measurable individual and systemic performativity than with the articulation of any kind of deeper educational values and visions.

The Transparent Quality Teacher

Maximizing educational efficiency also fundamentally depends upon ensuring transparency. From the moment an individual decides to become a teacher, her thoughts and actions are socially organized and managed in a set of infinitesimal principles and practices. Detailed data on teachers is used to compare individuals within and between departments, schools, cities, or countries, and provide proof and measure of performance. The need to know and compile data about the capabilities, interests, goals, and other personal and professional characteristics of the teacher, forms another regulatory technology. As Rose explains:

> To make calculations about a population necessitates the highlighting of certain features of that population as the raw material of

> calculation, and requires information about them…Calculation…
> depends upon the processes of 'inscription,' which translate the
> world into material traces: written reports, drawing, maps, charts,
> and pre-eminently, numbers (Rose 1989, p. 6).

Through transparency technologies, teachers are measured, assessed,
ranked, and divided. And as teachers as objects studied and known, they
are discursively constructed as visible and thus governable subjects.

Professional teaching councils and registration boards play a central
role in the collection of data and monitoring of teacher performance, by
compiling and maintaining registration lists of qualified teachers (General
Teaching Council, 2002a; Ontario College, 2002a; Queensland, 2002; Scottish Executive, 1999).[5] Registration requirements vary but generally
require proof of training, certification, and licensing, and in some cases
prior experience, citizenship, and language abilities. Some registration
boards also require personal letters and other proof attesting to a teacher's
character, fitness, and propriety to teach. For instance, in Queensland, an
applicant for registration must be able to prove that he or she is of good
character. An applicant is not of good character if "he or she behaves in a
way that does not satisfy a standard of behavior generally expected of a
teacher… or otherwise behaves in a disgraceful or improper way that
shows the applicant is unfit to be registered as a teacher" (Queensland,
1997, p. 2).

Teacher registers serve two main purposes. First, they provide a means
by which teachers' qualifications and status can be monitored and tracked.
Secondly, registers act as a mechanism to guard against incompetence and
misconduct in the profession. In this way, the register as a regulatory technology both enables and prevents individuals from teaching, by making
visible those who are qualified and deemed suitable, and those who are
not. In many jurisdictions, criminal checks on all new and registered
teachers are now compulsory practice. Policies to track teachers found
guilty of professional misconduct vary among the jurisdictions surveyed
here. Some registration boards prosecute individuals who claim to be
members of the profession while not registered (for example, South Australia). Others concentrate on investigating cases of registered members
accused of professional misconduct or incompetence and undertaking
prosecutions (Queensland Board, 2002; Ontario College, 2002a; Scottish
Executive, 1999).[6]

Lists of individuals prohibited from teaching, on medical, misconduct
or other grounds, have also been established in a number of jurisdictions.
This information, compiled by police departments, ministries or departments of education, is often shared with teacher registration boards. A few
overseas vetting schemes exist, whereby education employers in different
countries can check information about persons barred from employment
as teachers.[7] This allows teacher registration boards, or professional

teaching councils, to better monitor the "appropriateness" of persons employed as teachers and prevent those accused of crimes such as pedophilia from teaching (Queensland 1997, p. 10).

Most teacher registers are open for public scrutiny.[8] For example, at the Ontario College of Teachers' (OCT) website anyone can find data on each individual teacher's certificates, qualifications, letters of approval held, academic and employment history, and their status with the College. The last section is particularly pertinent, providing a disciplinary mechanism par excellence. A teacher in good standing has registered with the College, paid their annual membership fees and been issued a numbered certificate of qualification. (Box 7 contains my own 2003 membership status, now revoked for not paying fees, a consequence not of negligence, but of taking up a new university position and therefore no longer requiring OCT membership.)

Box 7 Registered Member Information	
Name: Marianne Larsen	**Status:** Suspended - Non-payment of fees
Name History: Larsen, Marianne Achen	**Type:** Certificate of Qualification
Reg. Number: 258110	**Initial College Certification Date:** 03/16/1992

Non-certified members, like myself, fall into a variety of categories: membership that has been canceled, revoked, or suspended for disciplinary reasons or non-payment of fees; or resigned or retired members. Life and death are bound up with certification status, as even deceased teachers are listed on the register. The teacher as data inscribed in a table, numbered and ranked, is made a transparent and calculable subject. The complete and continuous surveillance and tracking of the teacher is made possible by this technology, the web-as-panopticon.

Such technologies slice through the teacher, forming a myriad of identities. In the language of education policy reform, there is no such thing as 'the teacher' any longer, but a series of labels that divide and differentiate the teaching-subject.[9] Furthermore, distinctions are established through professional standards that establish codified, measurable criteria to calibrate and establish difference between teachers. These reforms as technologies individualize while imposing homogeneity on the group. Herein lies the paradox: while contemporary education reforms are concerned with teachers as a group, they simultaneously act to distinguish, divide, and discipline them. Through this process of differentiation, teachers are exhorted to demonstrate how they are better, and hence different from, their colleagues. The contradiction is that there exists simultaneously a foci on difference between individuals, and an insistence on uniformity and conformity (Foucault, 1977). We have moved beyond the mass/individual divide. Individuals, writes Deleuze become "*dividuals,* masses, samples, data, markets or *banks*" (Deleuze, 1990, p. 2).

The Quality Teacher as Self-Governing Subject

Registration boards and teacher registers, testing and performance appraisals provide transparent information about the individual and collective body of teachers. However, the collection of knowledge about teachers is achieved not only through external technologies of power. The teacher, through appraisal interviews, professional development plans, and learning portfolios also contributes to the construction of this data bank and of the self. While these reforms might appear to be empowered products of autonomous and independent individuals, they are better understood as a means to regulate the teacher's own behavior through self-governing practices. Teachers are encouraged to think about themselves as calculating individuals who take account of themselves and "add value" to themselves in order to improve their productivity (Ball, 2003, p. 217). Through these technologies of the self, teachers are exhorted to peer into their own souls to determine gaps and deficiencies that need to be filled. Perfection can never be achieved in the performativity game.

Through this new regime of truth, teachers begin to regulate their own behavior in line with external expectations. In his notion of panoptic surveillance, Foucault shows how invisible and unverifiable power makes the individual self-controlling, as she is conscious of being observed, assessed, and classified. Hierarchical observation as a whole produces power and distributes individuals within its continuous and permanent gaze. Individuals learn to judge themselves as if some external eye was constantly monitoring their performance, encouraging the internalization of the evaluative criteria of those in power, and thereby providing a new basis for control (Foucault, 1977, pp. 170–177; 195–209).

Panoptic power imparts a sense of always being watched, as teachers are subject to normalizing judgments of their students, peers, the principal/head teacher, parents or the inspector. If the gaze of others is felt to be inescapable and continuous, the teacher assumes responsibility for the restrictions of power, becoming a self-managing individual who has learned to internalize the gaze, observe, and govern him or herself. As an English Teacher Training Agency Board member acknowledged, "if your ultimate model is a profession which is of very high status, and achieving very high standards by any kind of international comparisons, then the only appropriate model for that is a very high degree of self-government and self-regulation" (Mahony and Hextall, 2000, p. 28).

Perhaps the word schizophrenic best describes the twenty-first century quality teacher. In this new regime of truth, the teacher must reconcile contradictory practices and principles, such as creating two sets of lesson plans: one to be filed away for future inspection, the other to be used in the classroom. This is the teacher who is expected to engage in the highest of professional relations with her colleagues, while at the same time competing against those same individuals through performance appraisal assessments, and self and peer reviews. This is the teacher who learns that what matters in terms of his/her own professional learning is measurable knowledge confined to classroom teaching and to raising outcomes, while encouraging her own pupils to study for the intrinsic love of learning, an immeasurable but no less important concept.

What is produced by these regulatory technologies is a spectacle of fabrications that is more important than the act of teaching and learning itself. Butler explains: "Such acts, gestures, enactments, generally construed, are *performative* in the sense that the essence or identity that they otherwise purport to express are *fabrications* manufactured and sustained through corporeal signs and other discursive means" (Butler, 1990, p. 136). Yet, according to Ball, these acts of fabrications are paradoxical as they "act and reflect back upon the practices they stand for. The fabrication becomes something to…measure individual practices against" (Ball, 2001a, p. 212). The act of fabrication, and not necessarily the practice it reflects, whether it is the performance appraisal interview, enrolling in a mandatory professional development course or sitting a qualification test, becomes the mechanism by which the individual teacher is constructed and governed.

As rational, reasoning and free individuals, it is difficult to accept that teachers' lives are regulated in such ways. However, the relationship between the free and autonomous subject, power and knowledge must be rethought. The paradox, according to Foucault, is that although it appears as if we are all free in modern society, this is a false autonomy. Our freedom is used as the means by which we exercise power on ourselves (Foucault, 1980, p. 98). Rose extends Foucault's hypothesis on power to illustrate the relationship between freedom and government. Challenging the foundationalist divide between freedom and government, Rose argues that freedom is not the opposite of governing, but one of its inventions and resources: "When it comes to governing human beings, to govern is to presuppose the freedom of the governed. To govern humans is not to crush their capacity to act, but to acknowledge it and to utilize it for one's own objectives" (Rose, 1999, p. 4).

Concluding Comments

Taken together, professional development courses, licensing and certification tests, registers and other divisions in status and rank, self and external assessment mechanisms — constitute a powerful set of technologies to govern and reshape the nature of teachers and teaching. Moreover, at the heart of these technologies, professional and ethical standards work to define and discipline the teacher. The U.S. government promise to guarantee a quality teacher in every classroom by 2005/06, signals that one commentator suggests is a "paradigm shift in our thinking about how we get the teachers we need" (Poliakoff, 2002, p. 1). Others have similarly noted how these education policy trends point to a profound shift in how we think about the teachers and teaching. As Ball writes, through these reforms, teachers are "*thought of* and characterised in new ways... [w]hat it means to be a teacher is fundamentally reconstituted in all this" (Ball, 1999, p. 8).

The emphasis in this comparative analysis has shifted to the effects of a set of regulatory technologies to reshape and govern the twenty-first-century teacher. How these reforms work themselves out on the ground differs from one place to another. Yet, while there are differences between and within the United States, Canada, New Zealand, Australia, and the United Kingdom in terms of how standards and accountability reforms have been established and implemented, the argument is that they function to create the teacher as a self-governing, visible, and calculable subject. And while others before me have argued that this is a struggle for the soul of the teacher (Ball, 1999, 2001b; Popkewitz, 1998; Rose, 1989), I would go further by asserting that this is a struggle for the whole of the teacher.

Two general categories of technologies have been reviewed in this chapter: external and internal. Through the latter, teachers internalize normative expectations and learn to self-govern, becoming the effect of power and at the same time, the element of its articulation. Other vehicles of power and knowledge work to constitute and govern the teacher, including principals/head teachers, and parents. However, this is not to say that the state has abandoned its efforts to control the teaching profession. The state, through the training institutions, legislated registration boards, and professional teaching councils, continues to closely govern and regulate the profession. In this new regime of truth, the disposition toward surveillance ensures the constant replaying of control and regulation. The combination of reforms discussed in this chapter comprise what Deleuze calls societies of control, where there is a sense of being never finished with anything, of "limitless postponements," continuous networks, permanence and perpetuality (Deleuze, 1990, pp. 2–4).

Within these societies of control, standards-based reforms such as performance appraisals, self-assessments, and teaching registers must be reconsidered as technologies of the self, whereby the teacher internalizes the gaze of the other, accepting the self-evident link between professionalism, accountability, and quality. In order for high-quality teaching standards to work, teachers must come to accept these reforms as a necessary element of professionalism. As the Australian Parliament's report *A Class Act* explains: "Without standards, a professional body is defenseless. A demonstrated ability to articulate standards for high-quality practice is an essential credential if a professional body wishes to be taken seriously by the public and policymakers" (Commonwealth Government, 1998, p. 4).

Such assumptions make it difficult to question critically these seemingly objective, benign, and neutral tools for teacher professionalization. However, this chapter has argued that standards-based education reforms govern and construct the teacher as a performing, transparent accountable subject. They are not always harmless suggestions to modernize or revitalize the profession. Self and external technologies function to intern and enclose the teacher within a particular set of normalizations that structure how we think, speak, and act toward the teacher. New, alternative spaces for envisioning teachers and teaching are opened up by making visible the rules and standards by which the twenty-first-century teacher is being re-made. This chapter therefore is an attempt to contest how we come to think, speak, and act toward the teacher and call into question those taken-for-granted possibilities of knowing.

Box 8
E-mail from my Principal after informing her of my decision to resign.

Dear Marianne,

I am heart-broken to hear of your decision. I wish I could think of something else but I am at a loss!!!! You have worked so hard and are so close, I understand completely your priorities. I just wish I could do SOMETHING!!!!!! If this is your decision, you will be truly missed. Although you were only here a short time, you gained my admiration, Marianne. You know that I would love to have you back, but some things are beyond my control.

Linda

Where am I positioned in this account? I left my career as a secondary school teacher, partly in protest over the regulatory nature of contemporary education reforms in the province of Ontario, and partly because I was unable to maintain the façade of fabrication. The final box on this page speaks to the diffuse ways that power now circulates in this new regime of quality, standards, accountability and control, and reminds me of the difficulty I had in making my decision to leave teaching and the consequences of that decision on others and myself.

Education reforms, like all disciplinary technologies, produce regimes of truth and subjects. The process of truth production is both enabling and constraining. While some of the enabling aspects of these reforms have been noted in this chapter (personal development learning plans to enable professional development, teaching registers to enable the tracking of pedophiles), much of the emphasis has been on the constraining elements. The constraining aspects of these technologies forced me to reconsider my own position within the teaching profession. My own experiences as a teacher have produced a reaction no less real, objective, valid, or 'true' than any other that I have come across in my 'academic' research on this topic.

Just as I cannot step out of my role as a teacher to write this 'academic' chapter, nor can I remove myself from the traditions of the field of comparative education. My experiences as a secondary school teacher, comparative education student, and university tutor influence how I think and write about teachers. Nealon writes that the key to a different logic is "the double necessity of working from within the institutional constraints of a tradition even while trying to expose what that tradition has ignored or forgotten" (Nealon, 1993 in Lather, 2001, p. 5). Lather calls this a "double(d) science" as both critique and complicity; a way to move beyond inside and outside (Lather, 2001, p. 5).

In moving beyond from within, I am responding to Broadfoot's call "to make the familiar strange" and challenge the taken-for-granted assumptions embedded in conventional comparative education discourse (Broadfoot, 2002, p. 5). Challenging the borders of intelligibility in conventional research means detaching oneself from some of the foundationalist assumptions outlined above and opening up new presently unimaginable spaces. This chapter is therefore also an attempt to open new paradigmatic possibilities for the field of comparative education research by questioning some of the self-evident certainties of the ways that we think and research the world.

The multidimensional nature of the study, incorporating my own experiences and reflections as a twenty-first-century teacher, derives from an acceptance that we always research and theorize from a socially situated position. This is not simply an issue of abandoning the search for understanding or offering up multiple, relative truths, but questioning how is it that we come to accept something as being true, and suggesting that there may be alternative ways to speak, think, and write about those who call themselves teachers.

Endnotes

1. While I refer to these countries in particular, I regard these processes to be a more widespread trend across Western societies. For instance, similar practices can be witnessed in Mexico, Wales, Northern Ireland and the Republic of Ireland, France, and South Africa.

2. There are two standards-based models: specific and general. The specific model is more prescriptive, outlining specific standards for each subject and grade or age of pupil. The *National Board for Professional Teaching Standards* has adopted this model, which sets out the standards for experienced U.S. teachers. Generic standards, which broadly describe a set of principles that should be present in all teaching regardless of the subject or grade level taught, are much more the norm. These standards have been adopted at the national government level in Australia, New Zealand, and England, and at the provincial/state level in Ontario, Alberta and British Columbia (Canada), and Victoria and Queensland (Australia).

3. Certification and licensing testing in North America is driven by free market principles, with a number of private companies providing off-the-shelf standardized assessments that are sometimes modified for state or provincial needs. The majority of U.S. states use the *Interstate New Teacher Assessment and Support Consortium* generic core standards and assessments as the basis for initial teacher licensing and certification. Additionally, the *American Board for Certification of Teacher Excellence* (ABCTE) was created to streamline and introduce free-market mechanisms into teacher licensing and certification. The ABCTE mainly competes against two other more established private companies: the *National Evaluation Systems* and the *Educational Testing Service* (ETS). The Ontario provincial government has contracted out the services of ETS to provide the first set of tests for new teachers beginning in September 2002.

4. Hextall and Mahony draw upon the notion of 'gateways,' noting that the teacher in England must pass Qualified Teacher Status (the first gateway into teaching), the induction period (the second gateway), and the final gateway of the performance threshold.

5. Teacher registers are maintained in New Zealand, England, Scotland, Ontario and British Columbia (Canada), and in the Australian states of Queensland, Tasmania, South Australia and Victoria, for example. There are no national registration boards in the U.S. and across Australia and Canada.

6. According to the Queensland Board of Teacher Registration, one of the important powers of a registering body is to discipline its registrants "in order to ensure that standards of behavior expected of the relevant profession are upheld" (Queensland, 2002). Details about cases of teachers accused of misconduct or incompetence and the results of the disciplinary inquiries are often made available to the public. The Discipline Committee of the Ontario College of Teachers investigates complaints involving members and takes appropriate disciplinary action. The College website includes details about disciplinary cases that have been fully investigated through a public hearing. A list of members found guilty of professional misconduct is posted on the website, with details of the charge and penalty imposed (Ontario College, 2002a).

7. In the United Kingdom, individuals prohibited from employment as teachers are included on the DfEE's List 99. The New Zealand Teacher Registration Board also maintains a list of former or current teachers convicted of punishable offenses. These lists are shared with other countries.

8. In some cases (such as the General Teaching Council in England), the public can only be informed whether the teacher is registered, while other information on the register is kept confidential. The Board of Registration (Queensland, Australia) provides information about all registered teachers to the public for a nominal fee of $1.

9. To draw upon the terminology used in the countries researched for this chapter, new teachers are labeled as Beginning Teachers, Newly Qualified Teachers, or Associate Members of the Institute of Teachers. Categories used to define classroom teachers include: Experienced Teacher, Leading Teacher Level II and Level III, Qualified Teacher Status (England), Fast-Track Teachers, or in the case of New South Wales an Accredited Practising Teacher (APT) I or II. Those few who become educational and managerial leaders in their schools are differentiated from their lower-ranking colleagues by title, salary, and responsibility. They are named APT III, Advanced Skills Teachers, Mentor, Master and Associate Teachers, and further up the administrative scale — the Department Head or Super-Head, and Principal or Head-Teacher, to name but a few categories of distinction. There are even proposals in the United States to categorize the retired teacher who comes back into the classroom, as the 'Faculty Fellow' or the 'Adjunct Teacher' (Archer, 2001; New Zealand, 1999; Ramsey, 2000).

References

Alberta Provincial Government. *Teacher Growth, Supervision and Evaluation Policy.* Calgary: Queen's Printer, 1999.

American Federation of Teachers. *Building a Profession: Strengthening Teacher Preparation and Induction.* New York: American Federation of Teachers, 2000.

Archer, Jeff. "Teacher Re-Creation." *Education Week* 20, no. 16: 46–50.

Australian College of Educators. *National Professional Summit on Teacher Standards, Quality and Professionalism: A Summary.* Deakin West: June 2001.

———. *Teacher Standards, Quality and Professionalism: Towards a Common Approach. Report of a National Meeting of Professional Educators.* Canberra: Australian College of Educators, April 2002.

Ball, Stephen J. "Global Trends in Educational Reform and the Struggle for the Soul of the Teacher!" *Paper presented at the British Educational Research Association Annual Conference,* University of Sussex, Brighton, September 2–5, 1999.

———. "Performativities and Fabrications in the Education Economy: Towards the Performative Society." In *The Performing School: Managing Teaching and Learning in a Performance Culture.* Edited by Denis Glesson and Chris Husbands, 210–26. London: Routledge/Falmer, 2001a.

———. 'The Teacher's Soul and the Terrors of Performativity.' *Journal of Education Policy,* 18 (2003): 215-228.

Broadfoot, Patricia. "Editorial: Structure and Agency in Education: The Role of Comparative Education." *Comparative Education* 38, no. 1 (2002): 5–6.

Butler, Judith. *Gender Trouble.* London: Routledge, 1990.

Commonwealth Department of Education Science and Training. *Teachers for the 21st Century — Making the Difference.* Canberra: Queen's Printer, 2000.

Commonwealth Government of Australia. *A Class Act.* Canberra: Queen's Printer, 1998.

Daley, Pat. *A Report on Teacher Testing.* Toronto: Ontario Secondary School Teachers' Federation, 1999.

Deleuze, Gilles. "Society of Control." *L'Autre journal* 59, no. 1 (1990): 1–4.

Department for Education and Employment. *Teachers: Meeting the Challenge of Change.* London, 1998.

Department for Education and Skills. *Professionalism and Trust — the Future of Teachers and Teaching.* 30. London, 2001.

———. *Threshold Standards: Proposed Handling of Analysis of Pupil Progress.* London, 2000.

Fenwick, Tara. "Teacher-Directed Supervision: Manufacturing Selves or Liberating Professional Practice?" *Paper presented at the Annual Meeting of the Canadian Association for the Study of Educational Administration,* University of Alberta, Edmonton, May 2000.

Fitzgerald, Tanya. "Potential Paradoxes in Performance Appraisal." In *Managing Teacher Appraisal and Performance.* Edited by Dave Middlewood and Carol Cardno, 112-24. London: Routledge/Falmer, 2001.

Foucault, Michel. *Discipline and Punish: The Birth of the Prison.* Translated by Alan Sheridan. New York: Vintage, 1977.

———. "Two Lectures: 7 & 14 January 1976." In *Power/Knowledge: Selected Interviews and Other Writings 1972–1977 by Michel Foucault.* Edited by Colin Gordon. New York: Pantheon, 1980.

———. "Practicing Criticism." In *Politics, Philosophy, Culture: Interviews and Other Writings, 1977-1984.* Edited by Lawrence D. Kritzman. New York: Routledge, 1988.

———. "Technologies of the Self." In *Ethics: Subjectivity and Truth.* Edited by Paul Rabinow, London: Penguin, 1994.

General Teaching Council for England. *Code of Professional Values and Practice for Teachers.* London: General Teaching Council, 2002a.

General Teaching Council for Scotland. *Professional Standards and Code of Conduct.* www.gtcs.org.uk 2002b.

Hextall, Ian, and Pat Mahony. "Just Testing? An Analysis of the Implementation of the 'Skills Tests' for Entry into the Teaching Profession in England." *Journal of Education for Teaching* 27, no. 3 (2001): 221–39.

———. "'Modernising' the Teacher." *Paper presented at the European Conference on Educational Research,* Lahti, Finland, September 1999.

Hickok, Eugene W., and Michael B. Poliakoff. "Raising the Bar for Pennsylvania's Teachers." In *Better Teachers, Better Schools.* Edited by Marci Kanstoroom and Chester E. Finn, Jr. Washington, D.C. Thomas B. Fordham Foundation, 1999.

Jeffrey, Bob, and Peter Woods. *Testing Teachers: The Effect of School Inspections on Primary Teachers.* London: Falmer Press, 1998.

Larsen, Dr. Judy. *Presentation at the Institute of Education, University of London on the Pricewater-houseCoopers' Teacher Workload Study.* London: March 19, 2002.

Lather, Patti. "Methodology with/in the Postmodern: Subversive Repetition and Double Science." *Paper presented at the American Educational Research Association,* New York: 1997.

———— "Getting Lost: Feminist Efforts toward a Double(D) Science." *Paper presented at the American Educational Research Association,* Seattle: 2001.

Mahony, Pat, and Ian Hextall. *Reconstructing Teaching: Standards, Performance and Accountability.* London: Routledge/Falmer, 2000.

Morgan, Wendy. "Electronic Tools for Dismantling the Master's House: Poststructuralist Feminist Research and Hypertext Poetics." In *Hypertext* (1999): 207–216.

National Board for Professional Teaching Standards. *What Teachers Should Know and Be Able to Do: Five Core Propositions.* Arlington, V.A.: NBPTS, 2003.

National Council for the Accreditation of Teacher Education. *Professional Standards for the Accreditation of Schools, Colleges, and Departments of Education.* Washington, D.C.: NCATE, 2002.

National Research Council. *Testing Teacher Candidates: The Role of Licensure Tests in Improving Teacher Quality.* Washington, D.C.: National Academy Press, 2001.

New Zealand Ministry of Education. *Teacher Performance Management.* Wellington: Ministry of Education, 1999a.

———— *Professional Standards: Criteria for Quality Teaching.* Wellington: Ministry of Education, August 1999b.

New York State Education Department Regents' Task Force on Teaching. *Teaching to Higher Standards: New York's Commitment.* Albany, New York: State Education Department, 1998.

Ontario College of Teachers. *Ontario College of Teachers Website* http://www.oct.on.ca Toronto: 2002a.

———— *Professional Learning Program.* Toronto: Ontario College of Teachers, 2002b.

———— *Standards of Practice for the Teaching Profession.* Toronto: Ontario College of Teachers, 2000a.

———— *Maintaining, Ensuring and Demonstrating Competency in the Teaching Profession: A Response to the Request from the Minister of Education re: a Teacher Testing Program.* Toronto: Ontario College of Teachers, 2000b.

Ontario Provincial Government. *Ontario Teacher Testing Program.* Toronto: Ministry of Education, 2002a.

———— *Supporting Teaching Excellence: Teacher Performance Appraisal Manual.* Toronto: Ministry of Education, 2002b.

Poliakoff, Michael B. "Walking the Walk of Excellence: American Board Certification for Teachers." *Paper presented at the White House Conference on Preparing Tomorrow's Teachers,* Washington, D.C. (5 March 2002): 1–4.

Popkewitz, Thomas S. *Struggling for the Soul: The Politics of Schooling and the Construction of the Teacher.* New York: Teachers College Press, 1998.

PricewaterhouseCoopers. *Teacher Workload Study.* London: Department for Education and Employment, 2001.

Queensland Board of Teacher Registration. *Board of Teacher Registration Website* www.btr.qld.edu.au. Brisbane: 2002.

Queensland Parliamentary Debates. *Teacher Registration and the Education and Other Legislation Amendment Bill.* No. 14. Brisbane: Queensland Parliamentary Library, November 1997.

Ramsey, Gregor. *Quality Matters — Revitalising Teaching: Critical Times, Critical Choices.* Sydney: Education Department, New South Wales, 2000.

Rose, Nikolas. *Governing the Soul: The Shaping of the Private Self.* London: Routledge, 1989.

———— *Powers of Freedom: Reframing Political Thought.* Cambridge: Cambridge University Press, 1999.

Scottish Executive. *Review of the General Teaching Council for Scotland: Final Report.* Edinburgh: The Scottish Office, June 1999.

Smyth, John and Alistair Dow. 'What's Wrong with Outcomes?' *British Journal of Sociology of Education* 19, no. 1(1998): 291–303.

Smyth, John and Alistair Dow. *Teachers' Work in a Globalizing Economy.* London: Falmer, 2000.

———— "What's Wrong with Outcomes?" *British Journal of Sociology of Education* 19, no. 1 (1998): 291–303.

Storey, Anne. A leap of faith? Performance pay for teachers. *Journal of Education Policy* 15, no. 5 (2000): 509–523.

Teacher Training Agency. *Computerised QTS Skills Test*. London: Teacher Training Agency, 2002a.

Travers, Cheryl L. and Cary L. Cooper. *Teachers Under Pressure: Stress in the Teaching Profession*. London: Routledge, 1996.

Troman, Geoff. "Teacher Stress in the Low-Trust Society." *British Journal of Sociology of Education* 21, no. 3 (2000): 331–53.

U.S. Federal Government. *A Quality Teacher in Every Classroom: Improving Teacher Quality and Enhancing the Profession*. Washington, D.C.: U.S. Department of Education: 2002.

Wellington Ministry of Education. *Professional Standards: Criteria for Quality Teaching*. Wellington: Government Printer, 1999.

World Bank Group. *Global Education Reform*. In http://www1.worldbank.org/education/globaleducationreform/. World Bank, 2001.

CHAPTER **8**

Power and Knowledge in Comparative Perspective: The Lysenko Affair

WILLIAM DEJONG LAMBERT

> When I was studying during the early 1950s, one of the great problems that arose was that of the political status of science and the ideological functions which it could serve. It wasn't exactly the Lysenko business which dominated everything, but I believe that around that sordid affair — which had long remained buried and carefully hidden — a whole number of interesting questions were provoked.
>
> *(Foucault, 1980, p. 109)*

At the close of a conference held at the Academy of Agricultural Sciences in Moscow in the summer of 1948, Trofim Denisovich Lysenko condemned genetics as Western, capitalist, imperialist science and declared his own "Michurinist" approach to the study of evolutionary biology as the only one acceptable for Soviet scientists.[1] Lysenko's speech was edited by Joseph Stalin himself, and afterward genetic researchers in the Soviet Union were forced to renounce their views and engage in self-criticism. The events which followed, including the imprisonment and murder of several genetic researchers in the Eastern Bloc, and the fact that the first courses in genetics weren't offered at universities in the region until the early 1960s (Gajewski, 1990; Kojevnikov, 2000), have caused the "Lysenko affair" to be considered one of the primary examples of the negative effects of communist totalitarianism upon academic research.

To understand Lysenkoism, however, as a manifestation of some dichotomy between ideology and objectivity, is to misunderstand the function of authority. Lysenkoism not only refers to the role of academia and the dynamics of knowledge production during the Stalin era, but it also informs an understanding of the way in which power functioned in the context of Soviet totalitarianism. The implications of this are by no means limited to any given historical or political context.

Laura Engelstein describes the relationship between the scientific community and the state apparatus in the Soviet Union as an "alliance" in which a "reconstituted technological elite was recruited as the system's social and ideological mainstay" (Engelstein, 1994, p. 231). A state ideology, claiming the objective authority of science, produced a situation in which "scientific standards" came to depend upon "Marxism for their own legitimization" (Engelstein, 1994, p. 231). This symbiotic relationship between power and knowledge was established in a context in which law had been criticized as an instrument of class domination. Thus, we are provided with an example in which institutions determining the perpetuation and development of knowledge are enlisted by the state to participate in the consolidation of power, and the legal framework of Western democracy is replaced by the legitimizing power of technological progress. From this perspective Lysenkoism may be understood as a framework with which we may compare methods of coercion within the opposing versions of modernity defining the second half of the twentieth century (Buck-Morss, 2000). Thus, the degree to which capitalist democracy and communist totalitarianism are legitimately perceived oppositionally, is again called into question.

As I describe in my conclusion, the notion of a more complex dispersion of coercion and authority is reinforced by developments in Russia since the downfall of communism. Foucault collapses the dichotomy between ideology and truth (meanwhile indicating the use of the term "scientific" as a synonym for the latter), referring instead to "the effects of truth ... produced within discourses which in themselves are neither true nor false" (Foucault, 1980, p. 118). Once the overtly "ideological" party apparatus had been vanquished, scientists in the Soviet Union came to question whether or not phenomena such as Lysenkoism did not perhaps have more to do with the way in which power had been, and continued to be, structured within the academic community (Gerovitch, 1998, p. 199). Therefore, we see that it was not political coercion, but the production of knowledge itself that was ultimately perceived as problematic.

Background

The first mention of Lysenko comes from an August 7, 1927 issue of *Prawda*, describing the achievements of an agronomist at an agricultural station in Azerbaijan, who had discovered a better way of fertilizing fields without the help of artificial chemicals. The article highlighted Lysenko's humble background, as the son of poor Ukrainian peasant farmers, who had been educated through correspondence courses at the Agricultural Institute in Kiev. The Communist Party's interest at this time in producing a new, anti-intellectual proletarian intelligentsia, is reflected in the depiction of Lysenko as resolving complex agricultural issues on the back of a scrap of paper. The Soviet government also strove to promote "heroes of agriculture" who were concerned with the practical application of scientific principles to food production, as opposed to bourgeois intellectuals only interested in theoretical pursuits (Joravsky, 1970; Amsterdamski, 1989).

Lysenko's advance to the forefront of what ultimately became the struggle between genetics and his own Michurinist theory, took place against the background of the disastrous results of collectivization and a general climate of terror as Stalin consolidated power in the Soviet Union during the 1930s. The first Five Year Plan set extremely unrealistic goals for industrialization, which led to severe famine as the military requisitioned nearly all of the wheat produced on the collective farms for sale on the world market. Pressure was thus put upon biologists to produce effective approaches to alleviating the food-shortages that resulted. Genetics as a science was compromised by the fact that it was actually a legitimate field of research. When Nikolai Vavilov, the leading Soviet geneticist was asked whether or not he could produce improved crop varieties, he replied in the affirmative but cautioned that it would take at least five years to do so. Lysenko meanwhile, recognizing the value of rhetoric over reality within the context of Stalinization, replied that he could do so immediately. Vavilov was arrested in 1940, sentenced to death and died two years later in a prison camp in northeast Siberia (Joravsky, 1970; Medvedev, 1969; Huxley, 1949).[1]

The culmination of the controversy between the geneticists and the followers of Lysenko finally came at the above-mentioned session of the Soviet Academy of Agricultural Sciences. This event became the model for various other ideological discussions in scholarly disciplines, designed to bring them under the control of the Party (Kojevnikov, A., 2000). Surviving the elaborate games of ideology and political maneuvering which took place in the Soviet Union during this period required great nerve as well as the ability to not surrender to justifiable paranoia. Lysenko was helped as a result of an attack by an inexperienced and naïve opponent, Iurii Zhdanov, whose father Andrei Zhdanov was the Politburo member most responsible for implementing the Party program among the artistic and cultural intelligentsia. The younger Zhdanov attacked Lysenko publicly for being insufficiently self-critical[2] and accused him of unnecessarily polarizing the debate between himself and the geneticists. The debate, according to Zhdanov, was not between "Soviet" and "bourgeois" sciences, but rather between two schools of Soviet biology. In response to Zhdanov's attack,

Lysenko appealed to Stalin as a humble, loyal Soviet scientist, unfairly derided by his enemies. Lysenko's appeal impressed Stalin to the degree that not only did he express his dissatisfaction with Iurii Zhdanov (whose father was soon to be purged from the Party and died under mysterious circumstances not long thereafter) (Rossiyanov, 2001), but he also allowed Lysenko to hold a meeting at the Academy from July 31 to August 7, at which Lysenko presented a report 'On the Situation in Soviet Biology,' which Stalin himself edited. The essence of Lysenko's report to the Academy was that there was a dispute in the world of biology (Stalin edited the word "Soviet," as a qualifier of "biology," from his address, possibly to imply that the dispute was universal) (Krementsov, 2000) between materialist, Soviet, Michurinism, and reactionary, idealistic distorters of Darwinism. The latter, according to Lysenko, had led to the development of eugenics, the politics of race, and the culture of imperialism. In his concluding remarks on the last day of the conference, which were subsequently reprinted in *Prawda*, Lysenko declared: "The Central Committee of the Communist Party has examined my report and approved it" (Krementsov, 1997, 2000).

Lysenko's Michurinism

The easiest way of understanding Lysenko's ideas is by examining the content of his attacks upon Western geneticists. Lysenko typically referred to genetics with a combination of epithets, including some combination of the names Weissman, Morgan and Mendel, all scientists who had been fundamental in the development of genetics. As he wrote:

> The bourgeoisie is interested in promoting Weismannism, which assumes a political significance through eugenics and various race theories. Weismannist (Mendelist-Morganist) genetics is a spawn of bourgeois society, which finds the recognition of the theory of development unprofitable because, from it, in connection with social phenomena, stems the inevitability of collapse of the bourgeoisie. Bourgeois society prefers the theory of immutability of the old, of appearance of something new only from recombination of the old or by happy chance. That is why this pseudoscience (was) such a useful tool in Hitler's hands for the promulgation of his monstrous racist theory.
>
> *(Medvedev, 1969, p. 120)*

Aside from the irony of the fact that Lysenko, in this passage, effectively blames Jewish scientists for Nazism, one also recognizes Lysenko's understanding of genetics as merely a scientific justification for bourgeois ideology. Among other things, Lysenko and his followers accused geneticists of "seeking nothing but the exploitation of nature," catering to the interests of "capitalist seed-firms" (Huxley, 1949, p. 46), endeavoring to mystify scientific knowledge in the interests of class oppression, and over-emphasizing natural selection ("survival of the fittest") to excuse the fact that in capitalist societies some people were allowed to live better than others (Fyfe, 1950).

Michurinism was based upon the notion of the inheritance of acquired characteristics. Lysenko insisted that through the application of his grafting techniques, different species could effectively be "taught" to survive in any environment by developing the necessary attributes, which could then be inherited by succeeding generations (Joravsky, 1970; Zirkle, 1949). The implication was that Soviet biologists could direct heredity and control nature for the benefit of the working class. This resulted, among other examples, in attempts to grow watermelons in Siberia and coffee trees in the Tatra Mountains of Southern Poland.

In terms of its depiction of the relationship between humanity and the natural world, Lysenkoism fit neatly into the framework of Marxist ideology[3] and may be understood to reflect aspects of Stalinist ideology as well. As "proof" of his theory that species of plants could be quickly and easily transformed, Lysenko published a photograph (later proven to have been faked) of a tree he had been able to produce, through transmutation, which was actually two species growing as one (Gakewski, 1990). This "natural phenomenon" may be seen to reflect a proposed "political phenomenon," described by Stalin in *Marxism and the National and Colonial Question* with reference to:

> The blossoming of cultures national in form and socialist in content under a proletarian dictatorship in one country, with the object of their fusion into a single, common socialist (both in form and content) culture, with a single common language…
>
> *(Stalin, 1934)*

At other times Lysenko seemed to fashion his ideas to directly challenge the ideological content he understood to exist within the science of genetics. For example, in his speculations concerning the possibility of planting trees to alter the climate of the dry, southern regions of the Soviet Union, he referred to the idea that the trees would cooperate, rather than compete for light and nourishment (Amsterdamski, 1989, p. 11). In fact he even claimed that the weaker trees would sacrifice themselves for the stronger, thus replacing Darwin's idea of natural selection with the notion of the individual sacrificing themselves for the collective good — science according to the dictates of ideology.[4]

Other examples of Lysenko's ideas are however, somewhat more difficult to understand with reference to ideology, and in fact seem to simply be instances of madness. At one point Lysenko was convinced that degeneration in various species was caused by weakness resulting from self-pollination. He sent a message to Jakovlev, the Soviet Agricultural Commissioner, announcing that he had discovered a method for eliminating this "problem" in wheat. Tens of thousands of collective farms were subsequently charged with implementing his approach, which involved over 800,000 peasants being sent out into the fields, armed with tweezers to remove the stamen from every ear of wheat to prevent them from self-pollinating. This project lasted for two years before being abandoned and then forgotten (Medvedev, 1969; Joravsky, 1970; Bikont and Zagorski, 1998).

Opposing Lysenko was fatal. Jakub Parnas was a Polish biochemist and professor at the University of Lwów (L'viv) before the war. During the occupation the Soviets offered him the opportunity to work in Moscow at the Institute of Molecular Biology. This position brought him into contact with Lysenko, whom he had the misfortune of contradicting during a session of the Academy in 1949. After Lysenko stated "*Gienow niet*" ("Genes do not exist."), Parnas lifted his head from the paper he'd been reading and stated "*Kakoj durak. Gieny suszczestwujut*" ("What an idiot. Genes do exist."). The next day, Parnas was visited by members of the NKVD (the Soviet secret police) who brought him to Lubjanka. Parnas was diabetic and his wife attempted to visit him in prison to bring him his insulin, but she was not allowed. Parnas died shortly thereafter (Bikont and Zagorski, 1998).

Science and the State

To understand the disciplinary role of the "scientific" in the context of totalitarianism, it is necessary to take into account the status of the *akademik* and the powerful influence of the notion of progress within the Soviet system. Lenin, when interviewed by H. G. Wells in the Kremlin in 1920, asserted that if life were discovered on other planets the revision to human ideas that would result would end the necessity for revolutionary violence. Science stood for objectivity in the lexicon of revolutionary socialism, and Lenin appealed for a "de-politicized solution" to the question of what constituted proper revolutionary practice, meaning science and technical expertise rather than class consciousness or ideology. For Lenin, ideology was identified with false consciousness, which is what distinguished it from that which he considered "science" to be. Meanwhile, historical materialism was understood as a form of philosophy used to change the world as scientific progress created a new notion of human potential.

Examples of the status of science in the context of Soviet ideology and its utopian possibilities are abundant. Marx's dialectical materialism was a self-styled scientific approach to history. Science fiction became popular in the Soviet Union as writers recorded social fantasies of interplanetary travel and immortality. In the realm of artistic production the Bolshevik

Revolution appropriated the futuristic utopian visions of the Russian avant-garde, elements of which were manifest in Lysenko's ideas as well. Children were christened in honor of the future they were borne into, bearing names such as "*Rebel*," "*Barikada*," and "*Elektrifikatsia*" (Smith, 1998, p. 37). There was also the scientific discourse of economic planning and the technological dynamism of the Space Race. Even Lenin's embalmed body in Red Square could be interpreted as the use of science to stop time and eliminate "historical transience by extending the recent past limitlessly into the future" (Buck-Morss, 2000, p. 71).

This official faith in science, in the context of a violent, authoritarian regime, often had negative consequences. The Party had little tolerance for what ideologues without any formal scientific background considered useless, theoretical debates. Science was forced into servitude as a cog in the machinery of industrialization. Most of the major physics and chemistry institutes were placed under state jurisdiction and forced to submit five-year plans of research that gave sufficient attention to the agenda of "socialist reconstruction" (Josephson, 2000).

This attention had the effect of reinforcing the social status of scientists as high priests, celebrating mass at the altar of materialism, miracle workers conjuring the future. Such a perception was in stark contrast to conditions under the tsarist regime, which had been fearful of modernization as a consequence of scientific advancement. Ironically, however, it was during this period that the paradoxes posed by relativity theory and quantum mechanics were becoming central to the study of physics. Soon scientists were subjected to the opinions of Marxist philosophers who criticized the failure of quantum mechanics and relativity theory to acknowledge class conflict. The outcomes in each discipline were quite different, however the Great Break at the end of the 1920s marks a point past which the biologists would most keenly feel the pressure to conform ideologically (Joravsky, 1961).

Lysenkoism in the West

The history of the Soviet Union has been described as being defined by "the mistake of Columbus," meaning that the Party "set sail" for socialism but instead arrived at Sovietism, thereby "landing Russia in an inverted modernity" (Malia, 1994, p. 15). This upside-down progress can be understood as a result of the attempt to put utopia in power (Heller and Nekrich, 1986) and govern individuals with reference to "the logic of history." Such a context was not particularly suited to the potentially tedious process of scientific inquiry, and helps to explain how it came to be that the ideocratic Soviet partyocracy would willfully isolate themselves from one of the most vital areas of scientific development in the Twentieth Century.

This goes some way toward accounting for the official support for someone who was often regarded by his contemporaries as a charlatan. One of the recurrent obsessions of the Soviet regime was to overtake the West — particularly the United States — a goal which was hindered both by the distance to be traversed, as well as the agonizing pace at which historical development, under the Russia tsars, had proceeded. Lysenko's rhetoric catered to these insecurities:

> Do we have the right to lose two to three years in anticipation of the verification of correct methods carried out on experimental farms? No, we don't have the right to lose even a day!
>
> *(Amsterdamski, 1989, p. 15)*

There were also practical reasons. Lysenko suggested that the problem of potato blight, an important issue in hot, dry climates, such as the southern part of the Soviet Union, had to do with the temperature at which the potatoes matured. He insisted therefore that they should be planted later. The approach recommended by the geneticists on the other hand, involved the selection, transportation, and cultivation of potatoes resistant to the blight. This solution was much more costly, and would have placed unsustainable demands on the Soviet railway system. Also, as absurd as Lysenko's ideas concerning proper cultivation may have been from the scientific perspective, they did not involve the use of artificial fertilizers, and were therefore much less costly, at least in the short term. In the long term, however, the application of Lysenko's methods did great damage to Soviet agriculture, not the least of which was the spread of potato blight to the Central Regions of the Soviet Union where it had previously not existed (Amsterdamski, 1989, p. 15).

It is also important to remember that Lysenko was not the only one to question genetics during this period. In fact, "Mendel-Morganism" was often characterized as being more theoretical than practical, and its adherents more interested in the laboratory than the concerns of individuals. Referring to the devastating effects of the Second World War upon Woronez, a town that changed hands throughout history between Poland and the Ukraine, the director of the Pomiculture Institute, Professor Plesiecki said:

> Our Morganists...occupy themselves with such capitalist problems as how many fruit flies died in Woronez during the war and what effect the war had upon them in terms of genetic transformation. And they occupy themselves with such great problems when our country lies in ruin.
>
> *(Amsterdamski, 1989, p. 14)*

Other academics took advantage of the ignorance and mistrust of the pre-Revolutionary Russian intelligentsia, an attitude characteristic of the post-Revolutionary power-elite. Ambition circumvented the necessity to conform to scientific methods, and dismal results were excused with accusations of sabotage that eliminated rivals. Such an environment was fatal to scientific advancement.

All of this does not account however for the motivations of Lysenko's advocates in places where the stakes of opposition were negligible or non-existent. Michurinist societies were established in France, England, Belgium, Argentina, and Japan. The *Association française des amis de Mitchourine* was particularly active, showing films and organizing lectures on the topic of Michurinism for French agriculturists. It is estimated that in southern France up to five thousand farmers were attempting to apply Michurinist principles under the direction of the Association, and various scientific institutes were engaged in attempting to replicate Lysenko's "experiments." One researcher, in the wake of an unsuccessful attempt to create new varieties of tomatoes using Michurinist principles, wrote in anguish to his colleagues:

> When an army fights one must not lament for those who are wounded or even for those who perish. I live in continual hope, that though I have been wounded, I will still belong one day to the avant-garde.
>
> *(Bikont and Zagorski, 1998, p. 14)*

One of Lysenko's more well-known supporters in the West was British Nobel Prize-winning playwright George Bernard Shaw, author of works such as *Man and Superman* and *Pygmalion*. Shaw was also a well-known socialist, and in 1949 published an article in *The Labour Monthly* entitled 'The Lysenko Muddle.' In this article he attempted to defend Lysenko by linking him to his own metaphysical notion of "Vitalism," which he described as "mystical, intuitive, irrational, poetic, passionate, religious, and Catholic." Shaw's sympathy for Lysenko, motivated by his Socialist politics, provoked derision from prominent Western geneticists, such as Theodosius Dobzhansky. In terms of discursively reaffirming the opposition between communism and capitalism, which the Lysenko controversy can be understood to represent, Shaw referred at the end of his article to the case of Sir Henry Dale, a British biologist who resigned from the Soviet Academy of Science in protest at Lysenko's tyranny. Shaw wrote:

> Sir Henry Dale's resignation of his membership of the Soviet Academy of Science on the Lysenko issue is entirely conscientious and honorable in intention. But the real issue is between the claim of the scientific professions to be exempted from all legal restraint in the pursuit of knowledge, and the duty of the State to control it in

the general interest as it controls all other pursuits. To my old question 'May you boil your mother to ascertain at what temperature a mature woman will die?,' the police have a decisive counter in the gallows. To Lysenko's question 'Can the State tolerate a doctrine that makes every citizen the irresponsible agent of inevitable Natural Selection?,' the reply is a short No. The Yes implied by Sir Henry Dale's resignation is a hangover from the faith of Adam Smith, who believed that God interferes continually in human affairs, overruling them to a divine purpose no matter how selfishly they are conducted by their human agents. Experience has not borne this faith *Laissez-faire* is dead.

(*Shaw, p. 20*)

The reference to "laissez-faire" in the above quote in effect articulates the criticism of order in the West, so often expressed by critics of liberal democracy. It also inadvertently reveals an important misapprehension of the role of the scientist-academic under Stalin. By enlisting the excesses of Nazi scientists as a comparative example, Shaw fails to perceive the more troubling implications of the state "control" of scientific development. The extent to which the authority of the state and the authority of science may be mutually reinforcing — with disastrous results — is what the case of Lysenkoism actually describes.

Just as Lysenko's rise to power had more to do with his utility to the state power apparatus, his decline as well was the result of politics rather than the discrediting of his ideas. Khrushchev supported Lysenko and in 1958 he received the Order of Lenin. However, after a visit to the United States, Khrushchev became enchanted with the notion that corn was the answer to Soviet agricultural problems, referring to it as "the queen of crops" (Heller and Nekrich, 1986, p. 547). In pursuing his corn program, he allowed for the application of agricultural methods derived from genetic research in the United States (Amsterdamski, 1989). Thus, the support Lysenko received came to be increasingly rhetorical rather than practical. Once Khrushchev was gone, Lysenko could only defend himself for so long. An article was produced for publication in *Prawda*, by a number of academics, including Nikolai Nikolaiovicha Siemionov, a Nobel Prize winning physicist and vice-president of the Soviet Academy of Sciences, criticizing Lysenko. The article actually attacked Lysenko primarily in ideological terms, as falsely presenting himself as a Marxist, rather than pursuing what one would think would be the simpler route of exposing him as a quack. Lysenko was able to marshal his last defenders to keep the article from actually being published in *Prawda*, but it did ultimately show up in another Party publication, *Science and Life* (Amsterdamski, 1989). At this point the steps splintered beneath Lysenko on the ladder of power, and he ended up below Moscow, in the considerably less-prestigious position of director of a collective farm. From there he sent periodic reports to the

Brezhnev regime, describing how thanks to his methods, the cows under his care produced more milk every year. This time however his claims were subjected to verification and dismissed as fabrications. Lysenko died in 1976.

Conclusion

When considering the coercive function of knowledge development and the pursuit of progress in the Soviet Union as a replacement for the role of "legality" in Western democracy, it is interesting to take into account the way in which the attitude of the Russian academic scientist has changed since the demise of the Soviet Union. Even well after the Stalin era, the scientific-academic community represented the most articulate and outspoken critics of the regime. This opposition reinforced philosophical assumptions concerning the link between free societies and the free pursuit of ideas. The collapse of the totalitarian state however, entailed a corresponding removal of the generous support to which academics in the Soviet Union had become accustomed. Thus, we now find that the scientific community has gone from being the most vocal supporters of liberal democracy, to being some of the most ardent advocates for a return to communism (Graham, 1998, p. 47).

As for academics in the West, many prominent scientists, such as Nobel Prize winning physicist Steven Hawking, have referred to the positive influence of Marxism on the development of their own ideas (Graham, 1998, p. 10). Whether Hawking is actually referring to "ideology," or simply alternatives recognized in a milieu isolated from the West, is an open question. The infiltration and interference of capitalist democratic governments vis-à-vis academia is by no means undocumented (Simpson, 1998), and the notion of "education as governance" has become a central aspect of post-structuralist analyses in the field of comparative education (Broadfoot, 2000). Thus, developing a fuller understanding, from a historical perspective, of the power-knowledge nexus in the Soviet Union may inform an understanding of this same dynamic existing in institutions of education existing in the context of democratic capitalism.

Two further points should be made in order to provide a fuller understanding of the implications of the "Lysenko affair," in terms of the way in which power functions in academic environments. The first has to do with essentializing the term "ideology" for the purposes of using it as a scapegoat, and the second to do with the establishment of an opposition between ideas that are "true," versus those that are "false," versus the perspective that the production of knowledge is a process in which such categories are constructed. With reference to the former, we may cite the immediate need by academics in the West to shelter Marxism-Leninism from the fallout of Lysenkoism. In *Science and Ideology in Soviet Society*, an edited collection published not long after the replacement of Khrushchev by Brezhnev, Loren Graham wrote:

> We are quite accustomed to saying, for example, that the controversy over Lysenko was a genuine blow to the strength of dialectical materialism. On close examination it becomes clear that the important issues in the Lysenko controversy have no direct connection to dialectical materialism. There is nothing in the formal framework of dialectical materialism about the inheritance of acquired characteristics, intraspecific competition, or the phasic development of plants.
>
> *(Graham, 1967, p. 101)*

The condemnation of Lysenkoism in the exact terms in which it was once perpetuated, reveals that it never was some "ideology" which was at issue in the first place, but rather a more elusive enactment of power.

As for the false opposition between truth and falsity, or rather, scientific objectivity and Lysenkoism, one need only refer to post-Lysenko outcomes in Soviet—not to mention U.S.—agriculture. Not only did the corn fields which compelled Khrushchev to allow for the use of genetic research in Soviet agriculture prove unsuitable to the climate of the Soviet Union, but government subsidization in the United States has introduced its own set of increasingly complex problems (Pollan, 2002). The current conflict between the United States and the European Union over genetically-modified food demonstrates the controversy developing beyond its initial Cold War context, (Leonhardt, 2003), and the "utopian" potential of genetic engineering, as currently described, speaks for itself and requires no citation.

In sum, rather than refer to the interference of "irrational" ideology in otherwise "objective" academic pursuits, we do better to recall the possibility that:

> Whereas myths in premodern culture enforced tradition by justifying the necessity of social constraints, the dreamworlds of modernity, political, cultural, and economic, are expressions of a utopian desire for social arrangements that transcend existing forms. But dreamworlds become dangerous when their enormous energy is used instrumentally by structures of power, mobilized as an instrument of force that turns against the very masses who were supposed to benefit. If the dreamed-of potential for social transformation remains unrealized, it can teach future generations that history has betrayed them. And in fact, the most inspiring mass-utopian projects, mass sovereignty, mass production, mass culture, have left a history of disasters in their wake.
>
> *(Buck-Morss, 2000, p. xi)*

Endnotes

1. Lysenko referred to his theory as "Michurinism" after I. V. Michurin, a Russian agronomist celebrated by the Soviet communists. His motivation for doing so was to gain credibility; even geneticists claimed to be followers of Michurin (Amsterdamski, 1989; Kojevnikov, 2000).
2. The Royal Society tried unsuccessfully to apply international pressure to save Vavilov by appointing him as a member in 1942. When Vavilov was posthumously rehabilitated in 1955, as Lysenko's career was heading into decline, it was revealed that the director of the All-Union Agricultural Institute, appointed by Lysenko, had been working for the NKVD (secret police) and had conducted an investigation against Vavilov (Amsterdamski, 1989, p. 24).
3. For a discussion on the behavioral processes of *kritika i samokritika* ("criticism and self-criticism"), see Alexei Kojevnikov, "Games of Stalinist Democracy: Ideological discussions in Soviet Sciences, 1947–'52." In *Stalinism: New Directions*. Edited by Sheila Fitzpatrick, 2000.
4. For a discussion of the relationship between Soviet Marxism, science and nature, see (Marcuse, 1961, pp. 128–129).
5. Lysenko also believed that Darwin had taken this idea from Malthus, who Marx criticized, along with Darwin, in terms of their analyses of human society Marx did not, however, challenge Darwin's ideas with regard to plants and animals (Amsterdamski, 1989, p. 11).

References

Amsterdamski, Stefan. *O Patologii ycia naukowego: Casus T.D. ysenko*. Warszawa: Niezalenie Oficynie Wydawnicza, 1989.

Bikont, A. and Zagórski, S. "Burzliwe dzieje, gruszek na wierzbie." *Gazeta Wybrocza*, 1998, sobota-niedziela 1–2 sierpnia.

Broadfoot, P. "Comparative Education for the 21st Century." In *Comparative Education*, 2000, 36(3) pp. 357–371.

Buck-Morss, Susan. *Dreamworld and Catastrophe*. Massachusetts: MIT Press, 2000.

Columbia University Oral History Project, Theodosius Dobzhansky Papers, The American Philosophical Society.

Engelstein, Lauren. "Combined Underdevelopment: Discipline and the Law in Imperial and Soviet Russia." *Foucault and the Writing of History*. Edited by Jan Goldstein. Cambridge, MA: Basil Blackwell Ltd., 1994.

Fischer, George, Ed. *Science and Ideology in Soviet Society*. New York: Atherton Press, 1967.

Foucault, Michel. *Power/Knowledge: Selected interviews and other writings, 1972–1977*. New York: Pantheon Books, 1980.

Fyfe, James. *Lysenko Is Right*. London: Lawrence and Wishart, 1950.

Gajewski, Wacaw. "Lysenkoism in Poland." In *Quarterly Review of Biology* 65/4 (1990), 423–434.

Gerovitch, Slava. "Writing history in the present tense: Cold War-era discursive strategies of Soviet historians of science and technology." In *Universities and Empire*. Edited by Christopher Simpson. New York: The New Press, 1998.

Gleason, Gregory. *The Central Asian States: Discovering Independence*. United Kingdom: Westview Press, 1997.

Graham, Loren. "Cybernetics." In *Science and Ideology in Soviet Society*. Edited by George Fischer. Cambridge, MA: MIT Press, 1967.

Graham, Loren. *What have we learned about science and technology from the Russian experience?* Stanford, CA: Stanford University Press, 1998.

Harding, Neil, Ed. *The State in Socialist Society*. Albany: State University of New York Press, 1984.

Heller, Mikhail and Aleksandr Nekrich. *Utopia in Power: A History of the Soviet Union from 1917 to the Present*. New York: Summit Books, 1986.

Huxley, J. *Heredity East and West: Lysenko and World Science*. New York: Henry Schuman, 1949.

Joravsky, David. *The Lysenko Affair*. Cambridge: Harvard University Press, 1970.

Joravsky, David. *Soviet Marxism and Natural Science, 1917–1932*. New York: Columbia University Press, 1961.

Josephson, Paul. "Stalinism and Science: Physics and Philosophical Disputes in the USSR, 1930–1955." In David-Fox, Michael and György Péteri Eds. *Academia in Upheaval: Origins, Transfers, and Transformations of the Communist Academic Regime in Russia and East Central Europe.* Conn., London: Bergin and Garvey, 2000.

Karpovich, Michael. *Imperial Russia, 1801–1817.* New York: Henry Holt and Company, 1959.

Kojevnikov, Aleksander. "Games of Stalinist Democracy: Ideological Discussions in Soviet Sciences, 1947–'52." In Fitzpatrick, Sheila, Ed. *Stalinism: New Directions.* London, New York: Routledge, 2000.

Krementsov, Nikolai. *Stalinist Science.* Princeton: Princeton University Press, 1997.

Krementsov, Nikolai. "Lysenkoism in Europe: Export-Import of the Soviet Model." In David-Fox, Michael and György Péteri Eds. *Academia in Upheaval: Origins, Transfers, and Transformations of the Communist Academic Regime in Russia and East Central Europe.* Conn., London: Bergin and Garvey, 2000.

Leonhardt, David. "Talks Collapse on U.S. Efforts to Open Europe to Biotech Food." *The New York Times.* www.nytimes.com. Downloaded June 20, 2003.

Malia, Martin. *The Soviet Tragedy: A History of Socialism in Russia, 1917–1991.* New York: The Free Press, 1994.

Marcuse, Herbert. *Soviet Marxism: A Critical Analysis.* New York: Vintage Books, 1961.

Medvedev, Z.A. *The Rise and Fall of T.D. Lysenko.* New York: Columbia University Press, 1969.

Pollan, Michael. "When a Crop Becomes King." *New York Times.* July 19, 2002, A17.

Rossiyanov, K. "Stalin as Lysenko's editor: Reshaping political discourse in Soviet science." The Department of the History of Science: Johns Hopkins University, 2001.

Shaw, George Bernard. "The Lysenko Muddle." *The Labour Monthly,* 31/1, 18–20, Jan. 1949.

Simpson, Christopher, Ed. *Universities and Empire: Money and politics in the social sciences during the Cold War.* New York: The New Press, 1998.

Smith, Martin, G. *Language and power in the creation of the USSR (1917–1953).* Berlin, New York: Morton de Gruyter, 1998.

Stalin, Joseph. *Marxism and the national and colonial question: A collection of articles and speeches.* New York: International Publishers, 1934.

Stalin, Joseph. "Marxism and Linguistics." In Franklin, B., Ed. *The Essential Stalin: Major theoretical writings, 1905–1952.* New York: Doubleday, 1950.

Taras, Raymond. *Ideology in a socialist state.* Cambridge, U.K.: Cambridge University Press, 1984.

Vaingurt, Julia. "Base Superstructures and Technical Difficulties in Maiakovskii's America." *The Harriman Review: Art, Technology and Modernity in Russia and Eastern Europe,* 12/4 (2000).

Williams, Raymond. *Marxism and Literature.* Oxford, U.K.: Oxford University Press, 1977.

Zirkle, Conway. *Death of a Science in Russia: The Fate of Genetics as Described in Prawda and Elsewhere.* Philadephia: University of Pennsylvania Press, 1949.

Lysenko also believed that Darwin had taken this idea from Malthus, who Marx criticized, along with Darwin, in terms of their analyses of human society. Marx did not, however, challenge Darwin's ideas with regard to plants and animals (Amsterdamski, 1989, p. 11).

CHAPTER 9

School Photographs as Tension: Reflections about Using Photographs in Comparative Educational Research

GUSTAVO E. FISCHMAN and GABRIELA CRUDER

The growing interest of scholarly inquiry into visual experiences, and the multiplication of studies of seeing and the seen, respond to unmistakable social and cultural realities: that images have become an omnipresent and overpowering means of circulating signs, symbols, and information (Fischman, 2001). Many of the everyday iconic events, such as watching movies, window shopping, and television consumption, are core cultural experiences of urban modernity and globalized capitalism. They demand from the viewer that s/he will be able to follow and understand implicit visual rules developed through the rapid trajectory of switching images.

However, the physical act of seeing the seemingly endless multiplication of images, and its saturating effects, are only one part of our daily visual experiences. In the matrix of the visual, it is also inscribed what is there that cannot be seen, through what lenses the visible and invisible become intelligible, and the spatial and temporal location of the observable and the observer, all of which constrain what is out there to see and not to see.

In the field of education specifically, images have become powerful components in the perception, evaluation, and popularization of ideas about schooling. Images about schools are influencing the public's perception of the goals of education and what are the means to achieve those goals (Giroux, 2000). Indeed, a rapid survey of mass media illustrates that changes in educational systems, whether curricular, evaluative, or financial, are often presented through the use of metaphors and images, perhaps even more than by the use of logical arguments. Even when images conflict with other sources of information, they appear to be extremely powerful in creating the public's perception in a particular direction. Moreover, as José Van Dijck argues in his study about the popularization of scientific knowledge, "beyond the invocation of *logos*, there are frequent appeals to *pathos* and *ethos* to persuade the general audience of the validity of a specific interpretation. Popular appeal often takes shape through the evocative use of mental pictures or compelling stories — or through *images* and *imaginations*" (1998: 10).

Yet the analysis of these popular images is rarely seen by comparativists as a relevant area of scrutiny.[1] A rapid review of several journals publishing comparative research shows that, with the exception of tables, maps, and some diagrams, there is almost no use of images. Visual aspects are, for the most part, reduced to the layout of the text.[2]

This neglect of the "visual" is most surprising, because of the increasingly sophisticated use of images in the majority of forms of information presentation in today's world. As Martin Jay notes:

> The model of reading texts, which serve productively as the master metaphor for objectivist interpretations of many different phenomena, is now giving way to models of spectatorship and visuality, which refuse to be redescribed in entirely linguistic terms. The figural is resisting subsumption under the rubric of discursivity, the image is demanding its own mode of analysis.
>
> *(Jay, 1996: 3)*

The model of spectatorship and visuality noted by Jay has been conceptualized at best as the "pictorial turn" and at worst as "the dictatorship of the images." In the words of TWJ Mitchell, "The Pictorial Turn looks at the way modern thought has re-oriented itself around visual paradigms that seem to threaten and overwhelm any possibility of discursive mastery ... In Europe one might identify it with phenomenology's inquiry into imagination and visual experience; or with Derrida's "grammatology," which de-centers the "phonocentric" model of language by shifting attention to the visible material traces of writing; or with the Frankfurt School's investigations of modernity, mass culture, and visual media; or with Michel Foucault's insistence on a history and theory of power/knowledge that exposes the rift between the discursive and the 'visible,' the seeable and the sayable, as the crucial fault-line in 'scopic regimes.'" (Mitchell: 1994, 9 & 12).

Very often the pictorial turn is associated with the use of postmodern and post-structural approaches and concepts, and this association appears to be one of the main difficulties for its critical incorporation into the field of comparative education. Anthony Welch, for example, a well-known comparativist, is opposed to the use of "imagery" in comparative education. He argues it is a manifestation of poststructuralist and postmodernity in the field, and those who use images cannot make qualitative distinctions between them. In Welch's own words:

> Much poststructural thought, in particular postmodernity, leaves us rudderless in a sea of blasé ironic detachment. We drift along as passive observers of the social world, watching the rising tide of imagery, but unable to distinguish between images of Third World poverty on the one hand, and the star-studded funeral rites of haute coutures such as Gianni Versace or Princess Diana on the other. Images all...

> *(Welch, 1999: 42)*

Welch and others (Massemann and Welch, 1997; Torres, 2000) argue that non-critical postmodern approaches offer very little in terms of improving our understanding and are no more appropriate tools for our field than non-critical modernist or Positivistic-oriented predecessors.[3] These well-known and reputable comparativists express important concerns and critical arguments about the political content and possible manipulation of images. These concerns coupled with the challenge of giving an *absolute* meaning to an image, are substantial problems for researchers of any field, and should be carefully considered in any research program attempting to use images. Moreover, we understand those critical positions as yet another indication of the importance of images in contemporary life. Indeed, we would like to argue that instead of dismissing the realm of the visual as a trendy style in social research, comparativists should critically incorporate analytical and methodological tools to use the information carried in images.

In a world of increased globalization and simultaneous fragmentation (in which the fixed borders of traditional communities and agencies such as the family, the school, and the nation are in constant disruption and relocation), it is necessary to develop other tools and methodologies that more fully expose the complexities of these transformations. One possible approach to understanding better the fragmentation of social contexts, the new social, political, and cultural dynamics, and their implications for comparative education, is to analyze prevalent and everyday cultural signs, such as the school photograph, as allegorical objects. This, as the next sections will elaborate, is not simply a trivial, idealistic or mechanical endeavor and requires the development of different ways of seeing (Berger, 1972).

What is in a Photograph?

Given the temporal gap between an object and its image, and since such an object has necessarily disappeared by the moment I look at the image, could it be some sort of fantas(magoric)tic game in there? Could it be possible that a photograph emerges as an *image in reverie*? Or even further, borrowing from Freud's famed metaphor, could we say that a photograph literally realizes the works of the unconscious? (Dubois, 1998:88)

Elsewhere, Fischman (2001) has analyzed an example of a school photograph from Argentina. It shows a schoolboy in white uniform posing and smiling in front of a shelf of books, which, as Fischman (2001) observed, were not real books, but were painted on a backdrop. These were books that cannot be read; wall-depicted books, fresco-books that are a synonymous-image with *well-kept books*. It is an image that in fact corroborates the discourse of the teacher, the one who takes care of books, keeps them out the reach of children by acting as the indispensable intermediary and custodian of knowledge at school; the privileged one who holds the code that may decipher them. Which possible viewpoints is the photograph actually handing out to the children's sight? Those were nothing but wall-painted books, bogus books that via the aloof language of the backdrop, exposed the impediment to their reading. Books proclaiming the closure to those possibilities for learning and thrill allegedly involved in every act of exchange and exploration... Non-book-books: in their remark, they reveal a limit.

The photo background introduces itself as a deliberate absence in all everyday tasks. Here, in image, an actual restitution takes place via the substitution of what is absent. Such a surrogate restitution attempts to balance the distance between the social prescription "we go to school to learn TO read and write," as opposed to what actually happens there. The photograph then enabled the parents to both make an excerpt, and read a moment in the process of enactment of the curriculum. The photograph, as a wedge at work between what is instituted and what is instituting, made apparent the tension amid the two.

The most favored shot for the yearly ritual of the school photo retrieves and puts at work certain elements, which from the standpoint of shared symbolism, would reveal what actually happens in this institution. The child holds a pencil, we assume he writes; we also notice books — children read at school. These material elements (objects-signs), ultimate symbols of the school culture, do play their parts in the plot. They have been arranged in such a way that our reading of the scene may at first glance suggest there seems to be a fairly free, autonomous handling of reading and writing activities in that place. We see a smiling child, and seduced by the spell of the predictable pseudo-instantaneous snapshot, we even go as far as assuming he reads and writes! And yet the chosen background cries out its truth, unveils itself, comes to light, and becomes the focal point. The background space encapsulates a cluster of meanings, and encapsulation, writes Metz, is "part of the passage mechanisms ... which facilitate the passing from one 'text' to another... from the latent to the apparent; A

passage that of course distorts the former while (it shapes) the latter."
(Metz, quoted in Gauthier, 1996: 157).

Fischman (2001) points out that the child in the photograph was at the
time enrolled in a special school for children with "mild retardation," in
which reading real books was considered too difficult for the children,
even though this particular boy was reading and creating comics at home.
When the boy's parents saw the photograph, they decided to enroll him in
a regular school the following year (Fischman, 2001). Had the parents'
sight leaned a bit toward the background of this photograph, over the
wall-depicted books, the image could have enabled them to analyze the
tension between the predictable and what was actually observed or happened. They would have noticed then the real distance prevailing between
children and books. In other words, this could have been their first step in
an inquiry that ultimately would have made apparent the persistent and
relentless mediation (control) the teacher puts forth during the reading
activities in the classroom.

Let's go back to the photograph of the child. He looks at us with a smile
that comes all the way from that moment. His smile remains fixed on
paper ever since he was photographed during his long past second grade
in special school. First, it is important to note that this is a photograph of a
real student, taken in a real school. In short, the viewers of this image are
inclined to understand the image within the boundaries or frames of reference of the so-called realistic photograph and this particular type of photograph has specific preoccupations. Baudrillard (1999, p.1) explains:

> So-called "realist" photography does not capture the "what is."
> Instead, it is preoccupied with what should not be, like the reality
> of suffering for example. It prefers to take pictures not of *what is*
> but of *what should not be* from a moral or humanitarian perspec-
> tive. Meanwhile, it still makes good aesthetic, commercial and
> clearly immoral use of everyday misery. These photos are not the
> witness of reality. They are the witness of the total denial of the
> image from now on designed to represent what refuses to be seen.
> The image is turned into the accomplice of those who choose to
> rape the real *(viol du reel)*. The desperate search for *the* image often
> gives rise to an unfortunate result. Instead of freeing the real from
> its reality principle, it locks up the real inside this principle. What
> we are left with is a constant infusion of "realist" images to which
> only "retro-images" respond. Every time we are being photo-
> graphed, we spontaneously take a mental position on the photog-
> rapher's lens just as his lens takes a position on us. Even the most
> savage of tribesmen has learned how to spontaneously strike a
> pose. Everybody knows how to strike a pose within a vast field of
> imaginary reconciliation.

The parent's sight decodes the readying of the setting; the depth of field exposes the set-up. It is precisely their sight that tears down the alleged spontaneity of the scene, which only then becomes montage. And this is how, ironically, the otherwise misleading effect of the background, turns into the very hard evidence of what really happened in the classroom, a reality that may well be part of an institutional mark.

Does a Photograph Show "Identity"?

Photography was initially developed in Europe in the early nineteenth century. It rapidly became a welcomed and popular tool, playing an important part in the construction of modern identity and the forces of Positivism. Unlike the social functions of mirrors or paintings in the pre-modern era which were meant to be seen by just a few, the multiplication and expansion of photographic images allowed many more viewers, and also and perhaps more important to look at a new subject, the modern consumer-citizen.

During this period, the multiplication of photographs of the urban crowd, the fair, the skyscrapers, the factory, and the school alluded to the notion of progress. The modern citizen, moreover, showed and emphasized, and thus made recognizable, the features of the self-knowing, homogenous and whole modern subject: the consumer of spaces, spectacles, and urban goods. During most of the modern period, photographic images attempted to show *reality*, and reproduction and representation were the two crucial aspects of how images functioned. However, as Baudrillard and others (Barthes, 1995; Hall, 1997; Jencks, 1995) explained, in the postmodern logic of this 'glo-calized' capitalism, image as simulation has replaced representation: "If they fascinate us so much it is not because they are sites of the production of meaning and representation — this would not be new — it is on the contrary because they are sites of disappearance of meaning and representation, sites in which we are caught quite apart from any judgment of reality" (Baudrillard, 1999: 237)

Baudrillard is referring to postmodern regimes of visuality and his position has as many defenders as detractors (Virilio, 1994, 1997), but the new regimes of visuality as sites of simulacra retain the quality of exposing objects and subjects. A photograph "exposes" the subject as a territory of inquiry. It is an analytical unit that develops a narrative or storyline, which are fragments of the exploration of the self. Furthermore, as a work in progress, a photograph urges us to search, ask, and glimpse, all at once, the spatial, selective, and integrative dimensions of our identity. To look at personal photographs involves transcending the literal in them and shifting the focus toward how subjectivity takes shape. Or, as Elkins notes, "Seeing alters the thing that is seen, and transforms the seer. Seeing is metamorphosis, not mechanism." (1997: 11–12)

Seeing photographic images implies a double metamorphosis. First, in the sight of the beholder, the other, laying on what has been sorted out, captured, framed, recorded in image. And yet, also the metamorphosis of the sight of the one who abides, who shows him or herself, who is shown, is in there too, looking directly at the camera while saying: ME. "The becoming of the self as other" (Barthes, 1995: 44) is right there, on the paper surface that altogether lodges the traces of the snapshot, the light measurement, and the click.

Analyzing the metamorphosis happening in photographs is an examination of both the relationships presented in the image, as far as its actual components, and the context of its enunciation. *I* look at the camera; *you* (the camera/photographer) look at me; *he/she* looks at the photograph, and only then does it "make sense"; the photograph produces meaning by way of the (imperative) sight of the other (social world).

I look at you; you expose yourself; she/he looks at me. Such is the everlasting triad of relationships involved in the photographic view. Images demand the sight of another. The other needs to be perturbed by the image in order to grasp the image's sense and meaning, because as Silva (1998, p. 108) notes:

> In Freudian jargon, perhaps the visual in the image alludes to the very moment when the 'libido' shows up. It is the shattering of consciousness required to access the unknown, the unconscious forces, or the new perception mechanisms not yet acknowledged at the level of the ordinary discourse… As an object of desire, a photograph urges us to go beyond all evidence, to disable the frame of obviousness in order to get what lays behind (Silva 1998, p. 108)

Silva's words are also an indication that photographs not only provide evidence, but also document, display, show, and hide meanings. In this process of hide-and-seek, we cannot assume that images are accurately absorbed by the viewer, that the meaning of each photo-image is instantaneously comprehensible and explicit in and of itself. The meaning of a photograph cannot be attained regardless of the context, or the circumstances of its production, circulation, and reception. (de Lauretis, 1984). Nevertheless, as Elizabeth Cowie (1977) appropriately comments (p. 18), meaning is never absolutely arbitrary in any text or image.

> Rather, the infinite conceivable process of attributing meanings and signification to an image is always, and only a theoretical probability. In practice, the image is always held, constrained in its production of meaning or else becomes meaningless, unreadable. At this point the concept of anchorage is important; there are developed in every society decisive technologies intended to fix the floating chains of signifieds so as to control the terror of uncertain signs.

Following Baudrillard (1999, p. 180), the photographic "event resides in the confrontation between the object and the lens, and in the violence that this confrontation provokes. The photographic act is a duel. It is a dare launched at the object and a dare of the object in return. Everything that ignores this confrontation is left to find refuge in the creation of new photographic techniques or in photography's aesthetics. These are easier solutions."

But there are no easy solutions. And yet, given the confrontation provoked in the photographic encounter, it is also possible to wonder whether there is an additional function: the use of a photograph as an "analyzer."

The Photograph: An Analyzer of the School Context?

According to Guy Lapasade (1979), an analyzer can be an artificial device (e.g., a microscope, an equalizer) or a natural device (e.g., the eye, the brain) that enables the dislocation of reality from its constitutive elements, with no conscious mind intervention. As Fernandez, following Lapassade, further explains, the concept of *analyzer* alludes to both contingent "events and occurrences as well as techniques tailored to induce the expression of information that may facilitate the revealing of formerly hidden signification." (1998, p. 43)

Since institutions function, too, according to implicit, silent, unwritten 'contracts,' comparative educators need to appropriate tools that may help in the "dislocation" of such elements. This is how photographs might become a "wedge," a stratagem, or a device, in the disabling of the tension that exists between what is instituted, and what is instituting. Once we access the epicenter of such a tension, which is what holds the disguised or latent significance, maybe then could we actually move on *to seeing*.

Seeing school photographs as analyzers, thus, embedded with information, meaning, and cultural tensions, requires also recognizing the presence of ambiguity. The *intrinsic ambiguity* of the status of images, as both material substance containing information, and iconic representation, turns our sight toward the it-seems-to-be relationship that all images embody. Photographs invoke a 'make-believe regime' based upon a categorical certainty about the actual existence of what is represented. The iconic status of a photograph, as a representation, and simultaneously as the very trace of what is represented, leads to an assumption, a socially extended and accepted fact, which establishes the framework for the relationship between the viewer and a particular discursive regime (Foucault, 1993). The photographic image is often read as if it were real, in the understanding that it is fully, 'truly,' and objectively informed by reality, hence its power of authentication.

A Photograph is also Illusion

To produce a photographic record requires the use of a specific technical device, the photographic camera. Such a device can be simple or complex, manual, automatic, or digital, but in all these variations there is a unifying characteristic. All cameras produce images, which are not just records of something, but signs, which belong to the realm of the production of meaning. The meaning-making process involves simultaneously subjective and social dimensions. No matter what social role an image plays (such as evidence in trials, personal identity in a passport, or the symbol of power, sex, or happiness in advertising), the creation of photographic images using a camera lens involves some degree of *subjective* choice though selection, framing, and personalization. But the subjective choice is understood in terms of the social role of the image because a photographic sign cannot be defined outside of its circumstances: photography cannot be conceived outside its references and its pragmatic effectiveness. In this sense a photograph is a social action and not only an expression of mere technical achievement. As Baudrillard (1999, p. 182) notes,

> This is the principle of imaginary experience (la loi de l'imaginaire). The image must touch us directly, impose on us its peculiar illusion, speak to us with its original language in order for us to be affected by its content. To operate a transfer of affect into reality, there has to be a definite (resolution) counter-transfer of the image.

The acts of measuring the light, framing, focusing, clicking, "freezing," and ultimately shooting capture what will become visible, and what will remain invisible, excluded, or cast out. What remains off-site, out of the photographic frame, is exactly what the image is not, what a photograph does not represent, and yet what supports its existence. The frame establishes the boundaries between the picture and everything else, and this boundary-making process allows the picture to exist. In this isolation, the inside of the photographic image recalls — and in some way stands for — everything that remains out of the picture (Calvino, 1988)

Photographs–What do you Reveal, What do you Hide?

Several perspectives that regard the possibilities of photography in the construction of identity suggest that the use of narrative proves an effective aide to the subjective process of elaboration of reality, through which every person fashions plots, storylines, and ultimately creates meaning (Vila, 1996). In this line of inquiry around the construction of meaning, many authors borrow from Michel de Certeau the notion of *event*, and apply it to the study of photography by analyzing how an event unfolds a given storyline within the photograph.

Michel de Certeau alludes to 'event' as the constitutive core of the text in historiography. The character of 'event' in an image — to the extent that it demands intelligibility — requires a subject who discursively situates it, so that it can respond to such a demand. In other words, this demand of intelligibility requires that the reproduced signs in an image, themselves become the very circumstances in which their contextual and associative structure shall work in their aim to effectively reproduce both the meaning and the emotional inflection of what is represented. It is important in this case that the subject must position him/herself within the discursive frame that simultaneously connects and explains an image. It is this positioning that makes room in photography for the process of the formation of subjectivity, hence room in the realm of pedagogy (Giroux, 1996).

Thinking of photography as having the preeminent function of an analyzer, allows it to be understood not merely in terms of what it is — presence, representation, and simulacra of what is absent — but also in its full possibilities of intervention on the actual present of the institutional time. What needs to be emphasized is the fact that it is precisely by highlighting its function as analyzer that photography may challenge the notion of "positive" time by means of tacitly comprising, in the very physicality of time a photograph embodies, the search for what has not been said, nor elaborated.

Whether a sign, object, or interpreter, a photographic snapshot actualizes the relentlessness of an object *taken* from its world. And yet it is there, in a snapshot, where we may foresee the chance to retrieve the condensing of tension that only the sight, any sight, can and may *do visible*: consciousness. Or as Regis Debray (1994, p. 98) states, "The secret power of images is unquestionably the power of our own unconscious (destabilizing as far as image, rather than structuring as language)."

Some may think this is just a matter of terminology; that the urge to regard a photograph as an *analyzer* and *event* may not make any difference after all. However, to perceive a photograph as an analyzer leads to a comprehensive exploration of the visible in its actual sophistication. It entails bringing up to light, to expose and foresee the possibility of passing through what is not revealed, though present. Furthermore, as an analyzer, a photograph opens up opportunities to unveil its inherent tensions; to deeply reflect on the possible transformation of the realm of school; to stress the *participant* core of the sight; and ultimately, to make full use of photography and its essential ambiguity.

Only as an analyzer can a photograph bring about the comprehensive exploration of the visible and its whole substantiality because as Jean Baudrillard (1999, p. 175) poignantly argued,

> Most images speak, tell stories; their noise cannot be turned down. They obliterate the silent signification of their objects. We must get rid of everything that interferes with and covers up the manifestation of silent evidence. Photography helps us filter the impact of the subject. It facilitates the deployment of the object's own magic (black or otherwise).

Photographs... So what?

This chapter proposed to reflect and discuss the challenges and possibilities of incorporating visual culture into the field of comparative educational research from a post-foundational and hybrid perspective. These reflections sprang out of a single photograph, and yet this perspective goes beyond the mere call of using photos, drawings, and other images as fashionable accessories of the almighty text. A critical incorporation, whether through the utilization and inclusion of visual technologies to record data, engaging in the study of the visual aspects of educational and cultural situations, or using graphic images (photo-essays, cartoons, and films) in the process of communicating the results of an investigation, requires attention, yet is not limited to the phenomena of vision and images.

Analyzing today's culture of images, as the manifestation of social, cultural, and economic changes in which the consolidation of global networks of entertainment-information and the impact of new technologies of imaging are key factors, should not be understood as a mere technical problem. What is at stake is a reorganization of regimes of visibility in which the images we can see and those remaining invisible have a key role in the reconfiguration of political, social, economic, and cultural procedures, traditions, and practices. This reconfiguration, Magaldy Téllez (2000, p. 195) points out, happens, following Paul Virilio's analysis, not for reasons of the apparently out of control quantity and quality of images, but because we are living in times in which the constantly mutating proliferation of images are simultaneously abolishing distances and creating instantaneous time, that is, creating a sense of the *now* without the *here*.

The new coordinates of time and space configure a logic that goes beyond the traditional perception of social differences. These differences displayed in the processes and practices of a visually inundated culture are circulating not only knowledge but also desires, and perceptual and interpretational schemas of the world and ourselves. When the symbolic horizon of modern public spaces such as schools is continuously challenged and therefore displaced by the hyper-consumption of images moving from and in all directions, those same images become key dis-organizers and re-organizers of perceptions, interpretations, knowledge, sensibilities, preferences, attitudes, loyalties, and allegiances.

One of the central arguments of this chapter is that in the matrix of the visual is also inscribed what is there that cannot be seen, through what lenses the visible and invisible become intelligible, and the spatial and temporal location of the observable and the observer, all of which constrain what is possible to see and not to see. Finally, my treatment of visual culture and comparative education is not limited to noting a "blind spot" in the field. This is not only an appeal that comparativists be more visually oriented, more self-critical, and especially not more "scientific." What really counts is whether the hybrid approach undertaken in this article helps in developing a post-foundational commitment, which reflects the sentiments about Foucault's genealogical work in that it (Foucault quoted in Margolis, 1993, p. 59):

> yields no criteria for thought or action; it only offers an attitude to life in every commitment. When we act or judge, we must do so as we believe. We favor legitimating such action in favoring such action; but we also guess, genealogically, that we cannot make that belief stick — universally, invariantly, necessarily, normatively, in any totalized way. For some, that will be enough; for others, it will be permanently disquieting.

This last quotation allows us to render intelligible a preliminary answer to the always important *So what?* The use of non-conventional methodologies — and their theoretical nuances — constitutes a challenge to the more traditional ways of doing comparative education. The incorporation of visual culture is a challenge, not a deliberate attempt to reinvent comparative educational research nor a wise way to proclaim, as in the old Spanish saying, that we are the one-eyed queen and king in the land of the blind. Our motivation is to investigate ideas and tools in order to overcome limitations in educational research, in the search to develop new questions while suggesting possible answers to our problems. This challenge has many colors, figures, voices and modalities, which can provide useful tools, ideas, and resources for researchers and practitioners alike. In short, the world of images should not be ignored, unless we want to avoid seeing the whole picture.

Endnotes

1. During the decade of 1990–2000, the field of comparative education saw the emergence of several works that critically inquired about topics and aspects related to visual culture and education, especially Novoa (2000) and the pioneering works of Paulston (1999). Yet, despite these noteworthy efforts, comparative education, understood as a field, has tended to avoid the examination of visual culture and the necessary debates about the epistemological value of images in educational research.
2. As in the case of William C. Cummings (1999), special use of layout in his article "The Institutions of Education." Another noticeable exception, in this case with regards the use of a drawing, can be seen in the same issue of the Comparative Education Review, in which Rolland Paulston analyzes the Comparative Education Review. See also Paulston (2000) about the use of "mapping" strategies.
3. Despite the multiple orientations present in the field of comparative education (Marxist, Feminist, Critical, Functionalist, etc.), in this chapter we would like to argue that Positivism is the dominant paradigm among comparative educators and researchers. According to Marianne Larsen, among the 988 presentations at the 2001 Annual Meeting of the CIES, only 24 could be considered postmodern in their approach and the rest were decidedly positivist and modernist.

References

Barthes, Roland. *La Cámara Lúcida. Nota Sobre la Fotografía*. Barcelona: Paidós, 1995.

Baudrillard, Jean. *Photography, Or The Writing Of Light.* Translated by Francois Debrix. A Translation of Jean Baudrillard, "La Photographie ou l'Ecriture de la Lumiere: Litteralite de l'Image." In *L'Echange Impossible* (The Impossible Exchange). Paris: Galilee, 1999, pp. 175–184.

Berger, John. *Ways of Seeing.* New York and London: Penguin, 1972.

Calvino, Italo. *Under the Jaguar Sun.* New York: Harcourt Brace, 1988.

Cowie, Elizabeth. "Women, Representation and the Image," Screen Education, 2–3 (1977): 5–23.

Cummings, William C. "The Institutions of Education: Compare, compare, compare!" *Comparative Education Review* (1999), 43: 413–437.

Debray, Regis. *Vida y Muerte de la Imagen. Historia de la Mirada en Occidente.* Barcelona: Paidós, 1994.

Dubois, Philippe. *El Acto Fotográfico. De la Representación a la Recepción.* Barcelona, Paidós, 1998.

Elkins, J. *The Object Stares Back. On the Nature of Seeing.* San Diego: Harcourt, 1997.

Fernández, Lidia. *Instituciones Educativas. Dinámicas Institucionales en Situaciones Críticas.* Buenos Aires: Paidós, 1998.

Fischman, Gustavo "Reflections about images, visual culture and educational research," Educational Researcher, 30 (2001) : 28–33.

Gauthier, Guy. *Veinte Lecciones Sobre la Imagen y el Sentido.* Madrid: Cátedra, 1996.

Giroux, Henry. *Placeres Inquietantes.* Barcelona: Paidós, 1996.

Giroux, Henry. *The Mouse that Roared.* Lanham, MD: Rowman and Littlefield, 2000.

Hall, Stuart. (Ed). *Representation: Cultural Representations and Signifying Practices.* Thousand Oaks, CA:Sage, 1997.

Jencks, Chris, Ed. *Visual Culture.* New York and London: Routledge, 1995.

Lapassade, G. *El Analizador y el Analista.* Barcelona: Editorial Gedisa, 1979.

Larsen, Marianne. "Global Resonance and Resistance: Affirmative Alternatives for Educational Policy, Practice, and Transformation." *Paper presented at the CIES Annual Meeting,* Washington, D.C. ,March 2001;

Lauretis, Teresa de. *Alice Doesn't: Feminism, Semiotics.* Cinema Bloomington, IN: Indiana University Press, 1984.

Margolis, J. "Redeeming Foucault." In *Foucault and the Critique of Institutions.* Edited by Caputo, J. and M. Yount. University Park, PA: Pennsylvania State University, 1993.

Mitchell, T. W. J. *Picture Theory.* Chicago: University of Chicago Press, 1994.

Novoa, Antonio. *Ways of Seeing.* Public Images of Teachers (19–20th centuries). Paedagogica Historica 36 (2000): 21–52.

Paulston, Rolland G. "Mapping Comparative Education after Postmodernity." *Comparative Education Review* 43 (1999): 438–64.

Paulston, Rolland G. Ed. *Social Cartography: Mapping Ways of Seeing Social and Educational Change.* New York: Garland, 2000.

Silva, Armando. *Álbum de Familia. La Imagen de Nosotros Mismos, Santa Fe de Bogotá.* Colombia: Grupo Editorial Norma, 1998.

Téllez, Magaldy. "Entre el Panoptismo y la Visiónica: Notas Sobre la Educación en la Videocultura." In Repensando la Educación en Nuestros Tiempos. Edited by Magaldy Téllez. Buenos Aires:Novedades Educativas, 2000.

Torres, Carlos A. "Social Cartography, Comparative Education and Critical Modernism: Afterthought." In *Social Cartography: Mapping Ways of Seeing Social and Educational Change,* edited by Rolland G. Paulston. New York: Garland, 2000.

Van Dijck, José. Imagination: Popular Images of Genetics New York:New York University Press, 1998.

Vila, Pablo. "Identidades Narrativas y Fotografías de la Vida Cotidiana," Causas y Azares, N°4, Buenos Aires, 1996.

Virilio, Paul. *The Vision Machine.* Bloomington, Indiana: University of Indiana Press, 1994.

Virilio, Paul. *Open Sky.* London: Verso, 1997.

Welch, Anthony. "The Triumph of Technocracy or the Collapse of Certainty? Modernity, Postmodernity, and Postcolonialism in Comparative Education." In *Comparative Education: The Dialectic of the Global and the Local.* Edited by Robert Arnove and Carlos A. Torres, Lanham, MD: Rowman and Littlefield, 1999.

CHAPTER 10

Postcolonial Theory in and for Comparative Education

PETER NINNES and GREG BURNETT

In recent years a number of authors have called for a reconceptualization of comparative education, based on their reading of social, cultural, and epistemological changes that are occurring on a global scale. Crossley (1999, p. 250) believes that these changes include

> dramatic changes in geopolitical relations; the intensifying pace of globalisation, growth of international consultancy and exchange programmes; advances in information and communications technology; demand for strengthened linkages between educational research, policy, and practice; growing tensions between the economic and cultural dimensions of social reform; postmodern challenges to dominant theoretical frameworks; and the symbolic impact of the turn of a new century.

The form that this reconceptualization should take has been the subject of some debate. Watson (1999) argues that comparative education needs to reassert itself because its traditional emphases on the historical and cultural contexts of education are necessary to offset the dominance of neo-liberal economic agendas in education. Broadfoot (2000) suggests that there should be a much greater emphasis on the processes of teaching and learning and less emphasis on the provision and organization of schooling. Cowen (2000) has argued that instead of asking what can be learned from studying other systems of education, we should be comparatively considering how historical forces, social structures, and individual identities combine to produce particular forms of education in particular sites. Popkewitz (2000) advocates that an important focus could be on how particular apparently universal rationalities of schooling and education, which construct certain notions of curriculum, childhood, learning and teaching, circulate across and between nations. Watson (1999) and Cowen (2000) both argue that theory should take a more central place in comparative education, particularly because of recent developments in social theorizing, with which comparative education has not fully engaged. Yet there is substantial debate about the place of new social theories in comparative education. Some authors, such as Watson (1998) and Welch (1999) see little place, for example, for postmodernism. Others, such as Paulston (1999, 2000), Rust (1991), and Ninnes, Mehta, and Burnett (Ninnes and Mehta, 2000; Mehta and Ninnes, 2000; Ninnes and Burnett, in press) suggest that a more detailed reading of 'post' texts in this field indicates that there are many interesting, valuable and challenging opportunities for comparative education arising from an engagement, particularly, with certain aspects of poststructuralism. Hoffman (1999) suggests serious engagement with the rethinking of 'culture' that has been undertaken in critical anthropology and Crossley (1999, 2000), Welch (1999) and Tikly (1999) argue that postcolonialism has much to offer comparative education. Of the latter three authors, Tikly provides the most detailed argument for considering postcolonial theories. However, in our view, Tikly makes a number of untested assertions concerning the relationship between comparative education and colonialism, neocolonialism, and postcolonialism. Furthermore, there are several relevant aspects of postcolonial theories that he does not consider. In this chapter, then, we examine Tikly's assertions and extend his arguments to cover a wider range of postcolonial theories and their applicability to comparative education.

We concur with Cowen (2000) that there are many comparative educations. In this chapter, we examine comparative education as practiced in English-speaking countries, and as represented by publications in primarily English language journals. We aim therefore to extend the dialogue concerning the implications of recent social theory on comparative education as practices in those particular contexts; we do not purport that our remarks apply to comparative education as practiced in other contexts, such as East Asia (see, for example, Gu Mingyuan, 2001).

Postcolonialism, like other 'post' perspectives, is not a unitary and homogenous body of thinking. Rather, it is a diverse set of ideas that have some overarching commonalities. We follow Gandhi (1998) in distinguishing between the condition of postcoloniality, and the theories of postcolonialism. Furthermore, following Hall (1996), we argue that the postcolonial is an era following the colonial era, in which sovereign power changed hands and the impacts and consequences of colonialism are still being felt and worked out. However, postcolonialism is not simply about describing the colonial era and its aftermath. Rather, it consists of a set of ways of thinking about, or knowing, colonialism and its consequences; it consists of a disruption of the dominance of Western ways of thinking and acting, a dominance that commenced with colonial expansion, conquest, and homogenization (Hall, 1996). We argue, too, that postcolonialism is not just about dealing with the past. We argue, as have others (e.g., McConaghy, 2000), that colonial relations of power and control continue to exist in many countries, such as in European settler societies where indigenous peoples are marginalized and oppressed. Thus, postcolonialism has important implications for studying education in many contemporary societies as well as on a global scale.

In this chapter we especially build on the discussion commenced in a substantive way by Hoffman (1999) and Tikly (1999). Hoffman has provided a useful review of the debates about culture and cultural analysis that have arisen in critical anthropology. In particular, she notes the problem of static, reified, and deterministic concepts of culture that essentialize individuals and the groups to which they belong. She also notes the mutually constitutive aspects of self-other relations and advocates for a comparative education that focuses on cultural practices, rather than culture and on learning *from* the other rather than learning *about* the other. Hoffman's review draws on key work in critical anthropology. Much of this work has informed postcolonial theory. However, postcolonial theory also draws on other traditions, some of which are used by Tikly.

Tikly argues that contemporary postcolonial studies differ from earlier colonial and anti-colonial works by its incorporation of postmodern and poststructural thought. He believes that comparative education has addressed colonialism mainly in the context of dependency theory and globalization theory, both of which inadequately theorize colonialism. Tikly argues that most of the discussions of colonialism in comparative education have been framed within neo-Marxist dependency theory perspectives. This work "provided a valuable critique of human capital and modernization theory, which had treated the colonial relationship as unproblematic" (Tikly, 1999, p. 609) and also linked colonialism, neo-colonialism, and education. However, Tikly identifies a number of limitations of dependency theory, including its fundamentally economic approach, which does not engage with issues of race, culture, identity, and language.[1] Furthermore, it tends to ignore the contradictory effects of relations between the colonized and colonizer and the development of alternatives and resistance. Dependency theory employs binary oppositions (colonizer/colonized; center/periphery) and uses the nation state as the unit of analysis, both of which are problematic because they oversimplify complex sets of social relations. Tikly suggests that there has been no systematic discussion in comparative education of the relevance of contemporary postcolonial theory and attempts to incorporate these ideas have been marginalized. Education literature concerning former colonies has an economic emphasis as a result of Jomtien. Non-economic issues such as race, identity, culture and language, which postcolonialism addresses, have been neglected. Finally, Tikly identifies two major areas of postcolonialism that could be fruitful for comparative education. First, postcolonialism deals with issues of racism, which comparative education has rarely addressed. Second, postcolonialism provides important insights into questions of culture, language, and curriculum with which the field could profitably engage.

We extend and develop Hoffman and Tikly's work in two major ways. First, we examine Tikly's claim that postcolonial theory has had little impact on comparative education and that neo-Marxist and dependency theory approaches continue to dominate the field. We do this by examining research, theoretical and essay review articles from six major comparative education journals published between 1991 and 2000. These journals are *Comparative Education Review, Comparative Education, International Journal of Educational Development, Prospects, Compare*, and *International Review of Education*. We searched reference lists and footnotes for references to neo-marxist and postcolonial works,[1] and scanned titles and abstracts for evidence of the themes of colonialism and postcolonialism. For each work which made some reference of these kinds, we carefully read each article and noted the kinds of ideas which were being employed, and tried to assess the extent to which the author was engaging with these ideas and their impact on the approach taken in the article. Second, we extend Hoffman's and Tikly's discussions by identifying a wider set of postcolonial theoretical concepts that we argue are of value to comparative education. Whereas Tikly particularly endorses postcolonial approaches to racism, culture and language, we address issues including self-identification through othering, ambivalence and desire, center and margin subject positions, resistance to and complicity in colonial practices, and issues of authority and speaking positions, all of which, we argue, have important and unsettling implications for comparative education.

Dependency and Neo-marxist Works

We examined citations of works by three writers in particular, namely Philip Altbach, Gail Kelly, and Martin Carnoy.[2] Some articles refer to these works predominantly in the process of providing a potted history or discussion of the future of comparative education (Watson, 1998; Crossley, 1999; Sweeting, 1999; Cowen, 2000; Hayhoe, 2000; Little, 2000). Others represent the views of these authors in primarily uncritical ways (Friederichs, 1991, 1992; Postiglione, 1991; Watson, 1991, 1994a, 1994b; Ginsburg, et al., 1992; Bray, 1993; Semali, 1993; Leach, 1994; Craft, Carr & Fung, 1998; Kempner, 1998; Raina, 1999; Bagnall, 2000).

A smaller number of authors critically engage with these neo-marxist approaches to issues of education and colonialism, including Tikly, whose critique of dependency theory is presented above. Williamson (1991) argues that there has been little study of colonized people's themselves, and the impact on colonial education of the local social context. He cautions against simplistic explanations of colonial education based on exclusive binaries of grateful recipients/passive victims and resistance/desire, and suggests that colonialism should be understood in terms of complex interactive processes between a range of participants, rather than in simplistic psychological terms in which the colonized experienced a "transformation from a people with a belief in themselves to those believing only in the capability of others such as colonial officials" (Williamson, 1991, p. 298). Luk (1991) provides a more complex reading of the colonial situation than most neo-marxist accounts. He points out that although in some cases the colonizers wished colonial schools to contribute to colonial power, colonial experiences, strategies, and consequences were highly diverse. Although in many cases indigenous cultures were greatly harmed by colonization, in other cases, certain aspects of indigenous cultures were able to thrive or be revived under colonial systems (Luk, 1991, p. 650).

Several authors critique dependency theory for its omissions. Bray (1994) argues that neo-marxist accounts say very little about processes of decolonization, while Bunwaree (1997) indicates that such analyses lacked a focus on gender. Chabbott (1998) believes they focus on power, dominance, and subordination but ignore organizational variables such as resource dependence, while Errante (1998) justifies her research project by arguing that neo-marxist accounts have paid little heed to the impacts of colonialism on the colonizers.

Postcolonial Engagements

The comparative education literature that we examined engaged with a number of contemporary postcolonial theoretical constructs, yet a number of important gaps remain. Recognition of the diversity of colonial practices and colonized peoples' experiences of colonization occurs in the work of Watson (1991), Tikly (1999), and Clayton (1998). Although Watson usually argues that colonization was uniformly and thoroughly destructive of indigenous cultures, in one piece (Watson, 1991) he cites Albert Memmi (1965) in the process of arguing that there were a range of motivations for colonialism, including psychological ones, and a range of policies for implementing the colonial order. Tikly (1999) cites Hall (1992) in regard to the critique of the essentialized black subject and the alternative view of a diversity of black identities as a way of demonstrating that colonial and postcolonial identities are hybrid, fractured, and unstable. Clayton (1998) cites novels by the Kenyan author Ngugi wa Thiong'o (1965) and the Nigerian Chinua Achebe (1959) to demonstrate a range of responses to colonialism, from collaboration to passive and active resistance. Clayton, however, ascribes discrete and homogenous identities to particular characters in these novels, and does not consider the possibility of multiple or hybrid identities, or the extreme ambivalence to the colonial order such as that experienced by the character Waiyaki in Ngugi wa Thiong'o's *The River Between* (1965, pp. 78–81).

Wright (1994) cites Ngugi wa Thiong'o (1986) to explain the impact of colonization on African cultures. Ngugi calls it a "cultural bomb" (Wright, 1994, p. 181). However, Wright acknowledges that there are varying views on how effective this cultural bomb was. He argues that some authors, such as Ngugi, are quite pessimistic. Others, such as Wole Soyinka, argue that Africans used European education for their own ends, and in most cases were not 'Westernized' by it (Wright, 1994, p. 192). Wright (1994, p. 192) also notes that "the issue of the effects of Western hegemony in general, and colonization, and colonial education in particular on Africans is a very complex one, and I believe the effects and Africans' responses varied and continue to vary according to location … whether one attended school or not, and the level of schooling, how traditional one's family was, etc."

Two pieces provide a more detailed analysis of the diversity of the colonial experience. Goodman (2000) focuses specifically on the colonial activities of a group of female colonizers, indicating that their particular gendered location in the colonial order resulted in particular sets of experiences. However, perhaps the most useful work we read, in terms of demonstrating a sophisticated engagement with contemporary postcolonial thinking about the diversity of colonial experiences, is the study by Errante (1998). She examines the experiences of various Portuguese colonizers, both within the colonies and within the metropole, and identifies race, ethnicity, gender, and social class as important signifiers of differential colonial experience. She further contributes to the breakdown of the binary of colonizer and colonized by revealing the ways in which the colonized exerted power over the colonizers.

Whereas neo-marxist accounts of colonialism provide a predominantly economic account of the process, some postcolonial theory examines the psychological side of colonialism. Matthews and Matthews (2000) cite Fanon (1968) to support their argument that colonialism instills a sense of inferiority in the colonized. Other authors note the desire that many colonized had for the knowledge and culture of the colonizers. Bunyi (1999), citing Ngugi wa Thiong'o (1985), argues that learning English was the key to gaining access to colonial power and decision making and concludes that is why parents wanted their children to learn English. Westley (1992), citing Achebe (1990), argues that in Africa many colonized peoples preferred to learn English, while at the same time the colonizers were favoring the use of vernacular languages in education. Wright (1994) argues that many students in Sierra Leone see the value of learning English, citing Fanon's (1967) idea that the mastery of language can result in the accrual of power. The power accrued through skillful use of the colonial language can thus be used to resist colonial forces. Sultana (1996), quoting Said (1993), argues that using the colonial language to pose alternatives to dominant ideas is part of a process of "writing back to the metropole" (Sultana, 1996, p. 105). Errante's (1998) work examines colonialism not in terms of the economic needs of the colonizing nation, but in terms of its psychocultural needs. Her argument is that colonialism was intimately tied up with the construction of national and individual pride, character, and identity.

The diversity of colonial experiences of the colonized and colonizers, and the psychological impact on both groups, reflect contemporary postcolonial thinking that colonialism is not a one-way process. Colonialism is not read as simply a process in which the colonizers homogenously and uniformly oppress the colonized. In addition to the variability of experiences, the colonized have some agency to respond to the diverse actions of the colonized. Clayton (1998) takes up this theme when he argues that the colonized are not uniformly mystified by the colonial experience to the extent that they become entirely passive victims. Rather, within particular constraints, they respond as, for example, collaborators or resisters. Demerath (1999), in his research into education in Papua New Guinea in the postcolonial era, argues that "in these struggles with modern forces, local peoples are able to combine seemingly disparate elements into their identities, and they demonstrate great imagination and resilience in the configuration of local/global relations" (p. 175). Thus, in the colonial era and in the postcolonial era of globalization, local responses to cultural dominance were and are not uniform, but variable, contingent, and contextualized (Appadurai, 1996; Hall, 1991). Wright (1994) develops this idea of agency in his proposal for educational reforms that allow students to come to voice. Here Wright draws on the work of hooks (1988), referring to coming to voice as "the act of speaking as an act of resistance, an act which develops and expresses critical consciousness and political awareness" (Wright, 1994, p. 191). Drawing on the work of Tuhiwai Smith (1992), Brady (1997) applies the issue of voice and agency to higher education contexts. She argues that indigenous academics, in working against colonial practices in contemporary 'settler' societies, have to create spaces for themselves and their students to define what counts as knowledge, how teaching occurs, who is researched, how and why. They need to pursue an academic life in which their own cultural knowledge and social systems count and which takes account of their aspirations and allows them to make a contribution to the wider world.

As we noted above, colonialism impacts on the colonized as well as the colonizer. It is a two-way process not only in the sense that both colonized and colonizer have some degree of agency, but also in the sense that the actions of the colonizers construct, prescribe, and constrain the identities of both the colonized and the colonizers themselves. This imperial construction of the 'self' and 'other' was clearly demonstrated in Said's (1978) work on Orientalism. Within the literature that we surveyed, only two articles take up these ideas in a substantive way. Goodman (2000) notes the way in which British women educationists employed constitutional, educational, familial, and religious discourses to construct themselves as authorities on colonial education, but at the same time there were ambiguities and contradictions in these constructions because of the differential gender relations within colonial societies. Errante (1998) notes also the ways in which the colonizers constructed identities for themselves and the colonized people in order to justify their hold on power. Part of the task of postcolonial analysis is to unpack these processes and products of colonial identity construction. This involves what Errante (1998), following Renan (1990), refers to as overcoming historical amnesia through a process of re-membering. Gandhi, paraphrasing Fanon, argues that this process involves unpacking the myths of Western progress upon which colonial empires were built by revealing the violence associated with colonial encounters:

> "industrialization tells the story of economic exploitation, democracy is splintered by the protesting voices of the suffragettes, technology combines with warfare, and the history of medicine is attached relentlessly… to the techniques of torture." (Gandhi, 1998, p. 21)

Several authors draw on postcolonial literatures to develop ideas about postcolonial or decolonizing education, which is a part of what Leela Gandhi (1998, p. 18) refers to as "postcolonial self-recovery." Wright (1994, p. 185) cites hooks (1984) and Spivak (1990) to support his suggestion that there is "an urgent need for marginalized peoples to move their discourses from margin to center." He proposes that formal education should include an engagement with critical African drama as a means for students to come to voice (see above). In doing so, he essentializes the role of drama in African cultures as "functional [and] performance oriented" (p. 187) and drama and orality as central in "Black creativity, theorizing and everyday life" (p. 191). These essentialisms, however, can be considered legitimate in the sense that they are constructed by subjugated peoples themselves and provide a means for subjugated peoples to affirm their identity and take control of their own educational futures (see, for example, Spivak, 1990, 1993).

Bunyi (1999) argues that African languages should be given a more prominent place in Kenyan schooling. She draws on Ngugi wa Thiong'o (1985, 1986) to show how English came to occupy the preeminent position in the curriculum. Bunyi argues that indigenous African languages and genres such as storytelling can make a positive contribution to social, economic, and political transformation in Kenya, noting in particular Fanon's (1967) assertion of the link between language and culture. In a somewhat less convincing way, Semali (1999) also argues for the incorporation of African literacies and knowledges into African classrooms. Westley (1992) also addresses the issue of language in postcolonial education. He notes Kenyan novelist Ngugi wa Thiong'o's switch from writing in English to writing in Gikuyu, and Wole Soyinka's (1987) suggestion that Nigeria use Swahili as a national language, as evidence of continuing struggles over language use in Africa.

Postcolonial Possibilities

As we noted above, Tikly (1999) endorses postcolonial approaches to racism, culture, and language. We signaled that we wished to extend his discussion by addressing issues such as self-identification through othering, ambivalence and desire, center and margin subject positions, resistance to and complicity in colonial practices, and issues of authority and speaking positions. In the articles that we analyzed, some of these issues, as well as others, have been engaged to some extent. These issues include language and the problematics of culture; the ambivalence of the colonized toward the colonial social order and in particular education, that is, the desire to mimic the colonizer mixed with the desire to resist; the possibilities of resistance, especially in terms of decolonizing education; the diverse impact of colonization on both the colonized and the colonizers, and the fracturing of this experience along gender, class. and ethnic lines. However, we also maintain that the following five sets of ideas, if taken up within Comparative Education, would further answer Tikly's concerns over neglect of what he calls the non-economic aspects of colonialism mentioned earlier.

Self-Identification Through Othering

Colonial interventions in the non-European world were based, in general, on a 'thicket of motivations' (Spivak, 1985, p. 132), including uneven combinations of ideological reasons and the desire for economic and territorial gain. However, underlying and enmeshed with these more readily identifiable reasons for European-dominated colonialism were other motivations that can be considered more central to the human condition. The colonial project also served to fashion notions of colonial identity. This occurred when the colonized 'other,' who was often perceived as fundamentally different, was used by the colonial 'self' for its own identity work. Based on Hegel's original master/slave dialectic (see Gandhi, 1998, pp. 16ff), JanMohamed (1985, p. 63) uses the term 'Manichean' to describe the way in which Europeans perceived themselves in relation to their non-European 'others' and the world they inhabited in terms of a great field of oppositions. JanMohamed describes this field in terms of several series of binary oppositions comprising:[3]

> Diverse yet interchangeable oppositions between black and white, good and evil, superiority and inferiority, civilisation and savagery, intelligence and emotion, rationality and sensuality, self and Other, subject and object (JanMohamed 1985, p. 63).

The European colonizers needed the colonized for their own self-identity work, that is, to formulate notions of the 'self' that would otherwise be impossible. The colonial enterprise therefore concerned itself with identifying 'difference' at every turn and using that difference to pronounce the European self's identity as superior to the other. Foucault (1970, pp.17ff) notes that around the end of the sixteenth century, the approximate beginnings of the European colonial period, there was a shift in European attempts to understand and interpret the natural and social world from an emphasis on resemblances to an emphasis on differences. In terms of the human world, John Frow (1995, p. 25), for example, has noted how colonial expansion and the consequent confrontation with a different other resulted in the construction of binary categories that affirmed notions of the superior European self. The beliefs concerning the 'self' and the 'other' that developed during the colonial period helped underwrite the Social Darwinism of the 1800s that perceived colonized people as primitive, exotic and in a more lowly position on the 'tree of man' than the European colonizers. More recent theories of modernization and development are also informed by constructions of the European 'self' as advanced and large parts of the non-European world as poor, struggling, and undeveloped. Significantly, the perceived 'gap' between self and other at each point of contact between the European and non-European world became the justification for a vast range of interventions, including education.

Therefore, as comparative educators, we need to be alert to the manner in which we encounter difference as our gaze is directed at education systems across boundaries of culture and ethnicity. We need to explore ways by which the 'other' can self-identify, and, democratically participate in the production of statements about education reforms and practices that purport to be transformative. As Hoffman (1999, p. 482) suggests, drawing on Clifford Geertz, it is possible to recognize difference but at the same time not create distance. In other words, we need to find ways to encounter difference without automatically constituting a hierarchical relationship between a 'privileged self' and a 'marginalized other.' Furthermore, in the statements generated about the education systems of 'others,' their perceived needs and the most appropriate interventions, we need to be alert to the particular aspects of difference between the 'self' and their 'others' that we highlight or erase. We also need to consider the extent to which the perception of difference is used to justify intervention, and the associated assumptions about the self and other that might otherwise remain hidden, unspoken, or ignored.

When moving across borders delineated by various perceptions of difference, we need to be alert to the motivational dynamics of 'othering' and the elements of self that intrude in the construction of the other. As Elizabeth Ellsworth (1989, p. 322) suggests, educational futures for everyone can more likely be worked out in proportion to the level of self-reflexivity present in the encounter:

> If you can talk to me in ways that show you understand that your knowledge of me, the world, and 'the right thing to do' will always be partial, interested, and potentially oppressive to others, and if I can do the same, then we can work together on shaping and reshaping alliances for constructing circumstances in which students of difference can thrive.

Ambivalence and Desire

Homi Bhabha (1994) has drawn attention to the 'ambivalent' nature of colonial attitudes toward the colonized other. These attitudes are often a mix of desire and repulsion that in effect disable the colonial project. This tension emerges when colonialists seek to re-make the 'other' in their own image, for example, in projects of assimilation and modernization. Bhabha (1994) describes this as mimicry, that is, the adoption by the colonized of the colonizers' values, knowledges, technologies, and so on. It is a form of flattery and thus is desired by the colonizer. On the other hand, there simultaneously exist feelings of repulsion (Bhabha, 1994). Too much change in the direction of the colonizer's values, culture, and so on is read by the colonizer as a menace and a threat to colonial dominance. We can observe this, for example, in colonial education systems that historically withheld English language instruction from all but a privileged few while simultaneously insisting that English language be used as the language of colonial administration and decision making (see, for example, Pennycook, 1998, Burnett, 2002).

While critiques of modernization and assimilation are common within comparative education, critiques of interventions that seek to maintain difference between, for example, the 'West' and the 'non-West' are less common. Marianna Torgovnick (1996) has identified a 'primitivism' in the rhetoric of many Europeans that yearns for an authentically indigenized subject, speaking indigenous languages and leading lives of "colourful alterity" (Gandhi, 1998, p. 85). This is what Rey Chow (1993) terms the "beloved object" of the traditional anthropological gaze; this gaze has the potential to museumize 'non-Western' people by re-locating them in some indeterminate but usually precolonial time frame. Johannes Fabian (1983, pp. 30ff) argues that confining non-Western people to an earlier time frame represents a denial of 'coevalness'. That is, the Western anthropological 'self' disallows its non-Western 'other' to exist in the same contemporary time frame. The result for many non-Western 'others,' when this anthropological discourse intersects with colonial governance, particularly in the form of education, is restricted access to positions of global and regional power.

When our comparative education work is based on a celebration of difference and emphasizes indigenizing the curriculum by incorporating Indigenous languages, local knowledges, and ways of knowing, we need to reflect on our own desires. We need to consider the extent to which our interventions, especially those that we view as 'cultural,' 'relevant,' and 'vocational,' are a result of our desire to see indigenous people doing Indigenous things. The resurgence in interest by many European linguists and educators for the preservation of near-lost Indigenous languages and their revitalization through schooling are relevant examples. While such desires for language maintenance are not necessarily inappropriate, language maintenance interventions need to be problematised for their potential to keep indigenous people in particular frames. Such interventions need to be examined for their potential to limit indigenous people's participation in wider, more powerful global discourses that are generated in Europe and North America. Recent work by Martin Nakata (1999) in the area of literacy education has disrupted the cultural relativist logic (McConaghy, 2000) that is still present in many educational settings today. For example, regarding the teaching of local languages in remote indigenous Australian communities, Nakata (1999) argues for an education system that equips children with language skills to circulate not only in an indigenous environment but also in a wider non-indigenous environment. To overemphasize difference and to let that difference dominate school curricula, as Nakata suggests, only leads to the further marginalization of people and a reinforced "dependence on the ideas and technologies of others" (Samoff, 1999, p. 412).

Center and Margin Subject Positions

Karen Mundy (1998) has demonstrated how within the field of comparative education there has been much critique of interventions across borders of culture and ethnicity that expose how those interventions seek to place indigenous people in relatively powerless positions within European/North American capitalistic systems (see, for example, Carnoy, 1974; Arnove, 1980; Altbach, 1982). Critiques that focus on indigenous marginality itself are less prevalent. Educational interventions across borders that are motivated by 'differential privilege' between centers and margins need to be tempered by recognition that marginality is socially constructed.

The identification of marginality by academics in the West, even when claimed to be grounded in some sort of empiricized lack, risks reinforcing, rather than interrogating, marginality. Even Said's (1978) *Orientalism* has faced the charge of disempowering non-Western others by unintentionally denying a differentiated and agential non-West and overemphasizing the discursive power of the West (see Gandhi, 1998, p. 81; McConaghy, 2000, p. 18). This tendency is also found elsewhere within postcolonial scholarship (Mukherjee, 1998). Some postcolonial perspectives, which seek to break down colonizer/colonized binaries, tend to equate subaltern silence with oppression. Mukherjee (1998) notes that some postcolonial theorists expect a particular form of 'resistance' from the periphery. When it is not forthcoming, discourses of oppression are assumed to have silenced it. Although silence could be read as resulting from colonial oppression, the silence could be read in other ways, for example, as a sign of other agendas. As Mimi Orner (1992, p. 81) has stated in connection to the 'critical' classroom:

> It is not adequate to write off student silence in these instances as simply a case of internalized oppression. Nor can we simply label these silences resistance or false consciousness. There may be compelling conscious and unconscious reasons for not speaking — or for speaking, perhaps more loudly, with silence.

Second, since Foucault (1978, p. 98) argues that objects of study are constituted through the play of asymmetrical power relations, marginality can be conceptualized as a socially constructed category. Spivak (1993, p. 55) has suggested this as a reason for marginality becoming what she calls a 'buzzword' in some academic circles. As she has argued, the relationship between center and margin is often a 'parasitic' one where the center, in the guise of the Western academy, needs the existence of the margin for what she calls 'institutional validation and certification.' In other words, the theoretical machinery that purports to identify and destabilize processes of self-identification through othering is itself not immune. Spivak particularly points to the personal gains made by some academics in terms of the "proliferating but exclusivist third-worldist job[s]" (1993, p. 55) available to these academics. Furthermore, it is not just European academics in the West who are implicated. Chow (1993, p. 13) has noted that some non-Western academics have employed a form of "self-subalternization" in order to give themselves an authority in the West while at the same time undermining any claim the oppressed might have to protest. Gandhi (1998, p. 128) has pointed out here an ironic reversal of Disraeli's idea, "the East is a career" (cited in Said, 1978, p. viii). Furthermore, a certain level of validation is helpful to academics who wish to distance themselves from Western academia's past and present complicity with imperialism and the project of (neo)colonial expansion and globalization. It may be that self-righteous identity work is done by some sections of the Western academy by bringing into existence a category called 'marginal' and clearing a space for those on the margins to speak.

Third, there is a possibility of perpetuating marginality under the belief of destabilizing it. In order to create and maintain its self-righteousness, the Western academy continually needs to have its object of desire marginalized. A very familiar tension exists between wanting to bring about justice yet wanting the injustice to remain. Such ambivalence is a hallmark of neocolonial oppression. This criticism is particularly justifiable when little or no political action or transformation results from the interrogation of marginality. Marginality discourse as articulated in the field of literary studies has faced this charge. Gandhi (1998, p. 56) quotes Ahmad (1995, pp. 16, 12) as describing such endeavors as a:

> Luxury based upon the availability of 'mobility and surplus pleasure' to a privileged few, while the vast majority of others are condemned to labor 'below the living standards of the colonial period.'

Resistance and Complicity

Tikly argues that postcolonial theory involves going beyond simplistic 'binary oppositions' of 'colonizer' and 'colonized' as a valid means of analyzing the effects of colonization. Drawing on Spivak (1985) and Hall (1992), Tikly (1999, p. 607) argues that postcolonial theory draws on a variety of factors, for example, gender, class, culture, location, and so on, to offer more nuanced explanations of the postcolonial condition. In a similar way, McConaghy (1998) suggests it is important to concede to multiple centers and margins and multiple oppressions.

Postcolonial theory has helped create a shift away from simplistic 'done to' (Chappell, 1995, p. 309) accounts of complex cultural interactions, which rob indigenous people of agency and contribute to a construction of them as simple, passive, and over-awed by the outsider's presence. It is too simplistic to perceive the colonial past in terms of a powerful colonizing presence that rolls juggernaut-like (Edmond 1997, p. 12) through indigenous societies, replacing indigenous languages, practices, values, knowledges, and so on with that of the colonized. Instead, postcolonial theory helps articulate notions of colonized resistance (Parry, 1994) and at time complicity (Gandhi, 1998), where colonized peoples were and are actively rejecting, appropriating, and modifying colonial values, technologies, practices and so on as they cross the border or the 'colonial beach' (see Dening, 1998, pp. 85ff on the 'colonial beach' as liminal space).

As comparative educators we need to be alert to the ways our own perceptions of educational contexts have the potential to rob local people of agency. We need to practice a high degree of reflexivity, as well as allowing local voices to invade our debates. By the same token, we need to be alert to the subtleties of these voices, both past and present. Bhabha (1994), for example, drawing on notions of Bakhtin's 'parody' and 'carnivale' (see Gardner, 1993) has warned that the mimicry of outsider values, technologies, and systems does not always mean compliance, but can be a subtle form of resistance to outsider interference. We also need to be alert to the ways that interventions across borders have often been 'hybridized' by those receiving them. Such interventions rarely remain in the form they were intended by outsiders. We need to recognize that local agency operates on interventions, modifying, rejecting, and appropriating educational technologies, aims, values, knowledges, and ways of knowing as they cross into local territory.

Authority and Speaking Position

Often debates that require the making of statements and interventions across borders of various kinds revolve around who has authority to speak on behalf of others and the oppositionality of so-called insiders and outsiders (McConaghy, 2000). Spivak (1988) has problematized the authoritative speaking position with her elusive search for the subaltern voice. She questions the means by which historians/investigators present themselves as authoritative in matters of the other, whether intellectuals should abstain from the investigation, whether there is a subaltern group that can speak for themselves and who are the true representative subalterns of history.

Few would challenge the need for a greater inclusion of the indigenous or local voice about education in indigenous settings. However, more consideration needs to be given to how speaking authority is constructed and legitimized among both 'outsiders' and 'insiders.' The field of anthropology and its 'participant observer' operating from the 'door of the tent' has been problematized widely (see McConaghy, 2000) in recent times for the ways in which it has historically constructed itself as authoritative in mostly non-Western settings. Many postcolonial critics have noted how many anthropologists have employed essentialized notions of identity (Ortiz, 1986/87; Minh-ha, 1986/87; Ellsworth, 1997; Appadurai, 1988; McConaghy, 2000) and have attempted to enhance their credibility by promoting themselves and their academies as aloof, neutral, value-free consumers of knowledge about the other. At the same time, traditional anthropology has constructed essentialized identities for the observed non-Western 'other' and, as a result, it has constructed ideas about what it means to be an authentic member of a particular cultural group. Not only is this a reductive process in that it fails to take into account the complexities of fluid multi-identities (Ortiz, 1986/87; Minh-ha, 1986/87; Ellsworth, 1997; McConaghy, 2000), it also fails to allow indigenous peoples to participate in the process of their own subject formation.

As comparative educators, we need to be alert to our own use of essentialisms and to be aware that stereotypes employed in such speech acts can contradict the experiences and identities of others who lay claim to an interest in a particular intervention. Within the field of comparative education we need to ask difficult questions about who gets to speak for whom about educational matters across various borders; and how we use our institutional affiliations (e.g. tertiary institution, NGO, member of a comparative education society) to subtly validate statements and interventions across borders.

Final Remarks

Comparative Education as a field has in its various manifestations almost always been concerned with an engagement with an 'Other.' For most of the last 150 years, such an engagement has not been problematized. In this chapter, we have sought to contribute to the reconceptualization of the field by extending the discussion commenced by Hoffman (1999) and Tikly (1999) about the place of postcolonial theory in comparative education. We have identified a range of concepts that neither of these two authors explored, each of which provides particular and unsettling challenges to the way we work as comparative educators.

Endnotes

1. Tikly (1999) points out that some approaches employed in comparative education, such as "socio-anthropological" ones, do address issues of culture and identity, but they tend to essentialize culture and view identity as fixed.
2. Our decisions about key works in neo-marxist and postcolonial theory were based on our own readings, as well as the works of Gandhi (1998) and Ashcroft, Griffiths, and Tiffin (1995).
3. We deemed the following works to be relevant to the analysis: Altbach (1971), Altbach (1975), Altbach (1977) (reprinted as Altbach 1982), Altbach (1980), Altbach (1984), Altbach (1985), Altbach (1987), Altbach (1988), Altbach (1990), Altbach (1993), Altbach and Kelly (1978a), Altbach and Kelly (1978b) (2nd edition 1984), Altbach and Selvaratnam (1989), Carnoy (1974), Kelly (1978), Kelly (1982), Kelly (1984), Kelly and Altbach (1978).
4. See also Blaut, 1993, p. 17 for a further list of common binaries.

References

Achebe, Chinua. *Things Fall Apart*. Greenwich, Conn.: Fawcett, 1959.

_____. "Literature of Celebration." *West Africa* 3779 (1990): 167–168.

Altbach, Philip and Gail Kelly. *Education and Colonialism*. New York: Longman, 1978.

_____. *Education and the Colonial Experience*. New Brunswick: Transaction Books, 1984.

Altbach, Philip and Viswanathan Selvaratnam (Eds). *From Dependence to Autonomy: The Development of Asian Universities*. Dordrecht: Kluwer, 1989.

Altbach, Philip. "Education and Neocolonialism." *Teachers College Record* 72 (1971): 543–588.

_____. "Literary Colonialism: Books in the Third World." *Harvard Educational Review* 45 (1975): 226–236.

_____. "Servitude of the Mind? Education, Dependency, and Neocolonialism." *Teachers College Record* 79 (1977): 187–204.

_____. "The University as Center and Periphery." In *Universities and the International Distribution of Knowledge*. Edited by Irving J. Spitzberg. New York: Praeger, 1980.

_____. "Servitude of the Mind? Education, Dependency, and Neocolonialism." In *Comparative Education*. Edited by Robert F. Arnove, Gail P. Kelly, and Philip G. Altbach. New York: Macmillan, 1982.

_____. "Distribution of Knowledge in the Third World: A Case Study in Neocolonialism." In *Education and the Colonial Experience*. Edited by Philip G. Altbach and Gail P. Kelly. New Brunswick: Transaction Books, 1984.

_____."Centre and Periphery in Knowledge Distribution in the Third World: The Case of India." In *A World of Strangers*. Edited by Edgar B. Gumbert. Atlanta: Centre for Cross Cultural Education, Georgia State University, 1985.

_____. *Higher Education in the Third World*. London: Sangam Press, 1985.

_____. *Textbooks in the Third World*. New York: Garland, 1988.

_____. "The Academic Profession." In *International Higher Education: An Encyclopedia*. Edited by Philip Altbach. New York: Garland, 1990.

_____. *Publishing in Africa and the Third World*. Buffalo, New York: Graduate School of Education Publications, State University of New York, 1993.

Appadurai, Arjun. *Modernity at Large: Cultural Dimensions of Globalization*. Minneapolis: University of Minnesota Press, 1996.

Arnove, Robert. "Comparative Education and World Systems Analysis." *Comparative Education Review* 24 (1980): 48–62.

Ashcroft, Bill, Gareth Griffith, and Helen Tiffen (Eds). *The Postcolonial Studies Reader*. London:Routledge, 1995.

Ashcroft, Bill, Gareth Griffith, and Helen Tiffen. "General Introduction." In The Postcolonial Studies Reader, edited by Bill Ashcroft, Gareth Griffith & Helen Tiffen. London:Routledge, 1995.

Bagnall, Nigel. "The Balance Between Vocational Secondary and General Secondary Schooling in France and Australia." *Comparative Education* 36 (2000): 459–475.

Bhabha, Homi. *The Location of Culture*. New York: Routledge, 1994.

Blaut, James M. *The Colonizer's Model of the World: Geographical Diffusionism and Eurocentric History*. New York: Guilford Press, 1993.

Brady, Wendy. "Indigenous Australian Education and Globalisation." *International Review of Education* 43 (1997): 413–22.

Bray, Mark. "Education and the Vestiges of Colonialism: Self–determination, Neocolonialism and Dependency in the South Pacific." *Comparative Education* 29 (1993): 333–348.

_____. "Decolonisation and Education: New Paradigms for the Remnants of Empire." *Compare* 24 (1994): 37–51.

Broadfoot, Patricia. "Comparative Education for the 21st Century. Retrospect and Prospect." *Comparative Education* 36 (2000): 357–371.

Bunwaree, Sheila. "Education and the Marginalisation of Girls in Post-GATT Mauritius." *Compare* 27 (1997): pp. 297–317.

Bunyi, Grace. "Rethinking the Place of African Indigenous Languages in African Education." *International Journal of Educational Development* 19 (1999): 337–50.

Burnett, Greg. " 'I-Matang, I-Matang, Ko na Aera?' Discourses of Colonialism in Kiribati Secondary Education." PhD thesis. Armidale: University of New England, 2002.

Carnoy, Martin. *Education as Cultural Imperialism*. New York: McKay, 1974.

Chabbott, Collette. "Constructing Educational Consensus: International Development Professionals and the World Conference on Education for All." *International Journal of Educational Development* 18 (1998): 207–18.

Chappell, David. "Active Agents Versus Passive Victims: Decolonised Historiography or Problematised Paradigm." *The Contemporary Pacific* 7 (1995): 303–26.

Chow, Rey. *Writing Diaspora: Tactics of Intervention in Contemporary Cultural Studies*. Bloomington: Indiana University Press, 1993.

Clayton, Thomas. "Beyond Mystification: Reconnecting World–System Theory for Comparative Education." *Comparative Education Review* 42 (1998): 479–96.

Cowen, Robert. "Comparing Futures or Comparing Pasts?" *Comparative Education* 36 (2000): 333–342.

Craft, Maurice, Ronnie Carr, and Yvonne Fung. "Internationalisation and Distance Education." *International Journal of Educational Development* 18 (1998): 467–72.

Crossley, Michael. "Reconceptualising Comparative and International Education." *Compare* 29 (1999): 249–67.

Crossley, Michael. "Bridging Cultures and Traditions in the Reconceptualisation of Comparative and International Education." *Comparative Education* 36 (2000): 319–332.

Demerath, Peter. "The Cultural Production of Educational Utility in Pere Village, Papua New Guinea." *Comparative Education Review* 43 (1999): 162–92.

Dening, Greg. *Readings/Writings*. Carlton South: Melbourne University Press, 1998.

Edmond, Rod. *Representing the South Pacific: Colonial Discourse from Cook to Gauguin.* Cambridge: Cambridge University Press, 1997.

Ellsworth, Elizabeth. "Why Doesn't This Feel Empowering? Working Through the Repressive Myths of Critical Pedagogy." *Harvard Educational Review* 59 (1989): 297–324.

Ellsworth, Elizabeth. *Teaching Positions: Difference, Pedagogy and the Power of Address.* New York: Teachers College Press, 1997.

Errante, Antoinette. "Education and National Personae in Portugal's Colonial and Postcolonial Transition." *Comparative Education Review* 42 (1998): 267–308.

Fabian, Johannes. *Time and the Other: How Anthropology Makes its Object.* New York: Columbia University Press, 1983.

Fanon, Franz. *Black Skin, White Masks.* New York: Grove Press, 1967.

Fanon, Franz. *The Wretched of the Earth.* New York: Grove Press, 1968.

Foucault, Michel. *The Order of Things: An Archaeology of the Human Sciences.* New York: Pantheon Books, 1970.

Foucault, Michel. *The Will to Knowledge: The History of Sexuality, Vol. 1.* New York: Pantheon Books, 1978.

Friederichs, Jane O. "Whose Responsibility? The Impact of Imminent Socio-Political Change on Hong Kong Education." *International Review of Education* 37 (1991): 193–209.

Friederichs, Jane O. Prospects for Educational Reform During Political Transformation in Hong Kong. *Compare* 22 (1992): 165–82.

Frow, John. *Cultural Studies and Cultural Value.* Oxford: Clarendon Press, 1995.

Gandhi, Leila. *Postcolonial Theory: A Critical Introduction.* St. Leonards: Allen and Unwin, 1998.

Gardiner, Michael. "Utopia as Critique." In *Bakhtin, Carnival and Other Subjects: Selected Papers from the Fifth International Bakhtin Conference.* Edited by David Shepherd. Amsterdam: Rodopi, 1993.

Ginsburg, Mark H., et al. "Educators/Politics." *Comparative Education Review* 36 (1992): 417–445.

Goodman, Joyce. "Languages of Female Colonial Authority: The Educational Network of the Ladies Committee of the British and Foreign School Society, 1813–1837." *Compare* 30 (2000): 7–19.

Gu, Mingyuan. *Education in China and Abroad: Perspectives from a Lifetime in Comparative Education.* Hong Kong: Comparative Education Research Centre, University of Hong Kong, 2001.

Hall, Stuart. "The Local and the Global: Globalisation and Ethnicity." In *Culture, Globalization and the World System.* Edited by Anthony King. London: Macmillan, 1991.

_____. "New Ethnicities." In *'Race,' Culture and Difference.* Edited by James Donald and Ali Rattansi. London: Sage, 1992.

_____. "When was the 'Post-colonial? Thinking at the Limit." In *The Postcolonial Question: Common Skies, Divided Horizons,* edited by Iain Chambers and Lidia Curti. London: Routledge, 1996.

Hayhoe, Ruth. "Redeeming Modernity." *Comparative Education Review* 44 (2000): 423–440.

Hoffman, Diane. "Culture and Comparative Education: Toward Decentering and Recentering the Discourse." *Comparative Education Review* 43(1999): 464–488.

hooks, bell. *Feminist Theory: From Margin to Center.* Boston: South End Press, 1984.

hooks, bell. *Talking Back: Thinking Feminist, Thinking Black.* Toronto: Between the Lines, 1988.

JanMohamed, Abdul R. "The Economy of the Manichean Allegory." *Critical Inquiry* 12 (1985): 59–87.

Kelly, Gail P. "Colonialism, Indigenous Society, and School Practices: French West Africa and Indochina, 1918–1938." In *Education and the Colonial Experience.* Edited by Philip G. Altbach and Gail P. Kelly. New Brunswick: Transaction, 1984.

Kelly, Gail P. and Philip Altbach. "Introduction." In *Education and Colonialism.* Edited by Philip G. Altbach and Gail P. Kelly. New York: Longman, 1978.

Kelly, Gail P. "Colonial Schooling in Vietnam: Policy and Practice." In: *Comparative Education.* Edited by Philip G. Altbach and Gail P. Kelly. New York: Longman, 1978

Kelly, Gail P. "Teachers and the Transmission of State Knowledge: A Case Study of Colonial Vietnam." In *Comparative Education.* Edited by Philip G. Altbach, Gail P. Kelly, and Robert F. Arnove. New York: Macmillan, 1982.

Kempner, Ken. "Post-Modernizing Education on the Periphery and in the Core." *International Review of Education* 44 (1998): 441–60.

Leach, Fiona. "Expatriates as Agents of Cross-Cultural Transmission." *Compare* 24 (1994): 217–31.

Little, Angela. "Development Studies and Comparative Education: Context, Content, Comparison and Contributors." *Comparative Education* 36 (2000): 279–296.

Luk, Bernard. H. "Chinese Culture in the Hong Kong Curriculum: Heritage and Colonialism." *Comparative Education Review* 35 (1991): 650–68.

Matthews, Catherine and David Matthews. "Languages of Scotland: Culture and the Classroom." *Comparative Education* 36 (2000): 211–221.

McConaghy, Cathryn. *Rethinking Indigenous Education: Culturalism, Colonialism and the Politics of Knowing.* Flaxton: Post Pressed, 2000.

Mehta, Sonia and Peter Ninnes. "Postpositivist Debates and Comparative Education: Resistance, Reinvention, Revolution." *Paper presented at the CIES annual conference,* San Antonio, Texas, March, 2000.

Memmi, Albert. *The Colonizer and the Colonized.* Boston: Beacon Press, 1965.

Minh-Ha, Trinh. "Introduction to She, the Inappropriate/d Other." *Discourse: Journal for Theoretical Studies in Media and Culture* 8 (Fall 1986/1987): 3–10.

Mukherjee, Arun. *Postcolonialism: My Living.* Toronto: Tsar Books, 1998.

Mundy, Karen. "Educational Multilateralism and World (Dis)Order." *Comparative Education Review* 42 (1998): 448–478.

Nakata, Martin. "Issues of Literacy in Indigenous Communities," Keynote address at Postcolonial Pedagogies for Community-Based Indigenous Teacher Education Workshop, 12–13 August. Armidale: NSW, University of New England, 1999.

Ngugi, Wa Thiong'o. *The River Between.* London: Heinemann, 1965.

Ngugi, Wa Thiong'o. "The Language of African Literature." *New Left Review* (April–June, 1985): 109–127.

Ngugi, Wa Thiong'o. *Decolonizing the Mind: The Politics of Language in African Literature.* London, J. Currey and Nairobi: Heinemann, 1986.

Ninnes, Peter and Greg Burnett. "Comparative Education Research: Poststructuralist Possibilities." *Comparative Education* (in press).

Ninnes, Peter and Sonia Mehta. "Postpositivist Theorising and Research: Challenges and Opportunities for Comparative Education." *Comparative Education Review* 44 (2000): 205–212.

Orner, Mimi. "Interrupting the Calls for Student Voice in 'Liberatory' Education: A Feminist Poststructuralist Perspective." In *Feminisms and Critical Pedagogy.* Edited by Carmen Luke and Jennifer Gore. London: Routledge, 1992.

Ortiz, Alicia D. "Buenos Aires" (excerpt). *Discourse: Journal for Theoretical Studies in Media and Culture* 8 (Fall, 1986/1987): 73–83.

Parry, Benita. "Resistance Theory: Theorising Resistance or Two Cheers for Nativism." In *Colonial Discourse/Postcolonial Theory.* Edited by Francis Barker, Peter Hulme and Margaret Iverson. Manchester: Manchester University Press, 1994.

Paulston, Rolland. "Mapping Comparative Education after Postmodernity." *Comparative Education Review* 43 (1999): 438–463.

_____. "Imagining Comparative Education: Past, Present, Future." *Compare* 30 (2000): 353–367.

Pennycook, Alastair. *English and the Discourses of Colonialism.* London, Routledge, 1998.

Popkewitz, Thomas. "National Imaginaries, the Indigenous Foreigner, and Power: Comparative Educational Research." In *Discourse Formation in Comparative Education.* Edited by Jurgen Schreiwer. Frankfurt am Main: Peter Lang, 2000.

Postiglione, Gerald A. "From Capitalism to Socialism? Hong Kong Education within a Transitional Society." *Comparative Education Review* 35 (1991): 627–49.

Raina, V. K. "Indigenizing Teacher Education in Developing Countries: The Indian Context." *Prospects* 29, 1 (1999): 5–25.

Renan, Ernest. "What is a Nation?" In *Nation and Narration.* Edited by Homi Bhabha. London and New York: Routledge, 1990.

Rust, Val. "Postmodernism and its Comparative Education Implications." *Comparative Education Review* 35 (1991): 610–626.

_____. *Orientalism: Western Conceptions of the Orient.* New York: Pantheon, 1978.

Said, Edward. *Culture and Imperialism.* London: Chatto and Windus, 1993.

Samoff, Joel. "No Teacher Guide, No Textbooks, No Chairs: Contending with Crisis in African Education." In *Comparative Education: The Dialectic of the Global and the Local*. Edited by Robert Arnove and Carlos Torres. Lanham, MD: Rowman & Littlefield, 1999.

Semali, Ladislaus. "Community as Classroom: Dilemmas of Valuing African Indigenous Literacy in Education." *International Review of Education* 45 (1999): 305–319.

Soyinka, Wole. "Meeting Point" (interview) *Courier* 102 (January–February, 1987): 2–4.

Spivak, Gayatri. "The Rani of Sirmur." In *Europe and Its Others: Proceedings of the Essex Conference on the Sociology of Literature*. Edited by Francis Barker. Colchester: University of Essex, 1985.

——————. "Can the Subaltern Speak?" In *Marxism and the Interpretation of Culture*. Edited by Carl Nelson and Lawrence Grossberg. URBANA: University of Illinois: Urbana, 1988.

——————. *The Postcolonial Critic: Interviews, Strategies, Dialogues*. New York: Routledge, 1990.

——————. *Outside in the Teaching Machine*. New York: Routledge, 1993.

Sultana, Ronald G. "Towards Increased Collaboration in the South: The Mediterranean Education Project." *Compare* 26 (1996): 105–10.

Sweeting, Anthony. "Doing Comparative Historical Education Research: Problems and Issues from and about Hong Kong." *Compare* 29 (1999): 269–85.

Tikly, Leon. "Postcolonialism and Comparative Education." *International Review of Education* 45 (1999): 603–21.

Torgovnick, Marianna. *Primitive Passions: Men, Women, and the Quest for Ecstasy*. New York: Alfred A. Knopf, 1996.

Tuhiwai Smith, Linda. "Ko taku ko ta te Maori: The Dilemmas of a Maori Academic." *Paper presented at the New Zealand Association for Research in Education/Australian Association for Research in Education conference*, Geelong: Deakin University, 1992.

Watson, Keith. "Teachers and Teaching in an Interdependent World." *Compare* 21 (1991): 107–26.

——————. "Caught between Scylla and Charybdis: Linguistic and Educational Dilemmas Facing Policy-Makers in Pluralist States." *International Journal of Educational Development* 14 (1994a): 321–37.

——————. "Technical and Vocational Education in Developing Countries: Western Paradigms and Comparative Methodology." *Comparative Education* 30 (1994b): 85–97.

——————. "Memories, Models and Mapping: The Impact of Geopolitical Changes on Comparative Studies in Education." *Compare* 28 (1998): 5–33.

——————. "Comparative Education Research: The Need for Reconceptualisation and Fresh Insights." *Compare* 29 (1999): 233–248.

Welch, Anthony. "The Triumph of Technocracy of the Collapse of Certainty? Modernity, Postmodernity, and Postcolonialism." In *Comparative Education: The Dialectic of the Global and the Local*. Edited by Robert Arnove and Carlos A. Torres. Lanham, MD: Rowman and Littlefield, 1999.

Westley, David. "Language and Education in Africa: A Select Bibliography, 1980–1990." *Comparative Education Review* 36 (1992): 355–67.

Williamson, Alan. "Breaking Down the Myths of Colonial Schooling: The Case of the Torres Strait Islands in Northern Australia." *Comparative Education* 27 (1991): 297–309.

Wright, Handel K. "Educational Change in Sierra Leone: Making a Case for Critical African Drama." *International Journal of Educational Development* 14 (1994): 177–193.

CHAPTER 11

A Postcolonial Rereading of the Contemporary Internationalization Movement of Japanese Education: The Construction of 'Japaneseness' in a Globalized World

YOKO MOCHIZUKI

While nations around the world are forced to cope with diversity and difference within their boundaries, Japan seems to be struggling with a problem of the contrary nature — conformity, homogeneity, and insularity. In this era of accelerated globalization, if the concern of most countries is to deal with diversity that already exists within borders and develop strategies for producing social cohesion, Japan's preoccupation seems to be with opening an insular country to the outside world and exposing its 'homogeneous' population to foreigners and foreign cultures.

The contemporary internationalization movement in Japan, *kokusaika* (which literally means 'internationalization'), is noteworthy for the unanimous support it enjoys. *Kokusaika* in the context of education constitutes a major restructuring movement in contemporary Japan, which must be discussed along with theoretical work on the construction of 'Japaneseness.' The popular discourse of internationalization is based on the widely shared assumption of Japanese homogeneity and uniqueness — that is, the belief that Japan is a monolingual, monoracial, classless society. In this chapter, I reinterpret from a postcolonial perspective the seemingly contradictory ways in which Japan's efforts to 'internationalize' its education system are intertwined with the construction of 'Japaneseness'. While examination of the colonial legacy in education is not a new approach in the field of comparative and international education, much of the writing on this theme was informed by dependency theory, emphasizing structural inequalities between the former colonizers and colonies and paying inadequate attention to issues of race, culture, difference, and identity (Tikly, 1999). Building on recent development in postcolonial studies,[1] researchers are beginning to uncover the colonial map underlying educational policies, practices, and discourses in former colonial empires (Steiner-Khamsi, 2000). Through examination of the Japanese government initiatives to cope with internationalization, I demonstrate the extent to which Japan's internationalization policies and practices are shaped by the historic fact that Japan was a non-Western colonizer. By recognizing the powerful influence which Western colonial discourse on the themes of race, culture, and difference has had upon the creation of a modern Japan, I attempt to show how the internationalization of Japanese education is not contradictory, but rather central to an ongoing project of constructing modern Japanese identity.[2]

Examining the interplay of Japan's internationalism and particularism in shaping its education policies is a meaningful project, not because Japan is an exceptional case, but because it provides a concrete and vivid example of "modernity's particular paradox of universalism and particularism" (van Loon, 1997, p. 160). As van Loon (1997) argues, Edward Said's *Orientalism* (1978) and Benedict Anderson's *Imagined Communities* (1983) have profoundly changed the way modernity is theorized, and recent postcolonial writings (see, for example, Chatterjee, 1993; Bhabha, 1994) have attested that particularism—racism, ethnocentrism, nationalism—is central to modernist universalism rather than antithetical to it. By recognizing Japan's self-positioning between the Western colonizers and the races subjugated by them, this chapter attempts to reveal how *kokusaika* operates to legitimate persistent inequitable relationships of power which involve race, ethnicity, and nationality. The purpose and significance of this chapter, however, does not lie in critiquing Japanese particularism underlying *kokusaika* in the name of 'cosmopolitanism'; rather, it lies in demonstrating even a well-intentioned critique of Japanese particularism serves to reinforce "neo-universalist internationalism" (Ashcroft, Griffiths, and Tiffin, 1995, p. 152) in an increasingly global world.

Theories of 'Japaneseness'

In post-war Japan, a popular publishing genre has developed devoted to analyzing the distinctiveness and uniqueness of the Japanese people and culture. These essentialist *Nihonjinron* ('theories of the Japanese' or 'discourse on the Japanese') texts focus on "the homogeneous, exclusivist, conformist, harmonious image of Japanese society, contrasting Japan and the Japanese with other (particularly Western), societies" (Goodman, 1990, p. 3). In response to a proliferation of Nihonjinron literature, there have been attempts to debunk the 'myth' of Japanese homogeneity and uniqueness by critically examining Nihonjinron (e.g., Dale, 1986; Mouer and Sugimoto, 1986; Yoshino, 1992, 1997). Since the mid-1990s, at least three edited volumes have been published explicitly challenging the notion of monocultural Japan (Maher and MacDonald, 1995; Denoon, et al, 1996; Weiner, 1997) and at least four books have been written by Japanese sociologists to debunk the myth of meritocracy in Japanese society and to challenge the notion of Japan as a classless society (Kariya, 1995; Takeuchi, 1995; Sato, 2000; Hashimoto, 2001).

In addition to a wealth of research on *burakumin*, Koreans and Ainu as Japan's minorities (see, for example, De Vos and Wetherall, 1974; Lee and De Vos, 1985) the increasing visibility of 'new minority groups' has also challenged the notion of homogeneous Japan. In particular, *kikokushijo* (Japanese-born, foreign-educated children returning from abroad where they have accompanied their parents on overseas assignments) and Japanese-Brazilian return migrant workers have captured much journalistic and academic attention. Although Japanese-Brazilian migrant workers and *kikokushijo* are ethnically Japanese, they tend to be regarded as 'non-Japanese' or 'less Japanese' and are constructed as new internal 'Others' to define and redefine Japaneseness.[3]

Few scholars of Japanese society now take *Nihonjinron* at face value. For critics of *Nihonjinron*, Japan is not so much a model nation that has successfully modernized while maintaining its unique cultural heritage, as a chauvinistic nation that has created a self-image of uniqueness. Critics of *Nihonjinron* point out that Japan as a modern nation state has constantly compared itself to and measured itself against the West, thereby allowing the 'us' Japanese category to be filled with all the desirable traits which 'they,' foreigners, do not possess (see Table 1). This line of argument that 'Japaneseness' is constructed in a self-conscious opposition to Western modernity is useful, and it partly explains why *kikokushijo* used to be—and still are to a certain degree—victims of ridicule for possessing 'Western' values and losing their 'Japaneseness.' This cannot explain, however, (1) why *kikokushijo* were transformed into a positive minority group in the popular and policy discourses of internationalization (Goodman, 1990), or (2) why the Japanese discriminate against the Japanese-Brazilians, who self-consciously retain their Japaneseness in Brazil, when they migrate back to Japan as unskilled workers (Tsuda, 1998; Hingwan, 1996).

By applying the dichotomy between Japaneseness and non-Japaneseness, both *Nihonjinron* writers and critics of *Nihonjinron* disregard racial hierarchies that exist between the First World and Third World countries. Although there is a recognition that *Nihonjinron* has developed as a response to Western cultural hegemony, the binary oppositions of self/other, Japanese/non-Japanese, insider/outsider, and tradition/modernity

TABLE 1. The construction of Japaneseness based on the dichotomy of self/other: Japaneseness and non-Japaneseness contrasted.

Japaneseness	Non-Japaneseness
In-group	Out-group
Japan	Other countries
Japanese	Foreigners
Japanese culture	Foreign cultures (particularly Western)
"Traditional" Japanese	"Internationalized" foreigners
Associated with pastness	Associated with modernity
Japanese language: *nihongo*	Language of the Other: English
Classless, unified society	Class-based, disunified societies

Source: Adapted from McVeigh, 1997, p. 84, Figure 4.1

virtually ignore the existence of the colonized.[4] In order to fully explain the complex dimensions of the process of constructing Japaneseness, we need an explanatory model that acknowledges Japan's self-positioning between the Western colonizers and the races colonized by them. Before taking a postcolonial approach to Japan's national identity and internationalization, I now critically examine the mainstream treatment of the internationalization of Japanese education and point out weaknesses in the existing literature.

The Dichotomy of the 'Actual' versus 'Ideal' of Internationalization

In the most naïve accounts of Japanese responses to the outside world, Japan is depicted as outrightly xenophobic as if the entire country were engaged in a concerted effort to keep foreigners and foreign cultures out (e.g., Lamont-Brown, 1994; Picken, 1986). Picken (1986, p. 60) writes that Monbusho's[5] attitudes toward the teaching of the English language reflect "xenophobic attitudes" and "fear of loss of cultural identity." Such a view of Japanese society, based on an uncritical acceptance of *Nihonjinron*, shows internationalization as an urgently needed measure to remedy Japanese insularity. *Kokusaika* is straightforwardly interpreted as a welcome move necessary to improve Japanese society. Citing Monbusho's policy measures designed to internationalize Japanese education, Scott (1993, p. 71) praises Japan's internationalization as "a serious and far-reaching endeavor."

Although Japan has successfully disseminated the idea of Japanese homogeneity both at home and abroad, many scholars do not regard *kokusaika* as an innocent project, resonating with the criticism of *Nihonjinron* as a nationalizing discourse. There is a body of education literature that treats 'internationalization' as an ideological apparatus to mask underlying, unchanging nationalistic projects of Japan. Some emphasize a nationalistic intention to gear Japanese education to the global economy (Spring, 1998), some stress a nationalistic project to reinforce Japanese identity (Lincicome, 1993; Parmenter, 1999; Parmenter et al., 2000), and some emphasize both (McVeigh, 1997). While Picken (1986) views a general lack of ability among Japanese people to communicate in English as a result of their xenophobic reaction to a foreign language, McVeigh (1997) argues that English language education in Japan is purposely and deliberately made ineffective for communicative purposes in order to reinforce Japanese identity vis-à-vis learning the non-communicative language of the Other.

While Japanese education enjoyed positive publicity in the United States especially when the Japanese economy was booming (see, for example, Cummings, 1982, 1989), many U.S. scholars have joined the Japanese leftist intellectual Horio Teruhisa[6] in a harsh attack on Japanese education in service to the economy and the state (e.g., Lincicome, 1993; Spring, 1998; Parmenter, 1999). It is not difficult to understand why U.S. scholars sympathize with Horio (1988), who views Japanese schools as authoritarian and anti-democratic. Japanese leftist intellectuals and progressive educators have interpreted many of the Monbusho initiatives as detrimental to the natural development of students (Okano and Tsuchiya, 1999, pp. 30–52), and their view is heavily indebted to the U.S. education philosophy that emphasizes "an Enlightenment legacy asserting liberty, the pursuit of happiness, human rights,...distrust of government, and repugnance toward orders and regulations that produce standardization and conformity," among other things (Wray, 1991, p. 469). In short, Japanese education almost perfectly represents what Americans and 'internationally-minded' Japanese see as an outdated education system that fails to contribute to personal development.

In a scholarly discussion of *kokusaika* in terms of education in Japan, taking place on both sides of the Pacific, official internationalization policies are unfavorably received or at least seen as in need of improvement. Not surprisingly, contemporary American scholars agree with Japanese 'progressives,' who have strongly identified with the "democratizing and decentralizing themes" (Cummings, 1982, p. 20) of the educational reforms instituted under the Allied Occupation (1945–52), about the need for 'genuine' internationalization in contemporary Japan. The dichotomy of the 'actual' and the 'ideal' of internationalization, then, closely parallels the binary opposition between a conservative state versus progressive individuals and groups. Conversely, the conflict between the conservative camp and the progressive camp (see table 2) is reduced to the dichotomy of nationalists versus internationalists. This downplays a critical point that the quest to make Japan 'international' has captivated a diverse set of actors despite their difference over definitions of 'internationalization'.

A Postcolonial Approach to the Debate over Internationalization

The move to internationalize Japanese education is unique because enthusiastic support is found across both conservative and progressive camps.

TABLE 2. Actors in Educational Policy Decisions in Japan.

	Traditional Conservative Camp	Progressive Camp
Central actor	Ministry of Education (*Monbusho*)	Japan Teachers Union (Nikkyoso)
Political party	Liberal Democratic Party (LDP)	Socialist and Communist Parties
Interest groups	Local administrators	Association of National University Presidents
	Business community	
Advocates	The Ad Hoc Council on Education (1984–87)	Leftist Intellectuals
		Morita Toshio (former director of the Citizens Institute for Educational Research affiliated with the Japan Teacher Union)
		Horio Teruhisa (Tokyo University professor)
Guiding Principle	State-instrumentalism; education in service to the economy and the state	Education for personal development, human rights, world peace

Sources: 64; Scott 1993, pp. 66–67.

The perplexing popularity of *kokusaika* can be understood by looking at the construction of 'Japaneseness' in the context of modern Japan's efforts to 'catch up' with the West. Not only does the dichotomy of a traditional, conservative state and liberal progressives contribute to minimizing the modernizing, progressive role which the Japanese state has played since the Meiji Restoration of 1868, it also discounts widespread cooperation and collaboration between the Japanese state and progressive individuals and groups — even during the ultra-nationalist years between 1931–1945 — driven by the shared belief in modernity (Garon, 1994). Moreover, the question of national identity in modern Japan was often a struggle between those who upheld the constitutional state and those (including intellectuals influenced by European Marxist thoughts) who were disillusioned by the modern Japanese state and instead turned to an "ethnicized" view of the Japanese (Doak, 1997). Debate over the internationalization of Japanese education, then, is not as clear-cut as it seems on the surface. If statists are those who espouse Western modernity and civilization, how can they also be ethnocentric nationalists, as critically described by advocates of internationalization for world citizenship? If anti-statists are those who try to create a Japanese nation distinct from the Japanese state based on ethnic nationalism, how can they be progressives who champion internationalism?

To solve this puzzle, we must acknowledge that those who embraced Western modernity and democratic values and those who rejected them were trapped in the Western racist paradigm in their effort to create modern Japanese identity.[7] Coming in contact with the Eurocentric world, where racio-cultural hierarchies were conceived in terms of polarization between the "Civilized White" and the "Barbarous Black" (Russell, 1992, p. 299), the Meiji Japan emerging from self-imposed isolation positioned itself between the enlightened white and the backward black in order to deal with its own racio-cultural status in the world (see Figure 1). Precisely because of their strong belief in Western values, Japanese supporters of Western democratic values uncritically embraced Western racial hierarchies. Fukuzawa Yukichi, a Meiji proponent of the right to democratic education as well as freedom of thought, regarded by Joel Spring (1990, pp. 47–48) and Wray (1991, p. 474) as a pioneer internationalist, is no exception. Fukuzawa (1875, as cited in Russell, 1992, p. 299) defined Japan and its Asian neighbors as "semi-civilized" *(hankai)*, positioning them between the "civilization" *(bunmei)* of the West and the "savages" *(yabanjin)* of Africa. Moreover, Fukuzawa (1885, as cited in Kobayashi, 1986, p.67) also advocated "de-Asianism" *(datsu-a)*, paving Japan's way toward isolation from—and the ensuing colonization of — its Asian neighbors.

Nobody would question that Japan has 'caught up' with the West at least in terms of modernization, but it is highly questionable whether Japan is ready to play a leadership role in the international community. Unmistakably, Japan's economic and educational 'miracles' challenged the underlying assumptions of modernization, that is, 'modern' attitudes and values are incompatible with 'traditional' ones. After all these 'miraculous' achievements, the Japanese are still obliged to feel somewhat 'uncivilized' and 'backward' in comparison with the West, precisely because of what the term 'miracle' implies — that is, the Western notion that *'they' Japanese* (or peoples in Korea, Taiwan, Singapore, and Hong Kong in the case of the East Asian Miracle) *are not supposed to be doing that well.*

Some argue that to negate this feeling of backwardness, the Japanese should assimilate more Western standards into the Japanese system (or achieve 'international standards' or 'global standards') and prove that they are not 'economic animals.' Meanwhile, others argue that the Japanese should be prouder of their tradition and culture. Contemporary Japan's urge to attain 'international standards' resonates with pre-war Japan's desire to be considered as an equal by European imperialists by way of turning itself into an imperialist. The historian Lewis Gann (1984, p. 502) writes that Japanese colonialism was "a matter of prestige" and Japanese nationalists regarded colonies as a "status symbol," pointing out that the Japanese colonizers lacked not only capitalist motives, but also self-confidence, national pride, missionary spirit, evangelical inspiration, and colonial romanticism equivalent to those held by their British, French, or German counterparts.[8] Writing on Japanese colonial education in Taiwan,

Civilized white
Idealized West
Symbolic power: modernity, rationalism, civility, enlightenment
colonizer

The model minority in the U.S., *Japanese-Americans* (distancing themselves from the Japanese). The 21 June 1971 issue of *Newsweek* reported Japanese Americans as "outwhiting the whites" (as cited in Takahash, 1997, 1).

Nonwhite Other

Positive minority *kikokushijo* (Japanese returnees categorized as a unified group with shared identifiable qualities associated with the West, such as individualism, directness, and the global language English) (Goodman, 1990).

Unique, Homogeneous Japanese
The non-Western Colonizer

Negative minority in Japan *Japanese-Brazilians* (return migrating to Japan as unskilled immigrant workers) (Tsuda, 1998; Hingwan, 1996).

Positive minority in Brazil *Japanese-Brazilians* (respected for high cultural and social status; strong identities as ethnic "Japanese") (Tsuda 1998)

Barbarous black
Nonwhite/Darker Other
"A symbolic counterpoint to modernity, rationalism, and civility" (Russell, 1992, 315).
colonized

Note: This model was constructed by the author based primarily on Russell's (1992) examination of how racial stereotypes of the black Other are constructed in contemporary Japanese mass culture. Based on my reading of a wide range of literature on minority groups who are ethnically Japanese, I positioned Japanese-Americans, *kikokushijo*, and Japanese-Brazilians in this model to show how different groups are constructed in popular and policy discourses of contemporary societies based on Western colonial discourse on race, culture, and difference.

Figure 1 The construction of 'Japaneseness' from a postcolonial perspective: Japan's discursive positioning vis-à-vis the West.

Tsurumi (1977) argues that the Japanese were preoccupied with making Taiwan a peaceful and prosperous "model colony" which could impress the Western colonizers.

With a postcolonial approach to the construction of Japaneseness in mind, we need to reframe the debate over *kokusaika* in terms of disagreement over strategies to prove Japan's modernity and civility to the world.

We can reach a more sophisticated understanding of cultural and political debates surrounding *kokusaika* by regarding them as the manifestation of Japan's ambivalence toward encouraging assimilation of Western standards to the point at which Japan, in effect, *becomes* the West. Seen in this light, advocating internationalization for global citizenship is not as lofty and sublime as the 'progressive' camp presumes. Assuming the benign superiority of the United States, for example, the 'progressive' camp tends to interpret the transformation of post-war Japanese education not as a successful local adaptation of imposed educational reforms, but as the unfortunate reversal of Occupation reforms.[9] The mainstream view among Japanese historians of post-war Japanese education has been that a series of education reforms under the Allied Occupation were not imposed by Americans but *voluntarily* implemented by the Japanese themselves *with the aid of Americans* (Katsuoka, 1999, p. 318). This interpretation downplays U.S. ethnocentrism and the project of Americanization, underlying the Occupation reforms, while emphasizing Japanese ethnocentrism and positing a state-instrumentalism, which allegedly prevented democratic reforms from materializing.

The Japanese racial paradigm — an "indigenized" (Appadurai, 1990) version of the Western racio-cultural paradigm — is so embedded in popular consciousness that 'we' Japanese cannot help but continue to distance ourselves from races subjected by Western powers. Japanese racism is evidenced by the Japanese politicians' crude racist remarks, which received extensive media coverage both in Japan and abroad. For example, at a National Study Council meeting of the Liberal Democratic Party on September 22, 1986, then Prime Minister Nakasone Yasuhiro attributed the declining "intelligence level" of the United States to the presence of Blacks, Puerto Ricans, and Mexicans (Russell, 1992, p. 296). Ironically, it was Nakasone who established *Rinji Kyoiku Shingikai* or the Ad Hoc Council on Education (hereafter AHCE) in 1984 and emphasized the need for internationalization. More recently, Ishihara Shintaro, the very popular governor of Tokyo, aroused criticism by making a derogatory comment on immigrants in Japan. Addressing a ceremony for the Ground Self-Defense Forces (SDF, the Japanese equivalent of an army) on April 9, 2000, Ishihara said that "*sangokujin*" — a term which literally means "people from third countries," but was used pejoratively to describe non-Japanese Asians after World War II — and other foreigners could stage a riot in the aftermath of a disastrous earthquake and called on the SDF to be prepared to maintain order in such an uprising.[10] It is not surprising, then, that Japan's internationalization is seen as full of ideological contradictions, manifesting the Japanese aspiration to elevate the Japanese race (either via cultivation of national pride or via assimilation of Western Enlightenment values) and their contempt for races subjugated by Western imperialists.

A Postcolonial Rereading of the Official Internationalization Policy

In this section I apply postcolonial theory in my review of policy measures developed by Japan's Ministry of Education to internationalize Japanese education, as a means to uncovering the colonial map that underlies the *kokusaika* in the context of education.[11] In its annually published white paper, *Monbukagakusho* (formerly Monbusho) succinctly addresses the question of how to cope with internationalization, along with other important educational issues. In Chapter 10 of the white paper published in 2002, *Monbukagakusho* (2002) discusses the need to continue to address the following four tasks to effectively respond to internationalization:

1. Cultivate a Japanese individual living in an international society (Section 2, Chapter 10)
   A. Promote education for international understanding
   B. Promote the teaching of foreign languages
   C. Improve educational programs for Japanese children living abroad
   D. Improve educational programs for Japanese children who have returned from a long stay overseas
2. Promote international exchanges to promote mutual understanding (Section 3, Chapter 10)
   A. Promote the exchange of students
   B. Promote international exchanges of teachers and youth
   C. Improve the teaching of Japanese to foreigners
   D. Promote the teaching of Japanese to foreign students in Japanese public schools
   E. Promote international exchanges and cooperation of culture
   F. Promote international exchanges of sports
   G. Promote bilateral exchanges
3. Cooperate on education development programs in developing countries (Section 4, Chapter 10)
   A. Domestic and international movements to promote education cooperation today
   B. Basic policies for international education cooperation and forms of cooperation
   C. Dispatch Japanese volunteers and experts to developing countries
   D. Develop human resources in development assistance
4. Promote international cooperation through international organizations (Section 5, Chapter 10)
   A. Participation in UNESCO's projects and cooperation with UNESCO

B. Participation in OECD's education projects
C. Cooperation with the Asia Pacific Economic Cooperation (APEC) in education projects
D. Cooperation with the European Union (EU)
E. Cooperation with the United Nations University (UNU)
F. Cooperation with the World Intellectual Property Organization (WIPO)

A Japanese Individual Living in an International Society

Policy Measure I-1 aims at promoting Japanese students' understanding of national history and traditional culture and encouraging them to nurture pride in and love for the nation, and at the same time, to cultivate abilities to live together with people of different backgrounds. Analyzing Monbusho's middle-school curriculum guidelines published in 1989, Parmenter (1999, p. 456) has found that Monbusho emphasizes "the role of education in developing students' self-awareness as a Japanese person and emotional attachment to the nation." Developing self-awareness as a Japanese individual is seen as an essential part of learning how to deal with people of different cultures in the context of "education for international understanding," not simply as an important goal of Japanese language and history education.

Policy Measure I-2 shows the Japanese government's attempt to make it easier for future generations of Japanese to deal with the outside — or English-speaking world. Nakasone's AHCE recommended an upgrading of English language education in schools mainly through greater emphasis on the communicative teaching method and the employment of foreigners and foreign-trained teachers. These suggestions have materialized, most notably through the 1987 inception and constant expansion of the Japan Exchange and Teaching (JET) program for improving the teaching of foreign languages in public secondary schools throughout Japan.[12] Table 3 shows the number of foreign college graduates invited as Assistant Language Teachers (ALTs) through the JET program.

The JET program, with an annual budget of more than $300 million, is what Japanese government officials proudly call "the largest initiative since World War II in the field of human and cultural exchange" and a "reverse Peace Corps" (McConnell, 1996, p. 446). The foreign teachers are "an important symbol of internationalization" and are treated as honorable guests (McConnell, 1996, p. 449). Preferential treatment of the ALTs clearly reflects the Japanese valorization of the white Other. Drawing on two-year fieldwork in Japan and interviews with ALTs, McConnell (1996, p. 453) has observed that the foreign teachers tend to expect that "Japanese teachers and administrators will come around to see the wisdom and sensibility of Western institutions and values" and regard "Japanese culture as somehow in need of 'development.'" The ALTs' demand that "the Japanese

TABLE 3. The number of Assistant Language Teachers (ALT) invited through JET Program, by Country (as of July 1, 2001).

	Country	Number	Percent
1	United States	2,347	42.0%
2	United Kingdom	1,325	23.7%
3	Canada	1,018	18.2%
4	New Zealand	345	6.2%
5	Australia	344	6.2%
6	Ireland	88	1.6%
7	South Africa	33	0.6%
8	Jamaica	22	0.4%
9	Singapore	13	0.2%
10	China	10	0.2%
11	France	9	0.2%
12	Germany	3	0.1%
13	Korea	3	0.1%
14	India	2	0.0%
15	Israel	2	0.0%
16	Italy	2	0.0%
17	Austria	1	0.0%
18	Finland	1	0.0%
	Unknown	15	0.3%
	Total	5,583	100%

Source: Adapted from Monbukagakusho 2002, Table 2–10–1.

reconstitute themselves and their society so as to make them more compatible with Western norms and expectations" (McConnell, 1996, p. 454) attests to the progressive role and Western superiority uncritically assumed by the foreign teachers.

Compared to I-1 and I-2, Policy Measures I-3 and I-4 affect only a fraction of Japanese children. Nevertheless, promoting education for overseas and returnee children is important as a sign of the government's commitment to 'internationalization.' Japanese policy regarding education of overseas children (I-3) is unique in that educational patterns are differentiated from those in developing countries (countries of the colonized Other) and developed countries (countries of the white Other). The Japanese government has established full-time and supplementary Japanese schools in certain foreign countries to educate overseas children since the 1970s, a policy which has created two distinct educational patterns for these children in the developing versus developed countries. In 'Third World' countries, the majority of students attend full-time Japanese schools. In 'First World' countries, the majority of students attend local (usually English-speaking) schools and supplementary Japanese schools on Saturday (Goodman, 1990; Kato, 1988; also see Table 4). One exception to this pattern is Africa. In Africa, a higher percentage of Japanese children attend *genchiko* (which literally means "local school") than in Asia, the Middle East, or Latin America, for "what are termed *genchiko* in Africa are in fact elite schools, dating from the colonial period, with lessons taught in English or French" primarily for Europeans by predominantly European teachers (Goodman, 1990, p. 35). These educational patterns of Japanese children living abroad clearly reflect Japan's racio-cultural paradigm. The Japanese overseas are willing to take advantage of educational systems of the civilized West (including those established for Western colonizers in Africa), while they see no merit in educating their children with children of the nonwhite/darker Other.

Policy Measure I-4 clearly shows the government's efforts to ameliorate the re-adaptation problems of returnee children or *kikokushijo*, as well as its utilitarian intention of producing 'international Japanese' who will serve to advance the national interests in the global economy. Although returnees vary tremendously in terms of age, duration, and place of sojourn, and the type(s) of schools they attended while abroad, *kikokushijo* are categorized as "a unified group with shared identifiable qualities often associated with Western values, such as individualism and directness" (Goodman, 1990, p. 212). Not all *kikokushijo* are returning from Europe or North America, and approximately one third of all school-age children residing abroad attend full-time Japanese schools (see table 4). As in the case of foreign teachers recruited through the JET program, it is their association with the idealized West that gives *kikokushijo* their symbolic value. As Goodman's (1990) study has demonstrated, preferential treatment of *kikokushijo*—most significantly special quotas set up to facilitate *kikokushijo's* entry into the top colleges and universities–damages the most celebrated achievement of Japan's postwar education system — equality — and also does little, to 'internationalize' the entire Japanese education system.

Given the accelerated international migratory movements in an era of globalization, the re-integration of *kikokushijo* into the Japanese education system must be discussed along with the integration of foreign students into Japanese public schools. Policy Measure II-4, "Promote the teaching of Japanese to foreign students in Japanese public schools," is an interesting development, for it shows that the Japanese government now recognizes the need for remedial language education or JSL (Japanese as a second language) education for immigrant students in public schools. Nevertheless, the inclusion of the measure under "international exchanges" also shows that consciously or unconsciously Monbukagakusho denies the possibility of foreign children's growing up as 'Japanese individuals'.

TABLE 4. Spread of Overseas Japanese Schools (as of April 15, 2001).

Area	Full-time Japanese Schools (Nihonjingakko)			Supplementary Japanese Schools (Hoshuko)			Total number of school-age accompanying children residing in the area
	Number of Schools	Student Enrollment	Percentage of Students enrolled in Nihonjingakko	Number of Schools	Student Enrollment	Percentage of Students enrolled in Hoshuko	
Asia	32	11,474	77.6%	16	503	3.4%	14,778 (29.1%)
North America	3	606	3.1%	83	13040	66.3%	19,666 (38.7%)
Central and South America	18	776	58.7%	10	137	10.4%	1,321 (2.6%)
Europe	23	3,344	28.4%	51	3673	31.2%	11,760 (23.2%)
Oceania	3	274	12.1%	10	496	22.0%	2,257 (4.4%)
Middle East	12	225	47.8%	7	46	9.8%	471 (0.9%)
Africa	5	144	26.7%	11	101	18.7%	539 (1.1%)
Total	96	16,843	33.2%	188	17,996	35.4%	50,792 (100%)

Source: Calculated from CLARINET (2001).
Note: North America includes Canada and the United States. In Canada there are 8 supplementary schools, which enroll 669 students and no full-time Japanese school.

International Exchanges for Mutual Understanding

The so-called "100,000 International Students Plan" is the government's attempt to increase the number of international students studying in Japan to a size appropriate for a developed nation with a powerful economy. This plan aims at increasing international students to the levels enjoyed by West Germany, the United Kingdom, and France (Hanami, 1995, pp. 113–115). While students from China, Korea, and Taiwan — three countries upon which Japan exerted a considerable influence as a colonizer — constitute 80 percent of foreign students in Japan, more than 60 percent of Japanese students abroad are concentrated in the United States (see Table 5 and 6). The influx of foreign students from Asia to Japan makes a sharp contrast with the efflux of Japanese students to English-speaking countries. China is the second most popular destination for Japanese students with about 20 percent of all Japanese students abroad, and this reflects the fact that, for over a thousand years, China had been the center of Asia and the civilized Other for Japan until Japan embarked on its modernization project.

Clearly, students from countries invaded or colonized by Japan find a Japanese degree desirable, while students from Western Europe and the United States—the white Other—do not seem to see merit in acquiring degrees in Japan.[13] This shows that, for the darker Other, Japan does represent modernity, cultural authority, and knowledge/power. For the civilized West, however, Japan belongs to the nonwhite Other (see figure 1). Interestingly, concerned with the long-term surplus of Japanese students studying in North America and Western Europe, Nakasone's AHCE even insisted that more Japanese university students choose Asia when they go abroad to study (Lincicome, 1993, p. 133).

Underlying the "100,000 International Students Plan" is Japan's desire to be recognized as a "civilized" nation which can make not only economic but also intellectual contributions to the international community. Through its internationalization policies, therefore, the Japanese government explicitly aims at strengthening the symbolic power and cultural authority Japan represents. Thus, policy Measures II-3 and II-5 promote the appreciation of Japanese heritage — language, arts, and culture — in foreign countries. Among business people, learning Japanese is regarded as a means to increase one's marketability, which is a product of Japan's economic strength. However, Japanese is not a *lingua franca* like English or French. Since Japan imposed the Japanese language upon its former colonies of Taiwan and Korea as part of its assimilation policy, proclaiming the intention of spreading the Japanese language to foreigners tends to be regarded as the manifestation of a hidden ambition for Japanese cultural hegemony, especially by the leftist Japanese intellectuals. To examine the nature and degree of the fear of 'Japanization' in Asia lies beyond the scope of this chapter, but it is important to recognize that Policy Measure II-3 is a project to add a 'universal' cultural value to the Japanese language.[14]

TABLE 5. The number of foreign students in Japan, by nationality (as of May 1, 2001).

	Country	Number		Percent
1	China	44,014	(1,713)	55.8%
2	Korea	14,725	(870)	18.7%
3	Taiwan	4,252	(-)	5.4%
4	Malaysia	1,803	(265)	2.3%
5	Thailand	1,411	(556)	1.8%
6	Indonesia	1,388	(554)	1.8%
7	United States	1,141	(147)	1.4%
8	Vietnam	938	(406)	1.2%
9	Bangladesh	805	(517)	1.0%
10	Philippines	490	(330)	0.6%
	Others	7,845	(3,815)	10.0%
	Total	78,812	(9,173)	100%

Source: Adapted from *Monbukagakusho*, 2002, Table 2–10–3.
Note: Figures in parentheses indicate the number of foreign students supported by the Japanese government.

TABLE 6. The number of Japanese students studying abroad, by country (various years).

	Country	Number	Percent
1	United States	46,406	61.4%
2	China	14,634	19.4%
3	United Kingdom	5,332	7.0%
4	Korea	1,871	2.5%
5	Australia	1,796	2.4%
6	Germany	1,788	2.4%
7	France	1,314	1.7%
8	Canada	774	1.0%
9	New Zealand	373	0.5%
10	Austria	359	0.5%
	Others	884	1.2%
	Total	75,580	100%

Source: Adapted from *Monbusho*, 2000, Figure 2-9-6.
Note: The year statistics were taken differs according to a country. The years span from 1993 to 2000.

Indeed, *Monbukagakusho's* (2002) intention to add "universal" value to Japanese heritage is evident in its particular reference, under Policy Measure II-5, to UNESCO's inclusion of eleven Japanese sites in its World Heritage List and proclamation of *Noh* (Japan's traditional performing arts) as one of the Masterpieces of the Oral and Intangible Heritage of Humanity. UNESCO's endorsement of Japanese heritage as "world heritage" and "heritage of humanity" gives instant validity to the claim that Japanese 'culture' has universal value. This strategy of deriving the civility and cultural authority of Japan from the universality and legitimacy of the United Nations is also apparent in Policy Measures III and IV.

International Cooperation

Policy Measures III and IV used to come under the same heading "international cooperation" (Monbusho, 2000). They reflect the Japanese government's desire to play the "civilizing" role in developing countries. After giving an overview of the international community's commitment to promoting basic education in developing countries, including the affirmation of the international goal "Education for All" at the Dakar 2000 World Education Forum (III-1) as well as different forms of development assistance (policy measure III-2), Monbusho highlights the civilizing role of Japan through bilateral cooperation (III-3, III-4) and active participation in the so-called 'international community,' namely, the United Nations organizations (IV-1, 5, 6), OECD (IV-2), and APEC (IV-3).

In the policy discourse of the Japanese government, "international cooperation" is usually used to signify Japan's support of the 'Enlightenment' project of the international community, while "international exchange" signifies all other kinds of exchanges between Japan and the rest of the world. *Monbukagakusho's* active role in financing the United Nations University (UNU) in Tokyo (IV-5) most vividly symbolizes Japan's support of the Enlightenment project of the United Nations. Altbach (1984, p.299) states that "[the] more 'modern' a nation is in terms of involvement with technology, industrialization, and current political and social thought, the more involved it is in an international system of knowledge." The primary function of UNU is to train scholars from developing countries for 'development.' In light of Altbach's (1984) view structured by a center-periphery model, the establishment of UNU in Tokyo reflects Japan's desire to be recognized as 'civilized' by way of making its capital into the center of an international system of 'development' knowledge.

Conclusion

As Ivy (1998, p. 93) describes it, Japan as a modern nation-state is "unimaginable outside its discursive positioning vis-à-vis the 'West.'" On the one hand, Japaneseness has been constructed within the Western colonialist discourse on race, culture, and civilization. Western hegemony has continued to influence the Japanese self-image; Japan's identity has been determined by its relationship to the White Other. Indeed, the "positioning of Japan's identity in Western terms" has established "the centrality of the West as the universal point of reference" (Sakai, 1989, p. 105) in defining Japanese difference, thereby reinforcing the universalizing master discourse of imperial Europe.

On the other hand, the construction of Japaneseness has always been a project to construct a 'modern'— yet not Western — national culture. As the nineteenth-century Japanese slogans 'Western Science, Eastern Morals' and 'Japanese Spirit, Western Technology' exemplify, Meiji Japan introduced Western-style schooling, science, and technology, while protecting against European and U.S. moral and political values. Science and technology belonged to the material "outside" domain — "a domain where the West has proved its superiority" — as opposed to the spiritual "inner" domain (Chatterjee, 1993, p. 4). While acknowledging Western superiority in this "outside" domain and achieving modernization, Japan has attempted to preserve its "inner" domain. The internationalization of Japanese education is not only a nationalizing movement to advance national interests but also indicative of Japan's willingness to let 'Western Morals' (e.g., individualism, democracy) finally touch this inner domain that has been exclusively associated with Japanese tradition.

Modernization theory has been attacked as ideologically biased and ethnocentric despite its "emphasis on measurable and *value-free* criteria" (e.g., industrialization, widespread literacy, economic growth), which would allow comparative assessment of the process of modernization across diverse politics (Garon, 1994, p. 342). Japan became 'modern' without becoming 'Western,' yet Japan is now under pressure from the international community to become 'international' on the grounds that Japanese insular culture should be made more compatible with Western moral and political values. Internationalization, then, is even more problematic than the concept of 'modernization' because it is more difficult to set up 'value-free' benchmarks of internationalization, and yet, it is almost impossible for researchers and practitioners in comparative and international education to dismiss value-laden criteria of internationalization (e.g., internationalism, human rights, social justice) merely as 'Western.'

Japan's internationalization has been roundly criticized by a number of Western and Japanese researchers primarily as internationalism based in 'Japaneseness.' It is important to recognize that Japan's racio-cultural paradigm guarantees not only a position of superiority for Japanese vis-à-vis the colonized Other but also a position of superiority for the Westerner vis-à-vis the nonwhite Other. Many critics of Japan's internationalization have reproached Japan for being chauvinistic, but they have not criticized Japan's conceptual complicity with the Western colonialist discourse, let alone the cultural hegemony the West tenaciously asserts. The very fact that the construction of 'Japaneseness' has been extensively discussed both by Japanese and non-Japanese scholars is indicative of the readiness with which academia is willing to critique self-aggrandizement on the part of Japanese people. This readiness to scrutinize 'Japaneseness' — Japanese ethnocentrism, Japanese racism, Japanese nationalism — stands in sharp contrast to the lack of "serious theoretical and critical attention" to the "power, valorization and experience of 'whiteness' as a form of contemporary ethnicity" (Williams and Chrisman, 1994, p. 17).

While such readiness itself is unmistakably a manifestation of Western universalism, what is more problematic is the production and consumption of knowledge driven by the civilizing desire to critique non-Western particularisms as symptomatic of 'backwardness' of those societies. When we as comparative and international education researchers attack internationalism based in 'Japaneseness' without challenging internationalism based in 'Western-ness' or the notion of the universal West, the ultimate convergence of the Japanese model of internationalization with Western models is construed as an evolutionary march toward a global village. Ironically, this approach leaves no possibility for countries of the nonwhite Other to become 'international' without becoming 'Western' despite its emphasis on 'genuine' internationalism and cosmopolitanism. Put more accurately, it is apparently — and only apparently — ironic and in actuality inevitable that *kokusaika* and the well-intentioned critique of *kokusaika* alike reinscribe colonial patterns of dominance and difference in our increasingly global world. The real challenge, if we are to develop new models of cultural exchange and development, is to avoid replicating the binaries of the Western colonialist discourse (e.g., 'First World' and 'Third World') on the one hand, and to evade giving away the colonial legacy and the undeniable fact of persisting disparities between the colonizer and the colonized on the other.

Endnotes

1. A detailed discussion of what constitutes postcolonial studies lies beyond the scope of this chapter. For edited volumes of important postcolonial writings, see Williams and Chrisman's (1994) *Colonial Discourse and Postcolonial Theory* and Ashcroft, Griffiths, and Tiffin's (1995) *The Post-colonial Studies Reader*. For discussion of the relevance of postcolonial theory for comparative and international education research, see Tikly (1999) and Ninnes and Burnett (this volume).

2. Although this chapter focuses on the relationship between Japan and the rest of the world, *kokusaika* is also about the relationship between Tokyo and the rest of Japan. For example, Robertson (1997) shows how Japan's countryside has been rediscovered and exoticized as Tokyo becomes internationalized. Robertson (1997) has observed: "Appeals to tradition underscore what Japanese culture has become (where tradition serves as a stable benchmark from which to measure the progress of modernity), while the rhetoric of internationalization emphasizes what it was (where the international-ness of the lifestyle is invoked to highlight and reify cultural practices and formations forfeited to the progress of modernity" p. 115. Robertson's observation has deep implications for the discussion of the construction of modern Japanese identity.

3. For discussions of how *kikokushijo* have been constructed as 'Other' in Japanese society, see Shibuya (2001, pp. 47–77) and Goodman (1990). Both Shibuya (2001) and Goodman (1990) pay close attention to the changing status of *kikokushijo*. For research on the immigration and integration of Japanese-Brazilian return migrant workers, see for example, Hingwan (1996), Tsuda (1998, 1999), and Brody (2002). The 1990 revision to the Immigration Control and Refugee Recognition Act granted *Nikkeijin* (descendants of Japanese emigrants) extensive immigration rights in Japan, including a right to legally engage in unskilled labor. Japan's official policy not to admit foreign unskilled laborers was compromised by allowing ethnic Japanese in Latin America to migrate back to Japan as unskilled workers. This led to an influx of *Nikkeijin* immigration from Brazil.

4. While discussing the construction of Japaneseness in terms of self-other, us-them polarities in his study focusing on Japanese business people, Yoshino (1997) states that "[the] Japanese sense of uniqueness should…not be confused with ethnocentrism, which is the belief that one's own group is central, most important, and culturally superior to other groups" (p. 141). Unlike critics of *Nihonjinron* who fail to recognize that, in the binary opposition of self/other, Japaneseness is constructed in relation to the dominant/universal Other (not the rest of the world), Yoshino (1997) is correct in pointing out that "Japanese elites long perceived themselves and their culture to be on the 'periphery' in relation to the 'central' civilizations (first that of China and then of the West) and constructed and reconstructed Japanese identity by stressing their 'particularistic' difference from the 'universal' Chinese and Westerners" (141). Nevertheless, he still fails to see Japan's complicity with Western racism in constructing Japanese identity.

5. Japan's Ministry of Education, Science, Sports, and Culture, *Monbusho* was reorganized as *Monbukagakusho* (Ministry of Education, Culture, Sports, Science and Technology) in January 2001.

6. In this chapter, Japanese names are given with the family name preceding the given name, in accordance with Japanese practice.

7. In her postcolonial critique of the founder of modern Japanese philosophy Nishida Kitaro, Arisaka (1997) analyzes how Nishida's philosophical universalism was complicit with Japan's colonizing project despite his opposition to imperialism. Just as the Japanese people's self-positioning between the Western colonizers and the races colonized by the West meant their complicity with European racism, Japanese philosophy's self-positioning vis-à-vis Western universalism served to justify Japanese colonialism on the grounds that Japan as "the bearer of [universal] truth" must free Asia from Western imperialism.

8. According to Gann (1987), Japanese colonialism cannot be explained adequately by existing theories of the origins of colonialism. Unlike European imperialists, Japan had neither "an excessive supply of savings that could most profitably be invested only abroad, under colonial auspices" (p. 499) nor "need for colonization as a prophylactic against rebellion from the poor" (p. 501); Japan mainly relied on agriculture for its income throughout its colonial expansion.

9. Issac Leon Kandel (1881–1965), a leading figure in comparative education, was a member of the United States Education Mission to Japan, which was responsible for post-war Occupation reforms. "Proponents of progressive education philosophy, which dominated American education from the 1930s through the 1950s, staffed the Education Division [of the Civil Information and Education Section (CIE), Supreme Command for Allied Powers (SCAP)]. Progressive educators possessed a confidence bordering on religious conviction that the new education was scientific, democratic, and modern. Conversely, they viewed traditional education as old-fashioned, unscientific, and authoritarian" (Wray, 1991, p. 448). Pollack (1993) writes that Kandel was concerned with what he saw as a missionary zeal of American progressive educators inexperienced with foreign education systems and said, "Hence, the imposition on Japan of the American system of education" (p. 779).

10. In an article entitled "Tokyo Chief Starts New Furor, on Immigrants," published in the *New York Times*, 10 April 2000, Calvin Sims reported that Ishihara's comments particularly shocked Korean residents by reviving painful memories of a massacre of innocent Koreans after a devastating earthquake in 1923 in Tokyo and Yokohama. After the 1923 earthquake, Korean residents were falsely accused of setting fires and looting, and several thousand Koreans were massacred by Japanese.

11. Although this section focuses on initiatives of the Japanese government, this is not to disregard the importance of institutional initiatives of Japanese and non-Japanese colleges and universities aimed at promoting internationalization. For brief discussions of 'branch schools' of the U.S. institutions in Japan, see Umakoshi (1997, pp. 269–271) and Lincicome (1993, pp. 134–5). To learn about the initiatives of Japanese private institutions to send their students abroad (including setting up overseas branch campuses of Japanese institutions), see Umakoshi (1997, pp. 265–6).

12. It is important to recognize the international politics as well as the politics within the Japanese government involved in the institution and implementation of the JET program. According to McConnell (1996), "the driving force behind the idea for the JET Program was the US-Japan trade crisis in the mid-1980s....The JET Program would allow the government to use surplus yen to deflect foreign criticism of Japan as a 'closed' society and an 'economic animal' reaping larger and larger annual trade surpluses" (p. 447–8). While the Ministry of Education is responsible for the educational portion of the JET program involving English teaching at the local schools, the Ministry of Foreign Affairs recruits ALTs and Ministry of Home Affairs controls budget and administration of the program through an office called the Council of Local Authorities for International Relations (CLAIR) (McConnell, 1996, p. 448).

13. This is not to disregard practical obstacles to pursuing graduate education in Japan, both for Japanese and non-Japanese students. The Japanese academic tradition that "a doctorate degree should only be awarded for major contributions to the field" requires doctorate students to put "the extraordinary effort" to earn a doctorate degree (Umakoshi, 1997, pp. 264–5). In many disciplines, aside from natural sciences and engineering, PhD degrees are not conferred at all, and it is customary to quit a doctorate program after fulfilling all doctoral requirements except dissertation or to obtain a PhD degree abroad.

14. Umakoshi (1997) states that, in 1982, the Japanese government established a "Preparatory Japanese Language Training Course" in China and Malaysia for their students leaving to study in Japan, and in 1984, started administering the "Japanese Language Proficiency Test" (JLPT) abroad (p. 259). According to the homepage of JLPT (http://www.iijnet.or.jp/jpf/jlpt/contents/home-e.html), the number of applicants to JLPT was 270,852 (the number of test-takers 227,593) worldwide in 2001, an increase of more than six times in nine years.

References

Altbach, Philip G. "The Distribution of Knowledge in the Third World: A Case Study in Neocolonialism." In *Education and the Colonial Experience.* Edited by Philip G. Altbach and Gail P. Kelly, 229-251. New Brunswick: Transaction Books, 1984.

Anderson, Benedict. *Imagined Communities: Reflections on the Origins and Spread of Nationalism.* London: Verso Press, 1983.

Arisaka,Yoko. "Beyond 'East and West': Nishida's Universalism and Postcolonial Critique." *The Review of Politics* 59, no. 3 (1997): 541–560.

Ashcroft, Bill, Gareth Griffiths, and Helen Tiffin, eds. *The Post-Colonial Studies Reader.* London: Routledge, 1995.

Bhabha, Homi K. *The Location of Culture.* London: Routledge, 1994.

Brody, Betsy. *Opening the Door: Immigration, Ethnicity, and Globalization in Japan.* New York: Routledge, 2002.

Lee, Changsoo, and George de Vos. *Koreans in Japan: Ethnic Conflict and Accommodation.* Berkeley: University of California Press, 1985.

Chatterjee, Partha. *The Nation and Its Fragments: Colonial and Postcolonial Histories.* Princeton: Princeton University Press, 1993.

Children Living Abroad and Returnees Internet (CLARINET), Ministry of Education, Science, Sports, and Culture, Japan. "*Kaigai no kodomo no doko (The Trend of Japanese Children Overseas)*" [www page] [cited 20 December 2001]. Available from http://www.mext.go.jp/a_menu/shotou/clarinet/data1.html.

Cummings, William K. "The Egalitarian Transformation of Postwar Japanese Education." *Comparative Education Review* 26 (1982): 16–35.

Cummings, William K. "The American Perception of Japanese Education." *Comparative Education* 25, no. 3 (1989): 293–302.

Dale, Peter N. *The Myth of Japanese Uniqueness*. London: Croom Helm, 1986.

Denoon, Donald, et al., eds. *Multicultural Japan: Palaeolithic to Postmodern*. Cambridge, UK: Cambridge University Press, 1996.

De Vos, George A., and William O. Wetherall. *Japan's Minorities: Burakumin, Koreans and Ainu*. London: Minority Rights Group, 1974.

Doak, Kevin M. "What is a Nation and Who Belongs? National Narratives and the Ethnic Imagination in Twentieth-Century Japan." *The American Historical Review* 102 (1997): 282–309.

Gann, Lewis H. "Western and Japanese Colonialism: Some Preliminary Comparisons." In *The Japanese Colonial Empire, 1895–1945*. Edited by Ramon H. Myers and Mark R. Peattie, 497–525. Princeton: Princeton University Press, 1984.

Garon, Sheldon. "Rethinking Modernization and Modernity in Japanese History: A Focus on State-Society Relations." *The Journal of Asian Studies* 53, no. 2 (1994): 346–66.

Goodman, Roger. *Japan's 'International Youth': The Emergence of a New Class of Schoolchildren*. Oxford: Clarendon Press, 1990.

Hanami, Makiko. "International Student Exchange Program at Hitotsubashi University: Policy and Perspective." *Hitotsubashi Journal of Social Studies* 27 (1995): 113–125.

Hashimoto, Kenji. *Kaikyu Shakai Nippon* (Japan as Class Society). Tokyo: Aoki Shoten, 2001.

Hingwan, Kathianne. "Identity, Otherness and Migrant Labour in Japan." In *Case Studies on Human Rights in Japan*. Edited by Roger Goodman and Ian Neary, 51–75. Japan Library, 1996.

Horio, Teruhisa. *Education Thought and Ideology in Modern Japan: State Authority and Intellectual Freedom*. ed. and trans. Steven Platzer. Tokyo: University of Tokyo Press, 1988.

Ivy, Marilyn. "Mourning the Japanese Thing." In *In Near Ruins: Cultural Theory and the End of the Century*. Edited by Nicholas B. Dirks. Minneapolis & London: University of Minnesota Press, 1998.

Kariya, Takehiko. *Taishu Kyoiku Shakai no Yukue: Gakureki-shugi to Byodo-shinwa no Sengo-shi* (The Future of Mass Education Society: The Post-war Japanese History of Educational Credentialism and a Myth of Equality). Tokyo: Chuuokoronsha, 1995.

Kato, Koji. "'*Hirakareta' nihonjingakko no sozo* (The Creation of 'Open' Japanese Schools Abroad)." In *Gendai Nihon no kyoiku to kokusaika* (Education of Contemporary Japan and Internationalization). Edited by Minoru Ishizuki and Masayuki Suzuki. Tokyo: Fukumura Shuppan, 1988.

Katsuoka, Kanji. "*Trainor no shiso to sengo kyoiku kaikaku* (The ideology of Joseph C. Trainor and post-war education reform in Japan)." In *Sengo kyoiku no sogo hyoka: sengo kyoiki kaikau no jitsuzo* (A Synthetic Evaluation of Post-War Education in Japan: Realities of Post-war Education Reforms). Edited by Publication Committee on a Synthetic Evaluation of Post-war Education in Japan. Tokyo: Kokusho Kanko-kai, 1999.

Kobayashi, Tetsuya. "The Internationalization of Japanese Education." *Comparative Education* 22, no. 1 (1986): 65–71.

Lamont-Brown, Raymond. "Internationalisation: Japan's Educational Challenge." *Contemporary Review* 265 (1994): 186-188.

Lincicome, Mark. "Focus on Internationalization of Japanese Education: Nationalism, Internationalization, and the Dilemma of Educational Reform in Japan." *Comparative Education Review* 37, no. 2 (1993): 123–151.

Maher, John C., and Gaynor MacDonald, Eds. *Diversity in Japanese Culture and Language*. London and New York: Kegan Paul International, 1995.

McConnell, David L. "Education for Global Integration in Japan: A Case Study of the JET Program." *Human Organization* 55, no. 4 (1996): 446–457.

McVeigh, Brian J. "Cultivating 'Ladylike' and 'International' Women at Takatsu." In *Life in a Japanese Women's College: Learning to be Ladylike*. London & New York: Routledge, 1997.

Monbusho (Ministry of Education, Science, Sports, and Culture, Japan). *Wagakuni no Bunkyo Seisaku Heisei 12–nendo* (Japanese Government Policies in Education, Science, Sports, and Culture 2000). Tokyo: Printing Bureau, Ministry of Finance, Japan, 2000.

Monbukagakusho (Ministry of Education, Culture, Sports, Science and Technology, Japan). *Monbukagaku Hakusho Heisei 13-nendo* (White Paper, 2001). [cited 1 September 2002]. Available from http://wwwwp.mext.go.jp/monkag2001/.

Mouer, Ross, and Yoshio Sugimoto. *Images of Japanese Society: A Study in the Social Construction of Reality.* London: Kegan Paul International, 1986.

Okano, Kaori, and Motonari Tsuchiya. *Education in Contemporary Japan: Inequality and Diversity.* Cambridge: Cambridge University Press, 1999.

Parmenter, Lynne. "Constructing National Identity in a Changing World: Perspectives in Japanese Education." *British Journal of Sociology of Education* 20, no. 4 (1990): 453–63.

Parmenter, Lynne, et al. "Locating Self in the World: Elementary School Children in Japan, Macau, and Hong Kong." *Compare* 30, no. 2 (2000): 133–144.

Picken, Stuart D. B. "Two Tasks of the Ad Hoc Council for Educational Reform in Socio-Cultural Perspective." *Comparative Education* 22, no. 1 (1986): 59–64.

Pollack, Erwin. "Isaac Leon Kandel (1881–1965)." *Prospects* 3, no. 4 (1993): 775–787.

Robertson, Jennifer. "Empire of Nostalgia: Rethinking 'Internationalization' in Japan Today." *Theory, Culture & Society* 14, no. 4 (1997): 97–122.

Russell, John. "Race and Reflexivity: The Black Other in Contemporary Japanese Mass Culture." In *Rereading Cultural Anthropology,* edited by G. E. Marcus. Durham: Duke University Press, 1992.

Said, Edward. *Orientalism: Western Conceptions of the Orient.* London: Routledge & Kegan Paul, 1978.

Sakai, Naoki. "Modernity and Its Critique: The Problem of Universalism and Particularism." In *Postmodernism and Japan.* Edited by Harry D. Harootunian and Masao Miyoshi. Durham: Duke University Press, 1989.

Sato, Toshiki. *Fubyodo Shakai Nippon: Sayonara So-churyu (Japan as Unequal Society: Farewell to a Middle-class Society).* Tokyo: Chuko Shinsho, 2000.

Schoppa, Leonard. "Education Reform in Japan: Goal and Results of the Present Reform Campaign." In *Windows on Japanese Education.* Edited by E. R. Beauchamp. New York: Greenwood Press, 1991.

Scott, Thomas J. "The Internationalization of Japanese Education: A Conflict Scenario." *International Education* 23 (1993): 67–75.

Shibuya, Maki. *Kikoushijo no Ichidori no Seiji: Kikokushijo Kyoiku Gakkyu no Sai no Ethnography (The Politics of Kikokushijo's Positionalities: Ethnography of Difference in Kikokushijo Education Classroom).* Tokyo: Keiso Shobo, 2001.

Spring, Joel. "Japan: Western Science, Eastern Morals." In *Education and the Rise of the Global Economy.* Mahwah, NJ: Lawrence Erlbaum Associates, 1998.

Steiner-Khamsi, Gita. "Transferring Education, Displacing Reforms." In *Discourse Formations in Comparative Education.* Edited by Jürgen K. Schriewer. Frankfurt & New York: Lang, 2000.

Takahashi, Jere. *Nisei/Sansei: Shifting Japanese American Identities and Politics.* Philadelphia: Temple University Press, 1997.

Takeuchi, Hiroshi. *Nihon no Meritokurah (The Meritocracy in Japan).* Tokyo: Tokyo University Press, 1995.

Tikly, Leon. "Postcolonialism and Comparative Education." *International Review of Education* 45 (1999): 603–621.

Tsuda, Takeyuki. "The Stigma of Ethnic Difference: The Structure of Prejudice and 'Discrimination' toward Japan's New Immigrant Minority." *The Journal of Japanese Studies* 24, no. 2 (1998): 317–59.

———. "The Motivation to Migrate: The Ethnic and Socio-Cultural Construction of the Japanese-Brazilian Return Migration System." *Economic Development and Cultural Change* 48, no. 1 (1999): 1–31.

Tsurumi, E. Patricia. *Japanese Colonial Education in Taiwan, 1895–1945.* Cambridge and London: Harvard University Press, 1977.

Umakoshi, Toru. "Internationalization of Japanese Higher Education in the 1980s and Early 1990s." *Higher Education* 34 (1997): 259–273.

van Loon, Joost. "Racism, Culture and Modernity." *Theory, Culture & Society* 14, no. 3 (1997): 157–164.

Weiner, Michael, ed. *Japan's Minorities: The Illusion of Homogeneit.* London and New York: Routledge, 1997.

Williams, Patrick, and Laura Chrisman, Eds. *Colonial Discourse and Postcolonial Theory.* Hemel Hempstead: Harvester Wheatsheaf, 1994.

Wray, Harry. "Change and Continuity in Modern Japanese Educational History: Allied Occupational Reforms Forty Years Later." *Comparative Education Review* 35, no. 3 (1991): 447–475.

Yoshino, Kosaku. *Cultural Nationalism in Contemporary Japan: A Sociological Enquiry.* London: Routledge, 1992.

———. "Cultural Nationalism and 'Internationalization' in Contemporary Japan." In *Global Convulsion: Race, Ethnicity and Nationalism at the End of the Twentieth Century.* Edited by Winston A. Van Horne, 131–146. Albany: State University of New York Press, 1997.

CHAPTER 12

Third-Space/Identity Montage and International Adult Educators

LEONA M. ENGLISH

The space that present-day global adult educators inhabit involves a daily negotiation of their identity. These are not the colonizers of an earlier time, nor are they totally disconnected from the white, Western world from which most of them originated. In the case of those from developing contexts in Asia and Africa, they resist the regulating discourse of the good worker, the good Muslim (or Christian or Hindu), and good woman or man, yet they still collude with it. Through reading their lives, we see how they resist these "rules of recognition" (Bhabha 1994, p. 100) through which they have been signified. While they may desire to be part of the culture, they both resist and embrace it simultaneously. Theirs becomes a critical engagement with the politics, the geography, and the people, whether it be in the West Indies, Africa, or Asia. Nomadic in every way, they operate between the worlds, and between the people, with their own identity constantly in flux.

In this chapter I use data from life history — interviews with global adult educators who daily resist being coded as homogenous white, Western colonizers and do-gooders, or as equally homogenous black, southern subalterns. I explore the cultural concepts of third space and hybridity as ways to explicate and complicate their lives and identities. Third spaces can be characterized as those arenas in which people on the margins create and re-create their identity, often in response to their marginalization (see Gutierrez, 1999). The implications of this third space theory for comparative and international education are discussed.

The Artist's Vision: Study Focus

The study participants were 13 women (9 from North America; 4 from Asia and Africa) who work in civil society organizations in the global sphere and who have done so for at least 5 years. These stories name a different kind of subaltern positionality, one that is both shifting and elusive. This identity politics interrupts and transgresses the status quo and suggests new directions for working with those who practice international adult education. These identities cannot be categorized — they are ambivalent and challenging, transgressing all centralized or mainstream sites, in favor of in-between fluid spaces that are alternately named third spaces (Khan, 2000). This research turns third space on its head because its focus is in a different direction (North America to Asia and Africa, and vice versa), and provides a critique of third space itself.

Montage — Shades of Third Space

In attempting to articulate third space, adult educators from North America who practice politics in developing contexts are revealed to be dislocated and dis-placed, working the hyphens (Fine, 1994) of what it means to be international and national, bilateral and unilateral, religious and spiritual, justice-oriented and caring. The third space they are part of is a site from where they may negotiate the locations of activism and development (see Routledge, 1996).

The post-colonial discourse of third space has been articulated most eloquently by Homi Bhabha in his numerous works on this topic (e.g., 1990, 1994). This is a discourse that is informed by Bhabha's own experience of being in diaspora, having migrated from Asia to North America. His work reflects the ambivalence of nationality and culture when one is dis-located and dis-placed from one's own home place. Third space is about identity politics, interrogating that most enigmatic space in our lives that makes us aware that identity is always in flux. It asks us to acknowledge the ways we collude and collide with structures, essentialisms, and mixed notions of identity (see Hollinshead, 1998; Soja, 1996); third space is a mucous-like (Todd, 1997) place that is at once transitory and transnational.

Painting Myself In: Still Life/Static Approaches to International Education

I first became interested in international cultural workers while teaching at St. Francis Xavier University in Antigonish, Nova Scotia, which has the distinction of being the home place of famed adult educator Moses Coady. Coady's modernist dream of a progressive abundant life for all resulted in the development of an international institute that has educated literally thousands of individuals from all over the globe, especially from Africa and Asia (see Welton, 2000). The focus of the Institute has since shifted from spreading the principles of his movement around the world to a more comprehensive and integrative view of cultural and international adult education work. This integrative and culturally sensitive view challenges some of the international development models that are operative in international non-governmental organizations. Yet, even in the local town, the Institute is little understood and common misconceptions exist about international adult education. Images abound of nuns in habits preaching to noble savages, and of self-effacing missionaries from North America who are teaching the rest of the world to become civilized.

As well, the general Western understanding of preparing for/sustaining oneself in comparative international work remains rooted in lists of steps and strategies one can take to prepare (e.g., Zieghan 2000); these lists are often couched in terms of globalizing culture and colonizing the lifeworld of those living in what was once problematically known as the Third World. These programs contain a mixture of cultural stereotyping and defense mechanism preparation. The focus is on the information that one needs to cope in a cross-cultural community, such as how to deal with culture shock (Brislin and Yoshida, 1994), rather than on how one might live and be ready for change, ambivalence, and transitions, as well as a sophisticated understanding of one's protean political, social, and spiritual identities.

Preparing the Canvas: Examining the Background

This chapter focuses on international adult educators. The latter is a term that I use to describe individuals who work in development education, literacy initiatives, and community development projects in countries that are economically challenged, in this case countries primarily in Asia and Africa. Although it is quite possible that questions of identity would be similar in a mixed gender grouping, I focused on women in this case and in so doing have excluded male colleagues who might do similar work and who might encounter similar issues of identity. The women in this study were variously educated, yet all held university degrees or at least a development diploma. They described the immediate preparation for their international placements as comprised of brief workshops and training, or a learn-as-you-go program. Participants were typically given modernist lists and prescriptions of what they might do to be ready for the development experience. In the case of the women from countries in Asia and Africa, preparation for work in their home countries was basically carried out by NGOs, training centers, and church sponsored organizations. While working in the non-profit organization, they received further training, and in the case of four of them, they continued this training by studying in Canada in a 5-month continuing education program. None of the participants reported being trained in a complex and comprehensive way for what they might encounter.

My interview questions for these women focused on a variety of issues, including questions of how they saw themselves, how they thought they were seen, and how their identities might have been complicated by their initial training. I sought to unpack this with questions about their growing up years (age, school, religious affiliation, etc.), and especially about significant events or people who influenced their international education work. I also delved how they had been prepared for their work. I inquired about how religion had influenced their decisions to do development work and if that was still an influence. I asked if their civil society organization work conflicted with their religious or political beliefs. These questions were developed by delving the existing literature on pre-departure training.

Significantly, the research on pre-departure training shows that there are a variety of approaches to training for the 'new' culture. Mendenhall and Oddou (1985), for instance, identify three of these: (a) self-orientation which is focused on building up personal resilience, (b) other-orientation, which is about building positive interactions and relationships in the host nations, and (c) perceptual-orientation, which is focused on understanding and knowing the views of a variety of cultures. Some programs employ a mixed approach to cross-cultural awareness (Brislin and Yoshida, 1994). Yet, many programs are designed to fortify the participants as opposed to helping them think, reflect, and be open to the experience.

Video — Capturing Moments of Transformation in Action

Often the experience of working in developing contexts was transformative for the participants and their worldview. The participants were generally unprepared for the disorienting dilemmas of working cross-culturally or being involved in development work, even if the context and the country were their own. Their awareness, that life-changing events were happening to them contributed to their political transformation. As a result of the burgeoning awareness they changed their life perspectives, how they lived, and how they characterized their educational work. For the women from North America, their heightened awareness of everything from church to the environment came as a result of the travel to developing contexts. For the women from Asia and Africa, transformations occurred, too, as a result of local challenges and their own questioning of indigenous assumptions and practices. Living globally appears to make it difficult to keep a provincial perspective. In the best sense, according to Berry (1988), it forces one to see the bigger picture, to envisage the world as an intricate web of relationships and people, in which humans have an intricate relationship to the universe, and a deep responsibility to the natural world. For the women in this study, dis-location and geographic dis-placement often resulted in a greater awareness of their life vocation — a heightened awareness resulting from being immersed in the local context. Take, for instance, Paula, a woman in her mid-thirties, who is now involved in local literacy work, and for several years worked in Mexico, Kenya, and most recently with a United Church of Canada initiative to return to Guatemala with displaced nationals who are fearful of their country's army. Her various international experiences have shaped all her later life decisions. Paula admits to not being too sure of why she went to Mexico, except to say it was the thing to do at the time. She now lives in a house in the woods that she built with friends. She believes that though she did not make monumental or deliberate decisions, her international experiences have resulted in transitions and transformations that have affected her life forever. In particular, they have helped her in "unlearning privilege" (p. 30) so that she can "become able to listen to that other constituency" (Spivak 1990: 42).

Reena, a native of India and a nun studying in Canada in a continuing professional development program, has an extensive education background (including a master's degree in sociology) and a long involvement in development. She spent years working in community development before she came to truly believe that her people could become "masters of their own destiny" (Coady, 1939). After years in her team-based center doing educational and community development work, she experienced a life-transforming event. In the middle of the night the women she had been working with took the initiative and organized themselves when one of them was gang raped. Rather than run to Reena's educational center for help, the women "got together in one village. They sent messages at night.... By morning there was 200 women and then they informed us that they were going to file the case and take up this issue. I think that was the day I enjoyed the most." It was then she realized that there was hope. In creating alliances within her own team, in working across differences, she has nurtured hope for educational practice.

These transforming events and moments where local voices followed local action had a decided effect on these women's identities. Their perspective transformations had urged them beyond personal transformation to a view of a societal change; negotiating that change was at times challenging to do. For some, this transformation was a "disorienting dilemma," but for many it was a gradual transformation (Mezirow and Associates, 1991). Support for and recognition of challenges such as these in the lives of adult educators may make transformations or disruptions more meaningful. These transformations are relevant in that they mark a turning point in these women's lives from which they cannot go back, and from which they move reluctantly and willingly into a third or ambivalent space in their lives.

Shaping a Politics of Knowledge
Given the ways they came to know about their work and their vocation (Collins, 1991; Palmer, 1998), one of the biggest challenges they had was negotiating the complexity of being part of systems and development

organizations, all the while maintaining a critical questioning eye on them. Boundary crossings occurred when they negotiate the complex politics of identity within their own culture and when they negotiate what it means to be part of a culture with which they both collude and collide.

Political displacement is not restricted to the women from North America. Selma is from Western Africa and does adult education and community development in her home country. In her mid-thirties, she is a Muslim woman who has been working with an NGO for 15 years, has had 2 years of training in community development, a year of study in politics in Cuba, and is completing a diploma in social development at an international development school in Canada. She and her husband, also educated as a social worker, are committed to improving the conditions of people, especially women, in their own country. They often, however, have conflict because of how the Islamic faith has been interpreted for women. Selma says it doesn't cause her any grief because she takes the essentials of Islam, whatever is helpful, and uses it in her own life. Every day away from home, she prays five times a day, just as she would at home. Yet, she is marginalized in not conforming to the norms of Muslim women in her county:

> So, the problem is they [my husband's family] are driving me away.... For instance, they say that I am married so they don't see why I should be following another man, so when they see me with my male fellow workers then they start to think...that I have some sort of relations with them. But in a sense I used to have that problem with my husband and I told him he shouldn't forget that he is also going to meet someone's wife somewhere who also assists him to do his work....So I just have to forget about them....

Selma works between cultural norms and taboos, in-law problems, a society that tells women what to do, and promotes an interpretation of Islam that she does not agree with. This puts her in a position of tension and constant negotiation. In order to do her work, she must be alert to the forces around her and yet find a way of resisting the occupation of her mind and body. In Khan's (2000) terms, this is "negotiating the ambivalence" of the situation, as well as making deliberate and personal choices about what to believe about religion and culture. Though not by choice, she is using her location to resist cultural stereotypes, patriarchy, and misogyny. This "fault line between cultures" (Dunlop, 1999: 57) allows her a third space that gives her some power and agency.

These women defy any stereotype of do-gooders or the stereotypical missionary — they are very much involved in self-critique of their own work and interrogating their own assumptions and cares. They have iterations and thoughts about their own desires and positions within and without cultural constructs that go back and forth. They think about what they do and visit and revisit their own ideas, signaling a fluidity of identification that counteracts dominant cultural stories of unitary subjectivity for women from North America. Paula is a Canadian literacy worker who routinely accompanies Central American nationals back home. She is aware of the contradictions in her life:

> Because I say these things, I am a vegetarian and I have respect for and love for non-humans but I also have leather on my Birkenstocks [sandals]. I think we always have to make compromises and that to live you have to kill if it's not a cow well then you may be killing carrots. So I acknowledge that there is no black and white and you can't get on a moral high horse about things . . .

The world of these adult education practitioners has become increasingly complex as a result of their work and life commitments. Class, race, and ethnic differences, as familiar as they are, are challenging for these women. Individually they trouble the categories (Lather 2001) of good woman, good worker, good Christian, Hindu, Muslim; they think about what they are doing, they understand the paradoxes in their lives, the limits of 'doing-good,' and how these affect what they are able to do.

As a consequence of their positioning, many of these women experience a dislocation and a disconnection. The dislocation symbolizes a disruption in a prescribed path of international work and in the constitution of their identities, be they based in spirituality or something else. The disconnection however, becomes a connective: They find support by coming together routinely to talk about their experiences, and their current social justice projects. These communities become a third space that nurtures political engagement and activism of various sorts, and from which they can "begin their presencing" (Bhabha, 1994: p. 5). This third space is a site of resistance and loving commitment in which they can "find or recognize the 'other' within her/himself" (Dunlop, 1999: 59). Like hooks (1990), they have been active in "choosing the margin [read third space] as a space of radical openness" (p. 153).

Laura, a white middle-aged woman who works at a development institute in Canada in which she teaches development workers from all over the world, talks about the ongoing dialogue that she has with herself in terms of being seen variously as a rich North American (by the participants at the Institute) and as a non-traditional baby boomer (by mainstream North America). Laura finds that she has constant thoughts and questions about her own work and her limits:

> I question that all the time actually. If you look within this organizational structure and how much I get paid for what I do and what direct or indirect impact of that actually has on anyone's life... you know, damn little. And some days I find that harder to live with and some days I think maybe there is a way better to contribute to

this and then some days I think the best thing people can do in the North is to get out of the way of people in the global South [developing contexts] — just stop screwing around with their economic and political systems.

Laura sees that though she is able to help other women, there is a limit to what she is able to do in her work; development work is complex, necessitating the involvement of the critically reflexive self (Brookfield 2000). So, there is an ongoing dialogue with herself as a result of her work that allows her to do her work. This interrogation of her own practices destabilizes the unitary self (Clark, 1999) and fractures notions of a monolithic identity for sojourners such as herself.

Artist's Inspiration: Third Space as a Reconstruction of Spiritual Identities

One of the strongest motifs in the interviews was the relationship that the woman had to spirituality (personal meaning-making, which may or may not be connected to religion) and religion (organized worship). In all cases, the women grew up in religiously-oriented homes, although this was not a condition for being interviewed. The early messages they received from religious figures often influenced their decision to undertake development work, regardless of which part of the world they grew up in. Yet, religion played itself out in markedly different ways for the women from North America and those from Asia and Africa. Spivak (1992), for instance, observes that "Western feminists have not so far been aware of religion as a cultural instrument than a mark of cultural difference" (p. 192). So, too, Walters and Manicom (1996) speculate that spirituality may be especially important to women who are "recovering womanist traditions and ethnic collectives [and who] draw on cultural and spiritual symbols in healing and transformative education" (pp. 12–13). When the women from North America were asked about the religious dimension of their lives they were surprised initially, given that this is usually a taboo subject in development circles (Ver Beek, 2000). Yet, the question elicited some of the most interesting data in the study.

These female adult educators have a strong desire to have their spirituality recognized and fostered in their lives and work. Yet, their beliefs often put them in conflict with organized religion, with their families or with employers, and make them challenge the hegemony of cultural institutions. For women from developing countries in particular, the choices they must make serve to push them into a third space, not unlike the descriptions given by Khan (2000) of Muslim women living in Canada. Whether they rejected religion, or accepted it on their own terms, it caused a major disruption for most of the women.

Many of the participants in the study were significantly influenced by their families, school teachers, or religious communities. This connection of justice work and early religious influences is established in the literature (e.g., Daloz et al., 1996; Tisdell, 2000). Many of the women in the study had been raised in religious traditions that strongly affected their choice to do overseas work. Sheila, a Canadian adult educator woman who worked for 20 years with a church-sponsored development organization, talked about being inspired to do justice work by the "many fun, dynamic, cool, intelligent women who were sisters [women religious]" in her high school. She was drawn to justice work because of these women, yet even her muse (one of the women religious) left the church a few years ago.

For many of the participants, their reasons for remaining committed to international adult education work are grounded in their deep faith in a Divine presence and are less connected to religious structures. Sheila described how this group of women influenced her when they taught her in school: "They knew I was going through a [rebellious] phase. And they let it go. Somehow I think all of that formed me to say it was all right to question, that you can challenge things." Sheila talked about how her "faith commitments have nothing to do with the institution of the church or much of its doctrine. I am a selective Catholic, in that I take those pieces of faith and doctrine that are meaningful to me and seem true and that is always in synch with doing work in international development and adult education." In selecting what is useful for her, she is neither Catholic nor non-Catholic; she is living "on the cusp" and has the ability to "deal with two contradictory things at the same time, without either transcending or repressing that contradiction" (Bhabha, 1995: 82).

The enduring influences of their families and religious institutions cause something more of a problem for those in developing contexts. Reena, a participant from India, who is also a Roman Catholic nun, talked about how she lives out her vows in a very traditional religious community, ever walking between her own free spirit, and the narrow conformist expectations around her.

> And there are days I don't get to say my prayers but I live it.... but I do follow the laws and there are sisters and if it will upset them, forget about it. I don't stand up like a revolutionist. I have elders and sisters that have just come and they would be upset. I make sure I am with them and say all the traditional things so they are comfortable. But as a person that is not going to define me.

Reena has learned not to cause too much disruption and conflict but to negotiate action and speech wherever she is, without sacrificing her own beliefs and convictions. Living in this space, she moves between the two worlds, and chameleon-like, changing appearances to accommodate the actors and herself.

For some of the women there was a sense that they were not just there to help out, but that this experience was much more concerned with their own deepest human connections. For example, the women sensed that their striving for justice was intricately connected to their spirituality. Spirituality is an integral part of learning and is intricately related to the concept of meaning-making. Therefore, 'faith' and 'spirituality' means the ability to make meaning. Although the need to address spirituality is new in adult education, the field has engaged for some time in understanding this need (see MacKeracher, 1996; English and Gillen, 2000).

Constructivism, or constructing knowledge/meaning from subjective and received sources, has long been seen as integral to female growth and development (Belenky, et al., 1986). My interviews appear to provide evidence that to make spiritual sense of life is to make meaning, which supports this theory. The women who participated in the study are fully aware that spirituality is part of their lives. Just as they are physical, emotional, sexual, and cognitive beings, they are also spiritual. All agreed that no direct attention was paid to their spiritual development, even those sponsored overseas by a religious organization. Karen, a middle-aged health educator, who works with a North American international training center, identified spirituality as the motivation and sustenance for her work. Karen is convinced, based on personal experience, that adult educators who work overseas need the opportunity to talk about their spirituality: "I think people are afraid to talk about spirituality in international development for fear of being labeled a proselytizer and evangelizer." This fear of being labeled is strong and is one of the reasons why the taboo regarding any discussion of religion and spirituality continues. This situation is unfortunate because adult educators have a need to make sense of their international experiences, to find meaning in their lives, and to be open to more than the physical and the technical. If co-workers and development agencies were able to recognize the spiritual dimensions of their being, this might be of help. In more than one case, the women went overseas to fulfill dreams but really came to significant learning about their own backgrounds, lives, and ways to be. In many ways, their "homelands" have disappeared as sites of refuge and comfort. Their homelands are elusive, and in many ways accessible only through creative acts of the imagination (Said, 1993).

The participants had personal convictions regarding the value of their work in development and they gave their time (usually underpaid or volunteer) because of their strong desire to contribute to the common good (Daloz, et al. 1996). Although these women had varied interests and perspectives, they invariably focused in some way on their own search to make sense or meaning of their lives, even if they did not always have a language to frame it. Karen talked about how she negotiated her ambivalent relationship to Catholicism, given that she is active in a religious development organization, and comes from a very traditional religious home. According to Karen, living in the South, adult educators "didn't mention Christianity, religion, spirituality, since it was a no-no. In fact, they would ask you if that were your motive and if you had that they got suspicious.... They were afraid people would evangelize." Yet, now living back in Canada and doing consulting work overseas, people still associate her with the religion of her youth, to which she is no longer strongly connected. She notes, "[Since my mother] passed away I don't have to go. I don't tell anyone I don't go. My aunt does not know. It is easier not to bring it up. ...Yet if someone asks 'who's Catholic?' I put up my hand."

Karen's identity is "always in flux, split between two or more worlds, cultures" (Spitta, 1995). Her silence is one of quiet resistance. It does not invite conflict; rather, it enables her to take a quiet stand and to engage in a personal project of freedom. Yet, she is aware that there are penalties for saying too much, given her family, work, and other links to organized religion.

> I tend to be somewhat careful on which side of the street I am walking on as to what I say. It all depends on what I want to do, what I want to accomplish.... When teaching a course in gender I hardly ever use [the word feminism]. That means you hate men [laugh]. It has all those connotations. I use it in company that I know understands it. I would very much identify myself as a feminist. Catholic feminist??? It is not often I would use the terms together.

Her resistance is "assembled out of the materials and practices of everyday life" (Routledge, 1996: 415), and for the most part it is individual and hidden. This resistance allows Karen to challenge the status quo, and to negotiate the complex terrain of her life. In many ways her belief in contributing to the common good strengthened and deepened over time, rather than changed radically and gave her support for her choices and her actions.

Critic's Review: Interpreting the Montage

In exploring these cases of female adult educators working both in Canada and overseas, I have come to a new awareness of the complexity of their identity and their politics. They are positioned in a third space where ambivalence obtains, where cultural and political identity is daily disrupted, and where cultures clash and collude (Khan, 2000). They are neither adult educators nor development workers, NGO employees nor independent spirits, but rather global travelers who negotiate daily the complexity of culture and identity. They may be from Asia or Africa or North America, old as well as young, institutionally based and nonaffiliated, humanist and liberatory in political orientation. The old codes and prescriptions for international adult educators are shaken and shifted, transgressed and transformed, enlivened and enervated. Rather than enumerating the cultural differences, comparative educators can learn from them to talk of connections across differences — race, gender, and nationality. They have mentored one another, created alliances between academics and practitioners, and challenged the notion of a bridge as a static, immovable structure (Thiesen, 1997).

As I listened to their stories, I was struck by the strategies of resistance that were employed by these women. Their political commitments and their varied identities enabled them to live as resistance fighters — raging against the state, globalization, domineering religious traditions, all the while struggling to be heard and to be a bona fide part of the civil society discourse to which they have much to contribute. They are involved in low-key political activities that directly affect the lives of local people and the communities in which they live. The strategies of resistance that enable them to be in the third space include silence, negotiation of difference, and creation of connections, in order to construct identity and to be able to act. In each case, when conflict reigned because they resisted family expectations (Marj) or religious expectations (Reena) or NGO apolitical commitment (Karen, Sheila), they kept a low profile and moved forward, directing their energies to their cause and not the resistance. This constant renegotiation of identity and position is the third space, where they work around the problem, using silence as a passport to integrity and effectiveness in their education work. They have become adept at negotiating difference, cultivating a support system around them. All these strategies have allowed them to construct identity and be able to act. This identity construction has been aided by their focus on the cultivation of Sumner's (1999) real capital. For some, this involves constant ambivalence (Laura) about living in a capitalist society, and a continuous critically self-reflexivity (Brookfield, 2000). Comparative educators can see in this the importance of the cultivation of networks and support structures that enable the participants to contribute their own identity construction and activity.

The moments of transition and identity negotiation that have been explicated here speak directly to comparative educators of the need for a more complex type of introduction to development work, one that moves beyond prescriptions of what to do and not to do overseas, to a more self-reflexive type of engagement with one's own story and background, since these dimensions seemed to be so formative in how these cultural workers live out their own lives. I suggest that critical self-reflexivity be a primary focus for pre-departure training. This might be enabled by journal writing (English and Gillen, 2001), critical autobiography (Randall, 1995) and other critically self-reflexive practices (Brookfield, 2000), which work less on the external changes one will encounter (e.g., food, culture) and more on how one is affected by these. Internal resources that may be of help in working with difference, one's own emergent beliefs, and potential conflict with others are also important here.

This type of preparation, which recognizes the unpredictable aspects of working in development contexts, allows the participants to become more active participants in their own stories, dealing with the intersections of conflicting cultures and ways of thinking, and being able to anticipate the inevitable moments of collision and collusion. In allowing one's own story to intersect with those of others, the performer can resist being coded, transgress the boundaries of culture, and practice education in a global (not globalized) context. Existing prescriptions and codes for adult education need to be abandoned so that adult educators can take multiple perspectives and positions on their work. This will allow them to "turn the landscape of national belonging into a more hybrid ethnoscape of transnational becoming" (Wilson 2001, p. 248).

This study shows how these adult educators moved from negotiation and influence in their families of origin to negotiate politics in the global spheres. Comparative educators can see here that identity is worked out differently for each woman in each place; they can learn that their task is less to control these shifts and more to support them as they occur. Although there is a sense that the women in the North have more boundaries to cross because they are moving physically away from their own cultures, comparative educators can be aware that negotiation is equally needed for the women of the South; negotiation of religious, cultural, and political identities is necessary for both groups of women.

Yet, third space as a conceptual construct has definite limits when superimposed on the life of the female international adult educator. While it captures the ambivalence of the actors and their rhetoric or performance of identity, it presupposes in many ways an active, engaged, and aware participation in third space. For some of the women, the ambivalence of third space is sometimes lived out on an unconscious level. In some cases conscious awareness occurred in the interviews or was interpreted by the interviewer as third space. Yet, third space theory comes closest to explicating the situation these women find themselves in. If, as Landis and Bhagat (1996) point out, there has been little progress in developing an effective intercultural training model, because there is "still the lack of theory — a theory that would tell us why certain training programs work, for whom, and when" (p. xiii), perhaps third space theory can be the theory that helps us understand it better. Third space can help comparative educators focus more on the complexity of identity and the inner struggles of those who work for progressive change in the global sphere. Comparative and international academics also can learn from these life stories of NGO workers in order how to create alliances, build bridges across differences of age and institution, and to be more responsive to change (Thiesen, 1997). Their life histories provide thick rich data that shows the intricacies of their struggle to be effective international educators.

Questions regarding the comparative nature of this study abound. This chapter has looked less for differences among the women of the North and South, and more to their points of interconnection, intersection, and boundary-crossing in areas such as type of work, motivation, support, and identity. The data support an "integrative feminist politics that welcome difference even as they heal divisions" (Miles, 1996: 140). These women's narratives call for a revisioning of binaries: spirituality from learning, spirituality from religion, and meaning from education (Ó Murchú, 1997). As comparative educators, we may learn from this study that there is more to be gained from focusing on, and examining, the issues of identity and the quest for meaning in the adult educators' lives. The "spotlight has been [on] the space of relational interaction at least as much as... the space of difference," says Freidman (1998, p. 104). Comparative educators may see that, in these stories difference has not been conceptualized as deviation. Rather, it has been conceptualized as a passage into a third space which then becomes a dynamic space of regeneration. As Dunlop (1999) says, we "need to unfix mindsets and unmap polarized notions of geography" (p. 58).

Comparative educators are challenged to think of the ways they can be open to accepting (not obfuscating) shifting and changing identities. Women and indeed all, who practice international development, experience daily conflicting identities, especially in terms of politics, family, and religion. Their narratives disrupt and decenter modernist lists and steps to preparation, and suggest that these approaches ignore the more complex and inviting issue — the person and identity of the adult educator, who cannot be "trained" or schooled for work in bilateral contexts. Their lives highlight their position as resistance fighters, positioned in a third space (Bhabha 1998) as non-static fluid shapeshifters (Haraway 1992), whose identity is shaped in time and place, and who situate themselves in the international contexts in multiple ways. They offer the field of comparative and international education exemplars of a practice that is inclusive, complicated, and yet effective.

References

Belenky, Mary Field, et al. *Women's Ways of Knowing*. New York: Basic Books, 1986.

Berry, Thomas. *The Dream of the Earth*. San Francisco: Sierra Club, 1988.

Bhabha, Homi. "The Third Space: Interview with Homi Bhabha." In *Identity: Community, Culture, Difference*. Edited by J. Rutherford. London: Lawrence and Wishart, 1990.

_____. "Translator Translated." *Artforum International* 33, no. 7 (1995): 88–119.

_____. "On the Irremovable Strangeness of Being Different." Publications of the Modern Language Association of America 113, no. 1 (1998): 34–39.

_____. *The Location of Culture*. New York: Routledge, 1994.

Brislin, Richard W. and Tomoko Yoshida. "The content of cross-cultural training." In *Improving Intercultural Interactions: Modules of Cross-Cultural Training Programs* (pp. 1–14). Thousand Oaks, CA: Sage, 1994.

Brookfield, Stephen D. The Concept of Critically Reflective Practice. In *Handbook of Adult and Continuing Education*. Edited by A. L. Wilson and E. Hayes. San Francisco: Jossey-Bass, 2000.

Clark, M. Carolyn. "Challenging the Unitary Self: Adult Education, Feminist theory, and Nonunitary Subjectivity." *Canadian Journal for the Study of Adult Education* 13, no. 2 (1999): 39–48.

Coady, Moses. *Masters of Their own Destiny*. New York: Harper and Row, 1939.

Collins, Michael. *Adult Education as Vocation: A Critical Role for the Adult Educator*. New York: Routledge, 1991.

Daloz, Larry, Keen, et al. *Common Fire: Leading Lives of Commitment in a Complex World*. Boston: Beacon Press, 1996.

Dunlop, Rishma. "Beyond Dualism: Toward a Dialogic Negotiation of Difference." *Canadian Journal of Education* 24, no. 1 (1999): 57–69.

English, Leona M., and Marie A. Gillen (Eds.). *Promoting Journal Writing in Adult Education*. New Directions for Adult and Continuing Education, # 90. San Francisco: Jossey-Bass, 2001.

English, Leona M., and Marie A. Gillen (Eds.). *Addressing the Spiritual Dimensions of Adult Learning*. New Directions for Adult and Continuing Education, # 85. San Francisco: Jossey-Bass, 2000.

Fine, Michelle. "Working the Hyphens: Reinventing Self and Others in Qualitative Research." In *Handbook of Qualitative Research*. Edited by Norman Denzin and Yvonna S. Lincoln. Thousand Oaks; CA: Sage, 1994.

Freidman, Susan Stanford. " 'Beyond' Difference: Migratory Feminism in the Borderlands." In *Mappings: Feminism and the Cultural Geographies of Encounter*. Princeton, NJ: Princeton University Press, 1998.

Gutierrez, David G. "Migration, Emergent Ethnicity, and the "Third Space" : The Shifting Politics of Nationalism in Greater Mexico." *Journal of American History* 86, no. 2 (1999): 481–517.

Haraway, Donna. "The Promise of Monsters: A Regenerative Politics for Inappropriate/d Others." In *Cultural Studies*. Edited by L. Grossberg, C. Nelson, and P. A. Treichler. New York: Routledge, 1992.

Hollinshead, Keith. "Tourism, Hybridity, and Ambiguity: The Relevance of Bhabha's 'Third Space' Cultures." *Journal of Leisure Research* 30, no. 1 (1998): 121–156.

hooks, bell. *Yearning: Race, Gender, and Cultural Politics*. Toronto: Between the Lines, 1990.

Khan, Shahnaz. *Muslim Women: Creating a North American Identity*. Gainesville, Fla.: University Press of Florida, 2000.

Landis, Dan. and Rabi. S. Bhagat (Eds.). *Handbook of Intercultural Training. 2nd Edition*. Thousand Oaks, CA: Sage, 1996.

Lather, Patti. "Troubling the Categories." *Paper presented at the AERA, Seattle, Washington, 2001*. Available online http://www.coe.ohio-state.edu/plather/papers/AERA2001/aera2001.htm.

MacKeracher, Dorothy. *Making Sense of Adult Learning*. Toronto: Culture Concepts, 1996.

Mendenhall, M., and G. Oddou. "The Dimensions of Expatriate Acculturation: A Review." *Academy of Management Review*, 10, no. 1(1985): 39–47.

Mezirow, Jack and Associates. *Fostering Critical Reflection in Adulthood*. San Francisco: Jossey-Bass, 1991.

Miles, Angela. *Integrative Feminisms: Building Global Visions 1960's–1990's*. New York: Routledge, 1996.

Ó Murchú, Diarmuid. *Reclaiming Spirituality: A New Spiritual Framework for Today's World*. New York: Crossroad, 1997.

Palmer, Parker. *The Courage to Teach*. San Francisco: Jossey-Bass, 1998.

Randall, William, L. *The Stories We Are: An Essay in Self-Creation*. Toronto: University of Toronto Press, 1995.

Routledge, Paul. "The Third Space as Critical Engagement." *Antipode* 28, no. 4 (1996): 399–419.

Said, Edward. *Culture and Imperialism*. New York: Knopf, 1993.

Soja, Edward W. *Thirdspace: Journeys to Los Angeles and Other Real-and-Imagined Places*. Malden, MA: Blackwell, 1996.

Spitta, Silvia. "Transculturation and ambiguity of signs in Latin America." In *Between Two Waters: Narratives of Transculturation in Latin America*. Houston, TX: Rice University Press, 1995.

Spivak, Gayatri Chakravorty. "Gayatri Spivak on the Politics of the Subaltern: Interview by Howard Winant." *Socialist Review* 90, no. 3 (1990): 81–98.

Spivak, Gayatri. "The Politics of Translation." In *Destabilizing Theory: Contemporary Feminist Debates*. Edited by M. Barrett and A. Phillips. Stanford, CA: Stanford University Press, 1992.

Sumner, Jennifer. "Adult Education Inc.: Globalization, the World Bank and Education." In Mohamed Hrimlech, *Proceedings of the 18th Annual Conference of the Canadian Association for the Study of Adult Education Proceedings*. Sherbrooke, Quebec, 1999.

Theisen, Gary. "The New ABC's of Comparative and International Education." *Comparative Education Review* 41, no. 4 (1997): 397–412.

Tisdell, Elizabeth J. "Spirituality and Emancipatory Adult Education in Women Adult Educators for Social Change." *Adult Education Quarterly* 50, no. 4 (2000): 308–335.

Todd, Sharon. Looking at Pedagogy in 3-D: Rethinking Difference, Disparity and Desire." In *Learning Desire — Perspectives on Pedagogy, Culture, and the Unsaid*. London: Routledge, 1997.

Ver Beek, Kurt Alan. "Spirituality: A development taboo." *Development in Practice* 10 no. 1 (2000): 31–43.

Walters, Shirley, and Linzi Manicom (Eds.). "Introduction." In *Gender in Popular Education: Methods for Empowerment*. London: Zed Books, 1996.

Welton, Michael. *Little Mosie from Margaree*. Toronto: Thompson Educational Press, 2000.

Wilson, Bob. Book review of Borders Exiles and Diaspora. *Journal of World History* 12, no. 1 (2001): 248–252.

Zieghan, Linda. "Adult Education, Communication, and the Global Context." In *Handbook of adult and continuing education*. Edited by Arthur L. Wilson and Elizabeth Hayes. San Francisco: Jossey-Bass, 2000.

CHAPTER **13**

Post-Development Theory and Comparative Education

JONATHAN MAKUWIRA and PETER NINNES

Introduction

Comparative education has engaged with the concept of 'development' for more than 40 years (see, for example, Kandel, 1961). As a result, development has become a substantial thread in the tapestry of comparative education; many comparative educators include a discussion of development issues in their courses, and work as consultants on small- and large-scale development projects. Part of the process of re-imagining comparative education, therefore, must involve an engagement with contemporary post-foundational theorizing in the field of development studies. In many cases, the ways in which comparative education has dealt with issues of development have mirrored the generation of ideas about the concept that have arisen in development studies. However, in this chapter we argue that key aspects of recent theorising in development studies have not found their way to any great extent into the comparative education literature. It is our aim therefore to identify and address these gaps. We first provide a brief overview of earlier perspectives on development, and then discuss a broad group of alternative development theories that are variously labeled 'alternative development,' 'alternatives to development' and 'post-development.' We examine the uptake of these theories in recent comparative education textbooks and explore their implications and applications for a re-imagined comparative education.

Theories of Development

'Development' as a concept related to social and institutional change has flourished in the six decades since the end of World War II. There is a wide range of views on the meaning of the concept (Thomas, 2000; Burkey, 1993; Escobar, 1995; Myers, 1999; Simon, 1999). Many definitions of development focus on individual and collective well being, as in Chambers' (1997, p. 9) notion of fostering "well-being for all" humans and Simon's (1999, p. 21) idea that development involves "enhancing individual and collective quality of life" in a sustainable and empowering manner that satisfies basic needs.

Modernization theories dominated early development thinking, and still permeate, albeit in sometimes more subtle forms, much of the work being done by various agencies around the world. Isbister (1991) observes that modernization theories mainly "focus upon deficiencies in the poor countries — the absence of democratic institutions, of capital, of technology, of initiative, and then speculate upon ways of repairing those deficiencies" (p. 33). For modernization scholars, development through economic growth is paramount (Burkey, 1993). They view 'undeveloped' countries as having lagged behind 'developed' countries because of traditional modes of living, which result in stagnation and backwardness. The cure for this stagnation is to embrace social, cultural, and economic systems from the 'developed countries,' and to become like the developed countries through growth-based innovations propelled by capitalist economic systems and democratic institutions and structures.

However, the critics of modernization argue that all the effort by the developed world to push the underdeveloped world to "be like them" has proven a failure. In the words of Sachs (1992, p. 1), one of the anti-development protagonists, "the idea of development stands like a ruin in the intellectual landscape. Delusions and disappointment, failures and crimes have been the steady companions of development and they tell a common story: it did not work.... But above all, the hopes and desires which made the idea fly, are now exhausted: development has grown obsolete." Such generalizations, however, have in turn been criticized by Nederveen Pieterse (2000), who argues for a distinction between big development, and smaller scale, grassroots activities. It is the former that many critics of development have targeted.

Dependency theory provided an early challenge to the assumptions and effects of modernization. Emanating mainly from Latin American economists and social scientists, the fundamental tenet of dependency theory is that the growth of rich nations, particularly European and North American countries, has impoverished the developing nations through the forces of capitalism (Peet and Harwick, 1999). The theory questions the assumed mutual benefits for countries on the 'periphery' of international trade with countries at the dominating 'center,' such as the U.S., Britain, and Japan. For dependency theorists, the 'third world' countries are not in a state of primitive fixation, but rather they have been constructed and framed through interaction with the 'powerful' nations. In other words, through these interactions, there is a latent development of underdevelopment, initiated, aided and abetted by a range of actors, including multilateral organizations such as the World Bank and the International Monetary Fund.

However, the center-periphery binary has been challenged by Isbister, who points out that many 'developing' countries have social structures entangled in the development of underdevelopment. In particular, local elites control the means of production and benefit from their relationship with foreign investors. Thus, while local elites reap the benefits of 'development' projects, the majority of people see little benefit from them (Isbister, 1991, p. 48).

There has been a range of responses to the criticism of modernization that dependency theories have raised. Some authors have argued that the problem of elite and outside interests dominating 'development' agendas and outcomes can be overcome by addressing at the grassroots the needs of the people who are meant to be the beneficiaries of development and by taking into account the specific or local contexts of people's lives (see, for example, Chambers, 1997; Maser, 1997; Myers, 1999; Burkey, 1993; Thomas, 2000). Participatory, people-centered, and transformational approaches are all part of a range of responses to bureaucratically cumbersome, top-down approaches. These responses are often referred to as 'alternative development' and have been championed by the likes of Friedmann (1992), Korten (1990), and Brohman (1996). Other authors, however, have argued for a somewhat more eclectic approach which while acknowledging and addressing local needs, fosters the participation of beneficiaries, and aims to be transformational, empowering and culturally appropriate, and also takes account of the workings and impact of national and global contextual elements, including the state and transnational agents such as multilateral organizations, global and regional trade agreements, and the like (see Mohan and Stoke, 1999).

Post-Development Theory

Post-development thinking involves a radical reassessment of the dilemmas of development. It is based on the premise that development has failed (Sachs, 1992). The failure of development is also attributed to its perceived subtlety as "the new religion of the West" (Rist, 1990, in Nederveen Pieterse, 2000, p. 175). Rahnema (1997, p. 392) argues that development has been highly intrusive in the lives of its "target populations," because so-called experts, although well-intentioned and promulgating messages of empowerment and participation, were working for the people rather than working with and learning from the people.

Post-development challenges to mainstream development and modernization took a major turn during the 1980's when the poststructural and postcolonial critiques of humanistic modernism and western imperialism articulated by thinkers such as Heidegger, Nietzsche, Husserl, Foucault, Said, Fanon, Bhabha, Spivak and others began to infiltrate development studies (for a summary of these ideas, see Peet and Harwick, 1999, pp. 127 ff). Their influence caused some development theorists and practitioners to rethink their ideas in several areas. First, there was a critical reassessment of terms such as 'progress,' 'improvement,' 'participation,' and 'development' (Peet and Hartwick, 1999). Poststructuralist development theorists problematized and examined the unintended consequences of the use of these concepts particularly in terms of relations of power, who had the authority to speak on the subject of development, and the discursive construction of developmental issues and problems (Escobar, 1992, 1995, 2001a, b).

Second, the issue of developmental process received attention. Poststructuralists disrupted the notion that development was somehow natural or inevitable if certain conditions were met, or indeed that development was universally desired. For poststructuralists, 'development' itself was an invention, a component of a language of power, and a social construction with a discursive or cultural history (Peet and Hartwick, 1999, p. 143; Escobar, 1995). In addition, Escobar argued, "development was — and continues to be for the most part — a top-down, ethnocentric, and technocratic approach, which treated people and cultures as abstract concepts, statistical figures to be moved up and down in the charts of progress" (Escobar, 1995, p. 44).

While post-development theorists may contend that their approaches are relatively radical, critics such as Nederveen Pieterse (2000) argue that post-development views are not new. For instance, Pieterse (2000) suggests that dependency theories also value autonomous processes and argue against economic, social and cultural dependency. He notes that whereas dependency theorizing privileges the nation-state, post-development thinking privileges the endogenous and places great value on local and grassroots actors and factors (Nederveen Pieterse, 2000, p. 181). Although Pieterse (2000) identifies many similarities between post-development and alternative development, Escobar (1995) advocates for "alternatives to development" rather than "alternative development," because, as noted by Nandy (1989, p. 270), "most of the [alternative development] efforts are also products of the same worldview which produced the mainstream concept of science, liberation, and development." According to Escobar (1995), alternatives to development can be found through the engagement with social and grassroots movements and recognition of their role as legitimate and authentic instruments to bolster the alternatives to development. Critics of this position, such as Pieterse (2000), warn that even when there is considerable effort to depart from mainstream development in favor of NGOs and other similar organizations, the NGOs themselves may depend on international aid agencies and multilateral organizations. As a result, Nederveen Pieterse (2000, p. 182) argues, there is a likelihood of propagating a new wave of "alternative managerialism," in which "lack of humanity" becomes the norm.

Another criticism directed at post-development theory concerns language and discourse. Peet and Harwick (1999) believe that discourse analysis tends to bring opposing theories into "quasi-coherent determining wholes" (p. 156). Yet this is a simplistic understanding of discourse and discourse analysis. Foucault (1972) at times defines discourse as the whole set of statements about a topic, and clearly this suggests not a quasi-coherent whole, but a collection of statements that may be contradictory to some extent (Ninnes, this volume). Another criticism is that the emphasis on discourse is little more than a language game (e.g., Pieterse, 2000, p. 183). This criticism suggests a shallow understanding of poststructural theories of language, especially the link between discourses and their social, political, cultural, and material effects (see, for example, McHoul and Grace, 1993). Recently however, Escobar (2001a) has argued that such criticisms are based on a privileging of the material over the discursive; he then disrupts this binary opposition by pointing out the substantial political consequences of language and meaning in the construction of the real or the material (Escobar, 2001a).

Rahnema (1997) mentions another dimension of the crisis facing development and his call for an end to development. He argues that the call for an end to development does not necessarily mean that there has to be an end to the search for better alternatives to change, provided it is change that neither dehumanizes nor destroys people's aspirations. He calls for change that requires "good people everywhere to think and work together" (Rahnema, 1997, p. 391). Partnerships, as a dimension of post-development and alternative development thinking, embrace change that is not "prepared and developed somewhere" else (Rahnema, 1997, p. 397). In a similar vein, Escobar resists calls for post-developmentalists to set down definitive agendas for generalizable alternative models of development. He argues (Escobar 2001b) that such normative practices have "always been present in all development discourse [and] this naturalized morality domesticates our ethical sensibilities, our thinking, and our actions in ways that can only serve the interests of those in power."

Theories of Development and Comparative Education

We now turn to a brief and indicative analysis of contemporary comparative education textbooks to examine the extent to which various theories of development are being deployed. It is beyond the scope and purpose of this chapter to provide an exhaustive analysis of a wide range of books and articles here, although that would certainly be a worthwhile and revelatory exercise. Rather we intend to demonstrate through selective analysis the ways in which particular development paradigms are used in what we consider to be key texts, and in so doing identify some gaps in the use of development theorizing by these texts. We focus on two textbooks, namely, *Comparative Education: The Dialectic of the Global and the Local* (Arnove and Torres, 1999) and *Learning from Comparing: New Directions in Comparative Educational Research* (Alexander, Osborn and Phillips, 2000), particularly volume 2, the focus of which is "Policy, Professionals and Development."

The latter part of the collected work by Arnove and Torres (1999) contains a range of chapters devoted to a generic discussion of education in particular regions of the world, namely Latin America (Arnove, Franz, Mollis and Torres, 1999), Asia (Su, 1999), Russia and Eastern Europe (Bucur and Elkof, 1999), the Middle East (Christina, Mehran and Mir, 1999), and Africa (Samoff, 1999). The only other chapter that has a geographical orientation focuses on particular aspects of education, rather than a generic discussion, and is entitled "The Political Economy of Educational Reform in Australia, England and Wales, and the United States" (Berman, 1999). The chapters by Arnove, et. al and Samoff in particular provide some theoretical treatment of development, whereas chapters such as the one by Su are quite atheoretical, laced with modernist assumptions without acknowledgement of even dependency theory explanations of problems with development.

Arnove et al. (1999) identify three stages in the changes in definitions of development. They argue that initially development was defined primarily in terms of economic expansion. Next, this particular focus was expanded to include ideas pertaining to the more equitable distribution of goods and services, democratic participation, cultural preservation, and political sovereignty. Finally, "In the 1970s... development was further defined to incorporate ideas of respect for the environment and conservation of non-renewable natural resources as well as more equitable relations between the countries of the South and those of the North" (p. 315). There are two clear gaps in this account. First, and most obviously, the account of development theories ends with ideas from the 1970s, two decades before the book was published. As a result, there is no engagement with development thinking from the 1980s and 1990s. Second, the analysis focuses primarily on normative definitions of development, that is, ideas about the purposes and desired outcomes of 'development.' There is very little discussion of the actual outcomes of particular approaches to development. However, earlier in the chapter the authors do frame their analysis in terms of dependency theory. They argue that education has a limited ability to foster social change in most of Latin America because most Latin American states are "dependent or 'conditioned' capitalist states" (p. 306) whose economies are built on alliances between state bureaucrats, state managers, transnational corporations, and the national bourgeoisie, all entangled in a context of U.S. hegemony.

Despite this attempt to frame the chapter in terms of dependency theory, much of the discussion suggests that modernization is the underlying paradigm being employed. A large section of the chapter is devoted to a discussion of enrollment patterns, access, teacher qualifications, student-teacher ratios, pay levels, income inequality, enrollment levels, gender access, illiteracy levels, and the status of indigenous peoples in education. The nature of the curriculum is covered only in very general terms. For example, the authors note "the curriculum contains little to engage the interest of children in the rural areas" (p. 309) and that "the language of instruction is invariably Spanish (Portuguese in Brazil)" (p. 311). They report "an impressive numerical expansion in [the secondary] level of schooling" (p. 311), and observe, "when we examine secondary student enrolments as a percentage of total enrollments, Latin America lags behind developing areas" (p. 311). Furthermore, "quantitative change generally has not been matched by a qualitative change in the aims, content, and pedagogy of secondary education" (p. 311). The implication here is that in some aspects of education, Latin America lags behind some unstated standard or benchmark, and that the purpose of educational reform efforts should be to match levels achieved elsewhere and to mimic some unstated standard in terms of aims, content, and pedagogy. Development then means more education of a kind found elsewhere. There are several absences in this argument. First, there is little cognizance of the notion that development might mean rethinking the purposes of education in terms of the needs and desires of students and their families in various local contexts, rather than in terms of system-wide indicators of access and enrollments. Second, the discussion implies a top-down, bureaucracy-driven model of reform and fails to consider rethinking the processes of framing educational change in terms of inviting participation of the supposed beneficiaries of educational reform or the creation of strategic partnerships with stakeholders such as local NGOs and other grassroots social organizations.

Samoff (1999) contributes a chapter on education in Africa to the Arnove and Torres volume. As with the Arnove et. al chapter, Samoff pays lip service to alternative models of development, but his discussion has substantial modernization assumptions and focuses. He argues that there are two sets of competing ideas about education and development in Africa. The minority view is that education should be "transformative, liberatory, and synthetic" (p. 413). The dominant view is modernist and utilitarian, arguing that the primary purpose of education is economic development. Samoff notes, too, alternatives such as Nyerere's education for self-reliance, localization of the curriculum in Zimbabwe, and the development of pan-African studies courses in some universities. Like dependency theorists and certain post-development thinkers, Samoff notes the failure of modernization as a model of development. He argues that in the immediate period after independence "progress was clear and dramatic" in education (p. 393). But "today, the most common refrain is crisis.... Schools and learning have deteriorated, and the situation is continuing to worsen.... For many, the objective is no longer broad improvement in the standard of living or self-reliance but simply survival." (pp. 393-95). Although there has been "some progress and, in some countries, very substantial achievements ... in much of Africa, many children get little or no schooling, illiteracy rates have ceased to decline (or have begun to rise), school libraries have few books, laboratories have outdated or malfunctioning equipment and insufficient supplies, and learners lack chairs, exercise books, even pencils" (p. 396). It is clear here that Samoff measures educational "progress" purely in Western terms. Indeed, the deficit assumptions underlying his argument are no clearer than when he claims that "Nearly all African countries started with an inherited education system that excluded most of the population." However, it could be argued that the imported and imposed colonial education systems excluded most of the population, but in many areas the long-standing indigenous education systems continued to function strongly. Samoff goes on to argue, "Africa came to independence with few educated people" (p. 402), as if all the local knowledge of the people counted for nothing. Furthermore, the blame for a lack of gender equity in schools lies primarily at the feet of the local social and cultural context. In considering why women do not comprise half of the school population, Samoff argues,

> The candidate causes are well known: parental attitudes, gender-differentiated expectations for future income... the labor and household responsibilities of women, the absence of role models at home and in school, explicit and implicit discouragement for pursuing particular courses of study, parents' educational achievement, family religious and moral precepts, sexual harassment and early pregnancy, and more (p. 409).

Samoff is clearly employing a deficit discourse characteristic of modernization approaches to development. Education is defined exclusively in terms of some imaginary Western norm, while indigenous knowledges and contexts are ignored or blamed for the failure of African education to live up to certain implied and externally derived standards.

The second work we wish to analyze is Alexander, Osborn and Phillips' collected work *Learning from Comparing: New Directions in Comparative Educational Research*. The second volume of this series has an entire section devoted to "Research, Education and Development." Alexander (2000) commences the section with a brief contextualization and overview of the contributions. He strikes a sobering note, observing that globalization may well be a two-edged sword that marginalizes as much as it liberates, and impoverishes as much as it empowers. He notes also the problematics of development research in postcolonial contexts. Thus, Alexander does not wholeheartedly subscribe to the new modernization discourses of some globalization enthusiasts; but nor does he in the limited space available canvas substantive issues in contemporary development theorizing.

The following chapter, by Michael Crossley (2000), shows a greater awareness than other authors of some of the problematics of development revealed by contemporary theorizing. He argues for the importance of taking local contexts and cultural differences into account, for an understanding of global aspects of context, as well as local and national aspects; for the problematization of terms such as 'developed' and 'developing'; and for a serious engagement with criticisms of the use of researchers from outside the South to research the South. Crossely argues that little application of post-modern perspectives is evident in education and development debates, yet there is an intensifying challenge to 'grand theory' (Crossley, 2000, p. 77).

Cheng Kai-Ming's (2000) chapter begins by observing that most development models have expanded from a sole focus on economic development to include issues such as basic needs fulfillment, equity, wealth distribution, political participation, and human rights. However, he argues that because of variations between nations, a uniform model of development is impossible. Cheng then goes on to privilege cultural difference as a key aspect that should be taken into account in studying development, and presents a culturalist account of China as an example. He argues for "an open mind to native perspectives and the sensitivity not to impose foreign frameworks on the researched" (Cheng Kai-Ming, 2000, p. 89) and for more South-South collaboration in research.

The issues of gender, education, and development are canvassed by Brock and Cammish (2000) in a quite substantial way. Their model includes geographical, socio-cultural, health, economic, religious, legal, political-administrative, and educational factors in a comparative analysis of Bangladesh, Cameroon, India (especially Gujarat and Orissa), Jamaica, Sierra Leone, and Vanuatu. They argue for the importance of local cultural effects in understanding communities' ability and willingness to promote change in girls' education, and argue for participatory approaches in research on girls' education. Yet the chapter rarely explicitly justifies its choice of development indicators, nor reveals how they came to be accepted as appropriate. There appears to be an assumed consensus and universality about these indicators that implies a modernization approach in the sense that the unstated purpose of development is to move communities in a particular direction which looks rather like the 'developed' West, in terms of girls' participation rates, the desired effects of literacy programs, and so on.

The section concludes with two chapters that attempt to critically engage with the previous chapters. Preston (2000) notes the impasse that developed once modernization's failure was apparent, and the potency of dependency theorists' critiques of modernization. Most significantly, Preston notes that the localized management development models and the large-scale cross-sectoral programs appear to be 1960s-style modernization in a neo-liberal guise. In particular, Preston argues that there is a "growing dependency of international and local voluntary organizations" on funding from large multilateral organizations. Yet there is no substantive engagement in this chapter with contemporary development theory. Finally, Schweisfurth's (2000) postscript to the section identifies key issues, but again does not engage contemporary post-development thinking.

Re-Imagining Comparative Education and Development

The comparative education texts examined above are not necessarily representative of the field as a whole. However, they are designed as introductory textbooks and as such implicitly purport to provide readers with a broad coverage of the major thrusts of the field. On the basis of this assumption, there is a vital need to reappraise the ways in which such introductory textbooks deal with issues of development. As the preceding analysis shows, the textbooks make little mention of contemporary post-development thinking. They do not, for example, canvas the whole problematic of development discourse, and the way language as a technology of power operating at a micro level influences what it is possible to think, say and do in development. Nor do they substantively address the issue of power at the macro level. There is very little problematization of the bureaucratic, top-down approaches to development that have been heavily critiqued by post-development theorists. A more sophisticated approach is required which more thoroughly engages with the complexities of the debates that have occurred in development studies in the past decade or two. This is not to suggest that we should completely abandon the understandings of the relationship between global capital, poverty, and 'underdevelopment' that dependency theory so powerfully provided in response to the failures of modernization. Rather, there is a need to provide a more substantive engagement with contemporary issues, and not cease our presentation of theory at a point in the distant past, such as the 1970s. In particular, there is, first, a need to problematize development discourses that normatively construct ideas about the aims of development, and especially the aims of developing education systems. Cheng (2000) has begun this process, albeit in a way that tends to reify culture. Second, we need to think through the role of comparative education in development. In particular, we need to critically engage with global organizations that impose normative, top-down, heavily bureaucratic models of development in a range of diverse contexts. We also need to consider our role as forming part of the critical mass of opposition to the "global forces threatening local spaces" (Peet and Harwick, 1999, p. 152); the extent to which we can or should direct our efforts toward supporting local grassroots initiatives; and the unintended consequences of colluding with organizations that co-opt and appropriate local people and local issues to serve wider and less locally productive agendas.

We do not advocate a utopian vision of pre-colonial societies, post-development critiques that involve "reappraising noncapitalist societies" (Peet and Harwick, 1999, pp. 152–153), We do argue that this element of the post-development critique suggests a need for an engagement with the marginalized. It suggests a need for 'development' work that seeks to listen to everyday people in villages and towns, not just the minders and local officials that often accompany consultants on their commonly brief visits to the field. Finally, we need to question the extent to which the projects we work on allow all affected parties an opportunity to contribute meaningfully to decision making, especially regarding issues of economic justice, changing lifestyles, materialism, morality, spirituality, and suitable responses to local, regional, and global forces.

References

Alexander, Robin. "Introduction: Research, education and development." In *Learning from Comparing: New Directions in Comparative Educational Research (Vol. 2: Policy, Professionals and Development)*. Edited by Robin Alexander, Marilyn Osborn and David Phillips. Oxford: Symposium Books, 2000.

Alexander, Robin, et al., *Learning from Comparing: New Directions in Comparative Educational Research (Vol. 2: Policy, Professionals and Development)*. Edited by Robin Alexander, Marilyn Osborn, and David Phillips. Oxford: Symposium Books, 2000.

Arnove, Robert and Carlos A. Torres. *Comparative education: The dialectic of the global and the local.* Edited by Robert Arnove and Carlos Torres. Lanham, MD: Rowman and Littlefield, 1999.

Arnove, Robert F. et al., "Education in Latin America at the End of the 1990s." In *Comparative education: The dialectic of the global and the local.* Edited by Robert Arnove and Carlos A. Torres. Lanham, MD: Rowman and Littlefield, 1999.

Berman, Edward H. "The Political Economy of Educational Reform in Australia, England and Wales, and the United States." In *Comparative Education: The Dialectic of the Global and the Local.* Edited by Robert Arnove and Carlos Torres. Lanham, MD: Rowman and Littlefield, 1999.

Brock, Colin and Nadine Commash. "Developing a Comparative Approach to the Study of Gender, Education and Development." In *Learning from comparing: New directions in comparative educational research (Vol. 2: Policy, Professionals and Development)*. Edited by Robin Alexander, Marilyn Osborn, and David Phillips. Oxford: Symposium Books, 2000.

Brohman, John. *Popular development: Rethinking the theory and practice of development.* Oxford: Blackwell, 1996.

Bucur, Maria and Ben Eklof. "Russia and Eastern Europe." In *Comparative Education: The Dialectic of the Global and the Local.* Edited by Robert Arnove and Carlos Torres. Lanham, MD: Rowman and Littlefield, 1999.

Burkey, Stan. *People First: A Guide to Self-reliant, Participatory Rural Development.* London: Zed Books, 1993.

Chambers, Robert. *Whose Reality Counts? Putting the First Last.* London: Intermediate Technology Publications, 1997.

Cheng, Kai-Ming. "Education and Development: The Neglected Mission of Cross-cultural Studies." In *Learning from comparing: New directions in comparative educational research (Vol. 2: Policy, Professionals and Development)*. Edited by Robin Alexander, Marilyn Osborn, and David Phillips. Oxford: Symposium Books, 2000.

Christina, Rachel, et al. "Education in the Middle East: Challenges and Opportunities." In *Comparative Education: The Dialectic of the Global and the Local*. Edited by Robert Arnove and Carlos Torres. Lanham, MD: Rowman and Littlefield, 1999.

Crossley, Michael. "Research, Education and Development: Setting the Scene." In *Learning from Comparing: New Directions in Comparative Educational Research (Vol. 2: Policy, Professionals and Development)*. Edited by Robin Alexander, Marilyn Osborn, and David Phillips. Oxford: Symposium Books, 2000.

Escobar, Arturo. *Encountering Development: The Making and Unmaking of the Third World*. Princeton: Princeton University Press, 1995.

_____. "The Making and Unmaking of the Third World through Development." In *The Post-development Reader*. Edited by Majid Rahnema and Victoria Bawtree. London: Zed Books, 1997.

_____. "Beyond the Search for a Paradigm? Post-development and Beyond." *Development*, 43(4) [online www.sidint.org/journal/online/], 2001a.

_____. "A Brief Response to Ray Kiely's 'Reply to Escobar.'" *Development* 43(4) [online www.sidint.org/journal/online/Escobar434.htm], 2001b.

Foucault, M. *The Archaeology of Knowledge*. London: Travistock, 1972.

Friedmann, John. *Empowerment: The Politics of Alternative Development*. Cambridge: Blackwell, 1992.

Isbister, John. *Promises not Kept: The Betrayal of Social Change in the Third World*. West Hartford, CT: Kumarian Press, 1991.

Kandel, Isaac. "Comparative Education and Underdeveloped Countries: A New Dimension." *Comparative Education Review* 4(3) (1961), 130–135.

Korten, David. *Getting to the 21st Century: Voluntary Action and the Global Agenda*. West Hartford, CT: Kumarian Press, 1990.

Maser, Chris. *Sustainable Community Development: Principles and Concepts*. London: St. Lucie Press, 1997.

McHoul, Alec and Wendy Grace. *A Foucault Primer: Discourse, Power and the Subject*. Carlton, Victoria: Melbourne University Press, 1993.

Mohan, Giles and Kristian Stokke. "Participatory Development and Empowerment: The Dangers of Localism." *Third World Quarterly*, 21 (2000), 247–268.

Myers, Bryant L. *Walking with the Poor: Principles and Practices of Transformational Development*. New York: Orbis Books, 1999.

Nandy, Ashis. "Shamans, Savages and the Wilderness: On the Audibility of Dissent and the Future of Civilisation. *Alternatives*, 14 (1989), 263–277.

Nederveen Pieterse, Jan. "After Post-development." *Third World Quarterly*, 21 (2000), 175–191.

Peet, Richard and Elaine Hartwick. *Theories of Development*. New York: The Guilford Press, 1999.

Preston, Rosemary. "Learning from Development Research in Educational Contexts." In *Learning from comparing: New directions in comparative educational research (Vol. 2: Policy, Professionals and Development)*. Edited by Robin Alexander, Marilyn Osborn, and David Phillips. Oxford: Symposium Books, 2000.

Rahnema, Majid. "Towards Post-development: Searching for Signposts, a New Language and New Paradigms." In *The Post-development Reader*. Edited by Majid Rahnema and Victoria Bawtree. London: Zed Books, 1997.

Rahnema, Majid and Victoria Bawtree. *The Post-development Reader*. Edited by Majid Rahnema and Victoria Bawtree. London: Zed Books, 1997.

Rist, Gilbert. "Development as a New Religion of the West." *Quid Pro Quo*, 1 (1990), 5–8.

Sachs, Wolfgang. "Introduction." In *The Development Dictionary: A Guide to Knowledge and Power*. Edited by Wolfgang Sachs. London: Zed Books, 1992.

Samoff, Joel. "No Teacher Guide, No Textbooks, No Chairs: Contending with Crisis in African Education." In *Comparative Education: The Dialectic of the Global and the Local*. Edited by Robert Arnove and Carlos A. Torres. Lanham, MD: Rowman and Littlefield, 1999.

Schweisfurth, Michele. "Postscript: Perspectives from the Fourth Seminar." In *Learning from Comparing: New Directions in Comparative Educational Research (Vol. 2: Policy, Professionals and Development)*, edited by Robin Alexander, Marilyn Osborn, and David Phillips. Oxford: Symposium Books, 2000.

Simon, David. "Development Revisited: Thinking about Practicing and Teaching Development after the Cold War." In *Development as Theory and Practice*. Edited by David Simon and Anders Norman. London: Longman, 1999.

Su, Zhixin. "Asian Education." In *Comparative Education: The Dialectic of the Global and the Local*. Edited by Robert Arnove and Carlos A. Torres. Lanham, MD: Rowman and Littlefield, 1999.

Thomas, Alan. "Meanings and Views on Development." In *Poverty and Development into the 21st Century*. Edited by Tim Allen and Alan Thomas. Oxford: Open University Press, 2000.

CHAPTER **14**

Mapping Diverse Perspectives on School Decentralization: The Global Debate and the Case of Argentina

JORGE M. GOROSTIAGA and ROLLAND G. PAULSTON

> The dissolution of the orthodox consensus has been succeeded by the Babel of theoretical voices that currently clamor for attention. One might distinguish three prevalent reactions to this seemingly disoriented situation of social theory. The first is a reaction of despair and disillusionment. A second might be described as a search for security at any cost: a reversion to dogmatism. The third response to the theoretical disarray of the social sciences today is almost exactly the opposite of the first. Rather than a reaction of despair, it is one of rejoicing: the diversity of theoretical perspectives is welcomed as testimony to the inherent fruitfulness of social theory. We cannot … achieve a closure of this diversity, nor should we seek to.
>
> *Anthony Giddens (1979, pp. 238–239)*

This study argues that school decentralization, as educational decentralization in general, is a contested issue, constructed by an interplay of different perspectives, or ways of seeing, that can be portrayed as a networked information-space at both theoretical and the practical levels. As with other conflicted educational issues where diverse knowledge communities make competing claims, practitioners, policy-makers and everyone involved in education seem to be in need of comparative research that contributes "to provisionally order and interpret today's multiple views of education and society" (Paulston and Liebman, 1996, p. 23).

The purpose of this chapter is to gain a better understanding of social cartography potentials via intertextual mappings of the phenomenon of school decentralization.[1] We investigate the meaning of school decentralization at the international, or global level, and in a particular national context, Argentina, from a critical pluralistic perspective that is sensitive to differences, i.e., to Gidden's " Babel," of multiple ways of seeing and being. The study focuses on the arguments and perspectives about school decentralization as they are constructed in texts. It includes arguments about what is (the origins, objectives, and implications of implemented policies) as well as claims concerning what ought to be central in school decentralization plans. With close reading of the texts, this study identifies and maps key arguments and major perspectives, and demonstrates via textual and visual interpretive representation of the debate field how comparative education inquiry today might be reinvented with close attention to rhetoric, texts, discourse, and to the spatial patterning of rhetorical difference.

Our main assumption is that the characteristics of discourses and debates significantly affect the way policies are planned and implemented. Discourse, "far from serving as a mere 'tool' for transferring meaning and intention, actually shapes what is thought and done" (Gottlieb, 1989, pp. 141–2). We also assume that different ways of seeing a phenomenon can reflect different values and interests, and may imply preferences for different policies on the issue. Accordingly, we choose to see a re-imagined comparative education as an agonistic space of contested interpretations and negotiated realities. It is in this new heterogeneous landscape that we must now begin to re-imagine and re-map our minds, our relations, our knowledge and values (Goodman, 2003, pp. 23–25).

So we have chosen to represent the discourse on school decentralization as a debate in order to illuminate tensions as well as coincidences between different positions. Moreover, the concept of debate allows interpreting discourse as a space where multiple perspectives enter into dialogue and confrontation, "as a site and object of struggle where different groups strive for hegemony in the production of meaning and ideology" (Paulston, 1995, p. 162).

Why the School Decentralization Focus?

Issues of centralization and decentralization are prominent in the current international debates on the governance of education systems (see Bray, 1994, 1999; McGinn, 1992). According to Reimers (1997), the model of traditional administrative decentralization lost appeal during the 1990s, "in part because it does not automatically lead to changes in the organization of the school and therefore of the teaching process" (p. 147). What has emerged, instead, is an interest in the idea of decentralizing decision-making to individual schools, whose link to the quality of teaching and learning processes has yet to be proved (Elmore, 1993; Reimers, 1997).

In general, the concept of school decentralization is seen as entailing the delegation (or devolution) of responsibility and authority to individual schools in different areas such as curriculum, instruction, and administration (budget, personnel, organization of time/calendar, use of space, etc.). The actual models vary in terms of what areas are decentralized, and what actors at the school level (i.e., principals, teachers, and parents) are given responsibility for decisionmaking (Murphy and Beck, 1995). The models may also vary in terms of the relationships of the school with other schools, the local district, and with municipal, provincial, and national governments (see Angus, 1993 for an example of the different roles that provincial governments may play in school decentralization).

The decentralization of education, including school decentralization, may respond to different rationales (see Lauglo, 1995; Prawda, 1993; Weiler, 1990). These include, but are not limited to, democratization, increasing efficiency, the development of professional community among teachers, shifting the cost burden of education to local governments and communities, and the integration of schools with local communities. Some of these rationales may be complementary, while others are seen to be contradictory to one another.

As stated above, the term "school decentralization" refers to processes of transferring responsibility and/or authority to the school from central levels (e.g., districts, provincial/state level, national level). Hanson (1997, p. 14) holds that "the basic premise behind decentralized schools is that educational decisions made at the local level are more quick, informed, flexible, and responsive to specific needs than decisions made in the capital city."

School decentralization comprises different kinds of arrangements concerning the authority and responsibility of different actors and various aspects of governance and administration. School decentralization is seen by some as part of a "struggle to reinvent schooling" (Murphy and Beck, 1995, p. 85). At the same time, it seems to relate to a broad set of educational and social issues, like school choice, privatization, the professionalization of teachers, the links between schools and local communities, organizational changes, the depoliticization of education, the crisis of the welfare, state and the rise of neoliberalism/neoconservatism, and the democratization of schools.

Our interrogation of the international literature on school decentralization (e.g., Angus, 1993; Reimers, 1997; Smyth, 1993) suggests that it constitutes a policy forum with different positions at the theoretical level and among social actors involved in education. As Hanson (1990) states, "as experience with the concept has begun to surface the awareness grows that

SBM (school-based management) means very different things to different people" (p. 523).

There is a limited understanding of school decentralization (and of educational decentralization in general). Usually, studies focus on how decentralization may be implemented in different ways to serve different objectives, but do not advance in the analysis and comparison of different perspectives (as ways of seeing) in the perception about what decentralization is and what ought to be. Lauglo (1995), for example, offers a comparison of eight types of educational decentralization (some of which involve decentralization to the school level), based on different rationales, which approximates to a mapping of multiple arguments, but he does not include arguments *against* decentralization, nor does he analyze the relationships among types.

When studies compare different perspectives, the comparison is usually made in terms of a binary, where one of the perspectives tends to appear as superior because of its implications for quality and/or equity. For example, Reimers (1997) reduces the debate on school decentralization to the "school choice" perspective and the "school-site empowerment" perspective, while Angus (1993) compares a neo-conservative discourse with a social-democratic approach to the decentralization of authority to schools, highlighting the perverse implications of the former. Exceptions can be found in the work of Lauglo (1995) (already mentioned), and in Plank (1995), where the Brazilian debate on decentralization is characterized as featuring four main positions (technocratic/authoritarian right, libertarian/laissez faire right, utopian left, and pragmatic left). Plank briefly describes each position without providing a deep analysis of the relationships between the different positions, and finally dismisses all four because of their "preoccupation with the control of means in the educational system" and their lack of serious attention to "the accomplishment of ends" (p. 146).

For the purpose of this chapter all perspectives or positions producing texts in the debate are taken into consideration, regardless of focus on means or ends and including perspectives both favoring and opposing decentralization. This study aims at contributing to the understanding of school decentralization by opening our view of the issue as an interactive field of diverse multiple perspectives, avoiding a hierarchical order or the prevalence of a particular view over all others.[2]

By focusing on the global debate, we attempt to represent and compare perspectives addressing a diversity of policies and proposals produced at local, national, and supranational levels. On the other hand, the mapping of the debate in Argentina allows us to situate arguments and perspectives in relation to the particular reform discourse field of a peripheral Latin American country, as well as the comparison of a national debate with a global debate.

In response to our editors' call to "re-imagine comparative education," we advocate a welcoming of diverse perspectives along with a social mapping practice to cope with the ensuing "Babel of ... voices" currently heard in the forum of educational policy debates. Accordingly, our task here will be to move beyond exhortation to the performance of a new methodological craft that, we contend, is both useful and necessary for the comparative and networking requirements of our disputatious time.

This chapter is organized around three questions:

1. How has the issue of school decentralization been understood and represented both at the global level and in the Argentine context? How do selected illustrative texts (including policy documents and scholarly texts) represent the complex realities and possibilities of school decentralization? How might texts be typed into major perspectives? What are the arguments about school decentralization, the worldview, and the defining rhetorical characteristics of each perspective? Here, we seek to implement a linguistic turn with an exegetic or close reading, of verbal texts.

2. How might the global and Argentine discourses on school decentralization be represented as open fields that include multiple perspectives and highlight the connections and differences among these perspectives? What kinds of relationships can be pictured between perspectives? Here we advocate a cartographic-pictorial, or spatial, turn.

3. What comparisons can be made between the case of Argentina and the global discourse on school decentralization? How does the Argentine map of perspectives relate to the global map? How well does our cartography of multiple perspectives perform our argument that social mapping is a useful tool to compare difference in our time?

The chapter focuses on the global debate since the 1980s to date, and on a single country, Argentina, which is experiencing a comprehensive reform of its educational system, including policies of school decentralization, since 1993. At the same time, the analysis aims at identifying the *major* perspectives on the general inter-textual debate according to the mappers' interpretation, therefore not all of the possible perspectives on the issue will be represented. In addition, the global debate is constructed through texts that mainly address the cases of English-speaking nations, and to a lesser degree Latin American countries, while for both the global and the Argentine debates, we focus on texts produced by academics and by governmental and multilateral international organizations.

The study does not consider which perspectives or arguments have more acceptance or power. Nor does it evaluate arguments in terms of their logic, coherence, empirical support, or any other evaluative criteria. Rather, it aims at representing how they construct meaning, and how various arguments and perspectives can be seen to interact in a field of difference.

In addition, this study provides an interpretation of how school decentralization is seen, not as a technical prescription for policymaking, but more akin to a *provisional* representation where arguments and maps change in response to the changing social and policy contexts, and new perspectives may be brought in through the incorporation of additional texts into the policy debate field.

Methodology

Our general approach to the research is interpretive and based on the view that:

> Order in the social world ... rests on a precarious, socially-constructed web of symbolic relationships that are continuously negotiated, renegotiated, affirmed or changed. The interpretive theorist's problematic is to understand the meaning and significance of this web of relationships, and how it exists as such (Morgan, 1990).

Within the interpretive tradition, this study draws on some elements of discourse analysis using a phenomenographic and comparative approach. Phenomenography is defined as "the empirical study of the limited qualitatively different ways in which various phenomena in, and aspects of, the world around us are experienced, conceptualized, understood, perceived, and apprehended" (Marton, 1994, p. 4424). This approach allows identifying and comparing multiple ways of seeing, advancing understanding about the heuristic representation of a phenomenon. "Through empirical studies as well as textual analysis, phenomenographic studies seek not to describe things as they are but to show how they have been presented as sedimentations of ways of thinking about the world" (Paulston, 1995, p. 159).

In this study, texts that inform the debate on school decentralization are considered as part of different discourses which can be seen — at the same time — as part of a general discursive framework and as competing truth claims. As Barnes and Duncan (1992) argue:

> Discourses are not unified, but are subject to negotiation, challenge and transformation. For power relations within a social formation are communicated, and sometimes resisted, precisely through the medium of particular discourses (p. 8).

Therefore, discourse analysis appears as an important approach for extending understanding of social and educational phenomena through examining how reality is variously understood or constructed through the use of words and ideas. Particularly relevant for this study is the notion of "close reading," which has been applied in previous comparative education studies by *inter alia* (Gottlieb, 1989; Paulston, 1995, 1999).

This study recognizes as well the influence of a post-modern sensibility that opens space to multiple perspectives without privileging any, moving away from exclusive modernist approaches that focus on binary oppositions, exclusions, and on essentialist notions of consensus and central tendency (see Paulston & Liebman, 1996). The focus on perspectives as part of an intertextual debate builds on Mausolff's (1996) mapping of perspectives on participation in rural development and on Paulston's (1999) mapping of comparative education discourse after postmodernity.

The database for our study is comprised of texts, including scholarly texts and organizational documents that address in a direct or indirect way the issue of school decentralization, and the arguments about school decentralization present in those texts.

We conducted a comprehensive review of texts on educational decentralization through database searches (ERIC, WorldCat, etc.) and a survey of some of the main U.S., British, and international journals from 1980 to the present (*American Educational Research Journal, British Journal of Sociology of Education, Comparative Education Review, Compare, Comparative Education, Educational Administration Quarterly, Educational Evaluation and Policy Analysis, Educational Policy, Educational Policy Analysis Archives, Educational Researcher, International Journal of Educational Research, International Journal of Educational Development, Journal of Education Policy, Prospects, La Educación, Review of International Education, The International Journal of Educational Management*, etc.). In addition, we used " snowballing," adding texts cited in the articles and books identified (Malen et al., 1990, p. 291).

At the global level, the survey of texts focused on the academic fields of international and comparative education, and educational policy, including organizational texts by the Inter-American Development Bank, World Bank, and UNESCO. Although there might be other relevant texts (e.g., newspaper articles), it is assumed that texts from such academic fields and organizations can provide a wide variety of arguments and perspectives. We recognized, however, that this results in a partial account of the educational discourse on decentralization.[3]

For the Argentine debate, we oriented the search to texts that were originally published in Argentina or that can be assumed to be addressed to local audiences, aiming to influence the discussion, design and/or implementation of school decentralization policies at the national level. The sources of texts included books, journals, reviews, newspapers, newsletters, web pages, and official documents. Library and database searches and surveys of educational journals, reviews, and newspapers were conducted by the first author, both in Argentina and in Pittsburgh. In addition, texts were also identified through conversations with the Argentine scholars

Inés Aguerrondo, Myriam Feldfeber, Mariano Narodowski, Silvia Senén González, and Guillermina Tiramonti; with Jorge Cardelli (representative of CTERA, the main national confederation of teachers' unions); and with Padre Juan Torrella (Catholic Education Office of the City of Buenos Aires), during the months of June and July of 2000.

For both the global and the Argentine debates, we attempted to include texts providing the broadest array of positions in the debates about educational decentralization. The main criteria for the selection of texts was comprehensiveness (illustrating all of the various ways of seeing the phenomenon) and diversity (covering as many arguments and ways of arguing as possible), until reaching redundancy. For the global debate, an attempt has been made to include in each perspective texts that discuss school decentralization in different (national and regional) contexts, including texts that address school decentralization in Latin America since it is the regional context for the Argentine case.

We gave priority to texts that have had an important diffusion and impact among educators (and the general public). Attention was given also to the identification of texts that suggest various kinds of relationships among different ways of seeing the phenomenon of school decentralization and, in the Argentine context, to texts that discuss school decentralization in relation to the global debate. Using these criteria, we selected 29 texts from a universe of some 100 texts that we identified for the global debate, and 14 texts for the debate in Argentina from a universe of 28 texts.[4]

Most of the texts in the global debate refer to English-speaking industrialized countries (e.g., United Kingdom, USA, Australia), in part because school decentralization has had important development in such countries, in part because our search of relevant literature has focused on texts in English (which facilitates the presentation of textual analysis in English), and has been limited by availability in a US university setting. The texts selected for the Argentine case are written in Spanish.

The analysis was conducted through discourse analysis involving a close reading of texts and using a phenomenographic approach. The selected texts were carefully examined in order to uncover their arguments, rhetorical characteristics, and worldviews, aiming at identifying the different ways of seeing the phenomenon of school decentralization in the global and Argentine discourses.

In our view, text analysis is performed as an interpretive exercise. As Fairclough (1992) points out, "one's analysis of the text is shaped and colored by one's interpretation of its relationship to discourse processes and wider social processes" (p. 199). Drawing on Ricouer's hermeneutics, Bjerrum Nielsen (1995) contends that "to read is thus to link the text's meaning together with another meaning, namely, the reader's experiences" (p. 9). In this view, texts are open to different interpretations, but interpretation is limited by the meaning of the text (its structure, its signs, and signals). This hermeneutical exercise takes into account the context in which the text has been produced, but also that texts can "have an importance beyond the initial context in which they were composed" (Barnes and Duncan, 1992, p. 6).

This study adopts an approach that gives more attention to the content or meaning of discourse while acknowledging the importance of the choices made in the use of language. The approach adopted here could be characterized as qualitative, as interpretive content analysis: "People who do content analysis study a set of objects (i.e., cultural artifacts) or events systematically by counting them or *interpreting* the themes contained in them" (Reinharz, 1992, p. 146).

While keeping a similar emphasis on ideas and arguments to the interpretivist approach (see Purpel and Shapiro, 1995; Anderson, 1998; Sayed, 1999), this study adopts a more phenomenographic approach that aims at identifying how different worldviews see various phenomena. As Paulston (1995) explains, "comparison of alternative perspectives seeks to identify distinctive characteristics ... of each conceptualization ... so they may be made visible, described, and mapped" (p. 159). Without necessarily ignoring the broader framework of the discourse on a particular subject matter or the role of dominant discourses in setting limits to what is said or written, a postmodern phenomenographic approach places the emphasis on the identification of perspectives or subdiscourses that are both at the center and the margins of dominant textual practices. Texts by Erkkilä (2000), Mausolff (1996) and Paulston (1999) exemplify this use of discourse analysis with a focus on ideas and the use of a phenomenographic approach. These works advance the idea of debates on particular issues, where various perspectives are seen advocating different and sometimes opposing ideas. In addition, all of them are examples of identifying arguments and/ or perspectives through a "close reading" of texts. Erkkilä (2000) uses argument as the unit of analysis to characterize different perspectives on entrepreneurial education. She reviews selected texts on the subject for three different countries in order to identify arguments, map the various perspectives in the debate in each country, and compare the three. Mausolff (1996) identifies — through an analysis and comparison of the ideas and worldviews of eight texts — four "ways of seeing" participation in international rural development texts. Paulston (1999) analyzes some sixty texts informing the postmodernity debate in comparative education, giving attention to ideas, worldviews, and rhetorical characteristics of texts, and identifies ten knowledge positions in the debate.

The identification of arguments is the most important element in this analysis, while the other elements (worldviews and rhetorical characteristics) are seen as significant for the processes of identifying and understanding the meaning of arguments, and for typing texts into different perspectives:

What is often called an "argument" is in fact the tip of the iceberg. The actual text of discourse given or explicitly presented by the proponent may make sense only because of background knowledge or assumptions shared by the speaker and her audience. Therefore, interpreting an argument from a given text in order to answer the question "What is the argument?" demands skills and techniques of "reading off" the argument from the discourse (Walton, 1996, p. 41).

The analysis aimed at identifying arguments about the origins and implications of current policies, about the forms that school decentralization should adopt, about the ways in which policies should be implemented, and about their general benefits and shortcomings. It is important to note again that we did not intend to conduct an evaluation of arguments in terms of their logic, coherence, empirical support, or any other criterion, but to represent how they construct meaning, and how various arguments and perspectives can be seen to interact in a field of difference akin to the notion of a cyber, or steering, space of interactive world views (Johnson, 1997).

In terms of rhetorical characteristics that contribute to the construction of arguments, the analysis of texts includes the following elements: (1) Issues of language, vocabulary, and rhetorical tone: what kind of language prevails (e.g., technical, poetic, political, etc.), what are some key and distinctive terms used, what is the prevailing tone of the text?[5] (2) Argumentative strategies, or the " logic of persuasion" (Hart, 1997, p. 82): how are different devises (quantitative justification, analogy, contrast, testimony, etc.) used to strengthen arguments and convince readers? (see also Perelman and Olbrechts-Tyleca, 1969; Summa, 1992).

The analysis of the text's worldview included their orientation to social change (i.e., from functionalist to conflict views), their ontological views (i.e., from objectivist to subjectivist views of reality), as well as claims related to central issues in comparative education and educational policy discourses, like distinctions between rational and interactive models of planning (Adams, 1988), and different views about the relationships among education, state, and social institutions (e.g., families, market, etc.) at local, national, and global levels (see Arnove, et al., 1997; Ginsburg, et al. 1990; McGinn and Cummings, 1997).

To the extent possible, texts were allowed to speak for themselves with the use of quotes. The use of quotes helps to show that the researchers' interpretation of the text is not arbitrary, and also to show the construction of argument in the texts' own words.[6]

In order to discuss various kinds of relationships among texts and perspectives, particular attention was given to what Fairclough (1992) calls the "manifest intertextuality" of each text, particularly in the form of quotes or statements that refer to other texts on the issue of school decentralization.

Following the technique developed by Paulston (1999), texts were compared to other texts and organized around common perspectives. This is, again, an interpretive exercise, and "drawing the boundaries of textual dispositions or genre categories is, of course, controversial" (Paulston, 1995, p. 174, n. 74). The identification and characterization of perspectives involved an iterative process of reading of texts, focusing mainly on arguments; provisional identification of major perspectives; selection of texts for illustrating perspectives; close reading of selected texts focusing on arguments, worldviews, and rhetorical characteristics; revision of perspectives; and adding/removing texts for illustrating perspectives.

Although the identification of perspectives represents a more open and flexible construct than a closed scientific typology, there are some criteria that merit consideration for the construction of typologies that can be relevant for the study we propose here. According to Tiryakian (1968), types are inductively arrived at and are essentially arbitrary: "the construction of a typology... entails, to an important extent, an initial creative act on the part of the researcher" (p. 179). There are three criteria for typological classifications that can be applied in an adapted way to the construction of perspectives in this study: comprehensiveness (all texts should be included), fruitfulness (heuristic value of classification) and parsimony (the analysis should identify the significant major perspectives, a limited number of types). In this study, the criterion of parsimony should be balanced with the idea of representing the widest possible range of positions and voices.

However, there is one important aspect in which identifying textual communities differs from typologies, that is the criterion that types must be mutually exclusive. In typing texts and arguments it is important to show how some texts or arguments can belong to more than one type or perspective. This may be derived from perspectives that are seen to use the same argument in different ways (e.g., in combination with different sets of other arguments), from texts that contain arguments that are seen as illustrating or informing more than one perspective, and from the intertextual features of texts and arguments (how they build on or respond to previous texts/arguments).

Two maps were produced to represent findings: an international and a national map of the perspectives and texts. The mapping of perspectives and texts has been done according to two dimensions, from Conflict to Equilibrium, and from In Favor to Against. These dimensions were identified as the most relevant through the analysis of texts. While the first dimension illustrates the position of perspectives and texts with regard to their general view of social and educational change (related to their worldviews), the second one indicates their position in relation to the general idea of school decentralization[7] (more related to the specific arguments about school decentralization). Both dimensions should be seen as continua.

A note here is in order, that might address the concern that maps, or mapping processes set up their own binaries. Binaries are oppositional and used to present 'either-or' relationships, for example, 'functionalism versus conflict.' They are useful accordingly, to support a *logic of exclusion* (that is, 'right or wrong,' 'male or female,' 'worker or owner).' In our maps we attempt a spatial display, a *desire for inclusion*. Accordingly, we reject binaries and choose dimensions instead. Dimensions are a measure of spatial extent between the poles of, for example, some ideas found in the texts. In this study, texts are read to see two dimensions, or points on a range, (i.e., the textual worldview from equilibrium to conflict, from positive to negative, including both). Dimensions open space to spatial patterning of difference, while binaries ground exclusions. Dimensions support a spatial turn opening opportunities for aletheistic (emergent, becoming) truths.

In addition to the maps, each perspective (at global and national levels) is explained (in terms of rhetorical characteristics, worldviews, and arguments) and exemplified with quotes from texts. For each perspective, we provide the analysis of two or more illustrative texts (again, in terms of rhetorical characteristics, worldviews, and arguments).[8] Two tables, one of perspectives (explaining their main features) and one of texts (identifying what perspective/s each text illustrates) enhance the presentation of findings for both the global and the national debates.

The Global Debate on School Decentralization

We have identified seven major perspectives in the global or international debate: Educational Markets, Efficient Systems, Local Empowerment, Pragmatic Balances, Democratic Participation, Effectiveness Critique, and Radical Critique. We claim that each perspective represents specific arguments about school decentralization, which in each case are related to a specific worldview. Table 1 presents the list of texts selected, and indicates their perspective(s) and geographic focus. Table 2 presents the main arguments of each perspective.

Although these tables may suggest that perspectives are closed entities with clear boundaries, a central argument of this study is for portraying the phenomenon of school decentralization as an interrelation of perspectives, as an intertextual field open to multiple interpretations and exchanges. With this purpose, we offer Figure 1, which shows a spatial patterning following the social mapping approach developed by Rolland Paulston of the perspectives and texts. This map is presented as one possible way (among others) of seeing the debate, as a heuristic device that may provide some guidance in our explorations of the discourse on school decentralization, and that remains open to re-mapping and counter-mapping by all readers. The map aims at representing the debate as an open space where perspectives have shifting boundaries and are in interaction with one another.

As mentioned earlier, the mapping of perspectives and texts has been done according to two dimensions, that is to say, from Conflict to Equilibrium

TABLE 1. List of the texts analyzed as part of the global debate on school decentralization.

Text (author, year, and title)	Perspective	Geographic Focus
Chubb & Moe (1990), *Politics, markets, and America's schools.*	Educational Markets	USA
Tooley (1996). *Education without the State.*	Educational Markets	UK
Finn, Manno & Vanourek. (2000). *Charter schools in action: Renewing public education.*	Educational Markets	USA
Caldwell & Spinks (1988). *The self-managing school.*	Efficient Systems	Global
Caldwell & Spinks (1992). *Leading the self-managing school.*	Efficient Systems	Global
Mohrman, Wohlstetter & Associates (1994). School-based management: Organizing for high performance.	Efficient Systems	USA
World Bank (1995). *Priorities and strategies for education.*	Educational Markets and Efficient Systems	Global, developing and poor countries.
Hess (1995). *Restructuring urban schools: A Chicago perspective.*	Local Empowerment	USA, Chicago
Bryk, Kerbow & Rollow (1997). Chicago school reform.	Local Empowerment	Chicago
Cookson (1997). School choice and the creation of community.	Local Empowerment	USA
Reimers (1997). The role of the community in expanding educational opportunities: The EDUCO schools in El Salvador.	Local Empowerment and Pragmatic Balances	Latin America, El Salvador
Nathan (1996). *Charter schools: Creating hope and opportunity for American education.*	Educational Markets and Local Empowerment	USA
Hanson (1997). Educational decentralization: Issues and challenges.	Pragmatic Balances	Global, Latin America
Ramírez, Webb, & Guthrie (1991). Site-based management: Restructuring decision-making for schools.	Pragmatic Balances	USA
Tedesco (1994). Changes in managing education: The case of Latin American countries.	Pragmatic Balances	Latin America
Fiske (1996). *Decentralization of education: Politics and consensus.*	Pragmatic Balances	Global
ECLAC/UNESCO (1992). *Education and knowledge: Basic pillars of changing production patterns with social equity.*	Pragmatic Balances and Efficient Systems	Latin America

(continued)

TABLE 1. (CONTINUED) List of the texts analyzed as part of the global debate on school decentralization.

Smyth (1996). The socially just alternative to the 'self-managing' school.	Democratic Participation	Global
Fine (1997 [1993]). [Ap]parent involvement: Reflections on parents, power, and urban public schools.	Democratic Participation	USA
Gadotti, M. (1996). Pedagogy of praxis: A dialectical philosophy of education.	Democratic Participation	Latin America, Brazil
Strike (1993). Professionalism, democracy, and discursive communities: normative reflections on restructuring.	Democratic Participation and Local Empowerment	USA
Chapman & Aspin (1997). Autonomy and mutuality: Quality education and self-managing schools.	Pragmatic Balances and Democratic Participation	Global, Australia
Malen, Ogawa & Kranz (1990). What do we know about school-based management? A case study of the literature — a call for research.	Effectiveness Critique	USA
Leithwood & Menzies (1998). Forms and effects of school-based management: A review.	Effectiveness Critique	Global
Elmore (1993). School decentralization: Who gains? Who loses?	Effectiveness Critique and Pragmatic Balances	USA
Whitty, Power & Halpin (1998). Devolution and choice in education: The school, the state and the market.	Radical Critique	Australia, England and Wales, New Zealand, Sweden, USA
Hartley (1994). Devolved school management: The 'new deal' in Scottish education.	Radical Critique	Scotland
Wells (2000). Where neoliberal ideology meets social context: A comparative analysis of U.S. charter schools and England's grant-maintained schools.	Radical Critique	England and USA
Angus (1993). Democratic participation or efficient site management: The social and political location of the self-managing school.	Democratic Participation and Radical Critique	Australia

Worldview, and from Favors to Opposes Decentralization. While the first dimension illustrates the position of perspective and texts with regard to their general view of social and educational change (related to their world-views), the second one indicates their position in relation to the general idea of school decentralization (more related to the specific arguments

TABLE 2. Main arguments of global perspectives on school decentralization.

Educational Markets	Proposes the decentralization of authority to parents (over school choice) and to individual schools (over educational programs and resource administration) in a system of competition among schools. Based on the idea that a quasi-market is the best mechanism for the regulation of schools, resulting in increased efficiency and quality.
Efficient Systems	Mainly concerned with increasing the overall efficiency of educational systems. The objective is to organize the educational system in a way that schools are able to produce higher quality "outputs" (student learning that responds to social demands and to the needs of the economy) with existing resources.
	School decentralization is seen as an administrative phenomenon that should be implemented within guidelines and accountability patterns set at national, state, and local levels.
Local Empowerment	Proposes the decentralization of decisionmaking power to parents and local community members. This decentralization can be in the form of school councils with authority over curriculum, general administration of the school, personnel administration, and/or budgeting, or in a more indirect way, through school choice mechanisms.
	Advocates local participation for the democratization of schools, "revitalization" of local communities, and the improvement of the quality of education.
Pragmatic Balances	A balance is sought between the power and responsibilities of different levels of educational governance — including national and local governments as well as schools — for the achievement of various goals (quality, efficiency, equity, democratization, etc.).
	School decentralization may have positive effects on the quality of education, provided that certain conditions are met, but may also have negative implications (inequities, fragmentation) in certain contexts.
Democratic Participation	School decentralization may provide opportunities for increasing participation of parents, teachers and community members in decisionmaking about substantial issues. The democratic conception of schools — stresses direct participation and the idea of school actors as active citizens — is affirmed by contrast or in opposition to other (prevailing) forms of school decentralization that focus on efficiency and on an instrumental participation of school actors.
Effectiveness Critique	School decentralization does not have a verifiable positive impact on the quality of education (student achievement). Decentralization as actually implemented can be considered as a political or symbolic response (from the government to various external pressures), most of the time not directly connected to pedagogic or instructional issues.
Radical Critique	Mainly concerned with challenging existing power relations and establishing egalitarian educational systems. The reform movements that promote school decentralization are seen as inspired by neoconservative and neoliberal ideologies that reflect the interests of the most powerful groups at the expense of disadvantaged groups.
	The main effects of school decentralization policies are the increasing of inequity/inequalities, and a concentration of schools on management, instead of educational, issues.

about school decentralization). Both dimensions should be seen as continua.

The Equilibrium Worldview pole corresponds to a functionalist view of society. As Morrow and Torres (1995) state, a functionalist approach "is especially concerned with the conditions that maintain social order and stability" (p. 20), with "adjusting the fit between education and what are assumed to be societal needs" (p. 36), where society is viewed as based on consensus. Functionalism stresses "*manifest* and selective *latent* functions of education and their overall *positive* influence upon social development" (p. 55, emphases in original). With regard to educational reform, functionalist approaches tend to endorse a " 'common sense' of reform [that] assume[s] that intervention is progress." A better world is to evolve as the result of new programs, new technologies, and new organizations that increase efficiency, economy, and effectiveness" (Popkewitz, 1991, p. 1).

Functionalism, at least in its purest forms, is closely related to a rational planning model–assuming consensus on what the problems are, believing that scientific and technical tools will allow one to identify optimal solutions which will ultimately benefit all members of society. "Planning, with its flow charts, manpower matrices, cost-benefit formulas, and engineering language suggests that a neutral scientific process is available that provides an algorithm for responsive, efficient change, … that models and methods have universal applicability or at least require little situational adaptability" (Adams, 1988, p. 411).

The Conflict pole, in contrast, represents a view of society and education characterized by structural contradictions, where oppressive relationships between social groups with different interests and levels of resources are characterized by coercion rather than cooperation. According to this view, "educational systems on the whole are biased toward the reproduction of existing power relations (involving class, gender, racial, and other social positions) and modes of consciousness that legitimate those relations" while "the task of social research and militant political action is to facilitate challenging these simple and/or complex reproductive tendencies" (Morrow and Torres, 1995, p. 35).

While there are five perspectives that tend to adopt — with different nuances — a functionalist stance (Educational Markets, Efficient Systems, Local Empowerment, Pragmatic Balances, and Effectiveness Critique), only two (Democratic Participation and Radical Critique) espouse a conflict view. At the same time, there are three perspectives that strongly advocate some form of school decentralization: Educational Markets, Efficient Systems, Local Empowerment; two that favor school decentralization, with some qualifications: Democratic Participation and Pragmatic Balances; and two perspectives that mainly argue against school decentralization: Effectiveness Critique and Radical Critique.[9]

In addition, using Rust's (1996) distinction between borrowing and critical relationships, we have identified various flows between

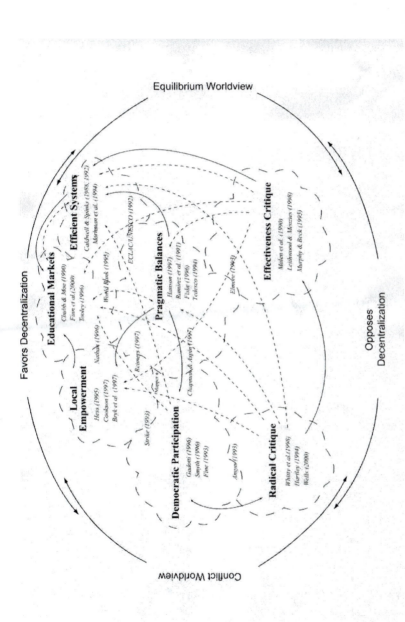

Figure 1. A map of major perspectives in the global debate on school decentralization presented as a relational intertextual field. Arrows indicate relations of interest between perspectives. Dashed lines represent critical relationships, while continuing lines represent borrowing relationships.

perspectives, which are shown in the map as continuing (borrowing relationships) and dashed (critical relationships) lines.[10]

The Debate on School Decentralization in Argentina

In this section, we map the debate on school decentralization in Argentina
during the 1990s, as an intertextual field. Then, we compare the debate in
Argentina with our mapping of the global debate. The analysis of the
debate in Argentina includes fewer texts than the global debate (see Table
3), but enough to illustrate the major perspectives for this single national
case (showing different ways of seeing school decentralization in a particular context).

We have identified — through the analysis of texts — six major perspectives in the Argentine debate: Educational Markets, Pedagogical Self-
management, Efficient Systems, Pragmatic Balances, Democratic Critique,
and Implementation Contexts. Three of them are perspectives that were
also included in the global debate, sharing the main assumptions and
worldviews. As in the global debate, we argue that each perspective represents specific arguments about school decentralization, which in each case
are related to a specific worldview. Table 4 presents the main arguments of
each perspective in relation to the Argentine context, while Figure 2 maps
textual perspectives using the same dimensions as the global debate map.

In the case of the debate in Argentina, we have identified five perspectives that tend to adopt — again, with different nuances — a functionalist
stance (Educational Markets, Pedagogic Self-management, Efficient Systems, Pragmatic Balances, and Implementation Contexts), and just one
(Democratic Critique) espousing a conflict view. At the same time, there
are three perspectives that strongly advocate some form of school decentralization (Educational Markets, Efficient Systems, and Pedagogic Self-
management); one that favors school decentralization with some qualifications (Pragmatic Balances); and two perspectives that argue mainly
against school decentralization (Implementation Contexts and Democratic Critique).

Both the global and the Argentine debates show how the arguments on
school decentralization inter-relate with other policy debates. The different contexts and policies that are discussed by the texts in the global
debate make it difficult to fully understand the relationships of the various
arguments and the whole implications of school decentralization, while
the analysis of a national case, like Argentina, allows us to see the arguments in a more situated way. In the global debate, however, it can be seen
that the issues of choice and of teacher professionalization, or more
broadly the status and control of teachers' work, are most significant. In
Argentina, choice does not appear to be so important, perhaps because
parents and students (particularly those of upper and middle-classes) have
traditionally had more flexible mechanisms for choosing among public

TABLE 3. List of the texts analyzed as part of the Argentine debate on school decentralization.

Text	Perspective
FIEL & CEA, 1993. *Descentralización de la escuela primaria y media: Una propuesta de reforma.*	Educational Markets
Llach (1997). *Otro siglo, otra Argentina: Una estrategia para el desarrollo económico y social nacida de la convertibilidad y de su historia.*	Educational Markets
Narodowski (1999). " Varias respuestas a diez objeciones efectuadas a las 'escuelas públicas autogestionadas': Un aporte al debate en la Argentina."	Pedagogical Self-management
Cicioni (1999). El movimiento de las *charter schools*: Una amenaza y una oportunidad para la educación pública argentina.	Pedagogical Self-management
Argentina (1996). Condiciones Básicas Institucionales: Nuevos contenidos en una escuela diferente.	Efficient Systems
Aguerrondo (1996). La escuela transformada: Una organización inteligente y una gestión efectiva.	Efficient Systems
Blanco Etchegaray et al. (1999). *La escuela protagonista.*	Educational Markets and Efficient Systems
Braslavsky (1993). *Autonomía y anomia en la educación pública argentina.*	Pragmatic Balances
Van Gelderen & López Espinosa (1996). *La escuela argentina en transformación: Ocho cuestiones y veintidós protagonistas.*	Pragmatic Balances & Efficient Systems
Revista Novedades Educativas (1997). El proyecto institucional o " de burocracias, formalidades y autonomías"	Implementation Contexts
Marquina & Trippano (1999). La escuela pública en manos de la sociedad civil.	Democratic Critique
CTERA (n/d). Las charter school.	Democratic Critique
Puiggrós (1999). *Educar entre el acuerdo y la libertad: Propuestas para la educación del siglo XXI.*	Democratic Critique
Filmus (1998). La descentralización educativa en el centro del debate.	Pragmatic Balances & Democratic Critique

schools (see Fiszbein, 1999; Narodowski, 2002), and because some "private" schools have been available at low cost (as the state subsidies these schools).[11] On the other hand, the school decentralization discourse in Argentina has been influenced by the issue of professionalism, and particularly by the debates about teachers' rights, the regulations of their work, and the criteria for teacher career advancement. In addition, the common emphasis across most perspectives in the Argentine debate on the need for increasing funds for education in general and for schools is noteworthy. It seems to be based on the perception that schools have been under-funded for many years, as well as the emphasis on the training of principals and

TABLE 4. Main arguments of perspectives on school decentralization in Argentina.

Educational Markets	Advocates the introduction of competition and choice, along with a substantial level of school autonomy, based on the assumptions of the efficiency of market mechanisms and of rational actors attempting to obtain maximum benefits.
Efficient Systems	Proposes increasing the autonomy of schools within central guidelines and controls, assumes consensus about the aims of education, and expresses the need for adapting educational system to demands from society and " the economy."
Pedagogic Self-management	Given a high level of authority, principals and teachers would be able to develop pedagogical innovations resulting in higher quality education, even responding to the learning needs of special groups. Influenced to certain extent by professionalism, but also advocating some community control over the work of teachers.
Pragmatic Balances	A balance is sought between the power and responsibilities of different levels of educational governance — including national and local governments as well as schools — for the achievement of various goals (quality, efficiency, equity, democratization, etc.). School decentralization may have positive effects on the quality of education, provided that certain conditions are met, but may also have negative implications (inequities, fragmentation) in certain contexts.
Implementation Contexts	Point to various limitations and difficulties in the implementation of school decentralization at schools: time-consuming process, external imposition that ignores the reality of schools, formal mechanisms that do not entail participation or improvement efforts, etc.
Democratic Critique	The reform movements that promote school decentralization are seen as inspired by neoconservative and neoliberal ideologies that reflect the interests of the most powerful groups at the expense of disadvantaged groups. The main effects of school decentralization policies are the increasing of inequity/inequalities, and the weakening of democratic mechanisms.

teachers as a critical element for an effective implementation of school decentralization.

One of the elements that we have tried to highlight in the discussion of perspectives and texts in both the Argentine and the global school decentralization debates has been the relationships among perspectives, which are sometimes represented in texts through direct references to other texts belonging to different ways of seeing. The combination of perspectives in a given text provides some indication that such perspectives can in some way be integrated, at least with regard to some of the arguments they advance. The identification of such imbricated texts, situated in an overlapping zone, helps to indicate the tenuous and imprecise borders of perspectives. In addition, as the arrows in the maps show, perspectives can be seen establishing different kinds of relationships to one another.

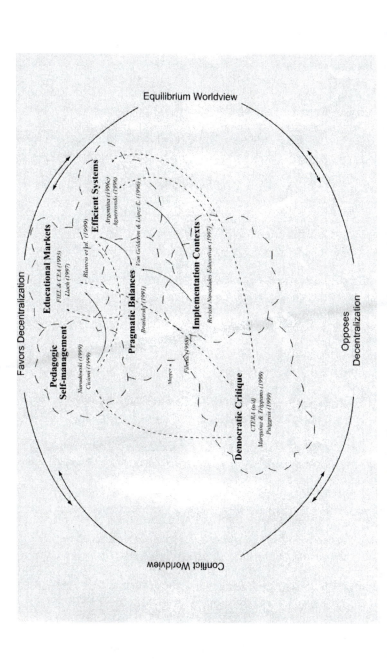

Figure 2. A map of major perspectives in the Argentine debate on school decentralization presented as a relational intertextual field. Arrows indicate relations of interest between perspectives. Dashed lines represent critical relationships, while continuing lines represent borrowing relationships.

Using Val Rust's (1996) distinction between borrowing and critical relationships, we have identified various flows between perspectives in both debates (see Table 1 and Table 3). At the global level, the Effectiveness Critique and Radical Critique perspectives establish critical relationships with all other perspectives, with perhaps the exception of the Democratic Participation way of seeing, whose proposals seem to remain mostly an ideal. On the other hand, several borrowing and critical relationships are simultaneously established by perspectives advocating school decentralization. The Local Empowerment and the Efficient Systems perspectives, for example, criticize (e.g., the inequities effects due to lack of state controls) and at the same time borrow (e.g., ideas of choice and competition) from the Educational Market perspective. The Pragmatic Balances way of seeing can be perceived as borrowing ideas of democratization of schools from the Democratic Participation, community control from the Local Empowerment, and centralization of goal setting and evaluation from the Efficient Systems perspectives, while criticizing the effects on equity of the marketization proposals of the Educational Markets perspective. It can also be seen that the Radical Critique perspective borrows from the Effectiveness Critique way of seeing arguments about the lack of impact of school decentralization over student achievement. Finally, it might be noted that the Democratic Perspective and the Radical Critique perspectives are very close, have a similar worldview and share a concern for equality and democratization. But while the first focuses on the possibilities of school democratization, the second concentrates on the critique of actual (non-democratizing and unequalizing) forms of decentralization. A relationship of mutual borrowing is established since main arguments in one perspective appear as supporting arguments in the other.

In the case of Argentina, similar flows seem to be taking place among perspectives (see Figure 2). More relevant, perhaps, are the relationships established with the global debate. Almost all perspectives reflect to some extent the global debate, placing the national discussion in an international context, especially in relation to Anglo-American experiences, and other Latin American cases. Examples and arguments from international cases and texts are used to: 1) legitimize reforms in the local context, although international cases are sometimes superficially discussed (e.g., Blanco Etchegaray et. al (1999) describe four international cases, without referring to any of the critiques that those experiences have received); 2) to criticize local proposals, remarking that proposals elsewhere have been implemented more carefully or with more resources, or have aimed at increasing quality for disadvantaged groups rather than at benefiting private educational firms (e.g., CTERA (n/d); and Puiggrós (1999), in the Democratic Critique perspective; or 3) to explain or criticize the rationales of school decentralization reforms proposed in Argentina (e.g., the Pedagogical Self-management perspective; Marquina & Trippano (1999) in the Democratic Critique perspective). The references to theories (e.g., effective schools) and policies (e.g., charter schools) that originated in central countries, and that have informed the global debate, are recurrent in the Argentine debate.

Summary

In this study, we have shown how the debate on school decentralization both at global and national levels can be portrayed as multiple perspectives or ways of seeing, through the analysis of academic and organizational texts. Our main objective has been to identify and juxtapose texts constructing phenomenon of school decentralization. A phenomenographic mapping approach has allowed us to move beyond binary oppositions and toward what might be called a post-paradigmatic view of the discourse on school decentralization. Here, we both represent and compare the inter-relation of various perspectives embodying different worldviews and arguments in an intertextual field of perspectives that under a more essentialist modernist approach might have been seen as incommensurable. In this way, we have offered a more inclusive and relational view of school decentralization than previous studies, without aiming at proving the superiority of any particular perspective over the others. Beyond the aims of this research is an evaluation of the actual weight of the different perspectives in the planning and implementation of school decentralization policies, although some of the arguments discussed suggest in some cases the influence they have had in policymaking.

This study builds on social mapping research developed by Paulston (1995; 1999; 2000), Mausolff (1996), and Erkkilä (2000), among others. This study, however, appears as the first attempt at using social mapping for comparing a national case to the global debate in a given issue. We have shown how the Argentine discourse borrows from, and to a considerable extent mirrors, the global discourse on school decentralization. This may well reflect the influence of globalization forces as examined by Green (1997) and Morrow and Torres (2000). At the same time, while the mapping of the global debate has shown a variety of arguments in relation to different geographic contexts, the analysis of a national case has allowed for a more contextualized view, and has helped to relate the arguments and perspectives to historical and social processes that are unique to a particular country.

This study has offered a combination of textual and visual representations for understanding of school decentralization as a contested issue, where we locate our point of view as social cartographers in the intertextual field, but do not identify our personal choice of the best " technical" solution or a superior alternative that provides the " best" answer to the policy dilemma, but multiple viewpoints shaped by conflicting values and worldviews. Again, it is important to keep in mind that both the textual and visual representations are constructed through the interpretation of texts, and do not necessarily reflect the views of the authors of these texts or the positions that they would personally choose in the maps.

The processes of constructing the map and identifying and characterizing perspectives influence one another. For instance, the visual representation reveals the existence of empty spaces in the intertextual field, which are open to the emergence of new perspectives that may locate into these spaces (Johnson, 1997). From the selection of texts to the design of the map, an iterative process takes place, a process that is open to continuing refinement. During this process, the positions of the various perspectives as well as our own position in the map changed as new perspectives were identified. Selecting the texts to be analyzed, constructing the different perspectives, and establishing the (provisional and shifting) boundaries among textual genres is a difficult process that requires the mapper to be aware of what is left out of the map (as a particular topic is chosen, specific dimensions are privileged, and particular kinds of texts are selected), and how his or her own biases inevitably influence any mapping process. Here social mapping may facilitate the individual process of " self overcoming" that is critical in all social learning and that should be at the heart of any project of self or professional renewal, or re-imagination.

Accordingly, intertextual maps would seem to work best when they remain open to refining and counter-mapping as "one purpose of mapping is to challenge the reader to do his/her own mapping" (Erkkilä, 2000, p. 191). In addition, the representations that we offer in this study could be further enhanced by designing other maps with different dimensions based on the same perspectives identified, or by identifying new perspectives that reveal differences along other new dimensions. An important next step would be testing the maps produced in this study with the knowledge communities that express the different perspectives identified and to remap more inclusively.

In addition, it would be worth exploring the value of the characterization and mapping of multiple perspectives for policy purposes. In contrast to closed positivist and ideologically reductionist views of policy research, it can be argued that in order to make more informed choices, it will be useful to have both intertextual debate maps and statistical hard data (See Watson, 1998). However, the possibility that a study like this will have an impact on policymaking depends on the willingness of comparative educators and policymakers to engage today's "Babel" of diverse worldviews and arguments.

We believe that the method of social mapping performed here has the potential of contributing to dialogues — as joint reflection and action — among different actors about research, policy, and practice (see Ginsburg & Gorostiaga, 2003). In order to achieve such dialogue, however, a study like this one should include more voices and views, particularly from those on the margins of discourse, from those who experience the policies of school decentralization firsthand. The mapping of the school decentralization debate is shown to enhance possibilities for such policy negotiations that take all of the different perspectives (and other views that social and educational actors may espouse) into consideration, thereby promoting a more thorough public debate, and making the policy process more inclusive, collaborative, and democratic. Opening space to include as many different positions as possible and uncovering textual inter-relations might well foster dialogue and better understanding among actors who see themselves occupying irreconcilable positions, for social mapping puts all in the same cartographic space. As with any map, however, it does not prescribe a particular path, nor guarantee that hegemonic power relationships and non-democratic mechanisms will not eventually prevail.

In reply to modernist critiques that postmodern social cartography abdicates any responsibility for moral judgments, we turn to Gitlin (1998, p. 72) and ask the reader to assess our methodological work here in light of what he proposes as an overarching postmodern concept, a politics of limits:

> Simply, there must be limits to what human beings can be permitted to do with their powers. The essence of a postmodern cultural politics must be rooted in three protections: 1) the ecological: the earth and (human) life must be protected; 2) the pluralist: the social group must be protected against domination by collectives; 3) the libertarian: the individual must be protected from domination by collectives. A politics of limits respects horizontal social relations — multiplicity over hierarchy, juxtaposition over usurpation, difference over deference, and finally, disorderly life in its flux over orderly death in its finality. The democratic, vital edge of the postmodern [as celebrated in our social cartography], the love of difference, ... and the exuberantly unfinished, deserves to infuse... [our reimagined comparative education]. Needless to say, this way of putting the matter leaves many questions unsettled, [many] conflicts and internal fissures... What kind of authority, what kind of difference is legitimate? Respect for uncertainties is of the essence.

On this paradoxical postmodern note, we suspend the discussion for now.

Endnotes

1. Hanson (1997), for example, uses the terms "decentralized schools" and "local school decentralization" to refer to processes of transferring of responsibility and authority from the center to schools. In different contexts these processes have been also labeled as "school-based management," "the self-managing school," and "school autonomy." We chose to talk about "school decentralization" because it appears as a broader concept and relates more clearly to the general discussion about decentralization. Debate can be defined as "the process by which opinions are advanced, supported, disputed, and defended" (Branham, 1991, p. 1). Debate entails the existence of different positions in disputation. Debates can be formal or informal, oral or written.

2. Here we seek to perform our interpretation of Friedrich Nietzsche's re-imagining project where he attempted a revaluing of the lifeworld after the patriarchal, technical, and logical dead certainties of high modernity. See Nietzsche (1994, pp. 92–96). This is among the most influential texts of early postmodern and poststructural thought and an exemplar of the creative imagination at work. In this widely influential study, unfortunately little cited in comparative methodology, Nietzsche's perspectivism argues that every view is an interpretation, which no view of the world is binding on everyone. He uses "genealogy" to reveal that behind their claims to be universally true and binding, all perspectives or world views attempt to promote their own special interests without admitting their partiality. Nietzsche also rejects nihilism: "Perspectivism does not result in the relativism that holds that any view is as good as any other; it holds that one's own views are the best for oneself without implying they need be good for anyone else. It also generates the expectation that new views and values are bound to become necessary, and the willingness to develop and accept…new schemes…to create new and better interpretations [i.e., situated mappings] better for particular people, at a particular time, for particular reasons." See Nehamas (1985, pp. 71–72).

3. As Cherryholmes (1988) notes, "educational discourse ranges from what is *said* in elementary classrooms, teacher education classes, and research findings reported at conferences and conventions to what is written in high school textbooks, assessment exams, and research articles in professional journals" (p. 3).

4. Determining the universe of texts implied also a selection process (mainly guided by the criterion of publication in academic journals or as books). In a simple search of the ERIC database, for example, we obtained 178 documents produced from 1979 to 2002 that included the term "school-based management" in their titles.

5. Hart (1997) provides various examples of different kinds of rhetorical tone.

6. "One way of showing this respect [for the text], of acknowledging the already written, of making it visible, is via quotations … There are still other reasons [to use quotations], of which one is the possibility to show that the already written *also* points in *other* directions than those [that the author quoting] concentrates upon" (Ekegren, 1999, p. xvi, emphasis in original).

7. Although school decentralization may take different forms and have different implications according to the contexts in which it is implemented, it can be argued that there is a general principle behind all of them that favors the granting of increasing autonomy to schools (or to one or more actors at the school level).

8. The discussion of each perspective and the analysis of the illustrative texts can be found in Gorostiaga Derqui (2003).

9. According to this view, "every society is based on the coercion of some of its members by others" (Dahrendorf, 1959, p. 162, quoted in Burrell & Morgan, 1979, p. 12).

10. Space constraints limit the extent to which we can convey the different arguments that each text presents. Readers are invited to go to the texts, contrast their own interpretations with ours, and construct their own maps of the debate. These texts do not necessarily have a richer or more complex view than texts identified as illustrating a single perspective. It needs to be kept in mind that perspectives are interpretive constructions. Using different criteria, different perspectives could have emerged and a text that appears in our mapping as sharing elements of two perspectives could be used to illustrate a single perspective.

11. Bonal (2003) makes a similar point for the case of Spain: "The size and the power of the private school sector and the absence of real control on school choice policies — which is itself a policy — makes it unnecessary to develop strong market-oriented policies and discourses" (p. 12).

References

Adams, Don. " Extending the Educational Planning Discourse: Conceptual and Paradigmatic Explorations." *Comparative Education Review*, vol. 32, no. 4 (1988): 400–415.

Aguerrondo, Inés. "La Escuela Transformada: Una Organización Inteligente y una Gestión Efectiva." In *La Escuela Como Organización Inteligente*. Buenos Aires: Troquel, 1996.

Anderson, Gary L. "Toward Authentic Participation: Deconstructing the Discourses of Participatory Reforms in Education." *American Educational Research Journal*, vol. 35, no. 4 (1998): 571–603.

Angus, Lawrence. "Democratic Participation or Efficient Site Management: The Social and Political Location of the Self-Managing School." In *A Socially Critical View of the* Self-Managing *School*. Edited by John Smyth. London: Falmer, 1993.

Argentina. *Condiciones Básicas Institucionales: Nuevos Contenidos en una Escuela Diferente.* Buenos Aires: Ministerio de Cultura y Educación, 1996.

Arnove, Robert, et al. "A Political Sociology of Education and Development in Latin America." In *Education in Comparative Perspective*. Edited by Y. W. Bradshaw. New York: E. J. Brill, 1997.

Barnes, Trevor J., and James S. Duncan. "Introduction." In *Writing Worlds: Discourse, Text and Metaphor in the Representation of Landscape*. Edited by T. J. Barnes and J. S. Duncan. London: Routledge, 1992.

Bjerrum Nielsen, Harriet. "Seductive Texts With Serious Intentions." *Educational Researcher*, vol. 24, no. 1 (1995): 4–12.

Blanco Etchegaray, Agustina, et al. *La Escuela Protagonista*. Buenos Aires: Fundación Grupo Sophia/Temas Grupo Editorial, 1999.

Branh;am, R. J. *Debate and critical analysis: The harmony of conflict*. Hillsdale, NJ: L. Erlbaum Associates, 1991.

Bonal, Xavier. "Managing Education Legitimation Crisis in Neoliberal Contexts: Some Peripheral Evidence." *British Journal of Sociology of Education* vol. 24, no. 2 (2003).

Braslavsky, Cecilia. *Autonomía y Anomia en la Educación Pública Argentina*. Buenos Aires: Flacso, 1993.

Bray, Mark. "Control of Education: Issues and Tensions in Centralization and Decentralization." In *Comparative Education: The Dialectic of the Global and the Local*. Edited by R. F. Arnove and C. A. Torres. Lanham, MD: Rowman & Littlefield, 1999.

—————. "Centralization/decentralization and Privatization/publicization: Conceptual Issues and the Need for More Research." *International Journal of Educational Research*, vol. 21, no. 8 (1994): 817–824.

Bryk, Anthony, David Kerbow, and Sharon Rollow. "Chicago School Reform." In *New Schools for a New Century: The Redesign of Urban Education*. Edited by D. Ravitch and J. P. Viteritti. New Haven and & London: Yale University Press, 1997.

Burrell, Gibson and Gareth Morgan. *Sociological Paradigms and Organisational Analysis: Elements of the Sociology of Corporate Life*. Portsmouth, NH: Heinemann, 1979.

Caldwell, Brian and Jim Spinks. *The Self-managing School*. London: The Falmer Press, 1988.

Caldwell, Brian and Jim Spinks. *Leading the Self-managing School*. London: The Falmer Press, 1992.

Chapman, Judith and David Aspin. "Autonomy and Mutuality: Quality Education and Self-managing Schools." In *Restructuring and Quality: Issues for Tomorrow's Schools*. Edited by T. Townsend. London and New York: Routledge, 1997.

Cherryholmes, Cleo. *Power and Criticism: Poststructural Investigations in Education*. New York and London: Teachers College Press, 1988.

Chubb, John E., and Terry M. Moe. *Politics, Markets, and America's Schools*. Washington, DC: The Brookings Institution, 1990.

Ciccioni, Antonio. "El Movimiento de las *Charter Schools*: Una Amenaza y una Oportunidad para la Educacion Pública Argentina. *Propuesta Educativa*, no. 20 (1999): 66–74.

Cookson, Peter W. "School Choice and the Creation of Community." In *Autonomy and Choice in Context: An International Perspective*. Edited by R. Shapira and P. W. Cookson, Jr. Oxford: Pegamon, 1997.

CTERA, Instituto de Investigaciones Pedagógicas. *Las Charter School*. In htpp://www.ute.org.ar/charter.htm (Retrieved October 2000).

Dahrendorf, Ralf. *Class and Class Conflict in Industrial Societies*. London: Routledge & Kegan Paul, 1959.

ECLAC and UNESCO. *Education and Knowledge: Basic Pillars of Changing Production Patterns With Social Equity*. Santiago: UNESCO, 1992.

Ekegren, Peter. *The Reading of Theoretical Texts: A Critique of Criticism in the Social Sciences*. London & New York: Routledge, 1999.

Elmore, Richard F. "School Decentralization: Who Gains? Who Loses?" In *Decentralization and School Improvement*. Edited by J. Hannaway and M. Carnoy. San Francisco, CA: Jossey-Bass, 1993.

Erkkilä, Kristina. *Mapping the Entrepreneurial Education Debates in the United States, the United Kingdom and Finland.* New York: Garland, 2000.

Fairclough, Norman. *Discourse and Social Change.* Cambridge, UK: Polity Press, 1992.

FIEL (Fundación de Investigaciones Económicas Latinoamericana) and CEA (Consejo Empresarial Argentino). *Descentralización de la Escuela Primaria y Media: Una Propuesta de Reforma.* Buenos Aires: FIEL & CEA, 1993.

Filmus, Daniel. "La Descentralización Educativa en el Centro del Debate." In *La Argentina que Viene.* Edited by A. Isuani and D. Filmus. Buenos Aires: Norma, 1998.

Fine, Michele. "[Ap]parent Involvement: Reflections on Parents, Power, and Urban Public Schools." In *Education: Culture, Economy, and Society.* Edited by A.H. Halsey, et al. Oxford, New York: Oxford University Press, 1997. [*Teachers College Record,* 94 (1993): 682–710.]

Finn, Chester E., Bruno V. Manno, and Gregg Vanourek. *Charter Schools in Action: Renewing Public Education.* Princeton, NJ: Princeton University Press, 2000.

Fiske, Edward B. *Decentralization of Education: Politics and Consensus.* Washington, D.C.: The World Bank, 1993.

Fiszbein, Ariel. "Institutions, Service Delivery and Social Exclusion: A Case Study of the Education Sector in Buenos Aires." Washington, DC: The World Bank. LCSHD Paper Series No. 47, 1999.

Gadotti, Moacir. *Pedagogy of Praxis: A Dialectical Philosophy of Education.* Albany, NY: SUNY Press, 1996.

Giddens, Anthony. *Central Problems in Social Theory: Action, Structure and Contradiction in Social Analysis.* Berkeley: University of California Press, 1979.

Ginsburg, Mark, et al. "National and World-System Explanations of Educational Reform." *Comparative Education Review,* vol. 34, no. 4 (1990): 474–99.

Ginsburg, Mark and Jorge Gorostiaga. "Dialogue About Educational Research, Policy, and Practice: To What Extent is it Possible and Who Should be Involved?" In *Limitations and Possibilities of Dialogue Among Researchers, Policy Makers, and Practitioners: International Perspectives on the Field of Education,* edited by M. Ginsburg and J. Gorostiaga. New York: RoutledgeFalmer, 2003.

Gitlin, Todd. Postmodernism: What are They Talking About. In *The Postmodern Presence: Readings on Postmodernism in American Culture and Society.* Edited by A. A. Berger. Walnut Creek, CA: Alta Mira Press, 1998.

Goodman, Jo Victoria. *Mapping Civic Debate after September 11, 2001: Civic Courage, Social Cartography and Curriculum Theorizing.* Doctoral Dissertation, University of Pittsburgh, Pittsburgh, PA, 280 p., 2003.

Gorostiaga Derqui, Jorge. *Mapping Perspectives on School Decentralization: The Global Debate and the Case of Argentina.* Doctoral Dissertation, University of Pittsburgh, Pittsburgh, PA, 198 p., 2003.

Gottlieb, Esther. "The Discursive Construction of Knowledge: The Case of Radical Education Discourse." *Qualitative Studies in Education,* vol. 2, no. 2 (1989): 131–144.

Green, Andy. *Education, Globalization and the Nation State.* London: Macmillan Press, 1997.

Hanson, Mark. "School-based Management and Educational Reform in the United States and Spain." *Comparative Education Review* vol. 34, no. 4 (1990).

_____. "Educational Decentralization: Issues and Challenges." Washington, DC: Inter-American Dialogue. PREAL, No. 9, 1997.

Hart, Roderick. *Modern Rhetorical Criticism* (Second Edition). Needham Heights, MA: Allyn & Bacon, 1997.

Hartley, David. "Devolved School Management: The 'New Deal' in Scottish Education." *Journal of Education Policy,* vol. 9, no. 2 (1994): 129–140.

Hess, G. Alfred. *Restructuring Urban Schools: A Chicago Perspective.* New York: Teachers College Press, 1995.

Johnson, Steven. *Interface Culture: How New Technology Transforms the Way we Create and Work.* New York: HarperCollins, 1997.

Lauglo, Jon. "Forms of Decentralization and their Implications for Education." *Comparative Education,* vol. 31, no. 1 (1995): 5–29.

Leithwood, Kenneth, and Teresa Menzies. "Forms and Effects of School-based Management: A Review." *Educational Policy*, vol. 12, no. 3 (1998): 325–346.

Liebman, Martin. "Social Mapping: The Art of Representing Intellectual Perception." In *Social Cartography: Mapping Ways of Seeing Social and Educational Change*. Edited by R. G. Paulston. New York: Garland Publishing, 1996.

Llach, Juan J. *Otro Siglo, Otra Argentina: Una Estrategia para el Desarrollo Económico y Social Nacida de la Convertibilidad y de su Historia.* Buenos Aires: Ariel, 1997.

Malen, Betty, Rodney Ogawa, and Jennifer Kranz. "What Do We Know About School-based Management? A Case Study of the Literature—a Call for Research." In *Choice and Control in American Education.* Edited by W. Clune and J. Witte. London-New York-Philadelphia: Falmer Press, 1990.

Marquina, Mónica, and Sergio Trippano. "La Escuela Pública en Manos de la Sociedad Civil." *Escenarios Alternativos* no. 6 (1999): 70–82.

Marton, Ference. "Phenomenography." In *The International Encyclopedia of Education.* Edited by T. Husen and T. N. Postlehwaite. Oxford: Pergamon Press, 1994.

Mausolff, Christopher. "Postmodernism and Participation in International Rural Development Projects: Textual and Contextual Considerations." In *Social Cartography: Mapping Ways of Seeing Social and Educational Change*, edited by R. G. Paulston. New York: Garland Publishing , 1996.

McGinn, Noel and William K. Cummings. "Introduction." In *International Handbook of Education and Development: Preparing Schools, Students and Nations for the 21st Century.* Edited by W. K. Cummings and N. McGinn. New York: Pergamon, 1997.

McGinn, Noel. "Reforming Educational Governance: Centralization/decentralization." In *Emergent Issues in Education: Comparative Perspectives.* Edited by R. F. Arnove, P. G. Altbach, and G. P. Kelly. Albany, NY: SUNY Press, 1992.

Mohrman, Susan A., Priscilla Wohlstetter, and Associates. *School-based Management:*

Morgan, Gareth. "Paradigm Diversity in Organizational Research." In *Theory and Philosophy of Organizations: Critical Issues and New Perspectives.* Edited by J. Hassard and D. Pym. London: Routledge & Kegan Paul, 1990.

Organizing for High Performance. San Francisco: Jossey-Bass, 1994.

Morrow, Raymond A., and Carlos A. Torres. "The State, Globalization, and Educational Policy." In *Globalization and Education: Critical Perspectives.* Edited by N. C. Burbules and C. A. Torres. New York & London: Routledge, 2000.

Morrow, Raymond A., and Carlos A. Torres. *Social Theory and Education: A Critique of Theories of Social and Cultural Reproduction.* Albany, NY: SUNY Press, 1995.

Murphy, Joseph, and Lynn Beck. *School-based Management as School Reform.* Thousand Oaks, CA: Corwin, 1995.

Narodowski, Mariano. "Socioeconomic Segregation in the Argentine Education System: School Choice Without Vouchers." *Compare* vol. 32, no. 2 (2002): 181–91.

Narodowski, Mariano. "Varias Respuestas a Diez Objeciones Efectuadas a las 'Escuelas Públicas Autogestionadas': Un Aporte al Debate en la Argentina." Buenos Aires: Fundación Gobierno y Sociedad, 1999.

Nathan, Joe. *Charter Schools: Creating Hope and Opportunity for American Education.* San Francisco: Jossey-Bass Publishers, 1996.

Nehamas, Alexander. *Nietzsche: Life as Literature.* Cambridge: Harvard University Press, 1985.

Nietzsche, Friedrich. *On the Genealogy of Morality.* Cambridge: Harvard University Press, 1994.

Paulston, Rolland G., and Martin Liebman. "Social Cartography: A New Metaphor/tool for Comparative Studies. In *Social Cartography: Mapping Ways of Seeing Social and Educational Change.* Edited by R. G. Paulston. New York: Garland Publishing, 1996.

Paulston, Rolland G. "Imagining Comparative Education." *Compare: A Journal of Comparative Education*, vol. 30 no. 3 (2000): 353–367. (Republished in *Comparative Education Reader.* Edited by E. R. Beauchamp. New York: RoutledgeFalmer, 2003.)

Paulston, Rolland G. "Mapping Comparative Education after Postmodernity." *Comparative Education Review* vol. 43, no. 4 (1999): 438–463. (Republished in *Comparative Education Reader.* Edited by E. R. Beauchamp. New York: RoutledgeFalmer, 2003.)

Paulston, Rolland G. "Mapping Knowledge Perspectives in Studies of Educational Change." In *Transforming Schools.* Edited by P. W. Cookson, Jr. and B. Schneider. New York: Garland Publishing, 1995.

Perelman, Chaim, and L. Olbrechts-Tyleca. *The New Rhetoric: A Treatise on Argumentation*. Notre Dame, IN: University of Notre Dame Press, 1969.

Plank, David. *The Means of Our Salvation: Public Education in Brazil, 1930–1995*. Boulder, CO: Westview Press, 1996.

Popkewitz, Thomas S. *A Political Sociology of Educational Reform: Power/Knowledge in Teaching, Teacher Education, and Research*. New York & London: Teachers College Press, 1991.

Prawda, Juan. "Educational Decentralization in Latin America: Lessons Learned." *International Journal of Educational Development*, vol. 13, no. 3 (1993): 253–264.

Puiggrós, Adriana. *Educar Entre el Acuerdo y la Libertad: Propuestas para la Educación del Siglo XXI*. Buenos Aires: Ariel, 1999.

Purpel, David E., and Svi Shapiro. *Beyond Liberation and Excellence: Reconstructing the Public Discourse on Education*. Westport, CT: Bergin & Garvey, 1995.

Ramirez, Rafael, Florence Webb, and James Guthrie. "Site-based Management: Restructuring Decision-making for Schools." In *Rethinking Effective Schools: Research and Practice*. Edited by J. R. Bliss, W. A. Firestone and C. E. Richards. Englewood Cliffs, NJ: Prentice Hall, 1991.

Reimers, Fernando. "The Role of the Community in Expanding Educational Opportunities: The EDUCO Schools in El Salvador." In *Education and Development: Tradition and Innovation*. Edited by J. Lynch, C. Modgil, and S. Modgil. London: Cassell, 1997.

Reinharz, Shulamit. *Feminist Methods in Social Research*. New York/Oxford: Oxford University Press, 1992.

Revista Novedades Educativas. "El Proyecto Institucional o 'de Burocracias, Formalidades y Autonomías.'" No. 82 (October 1997): 14–18.

Rust, Val D. "From Modern to Postmodern Ways of Seeing Social and Educational Change." In *Social Cartography: Mapping Ways of Seeing Social and Educational Change*. Edited by R. G. Paulston. New York: Garland Publishing, 1996.

Sayed, Yusuf. "Discourses of the Policy of Educational Decentralization in South Africa since 1994: An Examination of the South African Schools Act [1] [2]." *Compare*, vol. 29, no. 2 (1999): 141–152.

Smyth, John. "The Socially Just Alternative to the " 'Self-managing' School." In *International Handbook of Educational Leadership and Administration*. Edited by K. Leithwood, et al. Dordrecht, The Netherlands: Kluwer, 1996.

Smyth, John. (Ed.). *A Socially Critical View of the Self-managing School*. London: Falmer, 1993.

Strike, Kenneth A. "Professionalism, Democracy, and Discursive Communities: Normative Reflections on Restructuring. *American Educational Research Journal*, vol. 30, no. 2 (1993): 255–276.

Summa, Hikka. "The Rhetoric of Efficiency: Applied Social Science as Depoliticization." In *Writing the Social Text: Poetics and Politics in Social Science Discourse*. Edited by R. H Brown. New York: Aldine de Gruyter, 1992.

Tedesco, Juan C. "Changes in Managing Education: The Case of Latin American Countries." *International Journal of Educational Research*, vol. 21, no. 8 (1994): 809–815.

Tiryakian, Edward A. "Typologies." In *International Encyclopedia of the Social Sciences*. Edited by D. L. Sills. New York: Macmillan, 1968.

Tooley, James. *Education Without the State*. London: Institute of Economic Affairs Education and Training Unit, 1996.

Van Gelderen, Alfredo M., and Gustavo López Espinosa. *La Escuela Argentina en Transformacion: Ocho Cuestiones y Veintidós Protagonistas*. Buenos Aires: Santillana, 1996.

Walton, Douglas. *Argument Structure: A Pragmatic Theory*. Toronto: University of Toronto Press, 1996.

Watson, Keith. "Memories, Models and Mapping: The Impact of Geopolitical Changes in Comparative Studies in Education." *Compare*, vol. 28, no. 1 (1998): 5–31.

Weiler, Hans N. "Comparative Perspectives on Educational Decentralization: An Exercise in Contradiction?" *Educational Evaluation and Policy Analysis*, vol. 12, no. 4 (1990): 433–448.

Wells, Amy S. "Where Neoliberal Ideology Meets Social Context: A Comparative Analysis of U.S. Charter Schools and England's Grant-Maintained Schools." In *Challenges of Urban Education: Sociological Perspectives for the Next Century*. Edited by K. McClafferty, C. Torres, and T. Mitchell. Albany, NY: SUNY Press, 2000.

Whitty, Geoff, Sally Power, and David Halpin. *Devolution and Choice in Education: The School, the State and the Market*. Buckingham-Philadelphia: Open University Press, 1998.

World Bank. *Priorities and Strategies for Education*. Washington, D.C.: The World Bank, 1995.

Index

Index